T0384851

Handbook of Education, Training, and Supervision of School Psychologists in School and Community, Volume I

Handbook of Education, Training, and Supervision of School Psychologists in School and Community, Volume I

Foundations of Professional Practice

Edited by Enedina García-Vázquez,
Tony D. Crespi, and Cynthia A. Riccio

Routledge
Taylor & Francis Group
New York   London

Routledge
Taylor & Francis Group
270 Madison Avenue
New York, NY 10016

Routledge
Taylor & Francis Group
27 Church Road
Hove, East Sussex BN3 2FA

Printed in the United States of America on acid-free paper
10 9 8 7 6 5 4 3 2 1

International Standard Book Number: 978-0-415-96260-5 (Hardback)

Library of Congress Cataloging-in-Publication Data

García-Vázquez, Enedina.
  Handbook of education, training, and supervision of school psychologists in
school and community / Enedina García-Vázquez, Tony D. Crespi, and Cynthia
A. Riccio.
       p. cm.
  Includes bibliographical references and index.
    Contents: v. 1. Foundations of professional practice -- v. 2. Bridging the
training and practice gap : building collaborative university/field practices.
     ISBN 978-0-415-96260-5 (v. 1. : alk. paper) -- ISBN 978-0-415-96279-7 (v. 2. :
alk. paper)
    1. School psychologists--In-service training--Handbooks, manuals, etc. 2.
School psychology--Study and teaching. I. Crespi, Tony D. II. Riccio, Cynthia A.
III. Title.

LB3013.6.G37 2009
371.7'130683--dc22   2009017882

Visit the Taylor & Francis Web site at
http://www.taylorandfrancis.com

and the Routledge Web site at
http://www.routledgementalhealth.com

Contents

Volume II Contents

PART III
Difficult dialogues

PART IV
Professional issues

PART V
Into the future

Editors

Tony D. Crespi, EdD, ABPP, is presently a professor of psychology at the University of Hartford in Connecticut. A licensed psychologist, licensed marriage and family therapist, certified school counselor, and certified school psychologist, he holds board certification in school psychology from the American Board of Professional Psychology. A past president of Trainers of School Psychologists, he has published several books and approximately 100 professional articles, focusing on such areas as professional credentialing and clinical supervision, ethics and legal issues, and psychopathology in adolescents.

Tammy L. Hughes, PhD, is an associate professor at Duquesne University and the 2009–2010 president of the Division of School Psychology (16) of the American Psychological Association (APA). She is also the cochair of the School Psychology Leadership Roundtable and a past president of Trainers of School Psychologists, and serves on the APA Presidential Task Force planning the summit on the Future of Psychology Practice: Collaborating for Change. She is committed to solving the social issues that children face at school by bridging the gap between university teaching and field-based training. Dr. Hughes is an associate editor for *Psychology in the Schools* and serves on the editorial board of *The Journal of School Violence* and the *International Journal of Offender Therapy and Comparative Criminology*. She is the author and coauthor of numerous books, journal articles, chapters, and other publications on child violence, differentiating emotional disturbance and social maladjustment, and understanding the relationship between emotional dysregulation and conduct problems in children.

Judith Kaufman, PhD, ABPP, is a professor at Fairleigh Dickinson University (FDU). She holds a diploma in school psychology and currently serves as secretary of the American Academy of School Psychology and chair of the Advisory Board of Trainers of School Psychologists. Dr. Kaufman has held leadership positions in several national and regional organizations and has chaired several APA site visit teams. Prior to coming to FDU, Dr. Kaufman was director of school psychology training at Ferkauf Graduate School and also served as visiting faculty at the University of Wisconsin, Madison, and the Institute of Education, London, United Kingdom. Her research interests include supervision, cultural and individual differences, and risk and resiliency factors in emerging adulthood.

Cynthia A. Riccio is a professor, director of training for the School Psychology program, and a member of the neuroscience faculty at Texas A&M University. Her research interests include attention deficit/hyperactivity disorder, pediatric neuropsychology, and learning/language disorders. She also is involved in research related to autism spectrum disorders. Her current research has direct implications for the practice and science of school psychology across disability areas, with an emphasis on the developmental trajectory from middle school to high school and beyond.

Enedina García-Vázquez, PhD, associate dean/deputy director, leads the Information Sciences and Security Systems department of the Physical Science Laboratory at New Mexico State University. She holds tenure and full professor rank in the Counseling and Educational Psychology department. Dr. Vázquez serves as the editor of the *Trainers' Forum*, the journal of the Trainers of School Psychologists, a national organization concerned with the graduate preparation of future school psychologists. Dr. Vázquez is also the chair of the National Association of School Psychologists (NASP) Program Approval Board. In this capacity, she leads the process for school psychology programs seeking NASP approval.

Contributors

Christine M. Abbuhl, BA, is a school psychology doctoral student at Central Michigan University. Her primary research interest is deliberate self-harm in adolescents. Her writing in this book developed through working with a diverse group of professionals in creating a program to address the needs of local gay, lesbian, bisexual, transgender, and questioning (GLBTQ) youth.

Elsa Arroyos-Jurado, PhD, is an associate professor and director of training in school psychology at New Mexico State University. She earned her PhD in school psychology from the University of Iowa. Her interests include multicultural competencies in practice and training, neuropsychology, and mentoring of students and early career faculty.

Lynanne Black, PhD, is a certified school psychologist and assistant professor at Indiana University of Pennsylvania. She has taught numerous courses at the undergraduate and graduate levels in the areas of educational psychology, learning, behavior, assessment and intervention, and family–school relations. Her specialties include preschool assessment, parental involvement, and emergent and early literacy.

Stephen E. Brock, PhD, is a professor at California State University, Sacramento (CSUS). He worked for 18 years as a school psychologist before joining the CSUS faculty. Dr. Brock is the California representative to the National Association of School Psychologists (NASP) Delegate Assembly. In addition, he is a member of the National Emergency Assistance Team and cochair of the PREPaRE Crisis Prevention and Intervention Training Curriculum.

Carmen Broussard, PhD, is an associate professor of school psychology at Nicholls State University, where she also serves as program director for the Specialist in School Psychology program. Her research interests include assessment and intervention with early reading and mathematics, functional behavior assessment and intervention with disruptive behaviors in young children, and program evaluation of graduate training programs.

Ralph E. Cash, PhD, NCSP, is an associate professor of psychology at Nova Southeastern University (NSU), director of The NSU School Psychology Assessment and Consultation Center, a past president of the Florida Association of School Psychologists (FASP), and president of the National Association of School Psychologists. Dr. Cash recently received FASP's Lifetime Achievement Award for his service to the profession.

Ray W. Christner, PsyD, NCSP, is a school psychologist with South Middleton School District, Boiling Springs, Pennsylvania, and is on the faculty at the Philadelphia College of Osteopathic Medicine. He is coeditor of *School-Based Mental Health: A Practitioner's Guide to Comparative Practices* (Routledge, 2008) and *Cognitive-Behavioral Intervention in Educational Settings: A Handbook for Practice* (Routledge, 2005).

Schehera Coleman, MEd, is pursuing her PhD in school psychology at Temple University. Ms. Coleman is also a certified school psychologist currently working for the School District of Philadelphia.

Katurah Cramer, PhD, received her doctoral degree in school psychology at the University of Maryland. Her publications are on consultation supervision and instructional assessment. She currently provides on-line coaching for new instructional consultation team facilitators. She is on family leave until 2011 from the Howard County Public Schools, where she has been a school psychologist.

Tracy K. Cruise, PhD, is a professor of psychology at Western Illinois University (WIU). She is a certified school psychologist and licensed clinical psychologist who teaches and supervises Child Psychotherapy for the School Psychology and Clinical/Community Mental Health graduate programs at WIU. Dr. Cruise publishes and presents workshops in the area of child abuse (e.g., Child Abuse & Neglect: The School's Response) and internship supervision.

Kristen Cunningham, PsyD, is a clinical and adjunct faculty member at the Center for Psychological Studies at NSU. She is the acting director of the School Psychology Assessment and Consultation Center at the Psychology Services Center at NSU. Dr. Cunningham also serves as the chief psychologist at the Autism Spectrum Disorders Assessment and Diagnostic Clinic at the Unicorn Children's Foundation Clinic of NSU's Mailman Segal Institute for Early Childhood Studies.

A. Nichole Dailor, MS, is a doctoral student at Central Michigan University finishing her dissertation on the use of an e-mail discussion list to facilitate peer consultation for resolving ethical concerns. She completed her APA pre-doctoral internship in August 2008 through the Menta Group and currently is a school psychologist for the Bourbonnais Elementary School District in Bourbonnais, IL.

Scott L. Decker, PhD, specializes in neuropsychology and research methodology. He was a coauthor of the Bender-Gestalt II and taught neuropsychology and research methodology. He also served in a joint appointment at the University of Illinois at Chicago Neuropsychiatric Institute as a pediatric neuropsychologist. Currently, he is an assistant professor at Georgia State University.

Kathy DeOrnellas, PhD, LSSP, is an assistant professor in the School psychology graduate program and the director of the Specialist in School psychology graduate program at Texas Woman's University. She is a licensed psychologist. She also contracts with area school districts to provide psychological services and maintains a private practice where she provides assessment and therapy for children and families.

Panayiota Dimitropoulou, PhD, is a school psychologist working in a primary school setting. She is a member of the scientific team of the Centre for Research and Practice in School Psychology. Her research interests include mental health promotion, school-based prevention and intervention programs, and learning difficulties.

Daniel D. Drevon, BS, is a doctoral student at Central Michigan University. He conducts his research through the Center for Research, Training, and Consultation on GLBTQ Youth Issues at Central Michigan University. His research interests include GLBTQ youth issues and applied behavior analysis.

Frank J. Epifanio, PhD, NCSP, was a former associate professor in the School Psychology program at Rowan University, Glassboro, New Jersey. He was past president of the New Jersey Association of School Psychologists. He was also a school psychologist and director of special services. He died in November 2008 after a brief illness.

Thomas K. Fagan, PhD, is a 1969 graduate in school psychology at Kent State University and is professor of psychology and coordinator of the School Psychology program at the University of Memphis. He serves as historian to the National Association of School Psychologists and to the Division of School Psychology in the American Psychological Association. Dr. Fagan is a professor of psychology at the University of Memphis and has twice served as president of the NASP.

Ivelisse Torres Fernández, PhD, is an assistant professor in the Department of Counseling and Educational Psychology at New Mexico State University.

She earned her PhD in school psychology from the University of Iowa. Her research interests include social–emotional development in children and adolescents, resiliency, child and adolescent psychopathology, and multiculturalism and diversity.

Catherine A. Fiorello, PhD, received her doctoral degree in school psychology from the University of Kentucky in December 1992. She is an associate professor and director of the School Psychology program at Temple University. She specializes in assessment, especially developmental assessment in early childhood, assessment of children with disabilities, and cognitive and neuropsychological assessment.

Constance J. Fournier, PhD, is a clinical professor in the Department of Educational Psychology at Texas A&M University and is a licensed psychologist. She has appointments in the Special Education and School Psychology programs. She has numerous presentations and publications, and is active in the American Psychological Association (APA), NASP, and Council for Exceptional Children.

Abraham Givner, PhD, NCSP, is a professor of psychology and director of the Combined School-Clinical Child Psychology program, Yeshiva University, Bronx, New York, where he holds the Ferkauf-Silverstein Chair in School Psychology. Dr. Givner is a licensed psychologist in New York and New Jersey. He received his PhD in educational psychology from Yeshiva University in 1972. He is one of the founding members and the treasurer of the Consortium of Combined-Integrated Doctoral Programs in Psychology.

Robert M. Gordon, PsyD, has been working at the Rusk Institute of Rehabilitation Medicine at New York University Langone Medical Center since completing his doctoral degree at Yeshiva University's Child Clinical/School Psychology program in 1986. At the Rusk Institute, Dr. Gordon is the director of intern and postdoctoral fellow training and a clinical associate professor. He received a certificate in psychoanalysis and psychotherapy from Adelphi University in 1999. He has specialties in neuropsychological and forensic testing and psychotherapy with children and adults with physical and learning disabilities and chronic illnesses. He has published in the areas of ethics, supervision, relational psychoanalysis, dream interpretation, group therapy, and parental coping styles.

James B. Hale, PhD, MEd, ABSNP, is a licensed psychologist, certified school psychologist, and certified special education teacher. He is an associate professor and associate director of Clinical Training in the Department of Psychology at the Philadelphia College of Osteopathic Medicine.

Dr. Hale has pursued multiple lines of research, including studies that differentiate reading and math disability subtypes, challenge assumptions about the validity of global IQ interpretation, examine language and psychosocial functions associated with right hemisphere learning disabilities, and explore neuropsychological aspects of ADHD and medication response. Dr. Hale is an active researcher, practitioner, presenter, and author, including his coauthorship of the critically acclaimed, bestselling book *School Neuropsychology: A Practitioner's Handbook* (Psychology Press/Taylor & Francis, 2003).

Chryse Hatzichristou, PhD, is a professor of school psychology and director of the Center for Research and Practice in School Psychology at the Department of Psychology, University of Athens, Athens, Greece. She received her master's degree from Harvard and her PhD from the University of California, Berkeley. She chairs the Division of School Psychology of the Hellenic Psychological Society, and she has served as secretary of the Executive Committee of the International School Psychology Association. Her primary research interests include service delivery models, primary and secondary prevention programs in schools, school-based consultation, and cross-cultural and cross-national issues in school psychology.

George W. Hebert, PhD, is currently an assistant professor at the Louisiana State University Health Sciences Center in New Orleans, where he coordinates the APA-accredited Louisiana School Psychology Internship Consortium. Dr. Hebert is a licensed psychologist who has served in both urban and rural school settings. In addition, he served many years as the director of a public child/adolescent mental health clinic. His current research interests are focused on measurement issues surrounding various responses to intervention models. Dr. Hebert has always been active in the field of school psychology in both state and national professional organizations.

Sally A. Hoover, PhD, is currently director of pupil services at Quaker Valley School District, Sewickley, Pennsylvania. She is responsible for supervising psychology, guidance, and health service providers, including school psychology practicum students, and interns in a K-12 environment. Her responsibilities include providing universal screening in reading and math, coordinating direct services to general and special education students, and running special education programs.

Susan Jacob, PhD, is a professor of psychology at Central Michigan University (CMU). She is the author of numerous books and articles on ethical–legal issues in school psychology and also serves as the director of CMU's Center for Research, Training, and Consultation on GLBTQ Youth.

Aikaterini Lampropoulou, PhD, is a school psychologist working in a clinical setting. She is a member of the scientific team of the Centre for Research and Practice in School Psychology. Her research interests include mental health promotion, school-based prevention and intervention programs, and family–school partnership.

Mary Levinsohn-Klyap, PhD, who received her doctoral degree in school psychology from the University of Maryland, is the Howard County (Maryland) Public Schools district facilitator for problem-solving teams. Her work includes providing professional development in consultation and teaming with staff and interns. She has taught consultation courses at the University of Maryland.

Edward M. Levinson, EdD, NCSP, is the chair of the Educational and School Psychology Department and a professor of educational and school psychology at Indiana University of Pennsylvania. He has authored three books and more than 70 journal articles. His chapters on vocational assessment and/or transition appear in all five editions of the NASP's *Best Practices in School Psychology*, and his chapters on career development appear in both editions of the NASP's *Children's Needs*.

Emilia C. Lopez, PhD, is a professor and the director of the bilingual and multicultural specializations in the School Psychology program at Queens College, City University of New York. Her areas of interest are multicultural consultation, providing services via interpreters, bilingual School Psychology, and cross-cultural competencies.

Jeffrey R. Lovelace, MS, is a certified school psychologist with the West Hartford (Connecticut) Public Schools. He received his master's degree and specialist training in the School Psychology program at the University of Hartford. He has also completed course requirements for credentialing as a licensed professional counselor.

Clare N. Lowell, EdD, is an assistant professor of education at Marymount Manhattan College, New York City. She was a teacher and administrator in public education on Long Island for over 30 years. She earned her doctoral degree at Hofstra University, her master's in journalism at Columbia, and her master's in English literature at Adelphi.

Konstantina Lykitsakou, PhD, is a school psychologist working in a preschool setting. She is a member of the scientific team of the Centre for Research and Practice in School Psychology. Her research interests include mental health promotion, school-based prevention and intervention programs, systemic family therapy, statistics, and research methodology.

Denise Maricle, PhD, is an associate professor in the School Psychology graduate programs and the director of the Doctoral School Psychology graduate program at Texas Woman's University. Her research interests include school neuropsychology, neuropsychological assessment with children, role and function of school psychologists, and others. She teaches graduate level courses in school psychology and psychological tests and measurements for undergraduates.

Elise L. Martinez, MA, is a school psychologist in the Western Placer Unified School District in Lincoln, California. She is also a graduate student at CSUS. Ellie's research interests are in the area of crisis intervention with a specific interest in youth suicide postvention.

Anita Sohn McCormick, PhD, is a clinical assistant professor in the School Psychology program in the Department of Educational Psychology at Texas A&M University. She holds a PhD and a master's degree in school psychology. Her research interests include bilingual and cultural issues in assessment and evidence-based interventions for English language learner students.

Kara E. McGoey, PhD, is an associate professor and the director of the School Psychology Training program at Duquesne University in Pittsburgh, Pennsylvania. She is also a consultant to the Early Childhood Program at Children's Hospital of Pittsburgh and the University, Community, Leaders and Individuals with Disabilities Center at the University of Pittsburgh. Dr. McGoey's research interests and recent publications include topics on the assessment of and intervention with young children with behavior problems.

Sarah Meche, BA, has her bachelor's degree in psychology and is currently a graduate student in the School Psychology program at Nicholls State University. Sarah's research interests include autism spectrum disorders and the functional behavioral assessment and intervention with children with low-incidence disabilities.

Rosemary B. Mennuti, EdD, NCSP, is a professor and the director of School Psychology programs in the Department of Psychology at the Philadelphia College of Osteopathic Medicine. She is coeditor of *Cognitive Behavioral Interventions in Educational Settings: A Handbook for Practice* (Routledge, 2005) and *School-Based Mental Health: A Practitioner's Guide to Comparative Practices* (Routledge, 2008).

Daniel C. Miller, PhD, ABPP, ABSNP, NCSP, LSSP, is a professor in the School Psychology programs and chair of the Department of Psychology and Philosophy at Texas Woman's University, Denton. Dr. Miller is a licensed psychologist and a past president of the National Association of School Psychologists.

Jeffrey A. Miller, PhD, ABPP, is a diplomate in school psychology and the associate dean for graduate studies and research at Duquesne University. He is a past president of the American Academy of School Psychology and the current chair of the School Psychology Specialty Council. Dr. Miller's scholarship is in the areas of school psychology training and neuropsychology for teaching and learning.

Bonnie Kaul Nastasi, PhD, is an associate professor in the Department of Psychology at Tulane University. Dr. Nastasi's research focuses on the use of mixed methods research to develop culturally specific theories and evidence-based interventions. She is president-elect of Division 16 of the American Psychological Association.

LLecenia Navarro, PhD, is a practicing school psychologist in Sacramento, California. Her current interests include bilingual assessments, academic and behavioral interventions, and crisis intervention and response. She holds a BA degree in liberal studies and an MA in education from the California State University, Sacramento.

Rachel L. Navarro, PhD, is an assistant professor in the Department of Counseling and Educational Psychology at New Mexico State University. She earned her PhD in counseling psychology from the University of Missouri. Dr. Navarro specializes in multicultural vocational psychology. She teaches research methodology, career development, assessment, and counseling practicum courses.

Patrick Owen, PsyD, is a licensed psychologist and certified school psychologist working full time as a practitioner at Kershaw County School District in Camden, South Carolina. He is interested in how results from personality assessment measures inform the implementation of individualized education program goals. His previous publications address the usefulness of performance-based measures in the applied setting.

Constance Patterson, PhD, is a faculty member and field placement coordinator at Walden University. Dr. Patterson is interested in the range of issues involved in training school psychologists, especially as they enter the field during internship experiences. She lives in New Orleans, Louisiana.

LeAdelle Phelps, PhD, is a professor at the University at Buffalo, State University of New York, and has published three books and more than 75 journal articles and book chapters on adolescent health-related issues. She has been identified as one of the top 20 researchers in school psychology and received the 2006 Division 16 Jack Bardon Award.

Mary Ann Rafoth, PhD, is dean of the College of Education and Educational Technology at Indiana University of Pennsylvania. Her research interests involve learning skills, alternatives to retention, school readiness issues, and program and student learning outcomes evaluation. Dr. Rafoth has more than 30 publications and 50 presentations, including several chapters in the NASP's *Best Practices in School Psychology* series.

Robert J. Rimmer, EdD, is an assistant professor of educational leadership at William Paterson University, Wayne, New Jersey. He served for 32 years in public education as a teacher, counselor, principal, and superintendent of schools. He earned master's degrees from William Paterson in student personnel services and educational administration and his doctorate from Rutgers.

Margaret R. Rogers, PhD, is a faculty member of the School Psychology program at the University of Rhode Island. Her research interests include cross-cultural competencies of school psychologists, recruitment and retention of underrepresented students in psychology, and social justice.

Sylvia Rosenfield, PhD, is a professor at the University of Maryland and teaches the two-semester consultation course sequence to school psychology students. Her research and publications focus on instructional consultation and other forms of consultee-centered consultation. Her publications include *Implementing Evidence-Based Academic Interventions in Schools* (Oxford University Press, 2009), and *Instructional Consultation, Instructional Consultation Teams: Collaborating for Change* (Guilford Press, 1996).

Amanda Sinko, MA, is a school psychology graduate student and graduate assistant at Rowan University. She is currently completing her practicum in the Southampton Township School District in New Jersey and with the New Jersey Department of Education's Developing Safe and Civil Schools Project.

Jaime E. Slonim, MEd, is a graduate student completing her internship with the Seneca Valley School District in Harmony, Pennsylvania. She earned her master's degree in educational psychology from Indiana University of Pennsylvania in 2007. Her professional interests include neuropsychological assessment, executive dysfunction, trauma and resilience, and minority issues.

Julie Snyder, MS, is a doctoral student at the Center for Psychological Studies (CPS) at NSU. During her formal academic training she served as coordinator of continuing education at CPS. She is currently completing her predoctoral internship at the University of Miami/Mailman Center for Child Development.

Mark E. Swerdlik, PhD, ABPP, is a professor of psychology and coordinator of the School Psychology graduate programs at Illinois State University. He is a diplomate in school psychology and assessment psychology and a fellow of Division 16 (School Psychology) of the American Psychological Association. Dr. Swerdlik has more than 30 years of experience as a university educator. His scholarship is in the area of clinical supervision.

Jonnie L. Taton, MS, Ed, is a school psychologist with the Mt. Pleasant Public Schools, Mt. Pleasant, Michigan. She completed research on an instructional unit to foster more positive attitudes toward GLBTQ youth as part of her specialist degree studies at Central Michigan University.

Evelyn Teran, MA, completed her master's degree in school psychology at the California State University, Sacramento, after completing a double major in psychology and Spanish at the University of California, Davis. She currently works as a school psychologist with the Woodland Joint Unified School District.

Lea A. Theodore, PhD, is an associate professor in the School Psychology program at the College of William and Mary. Her research interests include developing classroom-based interventions for children with academic and behavior problems. Dr. Theodore is the vice president of professional affairs for the Division of School Psychology of the American Psychological Association and an associate editor for *School Psychology Quarterly.*

Yuma I. Tomes, PhD, is an associate professor and the director of the Master of Science School Psychology program at the Philadelphia College of Osteopathic Medicine. His research and teaching interests are multicultural/cross-cultural psychology, cognitive styles, and GLBTQ/diversity issues. Dr. Tomes is the author of several publications, book chapters, and reviews focusing on learning in diverse populations. Currently he is working on a cross-cultural text for mental health practitioners.

Sarah Valley-Gray, PsyD, is an associate professor and the director of continuing education at the Center for Psychological Studies at NSU. Dr. Valley-Gray spearheaded the development of the School Psychology programs at NSU and has served in a variety of leadership roles within the areas of training and credentialing.

J. Steven Welsh, PhD, is a professor of school psychology and the department head of psychology at Nicholls State University. He has presented and published articles on the topic of supervision in school psychology. He is a NASP program reviewer, has served as the chair of the NASP Special Interest Group in Supervision, and has consulted with school psychology training programs preparing for the accreditation process.

Barbara Bole Williams, PhD, NCSP, is a professor and the coordinator of the School Psychology program at Rowan University, Glassboro, New Jersey; the author of *Professional Ethics for School Psychologists: A Problem-Solving Casebook* (NASP Publications, 2008); a former member of the NASP Ethics Committee; a current member of the NASP's Ethics Advisory Panel; and the current national chair for revisions of NASP standards.

Michele Zaccario, PhD, is a licensed clinical psychologist employed as an assistant professor of graduate psychology at Pace University in New York City and as a pediatric psychologist at New York University Langone Medical Center's Rusk Institute of Rehabilitation Medicine and Neonatal Intensive Care Unit. She is a clinical supervisor of psychology doctoral students and leads multidisciplinary seminars on behavioral issues associated with medically fragile infants and children.

Roger D. Zeeman, PhD, NCSP, is the chair of education at Marymount Manhattan College, New York City. Previously, he was an associate professor and chair of special education at William Paterson University. Other professional experiences in New Jersey include school administrator, principal, and school and licensed psychologist. His degrees are from Harvard and Yeshiva.

Introduction

The field of school psychology is in a constant state of change. Demographics, definitions, disabilities, techniques, and strategies together with legislation and federal mandates are continuously shifting and creating new challenges for both education and training. At the same time, there are a core set of values shared by university and field-based trainers and practitioners that serve as the foundation of the profession. University training programs shape the future of the profession and simultaneously respond to the pragmatic needs of the populations we serve and the demands of the education system. While there have been several quality handbooks focusing on the history of school psychology, ethics, and professional practice and techniques, few, if any, focus on education and training issues and their translation to field-based practice. There is an explicit need to examine the essential tenets of the profession, critically review training and practice issues, and evaluate how the traditional and changing skills and issues translate into meeting the needs of children and the systems that serve them.

This two-volume handbook addresses the challenges of the training enterprise and its application. Volume I particularly examines contemporary issues of school psychology training at the university level. The topics explored range from broad considerations around the challenges of program development, considering various levels and models of training to the more specific issues of teaching of specialty skills and training for unique areas and special populations. Volume I serves as the template for the second volume of the handbook by way of raising questions and issues that ultimately play out in the field. Volume II is dedicated to bridging the training and practice gap.

Volume II examines issues critical to the practice of school psychology. Authors explore the nature of supervision at different stages of training (e.g., practicum and internship) and in a variety of settings. Each chapter raises issues, reflectively, for university training in a manner that facilitates the dialogue between university and field trainers. Problematic graduate student behaviors and the difficult dialogues that both university and field-based trainers encounter are responded to with an evidenced-based and direct approach. Volume II also considers issues of professional development, credentialing, and developing a professional identity, topics that predominate in practice settings yet are typically not addressed in any school psychology text.

Trainers of School Psychologists (TSP) are particularly proud to sponsor these two volumes. As an organization of university and field-based trainers representing school psychology programs at both the MA/specialist and doctoral levels of training across the country and internationally, we intend this handbook to serve our mutual goals in training the next generation of school psychologists. Specifically, the goal of this two-volume handbook is to support the TSP mission, which states:

> *TSP is committed to innovation and excellence in graduate training programs for specialist and doctoral school psychologists.... This is achieved by examining current trends in graduate education, providing professional growth opportunities to school psychology faculty, facilitating communication with field-based trainers and supervisors and initiating and supporting legislative efforts that promote excellence in training and practice.*

The contents of these volumes clearly support and further the mission of TSP and of the field itself. Each volume, while standing alone as an important resource, mirrors the other and enables issues and concepts to be translated from theory to practice. We invite all of our training colleagues to bridge the gaps.

Part I

Contemporary school psychology training

The university

1 School psychology as a profession

Introduction and overview

Cynthia A. Riccio, Enedina García-Vázquez, and Tony D. Crespi

INTRODUCTION

There is considerable and continuing concern with the quality of the educational system in the United States and the extent to which it is meeting the needs of the students (Rollin, Subtonik, Bassford, & Smulson, 2008). This is evident in the passage of recent legislation, including the No Child Left Behind Act of 2001 (http://www.ed.gov/policy/elsec/leg/esea02/107-110.pdf). At the same time, there is significant research to suggest that approximately 20% of children have or will have some type of disorder (Friedman, Katz-Leavy, Manderscheid, & Sondheimer, 1998) and would benefit from receiving psychological or other mental health services (Friedman, 2001). School psychological services have been in place for more than a century, dating back to 1886, when Lightner Witmer established the first psychological clinic, as well as a hospital-based school (Fagan, 2002; Fagan & Wise, 2007). Fagan (Chapter 2, this volume) provides a brief but detailed historical perspective on the profession. Children and adolescents spend a fair proportion of their waking time in school settings, second only to their home context. Consistently, there have been increased efforts to maximize parental involvement in the educational process (Carlson & Christenson, 2005; Ollendick, 2005; Pelco, Jacobson, Ries, & Melka, 2000). As such, school-based models for delivery of psychological services facilitate both student access to services and the potential for more generalized change within the contexts in which children and adolescents function, academically and socially (Riccio & Hughes, 2001). By providing a range of services—diagnostic, consultative, intervention, and prevention—in collaboration with educators, parents, and other professionals, it is possible to create safe, healthy, and supportive learning environments for all students that strengthen connections between home and school. School psychologists help children and youth succeed academically, socially, and emotionally by helping others to the best solution for each student and situation; they use different strategies to address student needs and to improve schoolwide and districtwide support systems. School psychologists work with students individually and in groups, directly and indirectly. They develop programs to train teachers and parents about effective teaching and learning strategies, techniques to manage behavior at home and in the classroom, working with students with disabilities or with special talents, addressing a range of problems, and preventing and managing crises (Barringer & Saenz, 2007; Riccio & Hughes, 2001). In many regards, other professionals often underestimate the broad roles and functions that school psychologists can fulfill (Gilman & Medway, 2007; Sheridan & Gutkin, 2000).

This volume, in a fundamental fashion, is intended to provide the reader with a critical overview of the profession and practice of school psychology in contemporary society. Assembling a team of acknowledged leaders in the field of school psychology, the reader will be exposed to critical concepts involved in educating and training future school psychologists. Developed under the auspices of Trainers of School Psychologists, a professional association of university training programs and university faculty, these two volumes address critical concepts in training and professional practice.

LITERATURE REVIEW

Roles of school psychologists

The roles of school psychologists are shaped in part by legislation, in part by the contexts in which the psychologists work, and in part by the training and experience of the individual school psychologist (Fagan, 2002; Gilman & Medway, 2007). Services provided by school psychologists include consultation, evaluation, intervention, prevention, research, and advocacy (Curtis et al., 2008). Traditionally, school psychology has been associated with evaluation and determination of eligibility for special services. In conjunction with the special education process, evaluation roles include the assessment of academic skills and aptitude for learning, as well as assessment of social-emotional development and mental health status for the individual. From an ecological perspective (Sheridan & Gutkin, 2000), the assessment role is not restricted to evaluation of the individual but includes examination of learning environments (i.e., the academic ecology and the school climate) and psychosocial variables that may have an impact on child adjustment.

Linked to assessment are the design and development of interventions. School psychologists also have a direct role in the provision of psychological counseling to help resolve interpersonal or family problems that interfere with school performance. This counseling may include direct training in social skills and anger management. School psychologists work directly with children and their families to help resolve problems in adjustment and learning; they help families and schools manage crises such as death, illness, or community trauma. One way that school psychologists do this is through their role as consultants.

As part of consultation, school psychologists collaborate with teachers, parents, and administrators to find effective solutions to learning and behavior problems. In this manner, they are able to improve the quality of services for all children by increasing the skills and knowledge base of those who work directly with children and families. They work to help others understand child development and how it affects learning and behavior, and they strengthen working relationships among teachers, parents, and service providers in the community. One way they strengthen these relationships is by developing partnerships of parents, teachers, and other professionals to promote positive child outcomes.

More recently, a focus for school psychologists has been that of fostering prevention activities and systemic change (D. N. Miller, George, & Fogt, 2005). These activities may include the design of various programs for children at risk of failing at school or who are at risk for adjustment problems. Programs may include those that promote tolerance, understanding, and appreciation of diversity within the school community and make schools safer and more effective learning environments. With the emphasis on prevention, consultation practices and involvement in policy development have taken on greater importance. School psychologists are in a position to work with school staff, administrators, and community agencies to provide services and programs directed at improving psychological and physical health for all children. Most importantly, school psychologists can facilitate the translation of research to practice (D. N. Miller et al., 2005).

The last role of the school psychologist is that of research and planning. The ability to provide all the other services is nested in advancing the knowledge base and establishing evidenced based practices for evaluation, intervention, prevention, and consultation. In order to ensure best practice, it is important for there to be ongoing and planned evaluation of the effectiveness of academic and behavior management programs. Psychology as a field can significantly contribute to fostering progress and addressing problems in educational and behavioral growth of children and youth; school psychology is uniquely suited to applying what is known from psychology to the educational context (Rosenfield, 2008).

Training for professional roles

School psychologists are highly trained in both psychology and education. Practitioners must complete a planned program that covers data-based decision making, consultation and collaboration, effective instruction, child development, student diversity and development, school organization, prevention, intervention, mental health, learning styles, behavior, research, and program evaluation. Minimally, this includes the equivalent of 3 years of full-time graduate study (beyond a bachelor's degree), a minimum of 60 graduate credits of coursework, and traditional coursework, as well as a practicum and year-long full-time internship. Training is rigorous, includes various professional examinations, and concludes with programs endorsing graduates for state Department of Education credentialing for practice.

This said, there are multiple models and levels of training within the field of school psychology (D. C. Miller, 2008); D. C. Miller, DeOrnellas, and Maricle (Chapter 4, this volume) and Givner (Chapter 5, this volume) describe some of the models and degrees offered. In general, school psychologists must be certified and/or licensed by the state in which they work; this may or may not be comparable to the certification available through the National School Psychology Certification Board. In some states, the entry level for certification or licensure is a minimum of a graduate degree program (approximately 65 graduate semester credits) that includes a 1,200-hour internship; this is most frequently referred to as a specialist or specialist in education (EdS) degree. Entry level for licensure as a psychologist in most states is restricted to those who obtain doctoral training (see Crespi, Chapter 13, Volume II).

Depending on their level of training and applicable laws governing certification and licensure, individuals trained in school psychology work in a variety of settings (Curtis et al., 2008). The majority of school psychologists, who are certified by departments of education, work in school settings; in fact, most individuals who complete a specialist or similar level program are often limited by law to the school setting. Individuals who obtain doctoral training in school psychology, however, can practice in a variety of settings, including public and private school systems, school-based health centers, clinics and hospitals, community and state agencies and other institutions, private practice, and colleges and universities. Despite the existence of these options, less than 15% of individuals trained in school psychology reported having a primary work setting other than a school setting (Curtis et al., 2008).

One component of training that has taken on increased importance in the last decade is related to evidence-based practice (Kratochwill, 2007). Research suggests that most training programs in school psychology are not adequately addressing evidence-based practices (Shernoff, Kratochwill, & Stoiber, 2003); one of the greatest challenges is in determining what constitutes an evidence-based practice for a given population or target behavior (Kratochwill, 2007). In order to continue to develop, establish, and demonstrate the evidence base, whether for assessment or intervention, students need a basic understanding of research methodologies. These methodologies cannot be limited to the use of randomized control groups but need to include understanding of how to conduct program evaluation, establish treatment integrity, and effectively conduct single-case or small n research. Kratochwill (2007) suggested four differing conceptual frameworks to improve the knowledge basis and practice—these included efficacy studies, transportability studies, dissemination studies, and system evaluation studies. Unfortunately, the extent to which research coursework is required and integrated into training and practice, even at the doctoral level, varies by training program (Rossen & Oakland, 2008).

PEDAGOGICAL/SUPERVISORY ISSUES

With more than 200 training programs throughout the United States and with a mix of part-time and full-time programs, as well as both doctoral and specialist programs, potential applicants have an array of options to examine when looking at training. Full-time or part-time? Traditional programs or distance learning models? Specialist or doctoral levels? Practitioner or research focused? For applicants, the field of options is wide. In addition, program faculty members have diverse applied and research interests, and programs also vary in focus, as well as in degrees conferred.

At present, approximately two-thirds of all programs are housed with schools of education, with the remaining housed with departments of psychology. Such differences can also relate to theoretical and programmatic focus, as well as degrees offered. Full-time programs at the specialist level can typically be completed in 3 years of full-time study and will include a mix of classes, practica, and a year-long internship. Full-time programs allow an interrupted sequence of coursework with minimal outside distractions but are not always feasible for applicants. At the doctoral level, students often find part-time options. Whether pursuing the PhD (doctor of philosophy), EdD (doctor of education), or PsyD (doctor of psychology) degree, the process may be drawn out over many years as personal, family, and professional responsibilities may delay timely degree completion. Ultimately, each applicant must personally choose whether a part-time or full-time option is best.

While school psychology programs historically occurred through traditional class delivery models, innovations in technology have increased the range of distance and integrated learning models. Whether distance learning models, online models, or "external" degree programs can best accommodate the acquisition of assessment and counseling skills remains unresolved. It is clear, though, that a growing shortage of school psychologists exists, it is clear that innovations in educational delivery systems have enhanced innovative graduate program degree offerings, and it is clear that many potential school psychologists are interested in alternative learning models. At present, for example, looking at clinical psychology, one sole distance learning program at Fielding Graduate University holds American Psychological Association (APA) accreditation and awards the PhD degree. In school psychology, National Association of School Psychologists (NASP) and APA approvals are likely to be explored by a growing number of such programs.

SUPERVISION

One hallmark of training as a school psychologist involves clinical supervision, typically through a cadre of practicing school psychologists who supervise practica and internship training components. In addition, many programs also complement this supervision with group, university-based supervision. Individual, face-to-face clinical supervision offers the ability to specifically focus on students' weaknesses; address assessment, counseling, and consultation issues; and specifically focus on strengthening the areas of weakness. Individual supervision is a hallmark of training in professional psychology.

Group supervision nicely complements individual supervision and offers a number of benefits, including vicarious learning of all participating; in effect, each student gets to experience at some level the issues that other students face in their field-based experience (Riva & Erickson Cornish, 2008). Based on survey results, it is likely that most students in psychology training programs will receive some form of group supervision, usually in conjunction with individual supervision; there is, however, little in the way of training available for the supervisors. In addition to case presentations, ethics and multicultural issues tend to be the most frequent topics addressed in a group format, with less emphasis on group dynamics (Riva & Erickson Cornish, 2008).

CASE ILLUSTRATIONS

Example 1: Susan Student, Specialist Student

Susan is a 22-year-old graduate of Old State University with a BA degree in psychology. Like the majority of applicants, she is a White female with a strong interest in children. She is not interested in private practice and envisions herself working in an elementary school setting. She explores both PhD and specialist (MA/MS and Sixth-Year Certificate/Specialist Degree) training options but is most interested in a 3-year specialist program. She is interested in pursuing graduate school while living in her home state.

Near her home, Susan compares an NASP-approved program at a private university and a program lacking NASP approval at a state university. Both require 66 credits. She is worried about the costs but is pleased to learn about the employability and state shortages of school psychologists. She accepts a research assistantship at the private university that will partially cover living expenses and pursues a range of student loans. With strong employability, she compares the 3-year program to that completed by law students and enrolls for the fall.

The 1st year involves a rigorous complement of classes, primarily in psychological assessment, school counseling, life-span development, and special education. She completes a comprehensive examination at the end of year 1. The 2nd year continues her coursework and includes a part-time practicum placement in a local high school. She earns her MA degree at the end of year 2. The 3rd year completes her final classes and includes a full-time, 5-day-a-week internship in a local elementary school. She earns a 6th-year/EdS degree at the end of year 3. Upon graduation, she completes the Praxis II examination, a national examination that, in this case, tests her knowledge of school psychology, and she accepts a position with a local school system.

Example 2: Maria Diligence, PhD Student

Maria is graduating from a small private university with a BA degree in psychology. A bilingual student, fluent in both English and Spanish, she is encouraged by her advisor to explore PhD programs in school psychology. She is most interested in PhD programs, as she is ultimately interested in a career involving university teaching and research. Because many PhD programs offer strong funding possibilities, she decides to apply solely to PhD programs.

Maria is accepted to the APA-approved school psychology program at State University. She had hoped for a minority, bilingual advisor, but none are employed in the program. She is matched, though, with a doctoral chair who seems supportive of her interests. The program is designed to be completed in 5 years.

Following the completion of her coursework, Maria accepts an internship in the local school system. While the internship is not APA approved—few public schools hold this approval—she feels that the proximity to the university best affords the ability to continue her dissertation research. In addition, the supervisor is a PhD with credentials as a licensed psychologist, which is important if she ultimately is interested in such a credential (see Crespi, Chapter 13, Volume II). Ultimately, she accepts a position with the school where she trained and completes her PhD in 7 years.

SUMMARY AND CONCLUSIONS

Schools are changing rapidly and are increasingly confronted by new challenges. From school violence to a growing mix of cultures, schools and school psychologists are facing a challenging population of issues. With approximately 20% of children demonstrating a disorder (Friedman et al., 1998) and a need for psychological or mental health services (Friedman, 2001), school psychology can be seen as a focus for assistance. With school psychological services dating to 1886, when Lightner Witmer established the first psychological clinic (Fagan, 2002; Fagan & Wise, 2007), school psychology has a strong presence in public education. At the same time, new challenges are growing. For example, there have been increased efforts to maximize parental involvement in the educational process (Carlson & Christenson, 2005; Ollendick, 2005; Pelco et al., 2000). In Connecticut, for instance, the first legislation has been passed to have the state Department of Education credential of School, Marriage, and Family Therapists for school practice.

Because of the growing numbers of mental health issues confronted by children and families, and changing family systems, schools are finding that school psychologists are a key service provider. This volume, in a basic way, is intended to familiarize readers, whether aspiring students of school psychology, current students, or interested educators and university faculty, with issues emerging in the profession.

RESOURCES

These two volumes provide an overview of a variety of topics; however, the preponderance of information that can be retrieved in any given search can also make it time-consuming and unwieldy. As you read the chapters, you may want to further explore the literature; to facilitate this, some useful resources are listed for each chapter. The list is by no means exhaustive, but it contains some of the most valuable materials that are currently available for the topic covered. Summaries are adapted, in part, from descriptive material provided in publication descriptions.

The National Association of School Psychologists
Suite 402, 4340 East-West Highway
Bethesda, MD 20814
(301) 657-0270
http://www.nasponline.org
NASP represents and supports school psychology through leadership to enhance the mental health and educational competence of all children.

Barringer, M., & Saenz, A. (2007). Promoting positive school environments: A career in school psychology. In R. J. Sternberg (Ed.), *Career paths in psychology: Where your degree can take you* (2nd ed., pp. 227–248). Washington, DC: American Psychological Association.
This chapter provides a discussion of school psychology as a career, what is required for academic preparation, financial outcomes, and personal experiences of two school psychologists.

Graves, S. L., Jr., & Wright, L. B. (2007). Comparison of individual factors in school psychology graduate students: Why do students pursue a degree in school psychology? *Psychology in the Schools, 44*, 865–872.
This article reports the results of a national survey of graduate students who have chosen to pursue a career in school psychology and discusses the implications for recruitment and retention of school psychology graduate students.

REFERENCES

Barringer, M., & Saenz, A. (2007). Promoting positive school environments: A career in school psychology. In R. J. Sternberg (Ed.), *Career paths in psychology: Where your degree can take you* (2nd ed., pp. 227–248). Washington, DC: American Psychological Association.

Carlson, C., & Christenson, S. L. (2005). Evidence-based parent and family interventions in school psychology: Overview and procedures. *School Psychology Quarterly, 20,* 345–351.

Curtis, M. J., Lopez, A. D., Castillo, J. M., Batsche, G. M., Minch, D., & Smith, J. C. (2008). The status of school psychology: Demographic characteristics, professional practices, and continuing professional development. *Communique, 36*(5), 27–29.

Fagan, T. K. (2002). School psychology: Recent descriptions, continued expansion, and an ongoing paradox. *School Psychology Review, 31,* 5–10.

Fagan, T. K., & Wise, P. S. (2007). *School psychology: Past, present and future* (3rd ed.). Bethesda, MD: National Association of School Psychologists.

Friedman, R. M. (2001). The practice of psychology with children, adolescents and their families: A look to the future. In J. N. Hughes, A. M. LaGreca, & J. C. Conoley (Eds.), *Handbook of psychological services for children and adolescents* (pp. 3–22). New York: Oxford.

Friedman, R. M., Katz-Leavy, J. W., Manderscheid, R. W., & Sondheimer, D. L. (1998). Prevalence of serious emotional disturbance: An update. In R. W. Manderscheid & D. L. Sondheimer (Eds.), *Mental health, United States, 1998* (pp. 110–112). Rockville, MD: Substance Abuse and Mental Health Services Administration.

Gilman, R., & Medway, F. J. (2007). Teachers' perceptions of school psychology: A comparison of regular and special education teacher ratings. *School Psychology Quarterly, 22,* 145–161.

Kratochwill, T. R. (2007). Preparing psychologists for evidence-based school practice: Lessons learned and challenges ahead. *American Psychologist, 62,* 829–843.

Miller, D. C. (2008). School psychology training programs. In A. Thomas & J. Grimes (Eds.), *Best practices in school psychology V* (Vol. 1, pp. clv–cxcviii). Bethesda, MD: National Association of School Psychologists.

Miller, D. N., George, M. P., & Fogt, J. B. (2005). Establishing and sustaining research-based practices at Centennial school: A descriptive case study of systemic change. *Psychology in the Schools, 42,* 553–567.

Ollendick, T. H. (2005). Evidence-based parent and family interventions in school psychology: A commentary. *School Psychology Quarterly, 20,* 512–517.

Pelco, L. E., Jacobson, L., Ries, R. R., & Melka, S. (2000). Perspectives and practices in family-school partnerships: A national survey of school psychologists. *School Psychology Review, 29,* 235–250.

Riccio, C. A., & Hughes, J. N. (2001). Established and emerging models of psychological services in school settings. In J. N. Hughes, A. M. LaGreca, & J. C. Conoley (Eds.), *Handbook of psychological services for children and adolescents* (pp. 63–88). New York: Oxford.

Riva, M. S., & Erickson Cornish, J. A. (2008). Group supervision practices at psychology predoctoral internship programs: 15 years later. *Training and Education in Professional Psychology, 2,* 18–25.

Rollin, S. A., Subtonik, R. F., Bassford, M., & Smulson, J. (2008). Bringing psychological science to the forefront of educational policy: Collaborative efforts of the American Psychological Association's coalition for psychology in the schools and education. *Psychology in the Schools, 45*, 194–205.

Rosenfield, S. (2008). Psychology and education, together again. *Psychology in the Schools, 45*, 257–259.

Rossen, E., & Oakland, T. (2008). Graduate preparation in research methods: the current status of APA-accredited professional programs in psychology. *Training and Education in Professional Psychology, 2*, 42–49.

Sheridan, S. M., & Gutkin, T. B. (2000). The ecology of school psychology: Examining and changing our paradigm for the 21st century. *School Psychology Review, 29*, 485–502.

Shernoff, E. S., Kratochwill, T. R., & Stoiber, K. C. (2003). Training in evidence-based interventions: What are school psychology programs teaching? *Journal of School Psychology, 41*, 467–483.

2 Putting school psychology training into historical perspective

What's new? What's old?

Thomas K. Fagan

INTRODUCTION

It is difficult to observe a characteristic of the field and name its origin with certainty. Although I generally avoid terms such as *first, earliest, only, never,* and *always*, there are some judgments that can be made about developments in the field, including those in the history of preparing school psychologists for practice (Fagan, 1986a, 1999, 2008; Fagan & Wells, 2000; Fagan & Wise, 2007). Contemporary school psychology training is vastly different from how it was decades ago. The number of U.S. institutions offering a school psychology program has grown from the first program at New York University in the late 1920s, to 28 at the time of the Thayer Conference in 1954, to approximately 100 at the time the National Association of School Psychologists (NASP) was founded in 1969, to 211 in the mid 1980s, to a recent estimate of 238 institutions (Fagan, 2008; Miller, 2008). Contemporary training programs share several characteristics. These include degrees offered and program requirements; models of training; program content; field experiences, including practica and internships; the influence of credentialing guidelines and accreditation; and miscellaneous descriptions, including descriptions of the faculty, students, and facilities. These areas are discussed and serve as a backdrop to some of the subsequent chapters.

AVAILABLE DEGREES AND REQUIREMENTS

Although contemporary training of school psychologists occurs exclusively at the graduate level, and most practitioners hold specialist level or doctoral degrees, this is a relatively recent characteristic. The earliest known program at New York University offered programs for school psychologists leading to the BS, AM, and PhD degrees (New York University, 1929). The 1954 Thayer Conference proceedings (Cutts, 1955) identified several programs at the graduate level and recommended graduate preparation in 2-year (master's) and 4-year (doctoral) programs for preparation as psychometrists and school psychologists, respectively. The varied levels of training for practitioners at that time were observed in the preconference survey data ($N = 468$): Almost 10% held only the BA degree, 25% held the doctoral degree (77% PhD, 23% EdD), and the remaining 65% held a master's degree, including several who were working toward a doctoral degree (Cutts, 1955, p. 119). Most school practitioners held a master's degree, with at least 28 different majors, and 25% held the doctoral degree, with at least 9 different majors (Division of School Psychologists, 1954). Thus, despite strong preferences for graduate degree training, many practiced with less preparation. Although some practitioners may have come from the New York University or other undergraduate programs, it is more likely that many were persons with undergraduate training in teacher education or psychology who completed additional course work or on-the-job training in psychoeducational testing.

The shift to graduate level preparation can be observed in the several published surveys of programs in the 1960s (Fagan, Delugach, Mellon, & Schlitt, 1986) and the NASP training program directories of the past 30 years. Although identified as an alternative to traditional PhD and EdD degrees almost 90 years ago (Hollingworth, 1918), the PsyD (doctor of psychology) degree has been available in school psychology only since the 1970s; the first was apparently in the professional program at Rutgers University (Brown & Lindstrom, 1977, p. 240). Available degrees in school psychology have contracted from undergraduate and graduate options to graduate degrees only but also have expanded to include a variety of graduate degrees, including the PhD, EdD, PsyD, MA, MS, MEd, MSEd, and the increasingly common EdS degree or an equivalent certificate of advanced studies (Thomas, 1998; Miller, 2008).

The training of early and well-known "school" psychologists was highly varied in content and length of preparation (Fagan, 1999). Graduate degrees were often completed in 1–3 years; they seem to have been more in a mentorial mode, where the overall completion of the program was decided by one's mentor, and specific requirements seem to have been fewer. In contrast, contemporary training is more specific, even prescriptive, and according to Thomas (1998) the typical degree lengths are 40 (master's), 66 (specialist), and 103.5 (doctoral) semester hours. The requirements for contemporary degrees have expanded from the earlier 1-year master's level degree to 2 years, and doctoral preparation has expanded to at least 4 years of study, not including the 1-year internship. The specialist degree, not available until the latter half of the 20th century, typically takes 2 years of graduate study and a year of internship.

Models of training

The early literature of school psychology reflects many opinions about the type of preparation school psychologists should receive, but there were no generally agreed upon training models. Discussions emphasized preparation in psychology and education, in basic and applied areas, and the importance of field experiences (Gesell, Goddard, & Wallin, 1919; Hollingworth, 1918; New York State Association for Applied Psychology, 1943). Long-standing tensions between the traditional research-oriented psychology camp and that of applied and professional psychology failed to achieve a national consensus on training until the scientist-practitioner model gained ascendancy from the 1949 Boulder Conference for clinical psychology (Raimy, 1950). That model was promoted at later conferences, including the 1954 Thayer Conference for school psychology (Cutts, 1955). Greater recognition of practitioner oriented training emerged from the 1973 Vail Conference, which encouraged the growth of professional programs granting the PsyD degree and the development of freestanding professional schools (Korman, 1974). Contemporary school psychology doctoral programs are organized to various degrees around these two training models. Nondoctoral programs are heavily influenced by state credentialing expectations and follow a pragmatic model (Fagan & Wise, 2007). Thus, broad models of training are relatively recent in the history of school psychology, and even more specific models of preparation (e.g., behavioral, ecological) are observed in most program descriptions.

Program content

Early training advocates consistently recommended doctoral preparation, and there was scant discussion of nondoctoral issues because such persons were considered unqualified unless under doctoral supervision. Of course, in the absence of credentialing regulations there were many practitioners with far less training. Early school practitioners were prepared in areas advocated by Witmer (1907), Gesell et al. (1919), and Hollingworth (1918), who identified the following areas as prerequisite to practice: clinical psychology, educational psychology, general-experimental psychology, mental hygiene, mental tests, teaching methods (reading, spelling, arithmetic), psychology and teaching of children with disabilities, practical and field experience, and social pathology (e.g., delinquency and mental deficiency); research, statistics, and thesis courses were also expected.

In addition, graduate students, especially doctoral students, often completed courses in related fields such as educational history and philosophy, sociology, medicine, and foreign languages. Many doctoral programs required proficiency in one more foreign languages, but this aspect of training seems to have disappeared by the 1970s or been supplemented with other "languages" (e.g., computer or sign language). The language requirement was appropriate in much earlier times, when some psychological publications had to be translated and when psychology students often completed doctoral training in Europe.

Training recommendations were provided by the New York State Association for Applied Psychology (1943), the Thayer Conference (Cutts,

1955), the Division of School Psychologists, the American Psychological Association (APA, 1981), and the NASP training standards. The New York State Association for Applied Psychology recommendations were spread across 10 areas and, although degree levels of training were not specified, a doctoral preparation was intended: advanced general psychology, experimental psychology, psychology and methods of teaching, problems or principles of education, educational measurement, psychology of growth, psychology of adjustment problems, clinical tests and procedures, clinical experience under qualified supervision (in both educational and clinical settings), and physical bases. Length of graduate preparation was not specified, but undergraduate work in the junior and senior years could be applied to meet requirements.

The Thayer conference proceedings recommended two levels of preparation, titles, and credentialing (the Thayer model) that has influenced the field for decades (Fagan, 2005). The University of Michigan's 2-year program (MSEd) was used as an example (Cutts, 1955, pp. 149–150) and included several prerequisite psychology and education courses and graduate courses totaling 35–37 hours and a 15-week full-time or equivalent part-time internship. Areas included measurements (9–10 hours, including statistics and individual testing), background courses (13 hours, including child development, mental hygiene of childhood and adolescence, personality development, education of exceptional children, educational and social control of mentally retarded children, and a course on medical information), and related courses (13–14 hours, including clinical study of atypical children; social learning; psychology of high school subjects; psychology and teaching of reading, spelling, writing, and arithmetic; physical growth of the child; experimental study of personality; and basic methods in psychology). A doctoral program example was provided by the program at the University of Illinois, which offered either the EdD or the PhD degree over a 3-year program and a 12-month internship (Cutts, pp. 168–170). The program of studies was divided into general orientation, educational and psychological diagnosis, dynamics and development of individual behavior, group and interpersonal relationships, and research planning and execution. Practicum experiences occurred across the years of study. Both program examples were jointly sponsored between units in education and psychology, emphasized special education and exceptional children, mental testing, and teaching methods, with a requirement of a teaching credential or equivalent training. Greater emphasis on research and diverse field settings were mentioned for the doctoral program.

The proposals of the American Psychological Association (APA) Division of School Psychologists (Bardon, 1963) were organized around five areas, allowing for some requirements to be met by undergraduate courses (proportions of training are in parentheses): (a) psychological foundations—theoretical and experimental (24 semester hours, 30%); (b) psychological methods and techniques (27 semester hours, 35%); (c) educational foundations—social, philosophical, historical; (d) school organization and program (18 semester hours, 25% for c + d); (e) electives (9 semester hours, 10%). Also recommended was a one semester (525 clock hours) or more supervised field experience, at least 50% of which was to be completed in a public school or university's campus school facility. The division's proposals were for preparation and credentialing of school psychologists at the doctoral level. Its proposed preparation for the "psychological assistant certification" was far less specific except for "an externship of at least 350 clock hours or equivalent experience." (Bardon, p. 714). Several years later, Division 16 published guidelines for both doctoral and nondoctoral programs undoubtedly developed to facilitate its longtime effort to achieve APA program accreditation (Division 16, American Psychological Association Subcommittee on Education and Training [Division 16], 1971, 1972a). The guidelines were comprehensive in their recommendations for facilities, faculty and student characteristics, as well as program content and field experiences. The nondoctoral expectations were not prescriptive and included five basic areas: "developmental psychology, learning, personality, measurement, research literacy courses. In addition, courses are desirable in abnormal, physiological, social, statistics and research design" (Division 16, 1971, p. 6). Practicum experience in campus and community school facilities was encouraged, and the internship recommendations followed from those of the Peabody Conference (Gray, 1963); doctoral internships were to be at least 1 school year and nondoctoral internships at least one semester. At the doctoral level content emphases were on a scientist-practitioner model, with preparation in psychology and education, and emphasis on theory and practice. Specific content courses were not listed, but the following description was offered:

> Training programs in school psychology have typically provided courses in what might be called "professional psychology." Among the most common offerings are courses in special problems in the practice of school psychology, psychodiagnostic procedures (group and individual), abnormal child psychology, learning problems, and interventional procedures, among them behavior modification, consultation, group techniques, parent counseling, techniques of psychotherapy, in-service activities, and educational remediation (Division 16, 1972a, p. 23).

Contemporary program content, strongly influenced by these earlier recommendations, has been all but standardized by the policies of the APA and the NASP. The APA efforts were observed in its specialty guidelines (APA, 1981) which recognized nondoctoral practitioners but, following APA policy, provided expectations only for doctoral trainees. Programs were to be at least 3 years of full-time graduate study, with

> didactic and experiential instruction (a) in scientific and professional areas common to all professional psychology programs, such as ethics

and standards, research design and methodology, statistics, and psychometric methods, and (b) in such substantive areas as the biological bases of behavior, the cognitive and affective bases of behavior, the social, cultural, ethnic, and sex roles bases of behavior, and individual differences. Course work includes social and philosophical bases of education, curriculum theory and practice, etiology of learning and behavior disorders, exceptional children and special education. Organization theory and administrative practice should also be included in the program. (p. 43)

Supervised practicum and internship were also expected, and the latter was to be a 1,200 clock hour internship, at least 600 of which were to be in a school setting.

The NASP put forth training standards in 1972 (NASP, 1972), formalized them in 1978 (NASP, 1978) for enforcement via the National Council for Accreditation of Teacher Education (NCATE), and for more than 20 years has required programs to organize content to be consistent with the editions of the school psychology *Blueprint* documents (National School Psychology Inservice Training Network, 1984; Ysseldyke et al., 1997, 2006). The earliest NASP standards emphasized specific areas of course content: individual assessment, individual differences, exceptional child, learning and remediation, personality theory and development, school organizations, and measurement/accountability/research (NASP, 1972). The later and more formalized standards (NASP, 1978) emphasized broad areas with specific core content areas: psychological foundations (human learning, child and adolescent development (normal and abnormal), human exceptionality and cultural diversity), educational foundations (organization and operations of the schools, instructional and remedial techniques, special education), psycho-educational methods evaluation (psycho-educational assessment, research design and statistics), intervention (consultation, behavior modification, counseling, organization and administration of pupil services), and professional school psychology (professional issues, standards and ethics in school psychology).

In adopting the *Blueprint* documents, NASP training standards shifted from specific content areas to domains of practice around which program content was to be organized. The original *Blueprint* (National School Psychology Inservice Training Network, 1984) specified 16 domains, while *Blueprint II* (Ysseldyke et al., 1997) specified 10, and *Blueprint III* (Ysseldyke et al., 2006) specified 8, with 4 in foundational competencies and 4 in functional competencies.

The changing content expectations reveal less specific course title expectations but increasing content expectations to be embedded within specialist level programs. Even doctoral programs may find it difficult to manage all the expectations in a standard degree format. Contemporary programs are also unique in content and courses in crisis intervention, psychopharmacology, several forms of consultation, specialized research designs, and statistical procedures (e.g., path analysis, meta-analysis). The specialized content follows upon advances in research design and statistics, assessment and interventions, and the broader events in society and American education. Where a course on juvenile delinquency might have been available in early training programs, courses in crisis intervention and diversity would be common today.

Practicum and internship

Field experiences and practical training have been recommended since the time of the first psychological clinic (Witmer, 1907). A structured internship akin to school psychology practice was initiated under Goddard at the Vineland Training School in 1908 (Morrow, 1946). The current expectations for at least one practicum experience in addition to practical applications components of skill-building courses (e.g., assessment) and for a school year of internship are extensions of earlier expectations. Practica were usually built into the skill-building courses, and any separate practicum experience was more akin to current internships. Supervised experiences in the community and its schools were often unavailable, and practicum experiences often occurred in campus-based clinics and/or the few available community facilities (Fagan, 1999). In much earlier times, the terms *practicum* and *internship* often connoted a similar type of field experience, often defined as clock hours of supervised practice. Hence, early programs had practical application components embedded within some courses and then had a separate field practicum. The expectation for a separate practicum and internship evolved over several decades and was recommended at the Thayer Conference. Contemporary programs are expected to have at least one separate practicum experience for nondoctoral training and several such experiences at the doctoral level.

As mentioned under program content, the Division of School Psychologists recommended that state education agencies require an internship of at least one semester (525 clock hours) for certification as a school psychologist and at least 350 clock hours for the psychological assistant certificate (Bardon, 1963). In its later training recommendations, the expectations were for at least one semester for nondoctoral trainees and at least 1 school year for doctoral (Division 16, 1971, 1972a).

Nondoctoral trainees were often expected to have a semester or less of internship experiences and, although preferring a school-year-long experience, a minimum of a 10-week, full-time internship appeared in early NASP guidelines (NASP, 1972). However, even prior to the founding of NASP, some states had greater expectations and required full-time, supervised internships of 1 school year. For example, Ohio had developed a statewide system of internships funded in part by and approved by the Ohio Department of Education by the mid-1950s (Bonham & Grover, 1961). Illinois also had a state-approved system, though not with as much state education agency support and oversight. Today, based upon the revisions of state education standards and the guidelines of both APA and NASP, the expectation of a 1-school-year supervised internship in a school setting is widespread for entry-level credentialing for school practice. Doctoral internships now require a minimum of 1,500 clock hours of supervised experience, and nondoctoral internships require a minimum of 1,200 hours.

Due primarily to the efforts of APA, its state affiliates, and the state psychology boards, a nationwide system of doctoral level internships has existed for many years. A clearinghouse for such internships has been managed since 1976 by the Association of Psychology Postdoctoral and Internship Centers. The system of internships is a major advancement in the overall predoctoral preparation of professional psychologists. Emanating from Veterans Administration settings at the time of the Boulder Conference, the system has expanded to a variety of settings, including school districts. This doctoral-level national system has no counterpart at the nondoctoral level. For the most part, nondoctoral training programs employ a system of internships developed in conjunction with the state department of education, but more often each program and its students seek out internships on an ad hoc basis each year.

Nondoctoral credentialing is done almost exclusively by state education agencies, influenced by program approvals conducted by the state education agencies (SEAs) through NASP's relationship with the NCATE. In this arrangement, school psychology has closely followed the models employed for teacher education as acknowledged in NASP's earliest guidelines (NASP, 1972, note, p. 4). Therein, colleges and programs, including their field experiences, are approved by the state or by a joint state-NCATE partnership. Comparable to student teaching, school psychology internships are developed by each program, and the appropriateness of sites is the responsibility of the program. The evolution of the two different internship oversight arrangements (doctoral and nondoctoral) is an example of the historical emergence and importance of the two worlds of school psychology (i.e., organized psychology and organized education).

The influence of credentialing guidelines

Credentialing requirements for school psychological personnel originated with large urban districts, then were developed by SEAs, and then by state boards of examiners in psychology (SBEPs). For example, the New York City Department of Education had an exam for psychologists that required a master's degree in psychology and 1 year's experience in mental measurement (Department of Education, 1925). (This flyer was posted to notify applicants of the procedures and requirements for the examination. In addition to posting an annual salary of $2,200, a statement regarding possible tenure was included. The requirements also listed citizenship, a physical examination, and that the applicant must be "over 25 and under 46 years of age" unless the applicant was already a New York City regular teacher.) It is likely that other major cities had specific hiring requirements as well. State level credentialing dates to the mid-1930s through the SEA in New York and in Pennsylvania. At that time there were no states with nonschool practice credentials formally granted by an SBEP. The New York and Pennsylvania requirements were rather specific about areas of study and practical experience. The following descriptions are extracted from those requirements and a related discussion (Fagan, 1999).

The Pennsylvania requirements applied to two levels: public school psychologists and public school psychological examiners (Pennsylvania State Council on Education, 1934). The overall requirements were "the completion of an approved college or university curriculum" and additional semester hours of study and practicum distributed across several areas (48 hours for the school psychologist, 36 hours for the examiner). The only difference in the requirements was 12 semester hours of experience.

Part I. Theory or content (24 semester hours in the following courses):

1. Educational psychology (6 semester hours, 4 in laboratory work and 2 in lecture courses)
2. Clinical psychology, abnormal psychology, psychology of atypical children, psychology of exceptional children, psychology of abnormal children, psychology and education of atypical or subnormal children (4 semester hours)
3. Psychology of childhood and adolescence (4 semester hours)
4. Tests and measurements (4 semester hours, to include individual and group tests, theory and application, interpretation)
5. Statistical methods (2)

Unassigned courses (4 semester hours) from "mental hygiene, social psychology, psychology of personality, and courses usually classified as sociological, studying the causes of poverty, dependence and delinquency" (Pennsylvania State Council on Education, 1934, p. 25).

Part II. Laboratory and practice (12 semester hours):

1. Clinical methods, practice, and diagnosis (4 semester hours)
2. Diagnostic teaching (2 semester hours)
3. Individual research in educational psychology (4 semester hours, including individual case research work)
4. Social service and field work (2 semester hours)

Part III. Experience (12 semester hours): "Experience in recognized and approved psychological work, including diagnosis and recommendation for care and remedial treatment shall be required. Equivalent—216 clock hours" (Pennsylvania State Council on Education, p. 25).

The 1937 revised Pennsylvania requirements included greater distinction between the two levels in five areas: general and theoretical psychology, psychometric techniques, other specialized techniques, related courses, and clinical practice (under supervision and allowable in several settings in addition to schools).

The New York SEA requirements, also adopted in 1934, provided for provisional and permanent certificates. The provisional certificate requirements included a 4-year BA or BS curriculum "offered by a recognized institution of higher education, and in addition 30 semester hours in approved graduate courses leading to the master's degree with a major in psychology or approved equivalent preparation; said preparation shall have included 52 semester hours in appropriate courses distributed according to the following schedule" (Cooper, 1935, p. 15):

General psychology (6 semester hours)

Education and educational psychology (21 semester hours) to include at least one course in each of the following areas: Group 1, methods of teaching, psychology of school subjects, remedial methods, guidance or similar courses; Group 2, history principles or philosophy of education; educational sociology, or similar courses; Group 3, educational measurements and statistics; Group 4, psychology of childhood, adolescence, learning, child development, or similar courses.

Clinical psychology (12 semester hours) may include individual psychology, abnormal psychology, psychiatry, social psychology, psychology of subnormal, psychology of superior children, delinquency, mental hygiene, mental adjustment, and social casework.

Clinical tests and procedures (3 semester hours) (no description given).

"Supervised practice in the giving of individual tests and in making reports involving interpretation and recommendation" (4 semester hours) (Cooper, 1935, p. 15).

Applied anatomy and physiology (6 semester hours) may include neuroanatomy, neuropathology, hygiene, and speech development.

The permanent certificate had additional expectations that "the psychologist shall have prepared 50 case reports which have been submitted to and approved by the State Education Department" and "shall have completed five years of appropriate experience, three of which, during the preceding five-year period, shall have been as a student psychologist in the public schools of New York State" (Cooper, 1935, p. 16).

The early Pennsylvania and New York requirements signify a high degree of coursework specificity in early credentialing and that expectations in the mid-1930s were increasing to the graduate level but allowing a mixture of undergraduate and graduate courses to meet the overall requirements. Both made mention of approved or recognized institutions and programs and considerable supervised field experience, suggesting a new form of oversight developing in the training-credentialing arena for school practice. The early SEA credentialing requirements were closely related to the needs of special educators for expert assistance in identifying children for services. The early requirements of New York and Connecticut SEAs reflected the difficulties in obtaining appropriate training and the need for two or more levels of recognition (Cornell, 1941; Cutts, 1943).

The Thayer Conference report identified 20 states and the District of Columbia that certificated school psychologists by "either school laws or the regulations of the state board of education" (Cutts, 1955, p. 108). The credentialing requirements were referred to as chaotic, with several levels of service provision and degree requirements from a "B.A. or a B.A. with a major in psychology, to the doctoral degree and APA membership" (Cutts, p. 109). "Twelve of these states and the District of Columbia require a teaching certificate as well as specific training in psychology, ... and seven of that twelve also require from one to three years of teaching" (Cutts, p. 130). The other eight did not require a teaching credential or experience. The requirement of a teaching credential and/or experience has all but disappeared over the past 50 years (Fagan, 2005). The Thayer recommendations formed the basis of the APA Division of School Psychologists' proposals for state certification (Bardon, 1963). Like the earlier state standards of Pennsylvania and New York, the Division's earliest proposal allowed for blending undergraduate and graduate courses to meet requirements. At present, all school psychology credentialing is based on graduate degrees and would recognize undergraduate courses only as prerequisites.

During the period 1930–1980, every state established credentials for school psychology personnel through their respective SEA and/or SBEP. Credentialing by an SBEP emerged slowly from a period of little or no regulation and was a central concern for applied psychologists and their state associations (see, e.g., Britt, 1941; Fryer, 1941; Hollingworth, 1922). A chronology of states approving licensing laws indicates that Connecticut was first, in 1945, and Missouri was the final state to do so, in 1977 (Committee for the Advancement of Professional Practice Centennial Task Force, 1992). Unlike SEA credentialing, SBEP requirements have evolved in close accord with the policies of the APA, have emphasized generic doctoral level practice based on APA policies, and, in some states, permitted a nondoctoral credential. The requirements blend basic psychology and professional psychology training, emphasize the scientist-practitioner and the professional models, and tend not to be prescriptive as applied to practice settings.

The SEA and SBEP requirements for credentialing are the most potent influences on the structure and content of contemporary training programs. Although it could be argued that a more potent force is the national level standards for accreditation and credentialing of the APA and the NASP, these are only enforceable when adopted by the state level agencies that have the authority to require them. Among the major changes over the course of school psychology training history has been the shift to developing training around the state credentialing agencies' requirements. This evolved as an increasing number of states secured the privilege of granting school psychologist credentials, as national-level training and credentialing standards were developed, and as the number of training programs rapidly increased after the 1950s to meet an increasing demand by school districts for psychologists to assist with special education assessments. Prior to that time, programs were far more likely to be developed in accordance with the philosophy of the administrative unit and program faculty and their judgment of the needs of school districts for psychological services.

As a consequence of this shift, the breadth of training appears to have narrowed, and programs, especially nondoctoral programs, have become almost entirely prescriptive. Few programs today could find room in the curriculum for many of the courses taken by early practitioners trained in an era of little or no regulation. Thus, the influence on school psychology training of credentialing agency requirements is an increasingly important development of the past 70 years. Perhaps the growth of graduate programs, and the accreditation–credentialing linkages, encouraged both the NASP and the Division of School Psychology-APA to abandon earlier efforts to encourage credentialing at several levels, including paraprofessionals (Division 16, 1972b; NASP, Training and Accreditation Committee, circa 1972). The recent clamor over the potential removal of the exemption for school psychologists in the APA's 1987 Model Licensing Act is a clear indication of the significance of national policy to state credentialing agencies. It is of historical note that the Model Certified Psychologists' Act of the American Association of Applied Psychologists (Committee on Legislation, 1939) proposed only doctoral certification but included an exemption for "any person certified by the Department of (Education) as a public school psychologist or psychological examiner in a public or private school" (p. 127).

Accreditation

The formal, external approval of training programs evolved over many decades, and the current national level system has state historical counterparts. For example, New York's SEA identified specific institutions whose training programs were consistent with its certification requirements (Cornell, 1942). Among the most recent of the major forces and changes in school psychology training has been the development of national level accreditation (Fagan & Wells, 2000). Accreditation by the APA, specific to doctoral school psychology programs, was not achieved until 1971. APA accreditation has followed the evolving policies and requirements of the APA's Committee on Accreditation, which takes a comprehensive perspective on training programs and their content as described elsewhere in this handbook. The content expectations are spread over broad areas, many of which are observed in earlier guidelines (see, e.g., APA, Committee on Accreditation, 2005, Domain B: Program Philosophy, Objectives, and Curriculum).

The accreditation history of programs via the NCATE preceded that of the APA and was applied to doctoral and nondoctoral programs. The NASP's affiliation with the NCATE dates to the early 1970s, and the process of NASP program approvals dates to 1988 (Fagan & Wells, 2000). The approval process via the NASP is also comprehensive, blending the domains of the *Blueprint II* with those of the NASP Training Standards (NASP, 2000).

Accreditation and program approvals have been a major force in shaping the content and structure of training programs. As indicated above, the accreditation requirements evolved from national level organizational policies that have reciprocally influenced, if not dominated, the development and revision of state credentialing requirements.

Miscellaneous comparisons

In general, early faculty were trained in general-experimental or educational psychology and took the few clinical courses that were available. For example, Arnold Gesell completed his doctorate under G. S. Hall of child study fame, and Lightner Witmer completed his under Wilhelm Wundt in Germany. Many of the persons who helped to develop contemporary training programs had backgrounds in clinical and educational psychology, came from varied undergraduate backgrounds, and held practitioner positions before joining the academy (Fagan, 1999). In contrast, contemporary school psychology faculty are more likely to have completed an undergraduate major in psychology, graduated with a doctoral degree in school psychology, and hold school psychologist credentials.

Earlier training programs were in psychology and/or education administrative units, sometimes offering degrees in both, and often included a campus demonstration school in which field experiences could be obtained. Technological advancements in instruction and communication are very noticeable, and contemporary program facilities share little in common with their historical counterparts except for classroom space and campus location. Even these are changing as programs turn to internet options for instruction and Web-based degree programs.

It is likely that current students come from less diverse undergraduate majors than in earlier times, and certainly fewer students are required to have teaching degrees and experience. It is difficult to judge whether the student population is younger, although many earlier school psychology trainees entered training after experience in other fields. Although women have held a strong presence throughout our history, the percentage of females among current graduate students seems higher than at any previous time.

The expectations of positive personal characteristics of students (mental stability, intelligence, responsibility, etc.) have been observed throughout the history of training (Fagan & Wise, 2007).

An assistantship to offset the cost of graduate training was awarded in 1890–1891 to Witmer with James McKeen Cattell at the University of Pennsylvania, and a fellowship to Gesell with G. S. Hall at Clark University paid $100 and a remission of all fees (Fagan, 1999). Hence the contemporary practice of providing financial assistance to graduate students dates to the beginning of the field.

Little has been found regarding the organization of school psychology graduate students in departmental associations, but many graduate programs now have such groups that are often connected to student affiliations embedded within the APA's Division of School Psychology and/or the NASP. A student affiliate group appears to have been initiated in Division 16 in the latter 1970s (Fagan, 1996). Student members comprise almost one fourth of NASP's entire membership.

Ironically, in the first 20 years of the Division's history, faculty memberships were not allowed unless the person had 2 years of service experience; hence the original title, Division of School Psycholog*ists*. This restriction was dropped in 1966, and the title was changed to School Psycholo*gy* in 1968–1969. The vast majority of current division members are trainers (Fagan, 1996), and the Division serves as a major representative of trainers' interests.

CONCLUSIONS

Early training programs were spurred by the advancements and applications of testing, especially that of intelligence and achievement. Contemporary programs continue to be developed around assessment, but of a broader nature, and around several important areas of intervention connected to both regular and special education. Nevertheless, most content areas of contemporary programs (see, e.g., Fagan & Wise, 2007, chap. 6) have historical antecedents. Unlike its early history, contemporary training has less overlap with related fields (e.g., clinical and educational psychology, school counseling, social work). Although earlier degree titles continue to be available, there has been an expansion of titles resulting from the availability of programs in both education and psychology administrative units, the expansion of training to the specialist level, and the emergence of professional programs offering degrees other than the PhD or EdD. However, the range of backgrounds from which practitioners come seems to have lessened since the time of the Thayer Conference, and there is a smaller proportion of school psychologists with prior teaching preparation and experience.

Content has changed considerably, though the major areas of psychological and educational foundations, professional courses, and field experiences remain. The length of preparation seems to have increased, and specialized content courses are more often required. Field experience requirements have increased considerably and surprisingly are consistent with recommendations made almost 90 years ago.

The evolution and changes in school psychology training of the past century occurred in the context of the regulatory impact of accreditation and credentialing. Since the emergence of SEA and SBEP credentialing, and later of accreditation, the training of school psychologists has been increasingly regulated. An analogous development in the practice of school psychology would be the impact of federal legislation, such as P.L. 93-380, Section 504 of the Rehabilitation Act, P.L. 94-142 (now the Individuals with Disabilities Education Improvement Act), and the No Child Left Behind Act. The interdependent relationships of accreditation at the national level and credentialing at the state level are the most powerful factors in the structure and curriculum of contemporary programs. That the national guidelines of the APA and the NASP and the state guidelines of psychology boards and state education agencies, respectively, are in most cases very similar is no accident (Fagan, 1986b). Over the past 50 years, the ideologies of the national level accreditors have heavily influenced the credentialing requirements and vice versa. It is virtually impossible for any current school psychology program to survive without at least meeting some form of oversight, especially SEA credentialing requirements for school-based practice. The agencies and organizations described in Fagan (1986b) and Chapter 7 of Fagan and Wise (2007) continue to dominate the professional and political determinants of many aspects of the field.

Contemporary students are better prepared in psychology and less likely to have been a former school teacher, and the cohort is more diverse ethnically and culturally. The current trainee cohort is judged to comprise more females than at any other time, especially at the doctoral level. This is even clearer at the level of training program faculty, and the increase has spread to leadership positions across the field.

Historical antecedents continue to influence the training of school psychologists but also to blend with societal events to pose several challenges. Can school psychology training programs close the gap between societal diversity and that of the training cohort? Will the emergence of nontraditional training options (e.g., Web-based programs) diminish the historical legacy of campus-based programs? Will the supply of doctoral school psychologists be able to meet the demand for faculty positions? Will the didactic content of programs become increasingly specialized, moving further away from our foundations in psychology and education? Will postdoctoral training become a necessity in order to meet the needs for future services? Will field experience requirements be forced to expand to meet these needs? Will the field ever resolve its long-standing conflicts of its two levels of training, credentialing, and practice? These and other challenges portend a complex but exciting future for the training of school psychologists. School psychology has struggled for more than a century to achieve its unique status among the specialties of professional psychology. It has survived the many challenges of its past and will continue to meet the challenges of the future.

RESOURCES

Fagan, T. K. (2008). Trends in the history of school psychology in the United States. In A. Thomas & J. Grimes (Eds.), *Best practices in school psychology V* (Vol. 6, pp. 2069–2086). Bethesda, MD: National Association of School Psychologists.
This is a documentary on the history of school psychology and its metamorphosis over the years. It provides a more detailed account of the historical perspective provided herein.

Reschly, D. J. (2008). School psychology paradigm shift and beyond. In A. Thomas & J. Grimes (Eds.), *Best practices in school psychology V* (Vol. 1, pp. 3–16). Bethesda, MD: National Association of School Psychologists.
Rather than a discussion of historical perspectives, this chapter focuses on the current paradigm shift and the socio-legal-political influences that shape school psychology practice.

REFERENCES

American Psychological Association. (1981). Specialty guidelines for the delivery of services by school psychologists. In *Specialty guidelines for the delivery of services* (pp. 33–44). Washington, DC: Author. See also *American Psychologist, 36*, 640–681.
American Psychological Association, Committee on Accreditation. (2005). *Guidelines and principles for accreditation of programs in professional psychology.* Washington, DC: Author.
Bardon, J. I. (1963). Proposals for state department of education certification of school psychologists. *American Psychologist, 18*, 711–714.
Bonham, S. J., & Grover, E. C. (1961). *The history and development of school psychology in Ohio.* Columbus, OH: Department of Education.
Britt, S. H. (1941). Pending developments in the legal status of psychologists. *Journal of Consulting Psychology, 5*, 52–56.
Brown, D. T., & Lindstrom, J. P. (1977). *Directory of school psychology training programs in the United States and Canada.* Stratford, CT: National Association of School Psychologists.
Committee for the Advancement of Professional Practice Centennial Task Force. (1992). *Milestones in psychology practice: 1892–1992.* Washington, DC: American Psychological Association.

Committee on Legislation, Board of Affiliates of the AAAP. (1939). Model "Certified Psychologists' Act." *Journal of Consulting Psychology, 3*(4), 123–127.

Cooper, H. (1935). *Certification bulletin No. 3, certification for school services. Laws, rules, regulations, and information.* Albany, NY: University of the State of New York.

Cornell, E. L. (1941). Certification of specialized groups of psychologists (School Psychologists). *Journal of Consulting Psychology, 5*(2), 62–65.

Cornell, E. L. (1942). *The work of the school psychologist* (Bulletin No. 1238). Albany, NY: Division of Research: New York State Education Department.

Cutts, N. E. (1943). Development of a certification procedure for school psychologists. *Journal of Consulting Psychology, 7*(1), 45–49.

Cutts, N. E. (Ed.). (1955). *School psychologists at mid-century.* Washington, DC: American Psychological Association.

Division 16, American Psychological Association Subcommittee on Education and Training. (1971). Standards and criteria for non-doctoral training programs in school psychology. *The School Psychologist, 26*(2), 2–11.

Division 16, American Psychological Association Subcommittee on Education and Training. (1972a). Standards and criteria for the accreditation of doctoral training programs in school psychology. *The School Psychologist, 26*(4), 17–32.

Division 16, American Psychological Association Subcommittee on Education and Training. (1972b). Proposals for state department of education certification of school psychologists. *The School Psychologist, 26*(4), 14–17.

Division of School Psychologists, American Psychological Association, Committee on Certification and Training. (1954). *Survey of school psychologists 1953–54, summary for the Thayer Work Conference August 1954.* (Available in the Ralph Tindall Papers, M 2006, Archives of the History of American Psychology, University of Akron, Akron, OH.)

Department of Education, City of New York, Office of the Board of Examiners. (1925, December 29). Examination for license as psychologist. New York: Author.

Fagan, T. K. (1986a). The historical origins and growth of programs to prepare school psychologists in the United States. *Journal of School Psychology, 24*(1), 9–22.

Fagan, T. K. (1986b). School psychology's dilemma: Reappraising solutions and directing attention to the future. *American Psychologist, 41*(8), 851–861. See also *School Psychology Review, 16*(1), 6–21, which includes responses by Bardon (22–26) and Lambert (27–30) and a rejoinder (31–35). A comment by D. K. Brown appears in *American Psychologist, 42*(7), 755–756.

Fagan, T. K. (1996). A history of Division 16 (School Psychology): Running twice as fast. In D. A. Dewsbury (Ed.), *Unification through division: Histories of the divisions of the American Psychological Association* (Vol. 1, pp. 101–135). Washington, DC: American Psychological Association.

Fagan, T. K. (1999). Training school psychologists before there were school psychologist training programs: A history 1890–1930. In T. B. Gutkin & C. R. Reynolds (Eds.), *Handbook of school psychology* (3rd ed., pp. 2–33). New York: Wiley.

Fagan, T. K. (2005). The 50th Anniversary of the Thayer Conference: Historical perspectives and accomplishments. *School Psychology Quarterly, 20*(3), 224–251.

Fagan, T. K. (2008). Trends in the history of school psychology in the United States. In A. Thomas & J. Grimes (Eds.), *Best practices in school psychology V* (Vol. 6, pp. 2069–2086). Bethesda, MD: National Association of School Psychologists.

Fagan, T. K., Delugach, F. J., Mellon, M., & Schlitt, P. (1986). *A bibliographic guide to the literature of professional school psychology 1890–1985*. Stratford, CT: National Association of School Psychologists (see section III-C).

Fagan, T. K., & Wells, P. D. (2000). History and status of school psychology accreditation in the United States. *School Psychology Review, 29*(1), 28–51.

Fagan, T. K., & Wise, P. S. (2007). *School psychology: Past, present, and future* (3rd ed.). Bethesda, MD: National Association of School Psychologists.

Fryer, D. (1941). Introduction: Contribution of certification to unified professional status in psychology. *Journal of Consulting Psychology, 5*, 49–51.

Gesell, A., Goddard, H. H., & Wallin, J. E. W. (1919). The field of clinical psychology as an applied science. *Journal of Applied Psychology, 3*, 81–95.

Gray, S. (1963). *The internship in school psychology: Proceedings of the Peabody Conference, March 21–22, 1963*. Nashville, TN: George Peabody College for Teachers, Department of Psychology.

Hollingworth, L. S. (1918). Tentative suggestions for the certification of practicing psychologists. *Journal of Applied Psychology, 2*, 280–284.

Hollingworth, L. S. (1922). Existing laws which authorize psychologists to perform professional services. *Journal of Criminal Law and Criminology, 12*, 70–73.

Korman, M. (1974). National Conference on Levels and Patterns of Professional Training in Psychology. *American Psychologist, 29*, 441–449.

Miller, D. C. (2008). Appendix 7. School psychology training programs. In A. Thomas & J. Grimes, *Best Practices in School Psychology V* (Vol. 6, pp. clv–cxcviii). Bethesda, MD: National Association of School Psychologists.

Morrow, W. R. (1946). The development of psychological internship training. *Journal of Consulting Psychology, 10*, 165–183.

National Association of School Psychologists, Training and Accreditation Committee. (Circa 1972). Competency continuum for school psychologists and support personnel. Washington, DC: Author.

National Association of School Psychologists, Training and Accreditation Committee. (1972). *Guidelines for training programs in school psychology*. Washington, DC: Author.

National Association of School Psychologists. (1978). *Standards for training programs in school psychology*. Washington, DC: Author.

National Association of School Psychologists. (2000). *Standards for training and field placement programs in school psychology*. Bethesda, MD: Author.

National School Psychology Inservice Training Network. (1984). *School psychology. A blueprint for training and practice*. Minneapolis, MN: Author.

New York State Association for Applied Psychology, Special Committee on School Psychologists. (1943). Report on the functions, training and employment opportunities of school psychologists. *Journal of Consulting Psychology, 7*, 230–243.

New York University. (1929). *New York University Bulletin, School of Education, Part I, Curricula and Schedule of Courses 1929–1930*. New York: Author.

Pennsylvania State Council on Education. (1934). Preparation standards for 1) public school psychologists, 2) public school psychological examiners. Harrisburg, PA: Author.

Raimy, V. C. (Ed.). (1950). *Training in clinical psychology.* New York: Prentice Hall.

Thomas, A. (1998). *Director of school psychology graduate programs.* Bethesda, MD: National Association of School Psychologists.

Witmer, L. (1907). Clinical psychology. *The Psychological Clinic, 1*(1), 1–9.

Ysseldyke, J., Burns, M., Dawson, P., Kelley, B., Morrison, D., Ortiz, S., Rosenfield, S., Telzrow, C. (2006). *School psychology: A blueprint for training and practice III.* Bethesda, MD: National Association of School Psychologists.

Ysseldyke, J., Dawson, P., Lehr, C., Reschly, D., Reynolds, M., & Telzrow, C. (1997). *School psychology: A blueprint for training and practice II.* Bethesda, MD: National Association of School Psychologists.

3 Creating a school psychology training program

The horse that became a camel, or what tail wags the dog?

Judith Kaufman

INTRODUCTION

School psychologists, together with teachers and administrators, are critical contributors to the nurturing, development, and education of our nation's children. The nature of training, the skills developed, and the attitudes and behaviors reinforced within the university setting and in partnership with field-based trainers can contribute to creating an educational milieu that facilitates positive growth. Providing professional education in any field that requires caregiving responsibility is an enormous challenge. Service delivery models are often shaped by the orientation and content of training, and services ultimately provided may be linked directly to the exposure and experience of the trainee. Balancing professional roles as gatekeepers versus comprehensive, ethical, and responsive service providers remains an ongoing challenge (Canter, 2006). Furthermore, in providing human services, there is an inherent social responsibility to include both knowledge of and representation of ethnic, racial, gender, and lifestyle diversity (Peterson, Peterson, Abrams, & Striker, 2006).

School psychology, as both a profession and a service delivery model, is considered to be on the brink of a paradigm shift, with changes in standards of practice, requiring new tools, and generating new dilemmas (Cantor, 2006). Thus, professional training programs must undergo serious examination as to how they are preparing professionals to meet the challenging needs of 21st-century school populations. There has been a "relative stability in the number and kinds of institutions offering programs" (Reschly & Wilson, 1995, p. 82); however, with the complexity of school-based challenges and the shortage of both practitioners and trainers, new programs and models of training may need to evolve, potentially incorporating extensive technology, creative scheduling, and broadening of internship opportunities. Thus, new roles for both university and field-based trainers may develop in response to the increased need of the populations to be served (Little & Akin-Little, 2004).

Accountability and evidence-based practice demands focusing on data-based outcomes are overriding themes in research and practice; as such, these themes may change the curriculum content of school psychology education. Although many training programs incorporate "problem solving models of service delivery" into their mission statements, a closer examination of the implications for training is essential, along with the inclusion of course experiences in consultation and intervention design. Demographics of children attending school have changed dramatically. Increased immigration, along with first and second generation children of immigrants, challenges cultural competence and responsiveness. Advanced medical research and its application permit children who formerly died young or were kept home and isolated to be included in public education. Response to intervention and prereferral models have shifted approaches to both assessment and special education placement. Given the increasing mental health demands in schools and families, many advocate for population-based or public health models for the delivery of services (Short & Talley, 1994). Irrespective of level of training, in order to be "successful," faculty may need to be soothsayers, foretelling the future trends so that responsive competencies can be integrated into the training program without annual curriculum modification. A critical decision point becomes whether a training program trains for "function" or for vision within the framework of the promulgated standards of practice, accreditation, program approval, and credentialing, the traditionally accepted hallmarks of quality training.

The National Association of School Psychologists (NASP) Web site (http://www.nasponline.org) suggests that selecting the "right" training program is one of the most important decisions to be made, once the profession of school psychology has been decided on. The program's orientation, philosophy, location, goals, and overall objectives are essential in evaluating what kind of school psychologist an individual will become and how he or she will shape the future of the profession. Among the considerations are the models and levels of training, theoretical orientation, professional roles emphasized, and population or age group emphasized. Faculty, too, are a significant influence on the graduate experience and can shape the culture of a particular training program.

How are graduate programs shaped and developed? What governs the design and development of the program? What are the fundamental philosophy and model of training? There are many issues, tensions, and potential conflicts facing both developing and existing university training programs and their associated field-based trainers. This chapter will highlight and discuss the common issues within the context of competing forces of models and levels of training, changing roles and functions, and diversity of populations with the requirements and tensions of credentialing and accreditation. A primary focus is answering the question of how training programs can be responsive to mandated criteria while maintaining philosophical and academic integrity.

REVIEW OF THE LITERATURE: FACTORS TO PONDER

Who are the architects and designers of professional training? What are the best practices in developing and maintaining quality graduate programs? Is master's plus certification sufficient to train our future school psychologists? How does a program determine who and what it wants to be?

STRUCTURE, LEVELS, AND MODELS OF TRAINING

Graduate programs in school psychology offer a variety of models and levels of training, including (a) a master's plus additional course work, leading to a specialist certificate called by different names in different places; (b) a PsyD, the practitioner/scholar/scientist in school psychology, a model potentially different from a research-focused degree; (c) a PhD in school psychology, following the scientist-practitioner focus that is the traditional approach to advanced training; or (d) a combined program that integrates two or more specialty emphases in a single program, such as school/child clinical or school/counseling (see Givner, Chapter 5, this volume).

An ongoing dialogue continues to exist between the Vail model (PsyD) and the Boulder model (PhD). While some believe that the only model for applied training should be the doctorate in psychology (PsyD), equivalent to the MD or JD, Kratochwill (2007) and others suggest that the scientist-practitioner model has been significantly neglected in our current training programs. This neglect may, in fact, contribute to the shortage of graduates entering academia, an area that will be discussed in greater detail later in this chapter.

There has been a growth of free-standing professional schools of psychology, most offering the doctorate of psychology (PsyD) in a variety of specialty areas. While concern has been expressed about the lack of multidisciplinary orientation in these professional schools, particularly the educational components in school psychology training (Swerdlik & French, 2000), the flexibility of course scheduling, the ability to attend part-time and the availability of Web-based courses and intensive summer programs permit individuals who otherwise could not attend doctoral programs on a full-time basis to continue their formal education. A majority of these schools are regionally accredited, and many do have American Psychological Association (APA) accreditation or are in the process of applying for it. The affiliate organization, the National Council of Schools and Programs of Professional Psychology, supports communication among programs but does not have any credentialing authority.

While there are those who believe that the doctoral level of training enhances one's skills and knowledge, there continues to be a reaffirmation, as Bardon stated in 1994, that nondoctoral school psychology is the primary, sufficient, and "only required level of training for practice in the schools" (p. 584). There is general agreement that the expansion from master's level to a specialist level was a critical step (1991) and is the minimal level for certification for school-based practice across the United States (see

Miller, DeOrnellas, & Maricle, Chapter 4, this volume). Unique challenges occur in training at the nondoctoral level. Most particularly, programs must make decisions regarding the range and specificity of coursework and experiences, whether to adhere to a generalist orientation in training, and the means for effective addressing of competencies as specified by *A Blueprint for Training and Practice III* (Ysseldyke et al., 2006). Talley, Short, and Kolbe (1995) presented an interesting perspective on levels of training. They suggested that the first 2 years of a (doctoral) program in school psychology would constitute the quality training in the field, and subsequent training would move away from school psychology to prepare professional child psychologists for service delivery both within and outside schools. Thus, this approach appears to affirm the nondoctoral level of entry to the profession, with the further doctoral level providing training to broaden the professional identity to incorporate competencies in primary health, public health and child clinical psychology. This is, however, only one perspective.

Recognition of specialties in professional psychology, until recently, was done on a de facto basis, and individuals identified themselves by joining a division within the APA or, for a small percentage, through the American Board or Professional Psychology (ABPP) diploma. In the late 1970s and early 1980s, the Commission for the Recognition of Specialties and Proficiencies in Professional Psychology (CRSPPP) was established, supporting the needs of both professional practice and academic programs. Over time, through APA and its subcommittees, CRSPPP and ABPP, specialty areas and criteria for recognition have been refined, resulting in a set of competencies for certification by specialty and not by individual. Such criteria are expected to be guideposts to professional training programs. These specialties and competencies pertain only to doctoral level training.

State departments of education (SDEs) maintain ultimate authority for the credentialing of school psychologists or school-based practice in most states, and as such maintain a forceful influence in the design of training programs. The structure and content of training programs are with the jurisdiction of SDEs, which ultimately determine the approval process (Swerdlik & French, 2000). Mandated or statutory courses are prescribed, varying from state to state, and therefore must be included in the curriculum if a program is going to train school psychologists who can be credentialed in the state with the approval of the SDE or other appropriate board.

Needless to say, entry level into the profession is a continuing source of discourse. In addition, "protection" and use of the title of *psychologist* typically, in most states and jurisdictions, are restricted to those with doctoral level education and licensed as such by the respective state board. Recent discussion surrounding the Model Licensing Act proposed by APA (Bradshaw, n.d.), indicating that a doctorate is necessary to hold the title of psychologist, exemplifies the ongoing entry level debate. While title is important publicly, one of the critical issues, often neglected, is whether nondoctoral programs are sufficient to accomplish the goal of training. There are specialist program requiring 84 credits of study, in contrast to some doctoral programs requiring only 96 credits. It is important for the training enterprise to carefully examine, as McFarland (2006) has asked, "What is so special about specialist training?" This question is further addressed in Chapter 4 of this volume.

ROLE AND FUNCTION

The discussion of the role and function of school psychologists has been pervasive throughout the literature since the profession was first identified. Edwards (1971) discussed the role and function of the school psychologist, indicating that it had "received considerable attention … during recent years" (p. 10). He indicated that the school psychologist had been viewed as an educator with additional training or as a clinical psychologist who happens to be working in the schools. Edwards argued that "an effective school psychologist must have extensive specialized training in the field of psychology as it relates to the educational process" (p. 11). He summarized the role as follows: "In terms of priority of functions, the school psychologist should first be a consultant to teachers and administrators with regard to any issues associated with improving the educational system" (p. 11). Contemporary practice recommends an extensive scope of training, ranging from legal knowledge to knowledge of school structure with assessment, intervention, and consultation as integral factors (Edwards).

The answer to the proverbial question, "What do school psychologists do?" is shaped by multiple factors. Is it determined by how they are trained, or are training programs shaped by what school psychologists need to do? Jackson (1997) suggested that "school psychologists at all levels work as applied scientists, interventionists and systems managers, providing assessments and diagnoses, overseeing interventions from individual counseling to group and family work, provide consultations, supervision, preservice and in service training, performing program evaluation and may also focus on primary prevention in the schools." The "bottom line in terms of role and function is the social context and individual creativity of the profession." The field of school psychology is like most wealthy adolescents—self-searching, sometimes in rebellion against authority, but constantly in transition and changing. The compelling question is whether training programs need to train for specific functions and current demands, or focus on the longer lasting process skills (metacognitive skills) that may be transferable over time and changing conditions; ideally, training programs would be able to effectively combine the two. How closely should training programs follow the newly revised *Blueprint for Training and Practice* (Ysseldyke et al., 2006), the NASP/National Council for Accreditation of Teacher Education

(NCATE) training standards, or, for doctoral programs, APA accreditation standards?

Kratochwill (2007) pointed out that "important agendas have been advanced for training psychologists who work with children and adolescents, including child clinical training, pediatric psychology knowledge, ability to provide services for children with serious mental disorders, serious learning disorders and the generic training for service delivery" (p. 829). Underlying all of these approaches is the emphasis on evidence-based practice (EBP), which could be considered to be a metaprocess critical to training for any role and function (Kratochwill). Just as proponents of diversity training support the infusion of such training throughout the curriculum, so too do Kratochwill and others urge the integration of the EBP knowledge base into the curriculum. In order to support an EBP model, Kratochwill also encouraged the expansion of training options into technology and expansion of models of research training to provide the necessary background for academic positions. In order to meet the challenging demands within the field of school psychology practice, Kratochwill, along with others (Nastasi, 2006) supported the recommendations of the recent futures conference. It is essential that we expand training in prevention science and incorporate public health- or population-based models that move beyond providing treatment for individuals and small groups in the face of limited resources and growing mental health needs.

Additional critical factors determining the role and function of school psychologists are state and federal laws, together with school-based reform initiatives. Major influences on practice have been special and regular education rules and standards, as well as the related federal and state laws governing public schools. With the passage of 94-142, the Education of All Handicapped Children Act (1975) the school psychologist was primarily involved with assessment of and intervention for children with handicapping conditions (Jackson, 2007) and sometimes offering counseling and consultation to teachers and parents. More recently, with contemporary changes in legislation, school psychologists are assuming expanded roles. Thus, knowledge and practice of curriculum-based assessment, monitoring student progress, providing initiatives for positive behavior support, as well as response to intervention skills are expected and in some states mandated. These expectations for school psychologists may have a direct impact on program curricula decisions, impacting on the employability of program graduates.

AREA NEEDS AND POPULATIONS SERVED

From both a philosophical and an ethical perspective, the development of cultural competency should be an essential outcome of school psychology training programs, together with the skills to interact with diverse populations. Both NASP and APA clearly specify training objectives and outcomes reflecting cultural diversity that are components critically evaluated in the credentialing process. Inclusiveness is a foundational value in both building and maintaining a training program (Bahr, 2000) and should be modeled, not only within a training program but throughout the university community. Collaboration to create change toward this goal is essential and involves the input of faculty, staff, students, and administrators as well. Cultural competence and skills in dealing with diverse populations have been negotiated using different models: specific course work, infusion throughout the content areas and reinforcement through practica experiences, or, most commonly, a combination of these two approaches. It should be noted that there are training programs that still do not offer specific course work in diversity issues and other programs where, because of location, students have limited opportunity to interact with clients from minority backgrounds.

While all programs should reflect an emphasis on cultural competence, there are those that have clearly identified themselves as multicultural training programs. Rogers (2006) examined the characteristics of school psychology programs that were noted for training students from such a perspective. One of the common characteristics of the 17 programs studied was that all employed an integration multicultural curriculum model (Rogers). The majority of the programs exposed students to clients of minority backgrounds during fieldwork, and many had a diverse body of supervisors. All of the exemplary programs had at least one faculty member engaged in research focusing on diversity issues. An additional critical finding was that those programs found support for diversity within the university community and found the climate to be compatible with their orientation and commitment. The two most difficult goals to achieve are the recruitment of a diverse student body and the hiring of faculty from diverse backgrounds, although programs are clearly committed to doing so. It is often difficult for training programs at all levels to meet the stipulations of APA and NASP standards, let alone meet the criteria of becoming an exemplary multicultural program. While the region of the country may limit exposure to minority populations, diversity training infused in course work and an emphasis on best practices in cultural competency are essential in providing ethical and professional training. Furthermore, diversity is a broader construct than solely minority issues and can include socioeconomic diversity, urban–rural issues, and lifestyle differences.

There is a clear and documented shortage of bilingual and culturally diverse school psychologists; there is a greater paucity of culturally diverse faculty. Recruitment, training, and retention of individuals from diverse backgrounds are ongoing challenges to the profession, but they are essential goals. Evidence exists that a diverse faculty assists in the recruitment of students of color to higher education (Antonio, 2000) and is important in attracting a diverse student body (Hagedorn, Chi, Cepeda, & McLain, 2007).

Furthermore, it has been substantiated that there are significant contributions of diverse faculties to new directions in scholarship and teaching. The need of universities to reaffirm their commitment to attracting both a diverse faculty and student body is a necessary but not sufficient goal. Having diversity present does not ensure that the development of cultural competency is taking place. Training programs need to be mindful of the preparation of *all* school psychologists to meet the needs of our rapidly changing student population.

THE ROLE OF THE FACULTY

Core school psychology faculty are the primary contributors in shaping a training program. Students will apply to training programs because of their knowledge of faculty along with the stated theoretical orientation and philosophy of a program. The influx of new faculty, along with the retirement of older faculty members, can shift the nature and direction of a training program over even a few years. Faculty are retiring at a greater rate than practitioners (Curtis, Grier, & Hunley, 2004); thus, the number of positions for academic school psychologists has been high (Akin-Little & Little, 2004). As a result, there continue to be many available academic positions, with an insufficient number of interested and qualified applicants. The increased number of students with fewer faculty can directly impact training, and as such, "the future work force may be more dependent upon the recruitment of trainers rather than trainees" (Canter, 2000, p. 15). Rather than hire faculty to reflect programmatic strengths or to shape the orientation of a particular program, because there are so few individuals seeking faculty positions, programs may hire a competent individual who may not fit in with the goals of the program, or the program may become more generalist, modifying its orientation to meet the interests of those who are qualified and available. Faculty may be hired just to teach courses and potentially from disciplines that do not reflect contemporary models of school psychology practice. Potentially, part-time or adjunct faculty could comprise the majority of faculty members, leading to inconsistencies within a training program and lack of sufficient student support. Even more difficult is the recruitment and retention of faculty who are minority and/or reflect diversity, a core training value.

There are those who feel that it is incumbent upon doctoral programs to include a commitment to train for academic careers (Kratochwill, Shernoff, & Sanetti, 2004) and to integrate that emphasis in the curriculum. The critical variables to attract students to faculty positions and to minimize the lure toward practice include "mentoring, modeling and money," (Shapiro & Blom-Hoffman, 2004, p. 365). At a recent focus group conducted with graduate students considering academia and new trainers with less than 5 years' experience (Kaufman, Hughes, & Wilson, 2007), barriers to seeking faculty positions that were expressed included the mystification of academia, the fear of "publish or perish" expectations, and the economic differences between academic and field-based practice. A number of individuals indicated that they had seen their mentors working constantly and thus perceived being a faculty member of as "having no life." Perhaps the Rosenfield (2004) article, "Academia: It's a Wonderful Life—Isn't It?" should be a required reading in all professional practice courses!

ACCREDITATION REQUIREMENTS: THE HEAVENLY BODIES

Accreditation is considered to be the hallmark of a quality training program. NASP/NCATE and APA, on the doctoral level, are the primary national accreditation organizations for school psychology programs. The most compelling factors in shaping the structure and model of training are the external credentialing agencies. Although oftentimes fraught with concerns (T. Fagan, personal communication, April 15, 2008), having accreditation not only shapes the program's direction but can determine the numbers of applicants and enrollment. From personal observation, as an APA site visitor, it seems that once a program receives APA accreditation, for example, not only is there a significant increase in the number of applicants, but in GPA and GRE scores. Obviously, certification standards are recognized as the benchmark of the best practices of a profession and the acknowledgment of the national professional organizations' recognition of quality, and not unlike the *Good Housekeeping* Seal of Approval, they have a positive impact. The proliferation of standards through organizations and governing authorities, state boards, and Nationally Certified School Psychologist certification, as well as requirements within the university, may create tensions between what is legislated and what is recommended by national organizations, which then may clash with what a program's need or philosophy is.

There are two primary networks in the field of school psychology, represented by the Division of School Psychology (Division 16) and by the NASP (Fagan, 1994). Most state psychology groups are affiliated with APA, whereas most state school psychology groups are affiliated with NASP. These networks have an impact on training, accreditation, and credentialing, where, for example, APA, a major accrediting body, is linked to psychology associations and state boards of examiners. NASP, a constituent member of the NCATE, is the major accrediting body for professional education programs and is linked to state education agencies. Although the networks do clearly overlap, each represents a philosophical strand in the development of school psychology. Fundamentally, although both support and acknowledge high standards to produce well-trained practitioners, the question of entry level remains the primary dividing issue. Credentialing will continue to remain a source of creative difference between and among organizations (Thomas, 1999); however, when the standards for NASP/ NCATE and APA are reviewed, it becomes apparent that the APA criteria have become less prescriptive. APA guidelines require a demonstration of a substantial understanding of and competence in breadth of scientific psychology, foundations of practice in the substantive area, diagnosing or defining problems through assessment and implementing intervention strategies, evaluating efficacy of interventions, integrating practicum and appropriate internship experiences, and responsiveness to cultural and individual differences (APA, 2004). A program can define itself as meeting specialty objectives if a cohesive theoretical and skill-based perspective is presented and demonstrated through clearly defined outcome measures and self-monitoring plan, thus creating a heterogeneity of approved programs (APA, 2004).

According to NASP, (2000) the purpose of its review is to provide a mechanism for the evaluation of programs by external peers and the recognition of programs that meet national quality standards. Program review also provides an important opportunity for self-evaluation and program development.

There is an integral relationship between NASP program approval and NCATE accreditation, where NASP is one of 19 NCATE-affiliated specialized professional associations. Although NCATE approves units and not programs, it does grant Nationally Recognized status to programs that have been approved by NASP. Alternatively, a program can be approved by NASP without NCATE approval. NASP/NCATE standards seem to have become more and more prescriptive and clearly delineated through domains of competency that must be reflected in course syllabi, program experiences, and all student evaluation forms. Although it has not been demonstrated, such a prescriptive approach could potentially create a lack of diversity among its accredited programs.

Two other professional organizations, Council of Directors of School Psychology Programs (CDSPP) and Trainers of School Psychologists (TSP) have a strong commitment to the training enterprise but have neither credentialing nor accreditation authority. Both organizations, CDSPP on the doctoral level and TSP on all levels of training, monitor trends in the profession, raising questions and providing input on critical issues. There are those who maintain that organizations composed of trainers should play a greater role in the promulgation of standards and in the credentialing and accreditation process.

It should be pointed out that national organizations do not have control over state regulations, although they can coordinate with states, with the Nationally Certified School Psychologist credential as a primary example. Furthermore, although the national organizations may promulgate accreditation standards, states need not follow those standards for a training program to be approved or for an individual to become certified. Those who are critics of the accreditation process indicate that setting specific standards of training diminishes the diversity of the field and raises the possibility of creating homogeneous training programs without specific program identities. Directors of training often bemoan the fact that they are "always" being reviewed or completing self-studies to submit to credentialing bodies and have suggested that there should be an integrated review process. In examining policy and standards of the various credentialing bodies, the reality is that the process is indeed daunting, the amount of data that needs to be generated overwhelming, and the accountability sometimes difficult. An enormous amount of creative and teaching time can easily be devoted to keeping up with reports and information required by the various credentialing bodies. It is particularly difficult for junior faculty, who are plagued with pressures to publish, present, and be available, to also be responsible for aspects of the credentialing process, which may happen at small institutions and relatively new programs.

On the other hand, while each credentialing unit provides criteria, standards, and competency domains or areas to be included in a training program, there is indeed considerable overlap among the bodies and sufficient flexibility for a program to develop its own identity. All too often, training programs interpret the criteria literally and evolve as having a course in every specified area, rather than considering exposure to content or experience with a subject, thus limiting program creativity, limiting specialization within the field, and extending graduate training beyond all possible limits. Within the structure of accreditation, it may be possible to create content modules, incorporating and integrating foundational content in a problem-based approach. For example, in considering the theoretical content of developmental psychology and theories of learning, overlapping assumptions and coordinated approaches can clearly be integrated, providing and enriching experience for students. An additional benefit is the ability to provide additional specialization courses, particularly within the nondoctoral framework. The process for credentialing at an individual level must also be considered and is covered in depth by Crespi (Chapter 13, Volume II).

OUTCOMES ASSESSMENT

Internal program review of context and content, which is a requirement of credentialing agencies, is also an iterative process of training programs. Emphasis on outcome and competency- or performance-based systems should be the driving force of any graduate training program in order to guarantee quality and not solely be for accreditation purposes. Performance-based systems foster the defining of philosophy, goals, objectives, and competencies for a training program, irrespective of external criteria.

Furthermore, in order to best determine outcomes, communication with the field is essential for the integrity of the training programs. Expectations and objectives can become collaborative, shaping training goals to meet contemporary practice needs and better prepare students to fulfill the challenging and changing demands of the profession. Students, field-based trainers and practitioners, and faculty can routinely have the opportunity for creative and productive collaboration for program change and program improvement. Although pass rates are not intended for this purpose, it should be noted that many programs do indeed require and publish their pass rates on both the licensing exam and Praxis, using those data, as well, in outcomes assessment.

SUMMARY

Developing and maintaining a quality training program, responsive to both conflicting and competing tensions while maintaining integrity and authenticity on any level, remains an ongoing challenge. Figure 3.1 illustrates the forces and factors that impact the creation, the development, and the evaluation of any school psychology training program, irrespective of level of training.

Among the contemporary training challenges to be considered are the following:

1. Level of training: What is sufficient education at the university level in training school psychologists?
2. Cultural competence: How do we train to serve a diverse student population with a relatively homogeneous work force while at the same time actively developing a diverse body of students and faculty to enter the school psychology profession?
3. Role and function: How do we effectively train school psychologists at the university and in partnership with the field to become comprehensive service providers, providing prevention, intervention, and consultative services within a realistic educational time frame?
4. Accreditation and credentialing: How does a training program meet the criteria of national, regional, and state credentialing bodies while maintaining program integrity and a unique identity?
5. Outcomes assessment: How do training programs creatively and effectively assess nature, quality, and result of training to ensure that we are appropriately training our students?

As we prepare practitioners and academics who will ultimately impact the next generation of children, as well as the professionals who serve them, we need to consider the challenges facing school psychology as a profession.

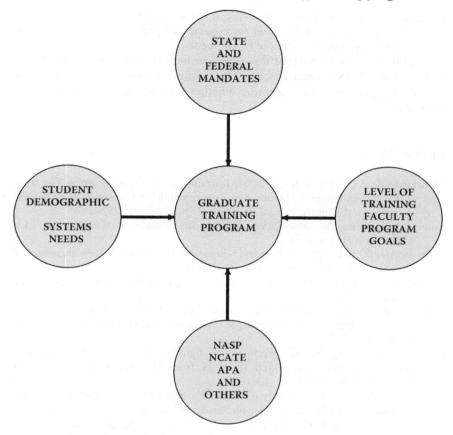

Figure 3.1 Forces and factors influencing program development.

We must also be concerned with our societal responsibility and to be mindful of how we can integrate the knowledge, skills, and attitudes to meet those challenges that can contribute to the development of an ethical and responsive professional workforce.

RESOURCES

Akin-Little, K. A., & Little, S. G. (Eds.). (2004). The state of developing university faculty in school psychology: Current status and perspectives on the future. *School Psychology Quarterly, 19*(4).
This miniseries is a collection of excellent articles focusing on the critical issues of academic faculty shortages, with suggestions for resolving the problem.

Ysseldyke, J., Burns, M., Dawson, P., Kelley, B., Morrison, D., Ortiz, S., et al. (2006). *School psychology: A blueprint for training and practice III.* Bethesda, MD: National Association of School Psychologists.

Blueprint III is an important document to help training programs define and meet the NASP competencies. The document can provide a checklist for existing programs to determine whether they are sufficiently broad in their training goals.

REFERENCES

Akin-Little, K. A., & Little, S. G. (2004) Introduction to the mini-series: The state of developing university faculty in school psychology: Current status and perspectives on the future. *School Psychology Quarterly, 19,* 295–296.

American Psychological Association (2004). *Site Visitor Workbook* (8th ed.). Washington DC: Author.

Antonio, A. (2000). Faculty of color and scholarship transformed: New argument of diversifying faculty. *Diversity Digest, 3*(2), 6–7.

Bardon, J. (1994). The identity of school psychology revisited. *School Psychology Review, 23,* 584–588.

Bahr, M. (2000). *Faculty perspectives on building a diverse, inclusive school psychology program.* Paper presented at the American Psychological Association, Washington, DC.

Bradshaw, J. (2008). School psychologists fight to keep title. *The National Psychologist.* Retrieved March 18, 2008, from http://www.nationalpsychologist.com/articles/art_v17n1_1.htm.

Canter, A. (2006). *School psychology. (COPSEE Document Number (B-4).* Gainseville, FL: University of Florida, Center on Personnel Studies in Special Education.

Curtis, M. J., Grier, J. E. C., & Hunley, S. A. (2004). The changing face of school psychology: Trends in data and projections for the future. *School Psychology Review, 33,* 49–66.

Education of All Handicapped Children Act, 20 U.S.C.§ 1401 (26)(A) (1975).

Edwards, R. P. (1971). The role and function of the school psychologist. *Journal of Education, 2*(3), 10–13.

Fagan, T. (1994). Guest editor's comments. *School Psychology Review, 23*(4), 584–588.

Hagedorn, L. S., Chi, W. Y., Cepeda, R. M., & McLain, M. (2007). An investigation of critical mass: The role of Latino representation in the success of urban community college students. *Research in Higher Education, 4,* 73–91.

Jackson, K. A. (1997). School psychology. *Eye on Psi Chi, 1*(3), 26–27.

Kratochwill, T. R. (2007). Preparing psychologists for evidence-based school practice: Lessons learned and challenges ahead. *American Psychologist, 49*(8)b, 829–843.

Kratochwill, T. R., Shernoff, E. S., & Sanetti, L. (2004). Promotion of academic careers in school psychology: A conceptual framework of impact points, recommended strategies and hopeful outcomes. *School Psychology Quarterly, 19*(4), 342–365.

Kaufman, J., Hughes, T., & Wilson, M. (2007). Forum for new trainers, National Association of School Psychologists, New York.

Little, S. G., & Aiken-Little, K. A. (2004). Academic school psychologists: Addressing the shortage. *Psychology in the Schools, 41*, 451–459.

McFarland, M. (2006, March). *What is so special about the specialist certificate?* Paper presented at the meeting of Trainers of School Psychologists, Anaheim, CA.

National Association of School Psychologists (2000). Standards for training and field placement programs in school psychology. Bethesda, MD: Author

Nastasi, B. K. (2006). Multicultural issues in school psychology practice: Introduction. *Journal of Applied School Psychology, 2*, 2–11.

Peterson, R. L., Peterson, D., Abrams, J. C., & Striker, K G. (2006). National council of schools and programs of professional psychology educational model. *Training and Education in Professional Psychology, S*(1), 17–36.

Reschly, D. J., & Wilson, M. S. (1995). School psychology practitioners and faculty: 1986 to 1991–92 trends in demographics, role satisfaction, and system reform. *School Psychology Review, 24*(1), 62–80.

Rogers, M. R. (2006). Exemplary multicultural training in school psychology programs. *Cultural Diversity and Ethnic Minority Psychology, 12*(1), 115–133.

Rosenfield, S. (2004). Academia: It's a wonderful life? Isn't it? *School Psychology Quarterly, 19*(4), 398–408.

Shapiro, E. S., & Blom-Hoffman (2004). Mentoring, modeling and money: The 3 M's of producing academics. *School Psychology Quarterly, 19*(4), 365–381.

Short, R. J., & Talley, R. C. (1994). Health care reform and school psychology. Half full/half empty: Health care and education advocacy. *The School Psychologist, 48*(4), 1.

Swerdlik, M. E., & French, J. L. (2000). School psychology training for the 21st century: Challenges and opportunities. *School Psychology Review, 29*(4), 577–588.

Talley, R. C., Short, R. J., & Kolbe, L. J. (1995) School health: Psychology's role. Washington, DC: American Psychological Association Center for Psychology in Schools and Education.

Thomas, A. (1999). School psychology 2000. *Communique, 28*(2), 28.

Ysseldyke, J., Burns, M., Dawson, P., Kelley, B., Morrison, D., Ortiz, S., et al. (2006). *School psychology: A blueprint for training and practice III.* Bethesda, MD: National Association of School Psychologists.

4 What is so special about the specialist degree?

Daniel C. Miller, Kathy DeOrnellas, and Denise Maricle

The field of school psychology has struggled, matured, and finally become a viable, strong, mature profession (Merrill, Ervin, & Gimpel, 2006). The role of the school psychologist has evolved significantly since its early beginnings, and today school psychologists are shaping practice, policy, and science. Rather than asking "What is so special about the specialist degree?" perhaps we should be asking "What is so special about school psychology and school psychologists?" Answering the second question leads to viable answers about the first one.

The question of what is so special about school psychology and school psychologists is easy to answer. School psychology has evolved to be primarily a practitioner-oriented field in which the majority of school psychologists are employed in practice settings, primarily public schools. The field of school psychology melds knowledge and skills from psychology, education, child development, family science, social psychology, and law in order to provide services to children, families, and educational organizations. School psychologists are highly trained professionals who:

- Use data-based problem solving methods to approach psychological, educational, social, behavioral, emotional, and cultural issues that face children and their families
- Conduct assessments ranging from the measurement of intellectual functioning or social–emotional functioning to the need for adaptive technology resources with disorders ranging from learning problems and behaviors associated with frequently occurring disorders to unique problems resulting from rarer conditions, such as selective mutism
- Conduct interventions, including individual counseling, group work, family therapy, parent education classes and/or support groups; behavioral education for parents, teachers, and administrators; and crisis intervention with children, with families, and in educational settings
- Conduct consultation with teachers, administrators, and parents regarding children, families, and programs
- Participate in the evaluation of educational programs and conduct research on the efficacy of interventions within the school setting

Crespi and Politikos (2004) summarize it this way: "The roles and functions of school psychologists have helped create a specific identity for the school psychologist, and partially solidify the uniqueness of school psychology among other psychological specialties" (p. 478).

There has never been a better time for undergraduate students to choose a career in school psychology. In the December 19, 2007, issue of *U.S. News and World Report*, school psychology was identified as one of the best careers of the decade and beyond. There are several reasons why a career in school psychology is so desirable, including a documented of shortage of school psychologists and a plethora of available jobs, increased need for the services provided by school psychologists, increased media focus on problems that children face, and federal legislation that mandates serving children with special needs and working with all children to prevent future learning and/or behavioral problems. With the changes to the Individuals with Disabilities Education Act, the tremendous increase in children diagnosed with autism, and the number of students involved in school violence, both as victims and as perpetrators, the need for school psychologists has never been greater. The American Psychological Association (APA) Public Policy Office (2008) reported that 10% of students have serious mental health problems, while another 10% have developing mental health problems in the mild to moderate range. As the only professionals on the school campus with training in both mental health and education, school psychologists are perfectly situated to provide mental health services in the schools. This, combined with federal law mandates for early identification and intervention, allows the role of the school psychologist to continue to expand. Unlike doctoral level school psychologists, who often find themselves fulfilling administrative roles or serving as trainers or supervisors, specialist level school psychologists work to meet the needs of students, teachers, and parents on a daily basis at the campus level.

BRIEF HISTORY OF THE SPECIALIST LEVEL OF TRAINING

In order to understand what is so special about school psychology and the specialist degree, a brief review of its history is necessary. A more extensive history of the profession of school psychology is provided in Chapter 2 of this volume.

The origin of the two levels of training

In 1954, the participants at the Thayer Conference recommended that there be two levels of training and practice: doctoral and nondoctoral (Cutts, 1955). The appropriate level of training at the nondoctoral level generated considerable debate; however, a minimum of 2 years of graduate study was generally considered to be acceptable. The APA has consistently held the position that the entry level graduate training into the profession of psychology is the doctoral degree. In 1969, the National Association of School Psychologists (NASP) was formed initially to represent the interests of nondoctoral school psychology practitioners. In 1978, NASP adopted the position that the entry level of training for the practice of school psychology should be raised to the specialist level from the master's level (Curtis & Zins, 1989). Brown (1989) pointed out that NASP endorsement of the specialist level of training coincided with NASP becoming a part of the National Council for Accreditation of Teacher Education accrediting process. In 1988, NASP further solidified its professional stance on the specialist level of training by establishing the Nationally Certified School Psychologist (NCSP) credential.

Differences between the doctoral and specialist levels of training

In 1989, Brown noted that "doctoral programs are considerably more heterogeneous in their curriculum than their specialist counterparts" (p. 14). Increasingly, specialist level programs are becoming more constrained by the high degree of specificity of the NASP training standards (2000). The primary difference between the specialist and doctoral levels of training in school psychology appears to lie in minor variations in curricula, with doctoral programs focusing on additional credits in statistics, research, and an area of specialization or minor. The primary reasons for individuals to seek the doctoral level of training are increased career opportunities (e.g., private practice, agencies other than public school, and academia), the desire to conduct research, a potential increase in salary, the desire for greater depth of knowledge or development of a specialty area, and a perceived increase in prestige.

Brown (1989) went on to point out that there was no evidence *at that time* that graduates of specialist level programs were more competent than graduates of master's programs or more or less competent than graduates of doctoral programs. Brown stated "the failure of both NASP and APA to fund substantial research in this area suggests that the entry level debate is merely political and guild related with neither organization desiring to empirically validate their arguments regarding levels of training" (p. 13). Brown, Swigart, Bolen, Hall, and Webster (1998) did evaluate differences between doctoral and nondoctoral school psychologists. They found no empirical evidence to suggest that doctoral school psychologists are more competent than nondoctoral school psychologists or vice versa. Some differences were found between the groups, such as the tendency of doctoral school psychologists to work in urban settings and to have higher salaries. No current research could be found to indicate that school psychologists trained at the specialist level are more or less competent as practitioners than those with doctoral training.

The projected trend toward doctoral entry

Some scholars in the field of school psychology have long held the belief that school psychologists would be increasingly trained at the doctoral level (Brown, 1989; Cobb, 1989; Fagan, 1986, 1989; Hodges, 1963; Phillips, 1990; Prasse, 1989). Brown predicted that "by the year 2000, the majority of school psychologists in training will be at the doctoral level. In fact by that time we may have a majority of doctoral level psychologists in school practice" (p. 12). The projected shift to doctoral training has yet to materialize. The specialist level of training continues to dominate the number of training programs and the number of students enrolled up through the 2007 sample of school psychology training programs (Miller, 2008).

Table 4.1 presents the changes in the number of U.S. school psychology training programs from a 1977 sample to the most recent 2007 sample. The number of graduate programs awarding only a master's degree has significantly declined from 63 in 1977 to only 3 in the United States in 2007. There has been a 54% increase in the number of graduate programs at the specialist level and a 55% increase in the number of doctoral school psychology programs during the past 30 years.

The real impact on the profession can be determined by evaluating the number of students enrolled in U.S. school psychology training programs during the past 30 years (see Table 4.2). Since 1977, there has been a 92% decline in the number of students enrolled in master's degree only programs, while the enrollment in the specialist level and doctoral programs has increased 57% and 51%, respectively. Contrary to prior predictions, 69% of all students enrolled in graduate school psychology programs are at the specialist level of training. These findings are consistent with the prediction by Reschly (2000) that "the specialist level will dominate school psychology practice in 2010 .... I think it is safe to assume that 70% or more of the practitioners in 2010 will be non-doctoral" (2000, p. 519).

Table 4.1 Changes in the Number of U.S. School Psychology Training Programs

	1977[a]	1984[b]	1989[c]	1998[d]	2007[e]
Master's	63	80	42	13	3
Specialist	143	174	164	193	220
Doctoral	64	69	67	82	99

[a] Brown and Lindstrom (1977).
[b] Brown and Minke (1984).
[c] McMaster, Reschly, and Peters (1989).
[d] Thomas (1998).
[e] Miller (2008).

Table 4.2 Changes in Student Enrollment of U.S. School Psychology Training
Programs

	1977[a]	1984[b]	1989[c]	1998[d]	2007[e]
Master's	1,774	1,466	750	220	150
Specialist	3,936	3,526	3,180	5,883	6,180
Doctoral	1,740	2,301	1,704	2,484	2,622
Total	7,450	7,293	5,634	8,587	8,952

[a] Brown and Lindstrom (1977).
[b] Brown and Minke (1984).
[c] McMaster et al. (1989).
[d] Thomas (1998).
[e] Miller (2008).

Reasons why the field has not moved toward a doctoral entry level

One reason that the field has not moved toward a doctoral entry level is that school psychology programs in general are often viewed by university administrators as expensive, particularly doctoral programs. In the NASP *Standards for Training and Field Placement Programs in School Psychology,* it is recommended that "the program maintains a no greater than 1:10 full-time equivalent (FTE) faculty to FTE student ratio in the overall program, as well as in practica and internship" (NASP, 2000). The *Standards* also recommend a minimum of three full-time faculty members. Thus, for example, with three full-time faculty and a recommended maximum 1:10 FTE faculty to FTE student, the average school psychology program should not exceed 30 full-time students.

The professional standards from NASP and APA that recommend faculty and student ratios are ideal and reflect the high-quality small group and individualized instruction needed to train school psychologists at the specialist and doctoral levels; however, many university administrators view school psychology program as expensive because of these external enrollment caps. At most U.S. public universities, school psychology training programs are under continued pressure to increase enrollment in response to the decrease in public state funding for higher education.

Brown (1989) identified several other potential roadblocks to the field moving to a doctoral entry level. One reason is that most states certify school psychologists through a state department of education rather than license them to practice through a state psychology licensing board. (Currently, two states are exceptions to this rule: Texas and Arkansas.) Certification in most states recognizes the NASP training standards and the specialist level entry requirements into the field. Because of the current shortage of school psychologists and the previously reported trends in programming, it appears unlikely that the states would adopt the APA standards, which require the doctoral entry level, any time soon.

Another reason the field has not moved toward doctoral entry level training for school psychologists was cited by Brown (1989) and Thomas (1998), who noted that most school psychology training programs are housed in universities and colleges that do not have doctoral degree granting authority. A specialist degree may be the highest degree that some universities are authorized to offer.

Finally, there appear to be social factors that contribute to the popularity of the specialist degree. In the early history of school psychology, the field was dominated primarily by men. Curtis, Hunley, and Chesno-Grier (2004) report that males dominated the field through the early 1980s, comprising 54% of all school psychologists. However, by 2000, women represented 70% of all school psychologists. This trend has continued, with almost 80% of all students enrolled in school psychology programs being women. This trend is seen in the all areas of psychology and has generally been referred to as the "feminization" of psychology. In a study by Graves and Wright (2007) examining why students pursue a degree in school psychology, a survey of graduate students in school psychology programs found that students in specialist level training programs were more likely than doctoral students to be influenced by job stability and the public school schedule. Consistent with trends among current practitioners, participants in this study were primarily White and female. With a mean age of 28, participants in this study may have been influenced by their current roles as women to choose a career that offers flexibility, such as school psychology.

Although these choices were not discussed by Graves and Wright (2007), on the basis of anecdotal information from past and present students, one can speculate that many women are interested in a career in school psychology because of its flexibility in meeting the needs of women. For example, public schools offer solid job security, good benefits, and a "great balance for combining a career with a young family due to schedule and hours" (Graves & Wright, p. 869).

BENEFITS OF THE SPECIALIST LEVEL OF TRAINING

One of the benefits of specialist level training is the ability to complete a 60-hour program in 3 years, with the 3rd year typically being a paid internship. The specialist level of training allows students to complete practitioner-oriented coursework without taking the research-based courses required of doctoral training programs. This allows graduates to enter the workforce sooner, with the option of returning for additional training at some point in the future. In addition, given the current requirements of the field for specialist level training, obtaining the specialist degree, above and beyond the master's degree, often provides a higher level of competency and prestige, and in some cases, remuneration.

Another benefit of the specialist level training is the ability to apply for the NCSP credential—the only national training standard for school psychologists. In 1988, NASP established the National School Psychology Certification System (NSPCS) as a means of ensuring that school psychologists meet minimum standards of training and are competent to perform entry level duties (Merrell, Ervin, & Gimpel, 2006). The specific goals of the NSPCS include the following:

- To promote uniform credentialing standards across states, agencies, and training institutions
- To monitor the implementation of NASP credentialing standards at the national level
- To promote continuing professional development for school psychologists
- To facilitate credentialing of school psychologists across states through the use of reciprocity
- To ensure a consistent level of training and experience in service providers who are nationally certified
- To promote the use of NASP *Standards for Training and Field Placement Programs in School Psychology* (2000) by training institutions
- To encourage school psychologists to seek national certification (NASP, 2008a)

The NSPCS grants the NCSP to applicants who have completed a NASP-approved or equivalent training program with internship and obtained a passing score on the National School Psychology Examination, administered by the Educational Testing Service. Although practicing school psychologists were initially slow to recognize the importance of obtaining the NCSP, currently there are more than 9,800 school psychologists with the NCSP credential (NASP, 2008b).

States vary significantly in their requirements and procedures for credentialing school psychologists, and the NCSP is the only national credential used for reciprocity (NASP, 2004). In our increasingly mobile society, reciprocity of credentialing is very important. As the NCSP has grown in popularity, it has become part of the standard for credentialing school psychologists in 31 states (NASP, 2008b). In 4 of those states (Delaware, Louisiana, Nevada, and Oklahoma) stipends are awarded to school psychologists who hold the NCSP (NASP, 2008a). For example, in Louisiana, having the NCSP entitles school psychologists to a $5,000 stipend annually. Individual school districts in some states, for example Indiana, Maryland, Minnesota, and North Carolina, offer salary incentives for school psychologists holding the NCSP (NASP, 2004).

DIVERSITY OF DEGREE TITLES, OR WHAT'S IN A NAME?

One of the challenges in the field of school psychology is how the public perceives the specialist level of training. The confusion comes from the wide diversity of titles that are awarded across the country that equate to a specialist level of training. Future graduate students, parents, educators, directors of special education, and human resource personnel are confused by the different degrees that are awarded to school psychology program graduates.

Miller (2008) reported a comprehensive list of 244 U.S. and Canadian school psychology graduate training programs. Of these total programs, 220 (90.2%) offer either a specialist level degree or a master's degree in school psychology. The majority of these nondoctoral programs (97%, or $n = 214$) are modeled after a specialist level of training (60 hours of graduate training as recognized by NASP, 2000).

A distinction needs to be made between a specialist level program and a program that awards a specialist degree (e.g., EdS). Because of credentialing restrictions in some states, the specialist degree may not be an available degree title. However, NASP will approve programs that meet specialist level criteria, including the minimum 60 hours of graduate training. Having established that semantic definition, Miller (2008) reported there are 71 school psychology programs that award a master's degree but are based on a specialist level of training. There were 143 school psychology programs that awarded a specialist degree. Note that some programs awarded a master's degree en route to the specialist degree; therefore, the number of the master's degree and specialist degree awarding programs does not add up to the total number of specialist level programs.

There are many titles that are awarded to graduates of specialist level school psychology programs (see Table 4.3). For potential students, the wide array of degree titles must be confusing. It is incumbent upon trainers to stress to potential students the importance of a specialist level of training and for the potential students to not be overly concerned about the title of the degree that is awarded.

FUTURE DIRECTIONS

School psychologists are in great demand as a result of their diversity of knowledge, variety of skills, and thorough training. Role diversity is one of the most appealing aspects of the profession. The sheer variety of opportunities within the profession often draws individuals to the field. This explosion in the diversity of roles of the school psychologist reflects the explosion of knowledge in the fields of both school psychology and psychology in general and appears to have provided the impetus for the increased training required of school psychologists.

Table 4.3 Frequency of Degree Titles of U.S. and Canadian Specialist Level
School Psychology Programs (*n* = 214)

Specialist Degree Title	Number (%)
EdS: Education specialist	89 (61.2)
CAS: Certificate of advanced study	18 (8.4)
CAGS: Certificate of graduate studies	13 (6.1)
SSP: Specialist in school psychology	6 (2.8)
CO: Certification only	2 (0.9)
PD: Professional diploma	2 (0.9)
SPsyS: Specialist in school psychology	1 (0.5)
MEd plus 45: Master's degree plus 45 additional hours	1 (0.5)
Specialist Level Programs That Award a Master's Degree	*Number (%)*
MA: Master of arts	36 (16.8)
MS: Master of science	24 (11.2)
MEd: Master of education	4 (1.9)
MSEd: Master of special education	4 (1.9)
MA/MEd: Master of arts or master of education	2 (0.9)
MS/MEd: Master of science of master of education	1 (0.5)

In the last 20 years, the evolution of school psychology and its diverse applications within educational settings have resulted in an increasingly diverse body of knowledge that school psychology practitioners are expected to master for entry into the field (Miller, DeOrnellas, & Maricle, 2007). Consequently, there has been an evolution from the master's level of training to the specialist level of training, and the preparation of school psychologists has changed dramatically over the course of about 30 years, which is a relatively short period of time in the life span of a profession, according to Curtis, Chesno-Grier, and Hunley (2004). Concurrently, there has been increased pressure to maintain professional skills and knowledge as the profession became more regulated through certification and licensure. Minimum standards for training school psychologists are delineated by NASP in the *Standards for Training and Field Placement Programs in School Psychology* (2000), which sets minimal levels of training required for NASP approval of school psychology programs. The training standards have typically reflected NASP's blueprint for training and practice, although the current standards for training have not yet been modified to resemble the most current blueprint, *School Psychology: A Blueprint for Training and Practice III* (Ysseldyke et al., 2006).

The challenge for trainers and their students has been keeping up with the depth of knowledge and skills required within each domain of practice (Miller et al., 2007). Fagan (2002) noted "that the point has been exceeded where a school psychologist can be trained to perform all roles and functions with competence" (p. 7). Hynd and Reynolds (2005) have further stated that "it is no longer possible for the school psychologist to master all of the areas of knowledge needed to function ethically and effectively in so many domains. The time for the development of specializations in school psychology has come" (pp. 11–12). Miller et al. believed that the increase in specialized knowledge within our field has led school psychology practitioners to choose (voluntarily or through necessity) to specialize within a particular area. Miller et al. acknowledged that there is a natural developmental progression that takes place within a profession, with specialization being viewed as a sign of maturity within the profession, and conclude, as did Fagan, and Hynd and Reynolds, that school psychology has reached this point.

Pleas for school psychologists to expand their roles and for training programs to provide the necessary preparation for a variety of expanded roles, in conjunction with increased training demands by accrediting and credentialing bodies, have the potential to lead to a change in the entry level requirement, perhaps moving, as previously predicted, toward the doctoral level (Brown, 1989; Cobb, 1989; Fagan 1986, 1989; Philips, 1988; Prasse, 1989). Given the practitioner orientation of the profession, the limitations of doctoral training in school psychology (primarily limited program availability and faculty shortages), as well as the acceptance of the PsyD degree in the fields of counseling and clinical psychology, perhaps the doctoral level practitioner degree may be warranted for the field of school psychology. Many specialist programs already require credit hours roughly equivalent to, or approaching, the PsyD level.

However, current trends would suggest the continued dominance of the specialist degree as the entry level for the profession for a number of reasons, including limitations of training programs and faculty shortages, the feminization of the field, economic limitations of the public education system, and student financial considerations, to name but a few. Regardless, further research is warranted to determine what level of training provides the most effective services, what are the economic implications of continued training requirements or of increasing the entry level degree requirements, and what are the barriers to additional education, such as at the doctoral level.

Another concern for the future of school psychology is the current shortage of school psychologists, which could have serious implications for the field in the years ahead. According to Curtis, Hunley, and Chesno-Grier (2004), the shortage of doctoral level school psychologists merits special attention. The potential implications of the disproportionate shortage of doctoral level school psychologists appear particularly ominous for university training programs. Vacant faculty positions in training programs will limit the ability of the profession to prepare new school psychologists, which is likely to compound the shortage problem. Facing unmet service demands as a result of unfilled school psychology positions, it is likely that some school districts will use alternatives to standard credentialing to hire individuals who have not completed a school psychology training program. There may be a move to reduce the credentialing requirements for school psychologists or to allow other psychology professionals access to the right to practice in the schools.

Also of concern is the feminization of the field of psychology. When feminization has occurred in other professional fields (for example, medicine and law), those fields have seen a decrease in prestige and a plateauing of financial remuneration. As women come to dominate the field of school psychology, might we not see a devaluation of the role of the school psychologists, the field of school psychology, and the remuneration available to school psychologists?

SUMMARY

Since school psychology has emerged as a distinct field, there have been attempts to predict what the future holds for the field. The future of school psychology and its entry level specialist degree will likely be shaped by many factors, among them state and federal education legislation, societal changes and demands, economic trends, and technology. As Curtis, Chesno-Grier, and Hunley stated in their 2004 article, "History would seem to suggest that we would be foolish in trying to gaze too far down the road. Any number of unanticipated developments such as sweeping legislation, major judicial decisions, significant changes in society, or key advances in any number of areas like technology, could dramatically alter our path and lead to a future not even considered" (p. 49).

RESOURCES

Fagan, T. K., & Wise, P. S. (2007). *School psychology: Past, present, and future.* Bethesda, MD: National Association of School Psychologists.
This introductory text for school psychology graduate programs reviews the history of school psychology and the role of the specialist level of training within the field.

Merrill, K. W., Ervin, R. A., & Gimpel, G. A. (2006). *School psychology for the 21st century.* New York: Guilford Press.
This introductory text for school psychology graduate programs reviews the history of school psychology and the role of the specialist level of training within the field.

Miller, D. C. (2008). Appendix VII: School psychology training programs. In A.
    Thomas and J. Grimes (Eds.), *Best practices in school psychology V* (pp. clv–
    cxcviii). Bethesda, MD: National Association of School Psychologists.
This is a comprehensive list of the 244 school psychology graduate training
programs within the United States and Canada. Program characteristics are
compared between doctoral and specialist level of training.

REFERENCES

American Psychological Association Public Policy Office. (2008). *Increasing access
    and coordination of quality mental health services for children and adolescents.*
    Retrieved April 13, 2008 from http://www.apa.org/ppo/issues/tfpacoord.html
Brown, D. T. (1989). The evolution of entry level training in school psychology: Are we
    now approaching the doctoral level? *School Psychology Review, 18*(1), 11–15.
Brown, D. T., & Lindstrom, J. P. (1977). *Directory of school psychology training
    programs in the United States and Canada.* Stratford, CT: National Association
    of School Psychologists.
Brown, D. T., & Minke, K. M. (1984). *Directory of school psychology training
    programs in the United States.* Stratford, CT: National Association of School
    Psychologists.
Brown, M. B., Swigart, M. L., Bolen, L. M., Hall, C. W., & Webster, R. T. (1998).
    Doctoral and nondoctoral school psychologists: Are there differences?
    Psychology in the Schools, 35, 347–354.
Cobb, C. T. (1989). Is it time to establish the doctorate entry-level? *School Psychology
    Review, 18,* 16–19.
Crespi, T. D., & Politikos, N. N. (2004). Respecialization as a school psychologist:
    Education, training, and supervision for school practice. *Psychology in the
    Schools, 41,* 473–480.
Curtis, M. J., Chesno-Grier, J. E., & Hunley, S. A. (2004). The changing face of school
    psychology: Trends in data and projections for the future. *School Psychology
    Review, 33,* 49–66.
Curtis, M. J., Hunley, S. A., & Chesno-Grier, J. E. (2004). The status of school
    psychology: Implications of a major personnel shortage. *Psychology in the
    Schools, 41*(4), 431–442.
Curtis, M. J., & Zins, J. E. (1989). Trends in training and accreditation. *School
    Psychology Review, 18,* 16–19.
Cutts, N. (1955). *School psychologists at mid-century.* Washington, DC: American
    Psychological Association.
Fagan, T. K. (1986). School psychology's dilemma: Reappraising solutions and
    directing attention to the future. *American Psychologist, 41,* 851–861.
Fagan, T. K. (1989). On the entry level debate. *School Psychology Review, 18,* 34–36.
Fagan, T. K. (2002). School psychology: Recent descriptions, continued expansion,
    and an ongoing paradox. *School Psychology Review, 31,* 5–10.
Graves, S. L., & Wright, L. B. (2007). Comparison of individual factors in school
    psychology graduate students: Why do students pursue a degree in school psy-
    chology? *Psychology in the Schools, 44*(8), 865–871.

Hodges, W. L. (1963). Certification of school psychologists. In M. G. Gottaegen and G. B. Gottaegen (Eds.), *Professional school psychology* (Vol. 2, pp. 331–343). New York: Grune & Stratton.

Hynd, G. W., & Reynolds, C. R. (2005). School neuropsychology: The evolution of a specialty in school psychology. In D. C. D'Amato, E. Fletcher-Janzen, & C. R. Reynolds (Eds.), *Handbook of school neuropsychology* (pp. 11–12). Hoboken, NJ: John Wiley & Sons.

McMaster, M., Reschly, D., & Peters, J. (1989). *Directory of school psychology graduate programs*. Bethesda, MD: National Association of School Psychologists.

Merrill, K. W., Ervin, R. A., & Gimpel, G. A. (2006). *School psychology for the 21st century*. New York: Guilford Press.

Miller, D. C. (2008). Appendix VII: School psychology training programs. In A. Thomas and J. Grimes (Eds.), *Best practices in school psychology V* (pp. clv–cxcviii). Bethesda, MD: National Association of School Psychologists.

Miller, D. C., DeOrnellas, K., & Maricle, D. (2007). Is it time for our organization to recognize subspecialties within school psychology? *Communique, 36*, 40–41.

National Association of School Psychologists. (2000). *Standards for training and field placement programs in school psychology*. Bethesda, MD: Author.

National Association of School Psychologists. (2004). *Nationally certified school psychologist: Advancing the profession, advancing your future* [PowerPoint slides]. Presentation at the NASP Public Policy Institute. Retrieved April 5, 2008, from http://www.nasponline.org/certification/NCSPPresentation.ppt

National Association of School Psychologists. (2008a). *NCSP legislation in state statutes*. Retrieved April 5, 2008, from http://www.nasponline.org/advocacy/ncspstatutes.aspx

National Association of School Psychologists. (2008b). *States that recognize the NCSP*. Retrieved April 5, 2008, from http://www.nasponline.org/certification/statencsp.aspx

Phillips, B. N. (1990). *School psychology at a turning point: Ensuring a bright future for the profession*. San Francisco: Jossey-Bass Publishers.

Prasse, D. P. (1989). Polarity: The past and the future. *School Psychology Review, 18*, 25–29.

Reschly, D. J. (2000). The present and future status of school psychology in the United States. *School Psychology Review, 29*(4), 507–522.

Thomas, A. (1998). *Directory of school psychology graduate programs*. Bethesda, MD: National Association of School Psychologists.

School psychologist: Executive summary. (2007, December 19). *U.S. News and World Report*. Retrieved April 5, 2008 from http://www.usnews.com/articles/business/best careers/2007/12/19/school-psychologist-executive-summary.html

Ysseldyke, J., Burns, M., Dawson, P., Kelley, B., Morrison, D., Ortiz, S., Rosenfield, S., & Telzrow, C. (2006). *School psychology: A blueprint for training and practice III*. Bethesda, MD: National Association of School Psychologists.

5 Combined–integrated training

An alternative to traditional school psychology training models

Abraham Givner

The nationwide shortage of doctoral-level school psychology faculty and practitioners, together with the apparent encroachment into the schools by clinical child psychologists, who have limited training in psychoeducational practices and attitudes and minimal exposure to the schooling environments, provides an exigent need to examine current and future models of training. There are currently 57 American Psychological Association (APA)-accredited doctoral level, traditional school psychology training programs. Of these, 51 adhere to a scientist–practitioner, Boulder model of training, and 6 follow a practitioner–scholar, Vail model. In addition, 10 other programs are accredited by APA as "combined" programs and meet APA accreditation requirements in at least two of the specialty areas. As of 2007, all 10 programs provided explicit training in school psychology. This chapter will address varied aspects of the combined–integrated (C-I) model of training and provide empirical support for its ability to meet the challenges to school psychology for the next generation in both traditional and nontraditional settings.

INTRODUCTION

The dominant training model for applied psychologists in the United States, known as the Boulder or scientist–practitioner model, developed after World War II. The Boulder model provided for training in psychological research and its application to practice. Boulder programs were oriented toward training students to be researchers—not practitioners. For more than 20 years following the Boulder Conference, the scientist–practitioner model was the only training model for educating psychologists (Peterson, 1997).

Despite the emphasis on the scientist–practitioner model, most students published no research, and few students felt well prepared for the professional work they were supposed to be doing (Peterson, 1985). In fact, more and more graduates of clinical and counseling psychology programs began to choose practitioner professions as opposed to becoming researchers (Peterson, 1997).

By 1967, the practitioner model and eventually the doctorate of psychology (PsyD) were introduced. Adelphi University was the first program dedicated to the training of practitioners in psychology. In 1968, the University of Illinois established the first doctor of psychology program (PsyD), and in 1969, the California School of Professional Psychology also began to train students in professional practice (Peterson, 1985). The 1973 Vail conference reinforced the movement toward the development of psychology programs that were primarily designed for practitioners. "The traditional PhD was suggested as the research degree and a new degree, the Doctor of Psychology (PsyD) degree, was recommended to identify those with professional practice preparation" (Beutler, Givner, Mowder, Fisher & Reeve, 2004, p. 913).

Currently, there are 300 PhD training programs and 72 PsyD training programs across the three specialty areas. Clearly, the C-I model has the smallest representation across specialty areas (10 of 372), yet the data presented below support the view that the C-I model provides a breadth of training and a functional and synergistic alternative to more traditional models. Graduates from C-I programs are well positioned to provide mental health and psychoeducational services across the life span.

Table 5.1 presents the number of PhD and PsyD programs in each specialty area. An embedded fact of importance is that all 10 C-I programs include training in school psychology that meets standards set by the training council for the C-I programs. Table 5.2 delineates the current C-I programs and year of accreditation as a C-I program. In 2008, Hofstra University's combined program was to have been transformed into a traditional clinical psychology program. The university's decision was partially based upon the need to meet the high standards for school psychology accreditation. Thus, as of winter 2008, there were 9 APA-accredited C-I programs. However, as events change rapidly, it is important to note that the University of South Alabama recently developed a combined–integrated clinical counseling program and Kean University developed a combined school–clinical program. Neither are yet accredited. South Alabama's program will be the first C-I program that does not include a school psychology specialization.

Table 5.1 Number of APA-Accredited Degree Granting Programs by Specialty Area

Degree	Clinical Psychology	Counseling Psychology	School Psychology	Combined/ Integrated	Total
PhD	173	69	51	7	300
PsyD	60	3	6	3	72
Total	233	72	57	10	372

Table 5.2 APA-Accredited Training Models/Programs and Year of Accreditation
of the Combined Program as of September 2008

Clinical-Counseling School Psychology	Clinical-School and School–Clinical Psychology	Counseling-School Psychology
Utah State University (1975)	Hofstra University (1980)	Florida State University (1995)
University of California, Santa Barbara (1990)	Yeshiva University (1998)	Northeastern University (1996)
	Pace University (1998)	James Madison University (1997)
	University of Toronto (2002)	University of Buffalo (1998)

The curriculum debate

Where there are proponents of different models, there is bound to be debate about the most effective model for training. One issue in this debate has focused on the core versus specific curriculum associated with each of the four APA-accredited specialty areas: clinical, school, and counseling psychology and a combination thereof. Cobb et al. (2004) examined the overlap in curriculum among the three specialties. They compared the curriculum from 10 accredited programs in each of the three practice areas and found that the programs were much more similar than different. They concluded this seminal article on the overlap of clinical, counseling, and school psychology programs by stating, "the considerable overlap ... in description, coursework, internships and employment—suggests that we should reconsider the meaningfulness of such distinctions for our profession, training, students and the public at large" (p. 953).

Some educators estimate that as much as 80% of the content in clinical, counseling, and school psychology programs overlaps (Bailey, 2003). This is partially due to the fact that all APA-accredited programs are required to teach a basic set of competencies, as noted in the APA Competencies document (Kaslow et al., 2007). Minke and Brown (1996) also found substantial overlap in curriculum requirements between child-clinical and school psychology programs. They continued to emphasize that the traditional separation of clinical and school programs into different academic units appears to be a barrier to the educational system. Thus, they advocated for "serious consideration of combined training approaches" (p. 634).

While attempting to find shared ground between specialties, the 1987 National Conference on Graduate Education in Psychology recommended that doctoral programs in professional psychology train for a common set of skills and common bodies of knowledge. More than twenty years later, we find that APA (2007) is promulgating an assessment of competency benchmarks model that focuses on delineating shared competencies

(Assessment of Competency Benchmarks Workgroup, 2007). This model uses the "competency cube" construct to address common competencies of knowledge, skills, and attitudes across the specialty areas. One of its strengths is that it attends to an expected developmental trajectory of training competencies across the life span of one's professional career and provides guidelines at each level.

The focus on competencies leads to two related, functional queries. First, how can we most effectively deliver empirically based training to the myriad of students seeking careers as health service providers? Second, given "the great difficulty one would have, even in the near future, in finding significant differences among the curricula of the three training practice areas" (Beutler et al., 2004, p. 924), is there a parsimonious and effective model for integrating both common and unique aspects of the three current specialty areas?

Genesis and reformulation of the C-I model

After World War II, a request from Veterans Administration officials for a list of programs that were qualified to provide clinical training led the APA to establish an accreditation system (Peterson, 2004). In 1947, the Shakow Committee of the APA began to develop accreditation standards and curricular content, including basic psychological sciences, professional skills in assessment and intervention, practica, and internships. Until 1975, APA accredited three specific specialty areas: clinical, counseling, and school psychology, all designated "general practice" and "health service provider" specialties. Then, in 1975, APA stated that

> combined professional scientific psychology is a new area of accreditation for programs that do not clearly fit the model for separate programs in clinical, counseling, and school psychology. This area of accreditation is defined as a combination of clinical, counseling, and/ or school psychology. (p. 1093)

The first combined training program was at Vanderbilt University's George Peabody College in 1974. The oldest extant program, however, is at Utah State University in the Department of Psychology. Currently, there are 10 APA-accredited combined–integrated programs; however, one of the programs, at Hofstra University, is being transformed into a traditional clinical psychology program. The change, as mentioned earlier, is partially due to Hofstra's difficulty in meeting standards in one of the two specialty areas. The programs and the dates of accreditation are as follows: Utah State (1975), Hofstra (1980), University of California, Santa Barbara (1990), Florida State (1995), Northeastern University (1996), James Madison University (1997), State University of New York, Buffalo (1998), Pace University (1998), Yeshiva University (1998), and University of Toronto (2002) (see Table 5.2).

All accredited C-I programs currently include training in school psychology in addition to counseling, clinical psychology, or both. A significant departure from this format will be the developing C-I program at the University of South Alabama. It will be the first program that will not include the school psychology specialty area.

Each of the specialty areas has its own council composed of its own training directors (the Council of University Directors of Clinical Psychology, the Council of Counseling Psychology Training Programs, and the Council of Directors of School Psychology Programs). Shealy (in Bailey, 2003) stated that until 2003, "combined programs have not had a formal voice, even though they are one of the four kinds of doctoral programs accredited by APA" (p. 36). The training council for the combined programs (Consortium of Combined–Integrated Doctoral Programs in Psychology [CCIDPIP]) was constituted in 2003.

The Consensus Conference on Combined and Integrated Doctoral Training in Psychology, held May 2–4, 2003, at James Madison University, was a historic step in the development of this training model. The training directors of the 10 active, APA-accredited programs attended the conference, along with representatives from two of the other training councils; APA's Education Directorate; the Committee on Accreditation; Association of Psychology Postdoctoral and Internship Centers (APPIC); the National Register of Health Service Providers in Psychology; past presidents of divisions 2, 12, and 29; National Council of Schools of Professional Psychology (NCSPP); American Psychological Association of Graduate Students; International Association of Applied Psychology; Association of Directors of Psychology Training Clinics; and Association of State and Provincial Psychology Boards.

The conference succeeded in articulating a common set of characteristics and principles that distinguishes the combined–integrated training model. Prominent among these principles are the following points:

1. Combined–integrated programs intentionally combine at least two specialties.
2. Combined–integrated programs provide intentional exposure to multiple theoretical orientations.
3. Combined–integrated programs provide intentional exposure to multiple practice settings.
4. Combined–integrated programs provide intentional exposure to the parameters of practice, including a variety of populations served, problems addressed, procedures, and settings, across the life span.

Two issues of the 2004 *Journal of Clinical Psychology* (Vol. 60, issues 9 and 10) summarized the 2003 Consensus Conference and provide theoretical and empirical support for the training model. Among the articles, Beutler et al. (2004) referenced Murray (2000), who found that growing numbers of doctoral students perceived a mismatch between their training and employment opportunities and that graduates felt ill prepared for assuming careers outside academia. Murray advocated broad training that would include combining two or more disciplines, in order to give professional students an edge in the job market.

Givner and Furlong (2003) stated that the value of a combined model is that students take classes, receive supervision, participate in fieldwork, and research activities with faculty and students who have complementary professional perspectives, such as clinical child and adolescent psychology, child development, special education, counseling, community psychology, public health, and others. The product of such training is a unique professional psychologist with interdisciplinary skills and knowledge and an appreciation for the synergies created by such training. This is in addition to the skills and knowledge that most traditionally trained professionals possess. Shrage, Blass, and Givner (2005) provided empirical support that graduates from the combined training programs are prepared at least as well as, if not better than, graduates from traditional specialty programs, across knowledge, intervention, and assessment domains.

The current status of C-I programs

Although the existing data on traditional psychology programs are available from APA's Center for Psychology Workforce Analysis and Research (ACPWAR), no data have been published and disseminated for C-I program. ACPWAR reported that 52,731 full-time students were enrolled in all doctoral programs in 2006–2007; 66.3% identified as being White and 23% as minority (APA OnLine: Center for Workforce Studies, n.d.-a). ACPWAR also reported (APA OnLine: Center for Workforce Studies. n.d.-b) that 3,189 PhD and PsyD degrees were awarded in clinical, counseling, and school psychology in 2005–2006. Of that number, 2,458 (77.1%) were degrees in clinical psychology, 411 (12.9%) in counseling psychology, and 320 (10%) in school psychology. No mention is made of graduates from C-I programs.

The demographic data concerning APA-accredited C-I programs have not been disseminated. The following information represents the first published database on the 9 of the 10 C-I programs that are currently accredited by APA in the *combined* category. The author requested that each doctoral program provide copies of its data that had been submitted to APA as part of its annual report. This information was collated and is presented in Table 5.3.

In summary, it appears that C-I programs are attracting significant numbers of applicants, admitting a highly selective, talented cohort, and training them to be extremely successful in internship competition. A small sampling of employment data for C-I graduates reinforces earlier information suggesting high employability across multiple domains. A full

Table 5.3 Demographic Information for Nine C-I Programs (2007)

Enrollment	N = 591
	Median = 61
	Range = 23–117
Applicants	N = 1350
	Median = 98
	Range = 55–331
Applicants accepted	N = 132
	Median = 9.8%
	Range = 5.2%-25.7%
Applied for internship	N = 85
Accepted for internship	N = 82 (96.5%)
GRE scores	Mean = 1218
	Range = 1088–1269
GPA	Median = 3.6
	Range = 3.33–3.73
Minority students	N = 120 (20.3%)
Gender (male students)	N = 109 (18.5%)
Core faculty:	N = 87
Minority:	N = 21 (24.1%)
Male:	N = 34 (39.1%)

employment database has not yet been compiled. Finally, minority and gender distributions of students and faculty in the C-I programs are comparable to those in traditional specialty programs.

Evidence-based research

The very small number of empirical studies that examined C-I training models have focused on surveying graduate students, interns, and alumni, as well as fieldwork supervisors. The studies have consistently found efficacious—though potentially biased—results that support the model. Nonetheless, the findings can inform those interested in developing future training models in school psychology (see the Resource section of this chapter).

Braxton et al. (2004) provided students' perspectives on doctoral training in C-I programs. They found that students are "generally well-rounded, pragmatic, and savvy to the historical and cultural differences between practice areas. Exposure to different settings, diverse and multiple professional goals, a strong generalist identity and marketability and flexibility were the defining characteristics of C-I students" (p. 988). These findings are supportive of Cobb et al. (2004), who suggested that C-I graduates may enjoy a wider range of employment possibilities than graduates from traditional programs.

Shrage, Blass, and Givner (2005) surveyed 51 interns from 9 C-I training programs and 26 directors of internship training who had supervised students from traditional clinical and school programs, as well as students from C-I programs. The findings indicated that C-I interns viewed themselves to be significantly better prepared than interns from traditional programs in all domains measured (assessment, intervention, consultation, cultural sensitivity, and professional development); directors of internship training rated C-I interns to be significantly better prepared in the domains of intervention, assessment, and consultation, with a trend toward significance for cultural sensitivity. Both groups were equally prepared in professional development. The findings lend credibility to the notion that C-I graduates are prepared at least as well as traditional students and may be better prepared in delivery of services. Further research is needed.

A reanalysis of data supplied by APPIC concerning the 2003 Internship Match process indicated that students from nine of the C-I programs participated in the 2003 APPIC MATCH and that 56 of the 63 students who applied for APA-approved internships received them (Beutler et al., 2004). This 88.9% acceptance rate was higher than that for any of the single specialty areas and provided initial support of the C-I model by both students and the professional community.

The cumulative data provided for the 2000–2006 internship application match process (Association of Psychology Postdoctoral and Internship Centers, n.d.) indicate that the average acceptance rate to APA-accredited internships, for all applicants from all academic programs, regardless of specialty (school, clinical, counseling, and combined), was 74.9%. This author examined acceptance rates for traditional school psychology programs and combined programs and found that the average acceptance rate for applicants from 47 United States-based traditional doctoral school psychology programs that reported more than 4 applicants during the 2000–2006 period was 68.4% (576 of 842 applicants). Sixty-eight additional applicants, from 31 school psychology programs, also applied for APA-accredited internships. Their acceptance data were not included in APPIC's summaries because fewer than five students applied from the specific program during the 7-year period. In summary, 910 school psychology doctoral students from 78 self-described school psychology programs applied for APA-accredited clinical psychology internships between 2000 and 2006. It is not known what percentage of the entire population of doctoral school psychology students these 910 applicants represent. It may be a small, moderate, or large proportion. Regardless of the descriptor, 910 school psychology students had a strong enough interest to go through the rigors of applying for a traditional clinical psychology internship and, by doing so, indicated a professional career choice that is not traditional. The tipping point may have been reached and needs to be respected.

The acceptance rate, during the same time period, for applicants from United States-based combined programs (*n* = 8), was 80.6% (397 of 492 applicants). Although the difference between the rate of acceptance from traditional and C-I programs (12.2%) falls short of being statistically significant, it is still of interest to current and future students and administrators. The data lend support to the premise that students from C-I programs are accepted in nontraditional school psychology internship settings at a rate that is comparable to students from clinical psychology programs and at a higher rate than those from traditional school psychology programs. Most importantly, the applicants from C-I programs are able to bridge the divide between schooling, clinical, and/or counseling settings and are recognized for these abilities.

Training for professional roles

The C-I model addresses two prominent training issues in professional psychology: breadth versus depth of training and the professional identity of its graduates. These issues are intimately linked to the pragmatic challenges of training students for the marketplace and for future professional development. Succinctly, C-I programs emphasize breadth of training, and its graduates identify as psychologists who have been trained with emphases across specialty areas.

C-I programs assume the following:

1. There exists a corpus of knowledge that cuts a cross all three specialty areas.
2. This body of knowledge can be taught in a graduate training program.
3. This corpus of knowledge and skills can serve as a foundation both for predoctoral specialization and for postdoctoral training in a more narrowly defined area of specialization. (Beutler & Fisher, 1994, p. 67)

The challenge to C-I programs is to provide a curriculum and integrated experiences that are graded for complexity, that speak to the breadth of training across more than one specialty area, and that also meet professionally defined criteria within each specialty; to do so within a reasonable amount of time; and for their graduates to have a professional identification. This challenge is immense, and yet the nine programs discussed in this chapter are currently meeting it.

Each C-I program has developed a curriculum and supervised field experiences that meet APA accreditation standards and the definitions delineated by the APA Commission for the Recognition of Practice Areas and Proficiencies in Professional Psychology. The case study on the following page presents one program's infrastructure and its pedagogical processes. Regardless of the combination of specialty areas, all programs meet the same set of criteria that define C-I programs.

The accepted reality is that there is significant overlap in content across the three specialty areas, that students from all specialty areas vie for the same employment opportunities, and that most graduates have the generic title of psychologist. The C-I training model is, by necessity and philosophy, pragmatic, flexible, and inclusive. It provides students with the opportunities to learn from mentors who were trained in multiple specialties, have differing conceptual orientations, and who have bridged the allied professional domains. It provides graduates with the skills, attitudes, and knowledge that are required for employment in all health care provider domains, without reference to specialty. In summary, it provides graduates with a valid reflection of the reality of professional life by providing a training program that emphasizes breadth of training.

There is very limited published research concerning the efficacy of C-I training, but the research that exists is all supportive of the model and its outcomes. In addition, we know very little about the current roles and functions or employment status of C-I graduates from all programs. Again, the case study below provides information about one C-I program. It is not known whether this data set is representative of all programs, and so a study by the current author has been undertaken to investigate the role and function of all C-I program graduates for the last 5 years.

A CASE STUDY: THE COMBINED SCHOOL–CLINICAL CHILD PSYCHOLOGY PROGRAM AT YESHIVA UNIVERSITY

Since its inception in 1965, as a Boulder model PhD program, the school psychology program at Yeshiva University has undergone several transformations and is currently an APA-accredited and National Association of School Psychologists-approved, Vail model, practitioner–scholar PsyD program in combined school–clinical child psychology. By 1969, the program was awarded a National Institute of Mental Health training grant to prepare school psychologists to work in the inner city. The program, which was initially located in the heart of Greenwich Village, is now located on the Albert Einstein College of Medicine campus in the Bronx, New York. Throughout the past 42 years, it has emphasized the development of knowledge, skills, and attitudinal competencies that are required to work in schools and mental health settings.

The program received APA accreditation in school psychology in 1988. At that time, it was clear that the curriculum overlap, noted earlier in this chapter, was prominent within the program, as was the multidisciplinary training of its faculty. We were a hybrid program in search of a clear identity that would be understood by the profession and the public. Subsequently, we requested a title change from "School Psychology" to "School–Clinical Child Psychology." After the state accrediting agency and APA approved the title changes, we applied for, and received, accreditation from APA as a combined school–clinical psychology program in 1999.

What kind of effect did this transformation have upon our school, and how might it affect the profession? The most dramatic result was a demographic one. In 1995–1998, while accredited as a traditional school psychology program, we received an average of 45 applications a year for admission. In 1999, we received 79 applications for admission into the newly accredited combined program. In contrast, we received 169 applications in 2007. Of the 44 students who were admitted into the program between 1999 and 2001, two were men and two were students of color. In contrast, 18.2% of the 2006 entering class were students of color, and 16% were men. Of equal importance, the average total GRE scores climbed from 1,069 in 2002 to 1,267 in 2007 and average GPAs climbed from 3.25 in 2002 to 3.52 in 2007. Those results indicate that the public is accepting our model and that more minority and male students, with higher GRE and GPA scores, will be available for future employment in both schools and clinical settings.

Our training program's strength emanates from its faculty, which mirrors a vision of interspecialty training. A faculty that supports a combined–integrated model of training must be divergent in its thinking and synergistic in its practice. To accomplish that goal and to provide supervision across specialty areas, each faculty member needs to demonstrate a commitment to diversity of training—in our case, combining school and clinical child psychology. We were fortunate that of the eight full-time faculty members, six had doctorates in school psychology, one in educational psychology, and one in developmental psychology; seven are certified school psychologists, and six had postdoctoral training in clinical psychology. In addition, our areas of expertise included early childhood development; adolescent and young adult development; family systems; neuropsychological, cognitive, and social emotional assessment; and multiculturalism. Our theoretical orientations included psychodynamic, cognitive behavioral therapy (CBT), and family models. In 2007, the program hired its first PhD clinical child psychologist whose areas of expertise mirror the program's integrationist mission and philosophy. She conducts research and training in two areas: promoting social–emotional and academic competence in early childhood and in parenting interventions, from a CBT perspective—specifically the parent–child interaction therapy and Webster-Stratton models.

Each of the nine full-time faculty members has training and experiences in both school and clinical psychology domains. This fact permits the faculty to model a natural integration of skills and attitudes that is so critical to training professionals. In addition, traditional boundaries between orientations become nonexistent, and a sense of inclusion and membership within multiple specialty areas is fostered. When supervised by this faculty, our students become part of a system that is problem solving and offering solutions from an integrative framework.

What is the process? All students are prepared to work in both schools and mental health facilities. Along the way they complete 114 credits (38 courses) in 4 years, accumulate 600–1,200 hrs of externship experiences in schools and 600–1,200 hr in mental health facilities prior to their final internship, in which they gain an additional 1,500–1,750 hr. In addition, they receive several hundred hours of class related assessment, counseling, therapy, and remediation practica through the school's clinic and complete two applied, doctoral research projects.

The program is cognizant and responsive to the demands of the cultural and professional context of the New York City (NYC) tristate area, which must be viewed as being different from those of, for example, Salt Lake City, or Dallas, Atlanta, or Harrisonburg, VA. To meet these demands, our students are required to work from multiple theoretical orientations including, cognitive-behavioral, psychodynamic and family systems models that are embedded within a cross-cultural and multiethnic matrix. One cannot escape the fact that NYC has always been a mecca for psychodynamic thinking and achievement. Although the empirical evidence that is regarded most highly by the current establishment is not as abundant for the psychodynamic model, it is still de rigueur in NYC for employment and internships in both schools and mental health facilities. As such, students are exposed to relational and play therapy models of treatment that have empirical support, in addition to the more recognizable treatments that emanate from behavioral and CBT orientations.

We follow a similar approach with regard to assessment. Although students are taught to use traditional and empirically supported assessment methods, they are also taught to use the Rorschach. We are aware of the controversy surrounding the validity of using the Rorschach, and yet, in NYC, a student would have difficulty receiving an APA-accredited internship in a mental health facility or in a school system without such training. Similarly, the program has been responsive to the current emphasis on response-to-intervention methodologies in the classroom and will incorporate them into our assessment and consultation sequences.

We are housed in a large urban area in which there is a significant multicultural, multiethnic, multilingual representation of students who may also present with diverse gender issues. These critical issues are discussed in all courses and are enacted during the 3,500 hr of required fieldwork in multicultural settings. In addition, we offer a bilingual extension to the school psychology certificate that is embedded within the doctoral program and that requires supervision from psychologists with similar training.

What evidence exists to support our model? On average, 83% of our students accept internships in mental health facilities, and 90% of them are APA-accredited internships. All graduates from the program are eligible for state certification in school psychology. Regardless of the type of internship that students accept, our data also indicate that within 3 years of graduation, 63% of all graduates work full-time in schools; 22% are in full-time private practice, and 15% remain in mental health facilities and college counseling centers. Although there may be an initial fascination and certain magnetism about APA-accredited clinical internships, the employment realities and the true nature of a profession in school psychology propel our graduates to work in the schools. The advantage of combined–integrated training that includes multiple theoretical orientations and multiple practica in schools and clinical settings is exemplified by the fact that almost 90% of our graduates also have private practices in which they coordinate their work with other school psychologists, psychopharmacologists, physicians, occupational therapists, college counselors, speech therapists, and rehabilitation counselors.

Our graduates have the experiences, knowledge, skills, and attitudes to work in any setting in which the psychoeducational needs of the child, adolescent, or family are paramount. Of the 33 students who graduated from the program in 2006 and 2007, 14 graduates are employed in schools, 7 in medical centers, 9 in community mental health centers, 1 in an early childhood center, and 1 in a child study center. Our outcome data are consistent with our model.

Supervisory and pedagogical dilemmas

One of the most critical training dilemmas that combined–integrated programs must confront focuses on supervision and mentoring of students. Yeshiva's program is not a traditional school psychology program, yet we train students to address psychoeducational issues and to work in schools where they are supervised by licensed psychologists who are also certified school psychologists. Similarly, we are not a traditional clinical psychology program, yet we train students to work in medical centers where they are supervised by licensed psychologists, psychiatrists, and other professionals who are not certified school psychologists. The dilemma is that from the first day of orientation until graduation, students are exposed to faculty, alumni, and peers who embrace the combined–integrated model, yet when these students are on externship and internship, their supervisors will probably be graduates of traditional programs themselves with little knowledge of combined models.

As emphasized throughout this volume, supervision is critical for the training of competent psychologists. The supervisor gains added importance by virtue of being in a direct, one-to-one formative relationship with a student and may gain power and influence that is equal to or greater than that of the academic faculty. It should be acknowledged that the academic and conceptual aspects of training, including the classroom and clinic experiences within a graduate school, may not be viewed by student to be as important or energizing as their daily interactions in the field. Students are eager and primed to work as practitioners, and when given the opportunity, they may imbue the supervisor with both real and idealistic powers, talents, abilities, and wisdom.

It is therefore critical that the training program establish quality control determinants over the complexities of the supervisory process. The program needs to remain involved, from the initial contract signing to continued evaluation of the supervisor-student relationship. The added difficulty for combined training programs is that of educating the supervisor about the very nature of the model.

Yeshiva's combined program utilizes state licensed supervisors for the following:

1. Assessment, remediation, and therapy experiences that are conducted within our school's clinic
2. Assessment, treatment, and consultation experiences in school placements
3. Assessment and treatment experiences in mental health settings

We also use graduate students, who have been trained by faculty, to supervise other students in assessment and remediation experiences.

The process begins with the development of an externship contract between the placement, the student and the academic program. We have adapted the Council of Directors of School Psychology Programs (CDSPP) Internship Contract as a template for all externship experiences. The field supervisor negotiates the contents of the contract with the student, who then reviews it with the academic program director for modification and approval. This procedure ensures quality control and predictability of function and roles from the outset of the experience.

Supervisors are informed of the program's mission, model, and objectives through written material, Web-linked information, and site visits from our faculty. It is critical that the supervisor perceives our students to have the knowledge, skills and attitudes, of a professional psychologist-in-training, not of either a clinical or a school psychology student. This altered perception permits the supervisor to enable the students to cross professional boundaries and to treat the child/adolescent and family from a broader perspective. This can only be beneficial for all involved parties.

Assessment supervision in our clinic

The Ferkauf Graduate School's Parnes Psychoeducational Clinic is the in-house clinic for all doctoral programs in the school. From the 1st year in the program, our students carry assessment, remediation, and therapy cases at the clinic and are provided with different levels of supervision by full-time faculty, adjunct faculty, and advanced graduate students. First- and 2nd-year students who conduct cognitive, academic and social–emotional assessment are provided with 3 hr per week of small group supervision by full-time and adjunct faculty who are licensed psychologists. The adjunct faculty are all graduates of our program and, as such, are fully knowledgeable of our model, and they are able to assist in the education and acculturation of the students. The criteria for selecting the supervisors are demonstrated excellence while a graduate student, continued professional development after graduation, and participation in the field. The adjuncts are supervised by the full-time faculty who are associated with the course. The students also meet in small groups with advanced graduate students to review scoring and administration issues. This level of peer supervision also carries with it a mentoring and acculturation component that is critical to the continued development of the students.

The 3rd-year neuropsychological assessment practicum is conducted by one full-time faculty member and two adjunct faculty, both of whom lead small group supervision sessions for 3 hr each week. The two adjunct faculty members are senior psychologists who are associated with medical centers in the area and who have private assessment practices. They are also experts in translating assessment data into psychoeducational guidance for teachers and other professionals. Their connection to school psychology and clinical psychology is transparent—both are clinical psychologists who have school psychology certification. Again, advanced, 4th-year students provide additional individual supervision to the 3rd-year student.

Our course on bilingual assessment, taken by 3rd- and 4th-year students, is taught by a bilingual clinical psychologist with school psychology training. Once again, the selection of supervisors is predicated on knowledge and experience with issues that are relevant to the intersection of school and clinical psychology.

Treatment supervision within the clinic

Second-year students are required to conduct reading and mathematics remediation through the clinic practica. This experience is supervised by a full-time faculty member and 3rd-year graduate students. The 3rd-year therapy practica is a significant crossroad for all students. Each student is required to carry two child/adolescent therapy cases for the year. There are two types of supervisory experiences. The first experience consists of small group meetings with two full-time faculty members. The second, intensive experience is one in which each student is assigned an individual supervisor, who has volunteered his or her time to meet with the student once a week at the supervisor's private office. These supervisors are licensed psychologists, in full-time private practice, who wish to maintain a professional connection with academia. In addition, they all have received significant postdoctoral clinical training across the life span. They are primarily responsible for the conduct of the case; however, they are in regular contact with the full-time faculty. The supervisors have varied theoretical orientations, which permits students to receive supervision from a psychodynamic, cognitive behavioral, or family systems orientation. The selection of the supervisors is based upon personal recommendations from known faculty and professionals and a careful review of their curriculum vitae. In synchrony with the program's model, the supervisors are either clinical child psychologists or school psychologists with extensive experience working with schools and mental health facilities. Supervisors are provided with materials and directed to the program's Web site (http://www.yu.edu/ferkauf/page.aspx?id=733&ekmensel=242_submenu_290_btnlink).

There are multiple methods and multiple sources to maintain quality control. The selection of supervisors is carefully monitored by program faculty and the program director. Supervisors are asked to evaluate students twice a year, and students are asked to evaluate the quality of the supervision at the end of the academic year. Program faculty and supervisors are in regular communication via telephone and e-mail to ensure continuity of information flow between the program and the supervisor.

All supervisors for assessment, remediation, and therapy practica that are conducted through our clinic are intimately associated with both school psychology and clinical psychology models and have professional associations with full-time program faculty. Their knowledge of the combined model is reinforced by students and faculty and by program-sponsored workshops that they are invited to attend throughout the year.

Supervision on externship (field placement)

The program has approximately 65 2nd-, 3rd- and 4th-year students completing 2-day-a-week externships in schools or mental health facilities (600 hr) in addition to approximately 20 students on full-time internship (1,500–1,750 hr), every year. In accord with CDSPP and APA guidelines, we require that each student receive a minimum of 2 hr a week of supervision by a licensed psychologist who is an employee or consultant to the facility where the student is externing. Many sites will provide more than one supervisor for each student, and so the program may have a professional relationship with more than 100 supervisors who are working with 85 students, each year. The task of educating supervisors about our model of training and maintaining contact and oversight is a daunting one.

Many of the externship placements have repeatedly accepted our students, thereby acknowledging the high quality of service that the students deliver. It is unclear, however, whether the supervisors understand the program's philosophy or the difference between traditional school and clinical programs and our own. We are in the midst of a research program to evaluate this issue. A prior study (Schrage, Blass, & Givner, 2005) that needs to be replicated found that externship supervisors evaluated students from C-I programs to be better prepared than students from traditional clinical and school psychology programs in the assessment and intervention domains. Nonetheless, it is our responsibility to disseminate information about combined programs, and we do so by having direct contact with supervisors, making site visits, sending written information to the sites, and sending the sites our best spokespeople, our students.

Although we cannot dictate the type of supervision that our students will receive, it is critical that the clinical psychologists in medical centers appreciate and integrate psychoeducational information into case conceptualization and not denigrate the roles and contributions of the practicing school psychologist. Similarly, it is incumbent on the school psychologist to integrate social emotional and clinical information into their conceptualization of academic problems. This focus on mutual respect and understanding across disciplines is critical to the delivery of quality wrap-around services for children and families.

SUMMARY

Students in the combined school–clinical child psychology program are trained to work in multiple settings. It is the program's philosophy that a child psychologist must be knowledgeable and competent to work with academic, social emotional, cognitive, neuropsychological, individual, and family issues within a multicultural and multiethnic matrix. An accompanying issue is one of professional identity. The compartmentalization of specialty areas and, with it, the artificial separation into knowledge and skills domains, are detrimental to the profession and its clientele. The C-I psychologist is a child psychologist with knowledge, skills, and attitudes that have been cross-fertilized by experiences in multiple settings with multidisciplinary professionals who practice from different theoretical orientations. The result is an integrated professional who is not the sum of his or her parts, but rather a person with a new perspective on working with children, teachers, and families.

RESOURCES

The Web address for the Consortium of Combined–Integrated Doctoral Programs in Psychology is http://www.jmu.edu/ccidpip. The list below provides a list of all C-I programs, degree offered, training director, and Web site.

If any institution is interested in discussing the issues and processes of transforming its own program into a C-I model or beginning a C-I program, the following members of the CCIDPIP's Executive Committee can be contacted:

Steven Pfeiffer, PhD, Chair
Florida State University
Pfeiffer@mail.coe.fsu.edu

Susan Crowley, former Chair
Utah State University
susan.crowley@usu.edu

Table 5.4 Program Names and URLs

Name of Program and Degree	Program's URL
Florida State University: Counseling and School Psychology (PhD) Dr. Steven Pfeiffer	http://www.epls.fsu.edu/psych_services/ PhD/about.htm
James Madison University: Clinical and School Psychology (PsyD) Dr. Harriet Cobb	http://www.psyc.jmu.edu/cipsyd
Northeastern University: School and Counseling Psychology (PhD) Dr. Barbara Okun	http://www.northeastern.edu/bouve/ programs/dcombinedschool1/ dcombinedschool.html
Pace University: School and Clinical Psychology (PsyD) Dr. Barbara Mowder	http://appserv.pace.edu/execute/ academic_psearch/display_program.cfm? Section=Curriculum&School=GAS&Cr ed=DSY&Maj=PSY&Location=NYC
State University of New York, Buffalo: Counseling and School Psychology (PhD) Dr. LeAdelle Phelps	http://www.gse.buffalo.edu/programs/ csep/1
University of California at Santa Barbara: School, Counseling, Clinical Psychology (PhD) Dr. Michael Furlong	http://www.psych.ucsb.edu
University of Toronto: Clinical and School Psychology (PhD) Dr. Nancy Link	http://hdap.oise.utoronto.ca/pages/ schoolClnChldPsych.html
Utah State University: Clinical/ Counseling/School Psychology (PhD) Dr. Susan Crowley	http://www.usu.edu/psychology/ programs/combined/index.php
Yeshiva University: School and Clinical Child Psychology (PsyD) Dr. Abraham Givner	http://www.yu.edu/ferkauf/page. aspx?id=733&ekmensel=242_ submenu_290_btnlink

Bailey, D. S. (2003). Combined and integrated. *Monitor on Psychology, 34*(7), 36–38.
This was the first review of the Consensus conference. It was an important article as an initial public recognition on a national level of the development of the Consortium of Combined–Integrated Doctoral Programs in Psychology.

Givner, A., & Furlong, M. (2003, Fall). Relevance of the combined–integrated model of training to school psychology: The Yeshiva Program. *The Trainer's Forum, 23*(2), 1–6.
This featured article was reprinted in *The School Psychologist* (2003, pp. 145–154). It discusses an alternative pathway by which professionals who are trained in a combined model can provide their expertise in the field

of school psychology. Yeshiva University's combined school–clinical child psychology program is used as a model for C-I training. An initial data set is presented to augment the efficacy of such training.

Shealy, C. N. (Ed.). (2004). Special issue: The consensus conference and the combined integrated model of doctoral training in professional psychology. *Journal of Clinical Psychology, 60*(9–10), 887–1125.
This two-volume series in the *Journal of Clinical Psychology* consists of 13 articles by leaders in the field of combined–integrated doctoral training. Part 1 of the series provides a historical perspective and explains the nature and scope of the C-I model. Part 2 discusses the implications and applications of the C-I model for professional psychology.

REFERENCES

APA OnLine: Center for Workforce Studies. (n.d.-a) *PhDs and PsyDs awarded in clinical, counseling, and school psychology, by type of program, 2005–06.* Retrieved September 16, 2008, from http://research.apa.org/doctoraled12.html

APA OnLine: Center for Workforce Studies. (n.d.-b). *Race/ethnicity of students enrolled full- and part-time in doctoral and master's departments of psychology, 2006–07.* Retrieved September 16, 2008, from http://research.apa.org/doctoraled16.html

Association of Psychology Postdoctoral and Internship Centers. (n.d.). *APPIC match: 2000–2006 Match rates by doctoral program.* Retrieved September 16, 2008, from http://www.appic.org/downloads/APPIC_Match_2000–06_by_State.pdf

Assessment of Competency Benchmarks Workgroup. (2007, June). *A developmental model for the defining and measuring competence in professional psychology.* Retrieved September 16, 2008, from http://www.apa.org/ed/graduate/comp_benchmark.pdf

Bailey, D. S. (2003). Combined and integrated. *Monitor on Psychology, 34*(7), 36–38.

Beutler, L. E., & Fisher, D. (1994) Combined practice area training in counseling, clinical and school psychology: An idea whose time has returned. *Professional Psychology: Research and Practice, 25*, 62–69.

Beutler, L. E., Givner, A. Mowder, B. A., Fisher, D., & Reeve, R. E. (2004). A history of combined-integrated doctoral training in psychology. *Journal of Clinical Psychology, 60*(9), 911–927.

Braxton, H. H., Volker, M. A., Loftis, C., Williams-Nickelson, C., Schulte, T., Kassinove, J. I., Tarquin, K., & Scime, M. (2004). What do students want? Perspectives from the front line of doctoral training in professional and combined-integrated psychology. *Journal of Clinical Psychology, 60*, 969–990.

Cobb, H. C., Reeve, R. E., Shealy, C. N., Norcross, J. C., Schare, M. L., Rodolfo, E. R., Hargrove, D. S., Hall, J. E., & Allen, M. (2004). Overlap among clinical, counseling and school psychology: Implications for the profession and combined-integrated training. *Journal of Clinical Psychology, 60*(9), 939–955.

Givner, A., & Furlong, M. (2003). Relevance of the combined-integrated model of training to school psychology: The Yeshiva University model. *The School Psychologist, 57*(4), 145–154. (Reprinted in *The Trainer's Forum, 23*(2), 1–6.)

Kaslow, N. J., Rubin, N. J., Bebeau, M. J., Leigh, I. W., Lichtenberg, J. S., Nelson, P. D., Portnoy, S. M., & Smith I. L. (2007). Guiding principles and recommendations for the assessment of competence. *Professional Psychology: Research and Practice, 8, 5*, 441–451.

Minke, K., & Brown, D. (1996). Preparing psychologists to work with children: A comparison of curricula in child-clinical and school psychology programs. *Professional Psychology: Research and Practice, 27*(6), 631–634.

Murray, B. (2000). The degree that almost wasn't: The PsyD comes of Age. *Monitor on Psychology, 31*(1).

Peterson, D. (1985). Twenty years of practitioner training in psychology. *American Psychologist, 40*(4), 441–451.

Peterson, D. (1997). The doctor of psychology degree. *Educating professional psychologists: History and guiding conception.* (pp. 77–93). Washington, DC.: American Psychological Association.

Shrage, A., Blass, L., and Givner, A. (2005, August). Interns' and internships directors' perceptions of combined and integrated programs. Paper presented at the annual conference of the American Psychological Association, Washington, DC.

Part II
Foundations of training

6   How much theory do we teach?

Bonnie Kaul Nastasi

The purpose of this chapter is to examine the role of theory in professional school psychology and, in particular, in the preparation of school psychologists.[1] The chapter is organized around several questions: Why is theory important in professional preparation of school psychologists? What theories are critical to preparing professional school psychologists? How do we integrate theory into professional preparation/development of "scientist~practitioners"? What are the implications for future research, practice and professional preparation/development?

WHY IS THEORY IMPORTANT IN PROFESSIONAL PREPARATION OF SCHOOL PSYCHOLOGISTS?

Establishing a rationale for including theory in school psychology graduate programs requires consideration of professional training standards and guidelines, models of professional competence, and definitions of the constructs of professionalism and scientist~practitioner.[2] To ensure program quality and credentialing, decisions about curriculum in school psychology require, at a minimum, adherence to training standards and guidelines set forth by professional organizations and credentialing bodies.

Current professional training standards and guidelines

Examination of current standards within psychology in general and school psychology in particular reveals consistency regarding preparation in

---

[1] For the purposes of this chapter, *professional preparation* (or *graduate education*) in school psychology is used generically to refer to both specialist and doctoral level programs. This is based on the assumption by the author that the inclusion of theory within graduate education does not require distinctions regarding level of training.

[2] The discussion here focuses primarily on the current zeitgeist in professional psychology. For those interested in a historical perspective, see Benjamin (2006), Fagan (2005), and Rubin et al. (2007).

foundations of professional practice (American Psychological Association [APA], 2003; Committee on Accreditation [COA], 2005; National Association of School Psychologists [NASP], 2000; Ysseldyke et al., 2006; Peterson, Peterson, Abrams, & Stricker, 2006). Training standards provide the basis for identifying competencies for professional practice. For example, training and practice standards set forth by APA provided the basis for a three-dimensional (cube) model for competency development, articulated by the Specialties and Proficiencies of Professional Psychology workgroup and adopted by the Council of Credentialing Organizations in Professional Psychology (Rodolfa et al., 2005). The three dimensions include (a) foundational competency domains: reflective practice/self-assessment, scientific knowledge and methods, relationships, ethical-legal standards and policies, individual-cultural diversity, and interdisciplinary systems; (b) functional competency domains: assessment/diagnosis/case conceptualization, intervention, consultation, research and evaluation, supervision and teaching, and management and administration; and (c) stages of development: doctoral education, doctoral internship, postdoctoral internship, fellowship or residency, and continuing competency (Rodolfa et al.). These dimensions encompass all professional specialties; differentiation of specialty is made on the basis of procedural and theoretical foundations and target problems, population, and settings (Rodolfa et al.).

NASP standards for training and practice, most recently interpreted by the Blueprint Task Force in *Blueprint III* (Ysseldyke et al., 2006), also address three dimensions of competence: (a) foundational competencies: interpersonal and collaborative skills, diversity awareness and sensitive service delivery, technological applications, and professional, legal, ethical and social responsibility; (b) functional competencies: data-based decision making and accountability, systems-based service delivery, enhancing development of cognitive and academic skills, and enhancing development of wellness, social skills, mental health, and life competencies; and (c) stages of development: novice (at completion of coursework), competent (at completion of internship), and expert (with postgraduate experience). The two models of professional preparation are summarized in Table 6.1. Noteworthy are the similarities with regard to foundational competency domains and the stages of development in the two models (Rodolfa et al., 2005; Ysseldyke et al.). The distinctions with regard to functional competency domains are indicative of specialty-specific distinctions that have implications for decisions about theoretical underpinnings of professional practice. These two models contribute to the proposed model for integration of theory in professional preparation, as depicted also in Table 6.1. Before turning to discussion of theoretical foundations for school psychology, two additional constructs relevant to professional identity warrant attention: (a) professionalism and (b) the scientist~practitioner.

Table 6.1 Professional Preparation: Competencies and Stages of Development

Dimensions	APA[a]	NASP[b]	Proposed model:[c] Theoretical Foundations
Foundational competencies	1. Reflective practice/self-assessment 2. Scientific knowledge & methods 3. Relationships 4. Ethical-legal standards & policies 5. Individual-cultural diversity 6. Interdisciplinary systems	1. Interpersonal & collaborative skills 2. Diversity awareness & sensitive service delivery 3. Technological applications 4. Professional, legal, ethical, & social responsibility	1. Biological & health foundations 2. Cognitive foundations 3. Social-cultural foundations 4. Developmental-ecological 5. Individual differences 6. Developmental psychopathology 7. Organizational/systems
Functional competencies	1. Assessment, diagnosis, case conceptualization 2. Intervention 3. Consultation 4. Research & evaluation 5. Supervision & teaching 6. Management & administration	1. Data-based decision making & accountability 2. Systems-based service delivery 3. Enhancing development of cognitive and academic skills 4. Enhancing development of wellness, social skills, mental health, & life competencies	1. Assessment 2. Intervention/prevention 3. Consultation/education 4. Management/supervision 5. Research/evaluation
Cross-cutting foundations			1. Interpersonal skills 2. Critical thinking 3. Ethics 4. Cultural diversity 5. Social responsibility
Stages of professional development	1. Doctoral education 2. Doctoral internship 3. Postdoctoral internship 4. Fellowship or residency 5. Continuing competency	1. Novice (coursework complete) 2. Competent (internship complete) 3. Expert (postgraduate experience)	1. Novice 2. Intermediate 3. Competent 4. Capable

[a] Interpretation of APA standards for training by Rodolfa, E., Bent, R., Eisman, E., Nelson, P., Rehm, L., & Ritchie, P. (2005). A cube model for competency development: Implications for psychology educators and regulators. *Professional Psychology: Research and Practice, 36,* 347–354, 2005, APA.

[b] Interpretation of NASP standards for training by Ysseldyke, J., Burns, M., Dawson, P., Kelley, B., Morrison, D., Ortiz, S., Rosenfield, S., & Telzrow, C. (2006). *School psychology: A blueprint for training and practice III.* Bethesda, MD: NASP.

[c] Author's interpretation and integration of competencies and stages of development as described in the following sources: APA, 2003; COA, 2005; Hatcher & Lassiter, 2007; Kaslow et al., 2007; NASP, 2000; NCSPP, Peterson et al., 2006; Rodolfa et al., 2005; Ysseldyke et al., 2006.

Professionalism

The definition of *professionalism* proposed by the Professional Development Workgroup (PDWG; Elman, Illfelder-Kaye, & Robiner, 2005) is adopted for the purposes of this discussion. The PDWG identified two dimensions of professionalism. The first of these, interpersonal functioning, is defined as the "operations or skills for relating effectively with others, developing one's own professional approaches and persona, and internalizing professional standards, ... [and] seeing oneself as a cultural being and understanding the impact of one's culture on interactions with others" (Elman et al., p. 369). The second dimension, critical thinking ("thinking like a psychologist"), includes

> [(a)] critical thinking and logical analysis; (b) being conversant with and utilizing scientific inquiry and professional literature; (c) being able to conceptualize problems and issues from multiple perspectives (e.g., biological, pharmacological, intrapsychic, familial, organizational/systems, social, cultural); and (d) being able to access, understand, integrate, and use resources (e.g., empirical evidence, statistical approaches, technology, collegial consultation). (Elman et al., p. 369)

The second dimension is particularly important to the concept of the scientist~practitioner as the primary identity for professional psychologists.

What is the scientist~practitioner?

The concept of "scientist~practitioner" within professional psychology has been the subject of much examination and discussion (Belar & Perry, 1992; Elman et al., 2005; Kratochwill & Shernoff, 2003; Nastasi, 2000; Sheridan & Gutkin, 2000; Stoner & Green 1992; Stricker & Trierweiler, 2006). Consistent with the notion of thinking like a psychologist are characterizations of the professional psychologist as (a) one who engages in disciplined inquiry (Peterson, 2006; Peterson et al., 2006); (b) a local clinical scientist (Stricker & Trierweiler); (c) a practicing scientist, reflective practitioner, or action researcher (Nastasi, 1998; 2000; Nastasi, Moore, & Varjas, 2004); and (d) one who integrates science and practice (depicted as *scientist~practitioner* or *scientist × practitioner;* Belar & Perry, 1992).

In order to reflect a more synergistic integration of science and practice of the capable professional psychologist, the term *scientist~practitioner,* proposed by delegates of the National Conference on Scientist~Practitioner Education and Training for the Professional Practice of Psychology (Belar & Perry, 1992), is adopted for characterizing the professional school psychologist in this chapter. The symbolism (~) of the scientist~practitioner is critical to the distinction between applied scientist and scientist in action. The applied scientist employs theoretically and empirically based knowledge in practice, thus utilizing evidence-based assessment and intervention tools. The scientist in action goes beyond the application of evidence-based practice (EBP) to the application of research methods for the purpose of advancing the theoretical and empirical/evidence base for practice.

The professional activity of the scientist~practitioner is characterized by praxis, or the ongoing interplay of theory, research, and action/ practice (Nastasi, 1998), described by social scientists in other fields such as applied anthropology (e.g., Partridge, 1985; Schensul, 1985). Belar and Perry (1992) describe scientist~practitioners as embodying "a research orientation in their practice and a practice relevance in their research" (p. 72). The scientist~practitioner (a) engages in problem solving, critical thinking, and reflection; (b) applies scientific methods to solving problems in the local context; (c) contributes to bridging the research-practice gap; and (d) generates new knowledge—theory and research evidence—that can be communicated to others (professional colleagues, policy makers, consumers/clients, and other stakeholder groups). (For more in-depth discussion of definitions of the professional psychologist as scientist~practitioner, readers are referred to the sources cited herein.) The construct of scientist~practitioner provides the basis for conceptualizing professional development in school psychology and exploring the role of theory in the lifelong learning process.

Model for professional development of the scientist~practitioner

Figure 6.1 depicts a model of professional development that is consistent with aforementioned training guidelines and definitions of competence. For the purpose of discussion, the foundations for development of integrated science~practice are categorized as scientific, practice/applied, and cross-cutting (see Table 6.1). The scientific foundations include theories, research, and methodology related to biological, cognitive, social-cultural, affective, and developmental aspects of behavior. The practice or applied foundations refer to the knowledge and skills in assessment, intervention (prevention to treatment for individuals, groups, organizations, systems), consultation, management/administration, supervision/teaching, and research and evaluation.

The cross-cutting competencies include interpersonal skills, critical thinking, professional ethics, cultural diversity, and social responsibility. These broad-based competencies are critical to integration of science and practice, and contribute to development of professional competence and professionalism of the scientist~practitioner.

The stages of development include novice, intermediate, competent, and capable. These levels are consistent with those proposed by Rodolfa et al. (2005), Ysseldyke et al. (2006), Kaslow et al. (2007), and Hatcher and Lassiter (2007). The fourth stage, capability, extends beyond competence to include the capacity to apply knowledge and skills to new clients (individuals, groups,

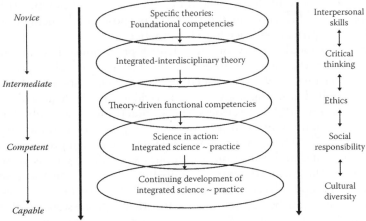

Figure 6.1 Role of theory in professional development for integrated science~practice of school psychology. Facilitating development from novice to capable integrated practicing scientist requires the following process: (a) introduction of specific theories through foundational coursework (i.e., development foundational competencies in biological, cognitive, social, developmental, individual differences, etc.), (b) fostering integrated-interdisciplinary theory as overarching framework for science-based practice (e.g., biopsychosocial [BPS], ecological-development, systems theories), (c) developing theory-driven functional competencies (i.e., assessment, intervention, consultation/education, management/supervision, and research/evaluation), (d) applying science to practice through supervised field training (practicum, internship), and (e) continuing professional development of an integrated science~practice approach. Concurrent with the development from novice to capable professional is development of cross-cutting competencies: interpersonal skills, critical thinking, ethics, cultural diversity, and social responsibility.

organizations) and settings, to generate new knowledge, and to engage in lifelong learning (Kaslow et al.). As such, this highest level is most consistent with the ideal scientist~practitioner or practicing scientist.

As depicted in Figure 6.1, progressing from novice to capable professional involves (a) acquiring knowledge of specific theories through foundational coursework (e.g., biological bases of behavior, cognitive bases of learning), (b) constructing an integrated theoretical framework as the basis for scientific~practice, (c) developing theoretically and empirically based functional competencies (e.g., assessment, intervention, consultation), (d) applying science to practice through supervised field training (practicum, internship), and (e) continuing professional development of an integrated science~practice approach. Concurrent with development of foundational and functional competencies is development of cross-cutting competencies that characterize professionalism (e.g., interpersonal skills, critical thinking). Before turning to issues of curriculum content and pedagogy, we first consider what theory or theories are pertinent to school psychology.

WHAT THEORIES ARE CRITICAL TO PREPARING
PROFESSIONAL SCHOOL PSYCHOLOGISTS?

An integrated science~practice model by definition necessitates a theoretically driven approach. The role of theory in professional practice can be characterized in the praxis cycle (cf. evidence-based practice) as follows: theory → case conceptualization → evidence-based intervention → evaluation + reflection → theory. The theoretical frame of reference informs how the professional school psychologist approaches (a) assessment and case conceptualization, (b) the selection and implementation of an evidence-based intervention, and (c) evaluation of the intervention. The evaluation, coupled with reflection, can subsequently inform the professional's theoretical base for future practice. This model is consistent with theory-driven data-based problem solving or decision making and with current models of evidence-based practice (APA Presidential Task Force on EBP, 2006; Kazdin, 2008; Kratochwill, 2007; Kratochwill & Stoiber, 2002; Nastasi & Schensul, 2005).

Some might argue that professional practice can be conducted atheoretically, guided by empirical evidence alone. In recent years, however, discussions have focused on questions regarding the preparadigmatic vs. paradigmatic stage of psychological science. Melchert (2007) contends that professional psychology has moved beyond preparadigmatic (i.e., characterized by competing individual theories) to solidly paradigmatic (characterized by an integrated theoretical orientation). Indeed, as Melchert argues, if professional psychology has not reached a paradigmatic stage in its development as a science, then "the claim that professional psychology is a science-based profession would be highly questionable" (Melchert, p. 37).

Integrated theoretical models

Assuming we have reached a paradigmatic stage in professional psychology, the question is, "What integrated theoretical model do we adopt for school psychology?" Melchert (2007) suggests that a comprehensive integrated biopsychosocial (BPS) perspective best characterizes our current understanding of human development and functioning. That is, human behavior can be understood best as the interaction of biological, psychological, and social (-cultural) variables. The BPS is consistent with the integrated models of human functioning in school psychology, namely ecological–developmental (Nastasi et al., 2004), ecological–transactional (Overstreet & Mazza, 2003), and systems–ecological (Christenson, 2003) models. What is consistent across these ecologically oriented integrated models (based on Bronfenbrenner, 1989) in school psychology is the attempt to provide a comprehensive framework for understanding the functioning of children and adolescents within the evolving contexts or systems in which they live. An ecological–developmental perspective requires consideration of biological, psychological (cognitive, affective), social, cultural, and contextual or systemic factors in gathering data for decision making (assessment, diagnosis, etc.), explaining behavior (e.g., case conceptualization), identifying appropriate interventions (i.e., selecting evidence-based interventions [EBIs]), and evaluating effectiveness of interventions. The developmental and systemic focus also necessitates interventions conceptualized within a continuum of services, from promotion/prevention/universal to treatment/intensive intervention. Finally, the ecological focus results in inclusion of contextual and systemic factors related to schools, families, peer group, communities, and the interactions of these systems.

Role of specific theories

If the professional psychologist adopts an integrated theoretical model, as suggested above, this leads to questions such as, Do specific theories have a role in professional psychology preparation and practice? Indeed, adoption of a comprehensive, integrated theoretical perspective does not preclude the teaching of specific theories nor the need for knowledge of the specific theories that comprise the integrated model. As reflected in the proposed model, education about specific theories relevant to foundational, functional, and cross-cutting competencies are critical.

Melcher (2007) makes an important distinction between an integrated theoretical model, such as biopsychosocial or ecological–developmental, for case conceptualization and intervention planning (EBP), versus selection of theory-specific EBIs.[3] For example, using the praxis cycle, the school psychologist might approach case conceptualization from an ecological–developmental perspective (e.g., gathering data on the individual's biological, cognitive, academic, social, and emotional functioning; cultural and familial background; and school and classroom contexts) but select an intervention on the basis of cognitive-behavioral principles because the data and the existing research support the use of the intervention.

Focus on multiple domains of functioning related to an individual and ecology necessitates extending the knowledge base of professional school psychologists beyond disciplinary or specialty boundaries. For example, Overstreet and Mazza (2003) contend that understanding community violence requires a cross-disciplinary theoretical model that includes other specialties of psychology (e.g., developmental, social, developmental psychopathology), as well as other disciplines, such as sociology and medicine. Similarly, Nastasi (2000; Nastasi et al., 2004) suggests that the

---

[3] For the purposes of this chapter, *EBI* refers to a specific intervention that has empirical or research-based support (for a discussion of what constitutes evidence, see Kratochwill & Stoiber, 2002). *EBP* refers more broadly to the practice of professional psychology based on "the integration of the best available research with clinical expertise in the context of patient characteristics, culture, and preferences" (APA, 2006, p. 273). EBP is thus consistent with engaging in science~practice versus selecting interventions with empirical support (EBI).

provision of comprehensive school-based mental health services requires partnership with professionals from "psychology (e.g., developmental, health, school, clinical, educational, social, community, organizational), medicine (e.g., pediatrics, psychiatry), behavioral health, public health, medical and educational anthropology, health education, sociology, and economics" (Nastasi, 2000, p. 544). Indeed, the complexity of learning, behavioral, and health problems increasingly necessitate the adoption of transtheoretical and transdisciplinary models for conceptualizing change. Furthermore, employing comprehensive integrated theoretical perspectives requires extending the foundations of scientific knowledge, which in turn has implications for professional preparation.

HOW DO WE INTEGRATE THEORY INTO PROFESSIONAL PREPARATION OF SCHOOL PSYCHOLOGISTS?

Integrating theory into professional preparation requires decisions about both curriculum content (What do we teach?) and pedagogy (How do we teach?). Although in practice, effective instruction depends on the seamless integration of content and pedagogy, for the sake of discussion, these topics are presented separately.

Curriculum content: what do we teach?

Figure 6.2 depicts a framework for integrating theory into curriculum content. Curriculum for preparing school psychologists should include content on specific theories (relevant to professional competencies), integrated theoretical orientations or model (relevant to science~practice), and theory generation (through research and evaluation). Although specifically directed toward graduate education, this model applies to professional development as a lifelong learning process and thus can guide decisions about continuing professional development as well. Thus, extant theories and new theoretical models generated through research and evaluation are expected to contribute to the professional's evolving comprehensive integrated theoretical model that guides science-based practice.

The integrated theoretical model is consistent with the construct of personal theory proposed by Brammer, Shostrom, and Abrego (1989) and applied to school-based professionals by Nastasi et al. (2004). The development of the professional's integrated theoretical model (personal theory) begins with what Brammer et al. describe as a creative synthesis of existing theories, resulting from graduate education, personal and professional experiences, and reflection. The professional's integrated theoretical model continues to evolve through continuing education and reflective science-based practice, or lifelong learning that embodies the integration of formal education with science~practice.

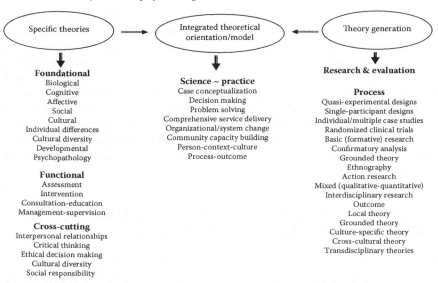

Figure 6.2 Theory within professional school psychology curriculum content: What do we teach? The professional development curriculum in school psychology should include content on specific theories, integrated theoretical orientations or models, and the process of theory generation. *Specific theories* refer to those relevant to foundational, functional, and cross-cutting competencies: for example, theories specific to domains of human development and change (e.g., cognitive, cognitive-behavioral). *Integrated theoretical orientations or models* are those that guide the science~practice, or praxis, cycle; for example, biopsychosocial (BPS) or ecological–developmental models of assessment and intervention. *Theory generation* refers to skill development in research and evaluation related to the process and outcome of theory generation activities: for example, ethnography for the purpose of developing culture-specific or local theories that can in turn guide local practice. Both specific theories and theory generation contribute to the development of coherent and comprehensive integrated theoretical models as the basis for integrated science and practice. Although primarily intended to guide graduate education, this model for integrating theory in curriculum can apply to the lifelong learning process.

As depicted in Figure 6.2, curriculum content pertaining to theory needs to include the specific theories that contribute to the foundational, functional, and cross-cutting competencies outlined in Table 6.1. Within the context of core courses in the foundational areas such as biological bases of behavior, cognitive psychology, developmental psychology, and professional ethics, students would acquire knowledge of the relevant theories (and related research). Similarly, skill-based or applied courses, such as school-based consultation or assessment of intelligence, would cover content relevant to the theoretical (and empirical) underpinnings (e.g., behavioral consultation, theories of intelligence). In addition, theories and related research germane to cross-cutting competencies would be covered in the relevant foundational or skill-based courses. For example, theories and research relevant to critical thinking might be covered in both cognitive psychology and courses related to decision making about academic interventions (e.g., response-to-intervention). In a similar manner, theories and research related to interpersonal skills could be included in a foundational course in social psychology and skill-based courses related to school-based consultation.

Professional practice of school psychology is ultimately dependent on science~practice that is grounded in an integrated theoretical orientation. Thus, curriculum content needs to include examination and/or development of integrated theoretical models. Specific integrated theoretical models, such as biopsychosocial or ecological–developmental, are introduced in foundational and skill-based courses and reinforced through application in field training (practicum and internship). Content relevant to theory generation is included in research and evaluation coursework, with subsequent application in field training and mentored research experiences. Critical to development of professional school psychologists are those theoretical or conceptual models that guide science~practice, such as those relevant to case conceptualization, decision making, problem solving, comprehensive service delivery, organizational or systems change, community capacity building, and understanding person–context–culture and process–outcome links (see Figure 6.2). Moreover, effective professional practice also depends on grounding in theoretical models relevant to development of critical thinking, interpersonal relationships, ethical decision making, cultural competence, and social responsibility (i.e., the cross-cutting competencies). Although specific assessment and intervention techniques (skill-based competencies) can be guided by specific theories, the complexity of evidence-based practice requires more comprehensive integrated theoretical orientations.

Theory generation within school psychology curriculum refers to skill development in research and evaluation related to the process and outcome of theory generation activities (Figure 6.2). As discussed earlier, the science~practice process involves development of local theory. Similarly, engaging in culturally sensitive practice requires generation of culture-specific, culturally appropriate, or cross-cultural theoretical models. Both local and culture-specific theories are consistent with the notion of grounded theory (Strauss & Corbin, 1990) as inductively derived or grounded in the experiences and worldview of members of the local context or culture. Transdisciplinary[4] theories are essential to the interdisciplinary

---

[4] *Interdisciplinary* refers to collaboration from discipline-specific perspectives or theoretical models; *transdisciplinary* refers to collaboration based on shared perspectives or theoretical models that reflect the integration of theories/models specific to each discipline (Rosenfield, 1999; Schensul, Nastasi, & Verma, 2006). Thus, transdisciplinary theory is used here to reflect a comprehensive integrated theoretical orientation based on theories from two or more disciplines (e.g., psychology and medicine).

nature of professional school psychology practice and the complexity of learning, behavioral, and health problems faced by school psychologists. For example, developing a comprehensive mental health service delivery system within a school district requires collaboration across multiple disciplines (psychology, education, public health, medicine, nursing, etc.). A transdisciplinary approach would require that the professional partners adopt an integrated theoretical model based on theories from the respective disciplines (e.g., learning problems could be conceptualized in terms of the biological, psychological, educational, and social-cultural factors, with interventions reflecting an integrated medical, educational, and psychological framework). Furthermore, for the professional school psychologist, developing an integrated theoretical model requires consideration of theory and research from other disciplines. For example, the psychologists might consult research literature in public health, anthropology, education, and psychology in developing a framework for addressing sexual risk or drug abuse in schools.

Development of skills for theory generation and science~practice requires that a research and evaluation curriculum include a wide range of research methods that extend beyond traditional quantitative designs. As depicted in Figure 6.2, graduate education curriculum should include quasi-experimental, single-participant, case study, randomized controlled trials (experimental), basic/formative, and confirmatory designs. In addition, qualitative research approaches, such as grounded theory and ethnography, are critical to development of grounded, local, and culture-specific theory. Similarly, action research provides an excellent research-based approach for developing models to address culture- and context-specific needs. Mixed qualitative–quantitative research designs hold promise for generating and adapting or translating evidence-based practice (Nastasi et al., 2007). Finally, development of transdisciplinary models involves grounding in professional literature beyond psychology, combined with interdisciplinary research and practice. The implication for curriculum content is the inclusion of required or recommended readings from professional literature in other disciplines and opportunities to develop skills for engaging in interdisciplinary research, for example, developing skills in negotiating consensus and building transdisciplinary models. (Schensul, Nastasi & Verma, 2006, provide an example of transdisciplinary collaboration in community-based research.)

Pedagogy: how do we teach?

Decisions about how to teach theory within school psychology curriculum involve considerations of (a) how to best present content (i.e., existing specific theories or integrated theoretical orientations), (b) how to apply theory to practice (i.e., establishing the science~practice links), (c) how to teach the process of disciplined inquiry (i.e., integrating theory in science~practice), (d) how to teach an approach to professional practice that involves both the integration of existing theory with practice and the generation of theory, and (e) how to foster development of what Elman et al. (2005) refer to as "professionalism" (interpersonal functioning and critical thinking) and other cross-cutting competencies (social responsibility, ethics, cultural competence), and the integration of these professional competencies with science~practice. Another consideration is perhaps the essential question: How do we address these considerations within an integrated pedagogy (i.e., the seamless blending of science, practice and professionalism)? Several authors have addressed the issue of establishing an integrated pedagogy in professional psychology (APA Presidential Task Force on Evidence-Based Practice, 2006; Belar & Perry, 1992; Gelso, 2006; Melchert, 2007; Peterson, 2006; Peterson et al., 2006). The following guidelines for pedagogy in professional school psychology preparation are based on common principles and strategies reflected in these sources (readers are encouraged to consult these sources for more detail and illustrations). Presented in the next section is an illustration of the application of these principles and strategies to school psychology.

1. Use a didactic structured inquiry approach to theoretical content relevant to foundational, functional, and cross-cutting competencies. Theoretical content is presented via lecture, assigned and recommended readings within specific competency-based courses. For example, theories relevant to development of and assessment-intervention for cognitive, behavioral, and social–emotional functioning are covered in foundation and skill-based courses, respectively. Similarly, theoretical models relevant to working with culturally diverse populations are covered via lectures and readings within specific multicultural coursework and/or across the curriculum.
2. Use a guided inquiry approach to theoretical content relevant to foundational, functional, and cross-cutting competencies. Foundational and skill-based courses include assignments that require independent readings to extend knowledge of theory or its application.
3. Provide opportunities for hypothetical and experiential application of theory to practice and theory generation. Using hypothetical "cases" (individual, group, system, organization, community) within coursework and real-life cases in supervised field training, include assignments that require students to consider and apply relevant specific and integrated theory to the praxis cycle: theory $\rightarrow$ case conceptualization $\rightarrow$ evidence-based intervention $\rightarrow$ evaluation + reflection $\rightarrow$ theory.
4. Provide opportunities for development and application of interpersonal functioning, specifically collaborative approach to science~practice. Introduce principles of and skills for effective collaboration using didactic approach. In particular, teach critical skills for engaging in collaborative problem solving and decision making, including

establishing relationships, communication, negotiating consensus, integrating discrepant viewpoints, and self-evaluation of group process (Nastasi et al., 2004). Facilitate application through collaborative case-based activities, such as small group problem solving, within course context or interdisciplinary collaboration in supervised field experiences.

5. Foster critical stance with regard to theory and its application to practice, such that structured didactic, guided inquiry, or case-based approaches involve examination of the research evidence relevant to the respective theories. For example, guided inquiry includes examining the research evidence to confirm or disconfirm existing theory.

6. Foster critical stance with regard to cultural appropriateness of theory and cultural validity of theory-based assessment instruments and intervention techniques/approaches. Within the context of both structured and guided inquiry, examine the empirical bases to support application/validity of evidence-based assessment or intervention strategies to diverse cultural groups, and critique their cultural relevance.

7. Provide opportunities for exploring theories from other disciplines, approaching cases from a transdisciplinary perspective, and generating integrated transdisciplinary models for science~practice. Include theories and research from related disciplines (e.g., public health, education, sociology) in lectures and required, recommended, or independent readings. Require that case-based activities involve exploration of theories and research from other disciplines (e.g., hypothetical cases), consultation or collaboration with professionals from other disciplines (e.g., real-life cases in field experiences), and/or interdisciplinary collaboration on hypothetical or real-life cases. Facilitate application of interpersonal skills to interdisciplinary collaborative activities, which include opportunities for self-evaluation and reflection.

8. Provide opportunities through structured and guided inquiry to examine social issues and develop attitudes and skills relevant to social responsibility. Incorporate content regarding social issues (e.g., social inequity, discrimination, poverty, racism, marginalization, oppression) in lectures and readings. Structure case-based activities to include social-cultural issues (e.g., examining socioeconomic factors and discrimination as factors in the poor interpersonal functioning of a high school student and planning interventions to address these factors).

9. Provide mentored experience in theory generation. Involve students in faculty-directed science~practice activities that include opportunities to engage in theory generation; for example, involve students in an action research project in the local schools, or an ethnographic study to develop a local culture/context-specific theory regarding promoting academic achievement of a culturally diverse student population.

10. Model the science~practice approach. In teaching, mentoring, and supervision roles, demonstrate an approach to professional psychology that exemplifies disciplined inquiry, critical thinking, effective interpersonal functioning, social responsibility, professional ethics, reflective practice, cultural competence, transdisciplinary collaboration, and commitment to lifelong learning and generating new knowledge.

Perhaps the ultimate challenge is to develop pedagogy incorporating all of the suggested principles and strategies. Achieving pedagogy characterized by seamless integration of science and practice, as described here, requires a commitment of faculty to lifelong learning, reflective teaching practice, and collaboration with professionals in psychology and other disciplines. Thus, an integrated pedagogy requires adopting and modeling the professionalism and science~practice that are the goals of graduate education and continued professional development.

CASE ILLUSTRATION: APPLYING THE SCIENCE~PRACTICE PROCESS IN SCHOOL PSYCHOLOGY

To illustrate application of integrated pedagogy in professional preparation of school psychologists, a case-based approach is adopted. The following activity could be incorporated in coursework as a hypothetical or simulated case study, or in field training as an actual case study. Key components include integration of theory with research and practice, application of an integrated theoretical model to the case, working within an interdisciplinary or transdisciplinary framework, and application of interpersonal functioning and critical thinking. In this example, *case* refers to school system; the goal of the activity is to develop a comprehensive service model (i.e., encompasses three-tiered model of universal, targeted, and intensive services) that builds organization capacity and student competencies to prevent or reduce school violence (school violence is the presenting problem); and the target professional competencies are those related to enhancing wellness, mental health, social skills, and life competencies (see NASP *Blueprint III*, Ysseldyke et al., 2006).

Figure 6.3 depicts the application of the science~practice or praxis process to hypothetical or real-life cases in school psychology. Components of the process are highlighted in this section, with illustration for developing system-wide school-based comprehensive services for violence prevention-reduction. The praxis process presented here is consistent with a participatory approach to generating or translating evidence-based interventions to the local culture and context, the Participatory Culture-Specific Intervention Model (PCSIM; Nastasi et al., 2004). PCSIM involves an integrated research-practice approach that is grounded in a recursive mixed qualitative–quantitative research design (Nastasi et al., 2007). (For

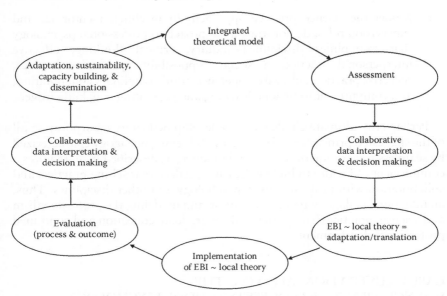

Figure 6.3 Case illustration: Application of science~practice process to hypothetical or actual cases within school psychology. Applying the science~practice process involves four phases: (a) integrated theoretical model; (b) case conceptualization, consisting of assessment and collaborative data interpretation and decision making; (c) evidence-based practice, reflected as adaptation of an evidence-based intervention (EBI) through integration of local theory, followed by implementation; (d) evaluation + reflection, which includes collection and analysis of process and outcome data, collaborative data interpretation, and decision making regarding further adaptations, program continuation, dissemination, and capacity building. The cycle concludes with reflection leading to modification of personal integrated theory. This approach is consistent with the Participatory Culture-Specific Intervention Model (PCSIM; articulated and illustrated in Nastasi, Varjas, Bernstein et al., 2002; Nastasi, Varjas, Schensul et al., 2002; Nastasi et al., 2004; Nastasi et al., 2007), which involves the integration of theory, mixed-methods research, and practice in the translation of evidence-based interventions to local culture and context.

those readers interested in more detailed guidance in the research and practice aspects, see Nastasi, Varjas, Bernstein et al., 2000; Nastasi, Varjas, Schensul et al., 2000; Nastasi et al., 2004, 2007).

The basic sequence depicted in Figure 6.3 is theory → case conceptualization → evidence-based intervention → evaluation + reflection → theory, in the context of a school-based collaborative approach. The first phase, integrated theoretical model, involves the articulation of a model based in psychology, and possibly other disciplines, to guide the process of case conceptualization, evidence-based intervention, and evaluation.

Assuming a collaborative approach, the theoretical model is negotiated with the other partners (team members; e.g., teachers, administrators, other mental health professionals, parents, students). For illustrative purposes, an ecological–developmental model is adopted.

The second phase, case conceptualization, involves (a) assessment of needs and resources specific to the individuals (e.g., students, parents, teachers) and their respective systems (e.g., peer group, family, classroom, school, community) and (b) collaborative data interpretation and decision making. The ecological–developmental model requires attention to individual factors (e.g., biological and psychological) and systemic factors at microsystem (e.g., classroom), exosystem (the school), macrosystem (local and societal public education values, norms, etc.), and mesosystem (e.g., home-school relationships) levels. Data are collected and analyzed using a mixed (qualitative–quantitative) methods approach, which could include observation, interviews, focus groups, review of school records, standardized tests, and self-report and informant-report ratings. Professionals with expertise in data analysis (e.g., school psychologist) prepare data for presentation to the partners/team members, who then engage in a collaborative process of data interpretation and decision making. The goal of the team process at this stage is to use data to understand the needs and resources at individual and systemic levels, develop a "local" theoretical framework, and identify targets or goals for intervention. Assuming a comprehensive service delivery model, the team makes decisions about needs regarding universal, targeted and intensive interventions, across the components of the ecological system. For example, the team may decide initially to target development of peaceful conflict resolution skills at the universal level, with inclusion of classroom, school-wide, and community components.

The third phase, evidence-based practice, is reflected as (a) adaptation or translation of EBI to meet the needs of local culture and context, and (b) implementation of the local adaptation. Based on the local theoretical model and goals, potential EBIs (i.e., interventions with empirical support) are identified by professionals with expertise in interventions and adapted to fit the local model. For example, evidence-based conflict resolution interventions grounded in cognitive-behavioral theory are identified and then modified to incorporate conflict situations and resolution strategies that are relevant to the specific population of students (e.g., urban African American and Latino middle school students, some of whom belong to gangs). Within a comprehensive service delivery model, intervention planning needs to include decisions about programming at universal, targeted, and intensive levels.

Implementation of the locally adapted EBI is coupled with ongoing data collection (using mixed methods) to monitor the acceptability, cultural validity, integrity, and impact/outcome of the intervention. Data collection and analysis inform necessary modifications to meet individual, cultural, or contextual variations. Critical to decision making about modifications in implementation is clear understanding of the mechanisms or components of the intervention that are responsible for outcomes (e.g., guided practice of communicating about differences of opinion) versus those components that can vary and not affect intervention effectiveness (e.g., topic of the communication). The professionals responsible for understanding the theoretical underpinnings of the intervention need to be involved in decisions about modifications; alternatively, other team members become knowledgeable through staff training. The plan for program implementation also should include plans for monitoring and adaptation, staff training, and decision making about modifications.

The fourth phase, evaluation + reflection, involves data collection and analysis, and team-based data interpretation and decision making about further adaptations, program continuation, dissemination, and capacity building. Evaluation addresses process and outcome, focused on acceptability, cultural validity, integrity, and effectiveness of intervention components. Analysis and interpretation focus not only on questions about the success or effectiveness of the intervention but also on questions about process–outcome links (e.g., What components of the interventions are critical to outcomes? What is the relationship between acceptability and effectiveness?). Consistent with initial assessment and monitoring, data collection and analysis involve the use of mixed qualitative–quantitative methods, followed by collaborative data interpretation by the partners/team. Critical decisions at this point include (a) further adaptations to strengthen or ensure expected outcomes, and/or meet unanticipated or emerging individual, contextual or cultural variations; (b) continuation and/or expansion of the program (e.g., scaling up to other schools in the district); (c) building capacity of the system or partners to continue these and related efforts; and (d) dissemination of findings to various stakeholder groups (e.g., professional audiences, policy makers, parents, community members). Finally, this last phase involves reflection on knowledge gained from the project experiences and, particularly for the professional school psychologist, further refinement of personal integrated theoretical orientation.

The application of the model depicted in Figure 6.3 within graduate education curriculum can occur in the context of coursework or field training. In the course context, assignments might include (a) final project that requires development of a written plan for school-wide violence prevention program; (b) activities focused on single phases of the praxis process (e.g., case conceptualization), or skill-based components of the process (e.g., simulation of collaborative decision making or developing a transdisciplinary theoretical model); or (c) a combination of (a) and (b), in which students participate in ongoing collaborative activity focused on developing group or individual projects (e.g., in-class small group work combined with independent individual or group assignments). Specific courses also could focus on developing the necessary skills; for example, practicing team-based problem solving in an instructional consultation course, or team-based case conceptualization in an assessment course. In field experience, assignments might include completion of some aspects of the praxis process during practica and completion of the full process during internship. Within field experience seminars, students could present their projects for discussion, collaborative decision making, and demonstration.

CONCLUSIONS: IMPLICATIONS FOR RESEARCH, PRACTICE, AND PROFESSIONAL DEVELOPMENT

This chapter addressed questions relevant to teaching theory in professional preparation of school psychologists, namely: Why is theory important in professional preparation of school psychologists? What theories are critical to preparing professional school psychologists? How do we integrate theory into professional preparation and development of scientist~practitioners? Training standards, models of professional competence, and definitions of constructs relevant to professional identity—professionalism and scientist~practitioner—provided the basis for inclusion of theory in graduate education and continuing professional development. The term *scientist~practitioner* was adopted to reflect the integration of theory, research, and practice as a cyclical process of evidence-based practice and knowledge generation, that extends beyond traditional notions of the applied scientist. The preparation of the scientist~practitioner with regard to theory was characterized as facilitating (a) knowledge acquisition of specific theories related to professional competencies; (b) development of a comprehensive, and preferably transdisciplinary, integrated theoretical orientation; and (c) skill development related to theory generation through research and evaluation. Thus, the curriculum content includes specific theories, integrated theoretical models, and skills for theory generation and further development of an integrated personal theory to guide professional practice. Pedagogy is characterized by a combination of structured didactic activities, facilitated disciplined inquiry, supervised research and field experiences, and opportunities for integrating theory development throughout the curriculum. Although the chapter focused on graduate education (coursework and field training experiences), professional development was characterized as a lifelong learning process through reflective practice. The integration of theory in a school psychology curriculum was illustrated by the application of the following cyclical praxis process to hypothetical or actual cases: theory → case conceptualization → evidence-based practice → evaluation + reflection → theory.

The proposed model for integrating theory in professional preparation has implications for research and practice in professional development.

Although consistent with existing models for graduate education, the proposed model extends the curriculum in several ways.

1. Curriculum content includes not only examination of existing theories but also skill development for theory integration and theory generation. This requires an expanded model of research training that includes quantitative, qualitative, and mixed-methods designs and mentoring experience within an integrated science~practice approach. In addition, students need preparation in developing integrated theoretical models that ideally include transdisciplinary collaboration, which has implications for structuring of learning opportunities to include interdisciplinary coursework, research, and field training.
2. The distinction between selection of EBIs on the basis of specific theories and the use of integrated theoretical models to guide the science~practice process needs further consideration and investigation. For example, researchers should examine the implications of using empirically validated assessment and intervention strategies on the basis of specific theories (e.g., behavioral) in the context of case conceptualization and evidence-based practice based on an integrated biopsychosocial perspective.
3. The influence of transdisciplinary collaboration and theory on decision making about case conceptualization and evidence-based practice warrants investigation. In addition, effective training models for fostering transdisciplinary collaboration in research, practice, and theory development need further development and validation.
4. The implications of consistencies and inconsistencies in training standards across professional organizations and credentialing bodies warrant discussion.
5. As with any recommendations that require expanding professional preparation programs, implications for inclusion in the curriculum warrant attention. Consideration for curriculum reform or revision includes future directions in professional practice and identity of school psychologists, evolution of professional psychology to a paradigmatic stage, and the call for pedagogy that integrates theory, research, and practice in more seamless ways.
6. Particularly important to any future developments in professional preparation for faculty are individual and organizational readiness for change, applicability of existing faculty competencies to new models, and willingness of faculty to engage in further professional development.

In conclusion, the integration of theory in professional development of school psychologists (as depicted in Figure 6.2) necessitates reconceptualizing professional preparation, particularly with regard to expanding current definitions of scientist~practitioner to include a more active science role. The scientist~practitioner, as depicted in this chapter, not only applies science (or evidence) to practice but actively engages, through research in local settings, in the generation of theoretical and empirical foundations for practice.

RESOURCES

Gelso, C. J. (2006). On the making of a scientist~practitioner: A theory of research training in professional psychology. *Training and Education in Professional Psychology, S,* 3–16.

This article describes a theoretical model for training of scientist~practitioners, with particular emphasis on creating a research environment as the context for preparing professional psychologists in an integrated research–practice model. Gelso presents evidence supporting the effectiveness of his theory of research training environment. He also describes specific evidence-based components of graduate education that foster preparation of research-oriented professional psychologists.

Melchert, T. P. (2007). Strengthening the scientific foundations of professional psychology: Time for the next steps. *Professional Psychology: Research and Practice, 38,* 34–43.

This article discusses the evolution of the scientific foundations of professional psychology through its preparadigmatic to current paradigmatic stage. The author presents what he refers to as a "unified science-based approach to professional psychology" (p. 39), with foundations in biopsychosocial (BPS) models of human functioning, and proposes BPS models as the basis for professional practice. He also discusses the implications of a unified model for future research, training, and practice.

Peterson, R. L., Peterson, D. R., Abrams, J. C., & Stricker, G. (2006). The National Council of Schools and Programs of Professional Psychology education model. *Training and Education in Professional Psychology, S,* 17–36.

This article describes the educational model proposed by the National Council of Schools and Programs of Professional Psychology (NCSPP), with regard to preparation of the professional psychologist as the local clinical scientist conducting disciplined inquiry, and the integration of research training as the basis for guiding critical thinking in practice and as a core element in a curriculum. The authors discuss the integration of science in a curriculum relevant to skill-based competencies (e.g., assessment, intervention, consultation) and core foundational competencies (e.g., biological bases of behavior). The authors conclude with a discussion of the implications of NCSPP model for both training and practice. The article contains specific strategies and considerations for curriculum planning.

REFERENCES

American Psychological Association. (2003). Guidelines on multicultural education, training, research, practice, and organizational change for psychologists. *American Psychologist, 58,* 377–402.

APA Presidential Task Force on Evidence-Based Practice. (2006). Evidence-based practice in psychology. *American Psychologist, 61,* 271–285.

Belar, C. D., & Perry, N. W. (1992). National Conference on Scientist-Practitioner Education and Training for Professional Practice of Psychology. *American Psychologist, 47,* 71–75.

Benjamin, L. T. (2006). American psychology's struggles with its curriculum: Should a thousand flowers bloom? *Training and Education in Professional Psychology, S,* 58–68.

Brammer, L. M., Shostrom, E. L., & Abrego, P. J. (1989). *Therapeutic psychology: Fundamentals of counseling and psychotherapy* (5th ed.). Englewood Cliffs, NJ: Prentice Hall.

Bronfenbrenner, U. (1989). Ecological systems theory. In R. Vasta (Ed.), *Annals of child development* (Vol. 6, pp. 187–249). Greenwich, CT: JAI Press.

Christenson, S. L. (2003). The family-school partnership: An opportunity to promote the learning competence of all students. *School Psychology Quarterly, 18,* 454–482.

Committee on Accreditation. (2005). *Guidelines and principles for accreditation of programs in professional psychology.* Washington, DC: APA.

Elman, N. S., Illfelder-Kaye, J., & Robiner, W. N. (2005). Professional development: Training for professionalism as a foundation for competent practice in psychology. *Professional Psychology: Research and Practice, 36,* 367–375.

Fagan, T. K. (2005). The 50th anniversary of the Thayer Conference: Historical perspectives and accomplishments. *School Psychology Quarterly, 20,* 224–251.

Gelso, C. J. (2006). On the making of a scientist-practitioner: A theory of research training in professional psychology. *Training and Education in Professional Psychology, S,* 3–16.

Hatcher, R. L., & Lassiter, K. D. (2007). Initial training in professional psychology: The practicum competencies outline. *Training and Education in Professional Psychology, S,* 49–63.

Kaslow, N. J., Rubin, N. J., Bebeau, M., Leigh, I. W., Litchtenberg, J. W., Nelson, P. D., Portnoy, S., & Smith, I. L. (2007). Guiding principles and recommendations for the assessment of competence. *Professional Psychology: Research and Practice, 38,* 441–451.

Kazdin, A. E. (2008). Evidence-based treatment and practice: New opportunities to bridge clinical research and practice, enhance the knowledge base, and improve patient care. *American Psychologist, 63,* 146–159.

Kratochwill, T. R. (2007). Preparing psychologists for evidence-based school practice: Lessons learned and challenges ahead. *American Psychologist, 62,* 829–843.

Kratochwill, T. R., & Shernoff, E. S. (2003). Evidence-based practice: Promoting evidence-based interventions in school psychology. *School Psychology Quarterly, 18,* 389–408.

Kratochwill, T. R., & Stoiber, K. C. (2002). Evidence-based interventions in school psychology: Conceptual foundations of the Procedural and Coding Manual of Division 16 and the Society for the Study of School Psychology Task Force. *School Psychology Quarterly, 17,* 341– 389.

Melchert, T. P. (2007). Strengthening the scientific foundations of professional psychology: Time for the next steps. *Professional Psychology: Research and Practice, 38,* 34–43.

Nastasi, B. K. (1998). A model for mental health programming in schools and communities. *School Psychology Review, 27*(2), 165–174.

Nastasi, B. K. (2000). School psychologists as health care providers in the 21st century: Conceptual framework, professional identity, and professional practice. *School Psychology Review, 29,* 540–554.

Nastasi, B. K., Hitchcock, J., Sarkar, S., Burkholder, G., Varjas, K., & Jayasena, A. (2007). Mixed methods in intervention research: Theory to adaptation. *Journal of Mixed Methods Research,* 1(2), 164–182.

Nastasi, B. K., Moore, R. B., & Varjas, K. M. (2004). *School-based mental health services: Creating comprehensive and culturally specific programs.* Washington, DC: American Psychological Association.

Nastasi, B. K., & Schensul, S. L. (2005). Contributions of qualitative research to the validity of intervention research. *Journal of School Psychology, 43,* 177–195.

Nastasi, B. K., Varjas, K., Bernstein, R., & Jayasena, A. (2000). Conducting participatory culture-specific consultation: A global perspective on multicultural consultation. *School Psychology Review, 29*(3), 401–413.

Nastasi, B. K., Varjas, K., Schensul, S. L., Silva, K. T., Schensul, J. J., Ratnayake, P. (2000). The Participatory Intervention Model: A framework for conceptualizing and promoting intervention acceptability. *School Psychology Quarterly, 15,* 207–232.

National Association of School Psychologists. (2000). *Standards for training and field placement programs in school psychology.* Bethesda, MD: Author.

Overstreet, S., & Mazza, J. (2003). An ecological–transactional understanding of community violence: Theoretical perspectives. *School Psychology Quarterly, 18,* 66–87.

Partridge, W. L. (1985). Toward a theory of practice. *American Behavioral Scientist, 29,* 39–163.

Peterson, D. R. (2006). Connection and disconnection of research and practice in education of professional psychologist. *Training and Education in Professional Psychology, S,* 47–57.

Peterson, R. L., Peterson, D. R., Abrams, J. C., & Stricker, G. (2006). The National Council of Schools and Programs of Professional Psychology education model. *Training and Education in Professional Psychology, S,* 17–36.

Rodolfa, E., Bent, R., Eisman, E., Nelson, P., Rehm, L., & Ritchie, P. (2005). A cube model for competency development: Implications for psychology educators and regulators. *Professional Psychology: Research and Practice, 36,* 347–354.

Rosenfield, P. L. (1999). The potential of transdisciplinary research for sustaining and extending linkages between the health and social sciences. *Social Science and Medicine, 35*(11), 1343–1357.

Rubin, N. J., Bebeau, M., Leigh, I. W., Litchtenberg, J. W., Nelson, P. D., Portnoy, S., Smith, I. L., & Kaslow, N. J. (2007). The competency movement within psychology: An historical perspective. *Professional Psychology: Research and Practice, 38,* 452–462.

Schensul, S. L. (1985). Science, theory, and application in anthropology. *American Behavioral Scientist, 29,* 164–185.

Schensul, S. L., Nastasi, B. K., & Verma, R. K. (2006). Community-based research in India: A case example of international and interdisciplinary collaboration. *American Journal of Community Psychology, 38,* 1–17. doi:10.1007/s10464-006-9066-z

Sheridan, S. M., & Gutkin, T. B. (2000). The ecology of school psychology: Examining and changing our paradigm for the 21st century. *School Psychology Review, 29,* 485–502.

Stoner, G., & Green, S. K. (1992). Reconsidering the scientist-practitioner model for school psychology practice. *School Psychology Review, 21,* 155–166.

Strauss, A., & Corbin, J. (1990). *Basics of qualitative research: Grounded theory procedures and techniques.* Newbury Park, CA: Sage.

Stricker, G., & Trierweiler, S. J. (2006). The local clinical scientist: A bridge between science and practice. *Training and Education in Professional Psychology, S,* 37–46.

Ysseldyke, J., Burns, M., Dawson, P., Kelley, B., Morrison, D., Ortiz, S., Rosenfield, S., & Telzrow, C. (2006). *School psychology: A blueprint for training and practice III.* Bethesda, MD: National Association of School Psychologists.

7 Teaching ethical and legal issues

Barbara Bole Williams, Amanda Sinko, and Frank J. Epifanio

Graduate programs in school psychology incorporate courses and topics in ethics and law pertaining to school psychology as a fundamental aspect of training. Those programs seeking the approval of the National Association of School Psychologists (NASP) are required to document that school psychology students have acquired prerequisite skills in the 11 *Domains of School Psychology Training and Practice* within the *Standards for Training and Field Placement Programs in School Psychology* (NASP, 2000b). One of these training standards is *School Psychology Practice and Development*, which covers ethical, professional and legal standards and emphasizes that school psychologists practice in ways that are consistent with these standards. More recently, *A Blueprint for Training and Practice III* (NASP, 2006) describes the domain of professional, legal, ethical, and social responsibility as one of the four areas of school psychology training and practice. This domain is foundational and permeates all aspects of professional practice. *Blueprint III* describes professional, legal, ethical, and social responsibility as follows:

> The issues addressed by this foundational domain are relatively straightforward but absolutely central to the efficacy of a school psychologist's work. School psychologists should be prepared to practice in ways that meet all appropriate professional (practice and ethical) and legal standards in order to enhance the quality of services and protect the rights of all parties. This includes adhering to due process guidelines in all decisions affecting students, maintaining accepted professional and ethical standards in assessment, consultation, and general professional practice; and fulfilling all legal requirements, including those in response to legislative and judicial decisions. (p. 17)

What are the best practices in teaching the important ethical, legal, and professional foundations of our profession? To respond to this question, this chapter will review various pedagogical strategies and offer suggestions as to how school psychology graduate educators can provide experiences for their students to help ensure that these future school psychologists will be prepared to integrate the ethical, legal, and professional standards into the fabric of their professional practice.

REVIEW OF THE LITERATURE

Case studies have long been regarded as effective tools for teaching ethics and law. McMinn (1988) described the advantages of using case studies in teaching professional ethics to psychologists in training. According to McMinn, case studies are interesting and showcase the importance of ethical principles, demonstrating how they are applied in everyday practice. Furthermore, case studies offer realistic situations and issues that students are likely to encounter in their future professional lives, thereby exposing the complexities of making ethical decisions. Johnson and Corser (1998) further explained that case studies can be used to draw attention to the fact that ethics codes provide only minimal standards, which may conflict with other professional and legal requirements.

In addition, Plante (1998) calls for the use of an ethical decision-making model for teaching ethics, which he sees going hand-in-hand with case studies. Many authors (Carlson, Thaler, & Hirsh, 2005; Helton & Ray, 2005; Jacob-Timm, 1999; Tryon, 2000, 2001) rely heavily on case studies in conjunction with decision-making models as a key method for teaching ethical and legal issues in school psychology.

What are the types of ethical and legal issues encountered by school psychologists? Jacob-Timm (1999) surveyed NASP members, asking participants to identify ethically challenging situations that they had encountered in the past 2 years. More than 200 incidents were identified and classified into 19 categories. Administrative pressure to act unethically was overwhelmingly the number one type of incident reported, with nearly a quarter (22%) of all incidents falling into this category. As a result, Jacob-Timm suggested incorporating two types of case studies into ethics training, highlighting professionals (a) in compliance with codes of ethics, and (b) in noncompliance with codes of ethics. Jacob-Timm's survey identified assessment and confidentiality issues as the next two categories, each with 14% of the total incidents reported.

In a more recent study, Helton and Ray (2005) also acknowledged the magnitude of administrative pressures to practice unethically as key issues facing school psychologists. Helton and Ray attributed the administrative pressures to practice unethically to the dual role school psychologists play as an employee of the school and as a child advocate. Helton and Ray conducted a national survey of school psychologists, drawn from members of NASP, and special education teachers, who were members of Council for Exceptional Children, asking how they would respond to four ethically challenging situations involving administrative pressure. Four general strategies for resisting pressures to practice unethically were identified: (a) preventing dilemmas from occurring, (b) educating and/or threatening others (i.e. by informing colleagues of special education laws), (c) involving others in solutions, and (d) combining strategies. Jacob-Timm (1999) and Helton and Ray are in agreement on the benefit of encouraging school psychology trainers to engage students in discussions regarding administrative pressures to practice unethically and strategies for resisting such pressures. Jacob-Timm specified that discussions need to include strategies for resisting administrative pressure to practice unethically, specifically to address issues of threats to job security, prestige, and future effectiveness. However, Tryon (2000) cautioned that ethics education has not yet been successful in reducing rewards associated with submitting to the pressures of acting unethically.

Another study conducted by Tryon (2001) surveyed school psychology graduate students on their beliefs about their preparation for and concern about dealing with 12 ethical issues, several of which also pertained to pressures to practice unethically. This study differentiated between students in later years of study versus those in earlier years of study, and also between those who had and had not previously taken an ethics course. Tryon (2001) concluded that students who had completed an ethics course felt more prepared to deal with ethical dilemmas than those who had not yet taken an ethics course; however, it did not decrease their concerns about dealing with future ethical issues. Furthermore, Tryon (2001) concluded that students in their later years of study felt more prepared to deal with ethical issues than their counterparts in earlier years of study. Finally, greater numbers of practica and internship hours were associated with less concern about dealing with ethical issues. Both Tryon (2000) and Jacob-Timm (1999) emphasized the importance of practica and internships serving as active learning experiences in which students can apply ethical decision-making skills. Tryon (2001) cautioned that knowledge of an ethical decision-making model did not necessarily mean graduate students used the model; therefore, students need to be encouraged to both know and apply ethical decision-making models.

Diversity considerations

A discussion on how to promote ethical and legal problem-solving skills in graduate students in school psychology would not be complete without considering the impact of school psychologists providing services to an increasingly diverse school-age population in our nation's schools. School psychologists face many new challenges and must be prepared for the realities of working in an increasingly ethnically and culturally diverse school environment. According to the U.S. Department of Education (2004), 5.5 million English language learners are attending U.S. public schools and speak more than 400 different languages. To address these challenges, multicultural training is needed to encourage school psychology graduate students to consider diversity issues in making decisions that are ethically and legally sound.

An example of one such challenging issue facing school psychologists and other educators is the overrepresentation of minority students in special education. Many (Hosp & Reschly, 2004; Oswald, Coutinho, Best & Singh, 1999) have cited this disproportionality of minority students, particularly associated with overrepresentation in the education classification categories of mental retardation and emotional disturbance. This consistent pattern of disproportionality in special education programs and the continued achievement gap between majority and minority students indicate that diversity considerations must be a primary concern for school psychologists. In response to disproportionality, the National Research Council (2002) advocated for sweeping changes in training for teachers, administrators, and related service personnel so that professionals can be more responsive to dealing with multicultural issues.

School psychology graduate training programs need to provide their students with increased training and experiences working with diverse groups in order to develop cultural competence in future school psychologists. Williams (2007) defined culturally competent services as skills and practices that enable school psychologists to work effectively to address the educational, social, behavioral, and mental health needs of students from diverse cultures. In response to the challenges of working with an increasingly diverse school-age population, NASP has developed resources to help train future and practicing school psychologists in meeting the needs of culturally diverse children. NASP's award-winning *Portraits of the Children: Culturally Competent Assessment Video/CD-ROM* (2003) is a multimedia resource package designed to promote effective culturally competent assessment practices when determining eligibility for special education.

Developing cultural competence in assessment and mental health practices among future school psychologists is a high priority for graduate training programs in school psychology. The legal and ethical basis for this is unquestionable. First, fundamental to educational law within U.S. public schools are the legal requirements for antidiscriminatory practices. Jacob and Hartshorne (2007) described federal grant legislation as statutes that provide funds to states under the condition that certain educational policies and procedures are followed. Examples of federal grant legislation are No Child Left Behind Act of 2001 and the Individuals with Disabilities Educational Improvement Act of 2004. The requirements for antidiscriminatory practices are central to both these laws and have direct implications for the practice of school psychology.

Second, ethical guidelines in school psychology also address respect for human dignity with regard to the rights of students and families to fairness and nondiscrimination. NASP's *Principles for Professional Ethics* (NASP, 2000b) operationalized the values of the professional association and describe the responsibility of its members to students, parents, teachers, and school systems:

> The principles in this manual are based on the assumptions that
> 1) school psychologists will act as advocates for their students/clients,

and 2) at the very least, school psychologists will do no harm. These assumptions necessitate that school psychologists "speak up" for the needs and rights of their students/clients even at times when it may be difficult to do so. (NASP, 2000a, I)

Moreover, the NASP's *Principles for Professional Ethics* states "school psychologists respect all persons and are sensitive to physical, mental, emotional, political, economic, social, cultural, ethnic and racial characteristics, gender, sexual orientation, and religion" (NASP, 2000a, III, A, #2). NASP made it clear that cultural competence is a key value for the professional association. It also expands the notion of diversity to include much more than racial and ethnic identity.

Furthermore, from the perspective of professional competence, NASP's *Principles for Professional Ethics* states that "school psychologists recognize the strengths and limitation of their training and experience, engaging only in practices for which they are qualified" (NASP, 2000a, II, A, #1). Therefore, school psychologists need and will continue to need explicit training in cultural competency. A school psychologist who lacks knowledge about working with students from diverse backgrounds is ethically obligated to obtain the knowledge and skills necessary to work with people from diverse backgrounds. Competence requires school psychologists to be "committed to the application of their professional expertise for the purpose of promoting improvement in the quality of life for children, their families, and the school community" (NASP, 2000a, III, A, #1). Furthermore, the ethics require that school psychologists protect the dignity and worth all of clients (NASP, 2000a, II, B, #1).

In terms of the school psychologist's relationship to the community, the *Principles for Professional Ethic* states that "school psychologists do not engage in or condone practice that discriminate against children, other clients, or employees (if applicable) based on race, disability, age, gender, sexual orientation, religion, national origin, economic status, or native language" (NASP, 2000a, III, D, #3). It is clear that professional ethics require school psychologists to become culturally competent. They cannot possibly meet the needs of students and families with diverse backgrounds if they do not strive for cultural competence.

PROFESSIONAL ROLES AND FUNCTION

As outlined in *Blueprint III*, professional, legal, and ethical standards are important in order to "enhance the quality of services and protect the rights of all parties" to whom school psychological services are provided. School psychologists need to adhere to legal requirements and ethical standards in the areas of "assessment, consultation and general professional practice." For the purposes of this chapter, reference to general professional practice encompasses the school psychologist's role in providing counseling and direct psychoeducational interventions with students. What are the key legal requirements and ethical standards as they apply to each of these areas in terms of the roles and functions of a school psychologist? Let us consider each area separately.

Assessment

Graduate students who are learning the intricacies of psychological assessment should be instructed in the ethical and legal guidelines related specifically to this area. Sattler and Hoge (2006) outline key ethical guidelines for conducting assessments of children and their families as including school psychologists who have (a) sufficient training and expertise in psychological assessment and theory that applies to understanding children and adolescents; (b) access to consultation with other knowledgeable professionals when necessary; (c) knowledge of state and federal laws regarding assessment, including informed consent; (d) awareness of their own personal biases; (e) an understanding of confidentiality and disclosure of information; (f) multiple methods of data gathering; (g) knowledge and expertise in interpretation of data and report writing in order to explain assessment findings; and (h) knowledge of regulations and policies regarding the maintenance of raw data, test protocols, etc.

Embedded within what Sattler and Hoge refer to as ethical considerations are also knowledge and understanding of the legal requirements pertaining to psychological assessment. Throughout NASP's *Principles for Professional Ethics,* there are explicit statements that school psychologists follow state and federal laws in all areas of practice. Having a working knowledge in the requirements of the Individual with Disabilities Improvement Education Act of 2004 (IDEA 2004), section 504, and state rules and regulations governing assessment presents a challenge to even the most astute school psychology graduate student and requires experienced school psychology practitioners to participate in ongoing professional development in both federal and state regulations.

Consultation

When school psychologists are providing indirect services to students through consultation with parents, guardians, teachers, and other professionals, there are several ethical guidelines that are important to incorporate into their practice. Within a consultative relationship between a school psychologist and a teacher or parent, perhaps the most crucial ethical principles to be aware of are the issues of integrity in professional relationships and confidentiality. Jacob and Hartshorne (2007) explained that integrity in professional relationship is characterized as one based on trust. A school psychologist-client relationship is a *fiduciary* one, that is, a relationship based upon trust.

Maintaining confidentiality in a consultative relationship between a school psychologist and a teacher is an example of this fiduciary relationship. When a school psychologist is consulting with a teacher, confidentiality applies to that relationship. The confidential nature of information exchanged between the school psychologist and teacher must be established at the beginning of the consultation process. According to NASP's *Principles of Professional Ethics*, "school psychologists inform children and other clients of the limits of confidentiality at the outset of establishing a professional relationship" (NASP, 2000a, III, A, 11). Likewise, the limits of confidentiality must also be discussed, so that the client understands under what conditions and to whom information will be shared. In addition, Jacob and Hartshorne (2007) stated that it might be necessary to breach confidentiality in a consultative relationship in those unusual circumstances when the actions of the consultee (teacher or other professional) could be considered harmful to the client (student). Novice school psychologists should be cautioned that when confidentiality is breached in the consultative relationship with the teacher in other than these extraordinary circumstances, there is likely to be a loss of trust between the school psychologist and the teacher that could interfere with future interactions.

An example of a major pitfall often encountered by novice school psychologists during consultation is when an unknowing principal or other administrator (i.e., someone unaware that a confidential relationship exists) requests information from the school psychologist regarding the consultee's (teacher's) skills, e.g., behavior management or ability to differentiate instruction, for the purposes of using this information in a performance evaluation of the teacher. Unbeknownst to the principal (unless this is explained), the information garnered during the consultative relationship is confidential and should not be shared without permission from the consultee.

Counseling

A school psychologist has many legal and ethical obligations to the student prior to beginning a counseling relationship. Among these are securing parental consent for counseling, understanding guidelines for sharing information with parents and teachers, and counseling culturally diverse students and families. In addition, there are those situations that may be particularly troublesome and present challenges in dealing with specific situations involving substance abuse, criminal behavior, and pregnancy. Jacob and Hartshorne (2007) provide a comprehensive review of these topics, and every school psychology graduate student and practitioner should have a copy of this indispensable text in his/her library. Many ethical and legal questions regarding a school psychologist's role and function in counseling and other areas can be answered by referring to this text.

Confidentiality is a premiere consideration for the school psychologist when entering into counseling relationship with a student. Consistent with

NASP's *Principles of Professional Ethics* (NASP, 2000a, III, A, 11; as quoted above), school psychologists must inform clients (students and their parents) of the limits of confidentiality from the beginning of the counseling relationship. It is commonly believed that most information shared within a counseling relationship between a school psychologist and a student can be held confidential; however, Jacob and Hartshorne (2007) outlined three conditions under which that confidential information can be disclosed; they are (a) when the information involves a danger to the student or to others; (b) when the student requests it; or (c) when there is a legal obligation to testify in court. Information that is less well known and should be emphasized with school psychology graduate students during their counseling training is that, according to Jacob and Hartshorne, "a student who is a minor has no legal right to confidentiality independent of the parents" (p. 64). Jacob and Hartshorne went on to emphasize the critical importance for the school psychologist who will be providing counseling to a student to explain to the parent the importance of a promise of confidentiality to the student in order to establish a relationship based upon trust and thus be helpful to the child. A school psychologist should explain to the parent and gain agreement that the school psychologist "will not disclose specific confidences shared by the child with the parent without the child's assent to do so" (p. 64). The school psychologist can reassure the parent that he or she will be informed immediately if a serious situation occurs (as outlined in the limits to confidentiality above).

PEDAGOGICAL ISSUES

There are a variety of pedagogical methods and strategies that we will discuss to teach ethical, legal, and professional competencies to graduate students in school psychology. However, before doing so, we would like to offer a more general recommendation as to how ethical codes and legal issues should be introduced and reinforced with graduate students in school psychology. The lead author of this chapter would advocate that ethical codes and legal requirements should be explicitly taught in an introductory course that includes ethics and law in school psychology. Beyond that, consistent with Tryon's (2000) belief, ethical issues should be addressed across the curriculum during graduate school. Practica and internship experiences are critical points in which ethics and legal issues should be discussed as graduate students encounter and actively engage in real-life experiences with students, parents, and teachers. Thus, although there may be a single flagship course that introduces ethical and legal issues, there should be an ongoing thread of discussion related to ethical and legal decision making and problem solving that permeates graduate courses in school psychology.

What are the pedagogical methods that promote the development of effective ethical and legal problem-solving skills among school psychology graduate students? Among those strategies that have proven to be most effective are (a) exposure to scenario-based case studies, (b) an ethical and legal decision-making model, (c) ethical diaries, (d) ethical autobiographies, (e) reflection papers, (f) a mock ethics committee, (g) "strengths and weaknesses" exercises, (h) ethics rounds, and (i) role playing.

Ethical and legal decision-making model

Williams, Armistead, and Jacob (2008) advocated for the use of a decision-making model in school psychology in order to examine ethical and legal dilemmas from a critical-evaluative perspective. Such a model helps to ensure that the outcome of the decision-making process is principled, is reasoned, and can be applied to similar situations. Rather than relying on initiative judgment alone when a school psychologist is faced with complex, sometimes emotionally charged situations, applying a logical problem-solving model with a systematic step-by-step approach can be helpful. Williams, Armistead, and Jacob presented this decision-making model (see Table 7.1) that is based on the earlier work by Koocher and Keith-Spiegel. These authors believe that using such a model will help

Table 7.1 Ethical and Legal Decision-Making Model

---

1. **Describe the problem situation.**
   Focus on available information and attempt to objectively state the issues or controversies.

2. **Define the potential ethical and legal issues involved.**
   List the ethical and legal issues in question.

3. **Consult available ethical and legal guidelines.**
   Research the issues in question using reference sources.

4. **Consult with supervisors and colleagues.**
   Talk with your supervisor and knowledgeable colleagues who are familiar with the legal and ethical guidelines that apply to school psychology. Brainstorm possible alternatives and consequences and seek input from those whose opinions you value.

5. **Evaluate the rights, responsibilities, and welfare of all affected parties.**
   Consider the implications for students, families, teachers, administrators, other school personnel, and yourself. How will the various alternative courses of action affect each party involved?

6. **Consider alternative solutions and consequences of making each decision.**
   Carefully evaluate in a step-by-step manner how each alternative solution will impact the involved parties.

7. **Make the decision and take responsibility for it.**
   Once all the steps are completed, make a decision that is consistent with ethical and legal guidelines and one that you feel confident is the best choice.

Source: Williams, B. B., Armistead, L., & Jacob, S. (2008). *Professional ethics for school psychologists: A problem-solving model casebook.* Bethesda, MD: NASP Publications. (Adapted from Koocher and Keith-Spiegel, 1998.)

school psychologists become more proactive, effective problem solvers and decision makers.

Exposure to scenario-based case studies

Using scenario-based case studies in conjunction with the application of a decision-making model offers school psychology graduate students opportunities to practice with real-life situations. Williams, Armistead, and Jacob (2008) utilize this approach throughout their book by using situational ethical and legal dilemmas taken directly from the professional lives of school psychologists and applying the decision-making model to them. As a basis for their book, these authors asked school psychologists to submit actual dilemmas from their practice of school psychology, and the result was at times stranger than fiction.

Ethical diaries

An extension of the use of the problem-solving model is to require more advanced students in school psychology to keep an ethical diary. During their practicum and internship experiences, school psychology graduate students can be encouraged to reflect upon situations they are encountering in their school-based experiences by writing about them and applying the decision-making model as they attempt to solve them. The lead author of this chapter has used this technique in graduate courses asking the school psychology students to substitute their *own* experiences for those ethical and legal dilemmas and case studies presented and discussed during class. Student feedback indicates that keeping ethical diaries helps them examine situations from multiple perspectives, rather than resorting to the most expeditious decisions.

Ethics autobiography and reflection papers

Bashe, Anderson, Handelsman, and Klevansky (2007) contended that the ethics autobiography is not new; however, they adapted the traditional assignment to their acculturation process of ethics training. They encourage students to examine their personal view of ethics, their ethnic and religious background, and their knowledge of professional psychology ethics. Students are challenged to reflect on how their own personal values and backgrounds may interact or conflict with professional ethical principles. The authors provided a number of questions to guide students' writing.

In addition to an ethics autobiography, Bashe et al. (2007) asked students to write reflection papers throughout the semester. Reflection papers can be reactions to readings or class discussions, and the students' acculturation process is expected to be considered. Through discussion papers, students examine their changing and growing professional identities. Often students' last reflection paper of the semester is a revision of their ethics autobiography.

Mock ethics committee

Johnson and Corser (1998) described a technique implemented to enhance general case study use in the teaching of professional ethics in psychology. After students develop a basic knowledge of ethics by examining professional codes of ethics, such as that of the American Psychological Association (APA), and models of ethical decision making, students form a mock ethics committee. Students rotate membership on a class ethics committee, with about three or four members, and one student is randomly chosen to represent a psychologist accused of various ethical violations. The remainder of the class observes the formal complaint hearing, which results in official rulings and appropriate penalties. At the close of the hearing, the entire class engages in in-depth discussions of the relevant ethical issues.

Strengths and weaknesses exercise

In the strengths and weaknesses exercise by Bashe et al. (2007), students are asked to identify and describe characteristics, values, motivations, principles, behaviors, and/or skills they think will be their greatest strengths as an ethical psychologist. Students are then challenged to consider how these strengths may actually be their greatest weaknesses. This encourages more complex self-exploration and also helps students stride toward an integration of personal and professional ethics.

Ethics rounds

Bashe et al. (2007) described another activity used in class called ethics rounds. Ethics rounds are a series of class discussions during which students are asked to describe ethical dilemmas and situations they have previously encountered. Then they are asked to report on how they handled these situations, often at a time in their lives when they would have had little or no knowledge of professional ethics. This process helps students reflect on their own personal ethics of origin.

Role playing

Tryon (2001) cited several studies that describe situations when graduate students and practicing school psychologists might not confront or report colleagues who were practicing unethically. In addition to practicing ethically themselves, Tryon suggested that school psychologists must ascertain that their colleagues practice ethically even if professional friendships are jeopardized. Tryon identified role-playing that offers an opportunity to practice confronting colleagues as an effective means for training future school psychologists. Along with role playing, Tryon suggested discussing possible outcomes of reporting or not reporting their colleagues' ethical violations.

CASE ILLUSTRATION

The case illustration that follows is an example of the use of the decision-making model embedded with scenario-based case study recommended by Williams, Armistead, and Jacob (2008). In addition, at the end of the illustration, other types of pedagogical methods are suggested that might be considered as alternative strategies to use with this example for promoting ethical and legal problem solving among graduate students in school psychology.

The case of Jane and the director of special services: a step-by-step problem-solving model example

Jane is an experienced school psychologist who has been employed in her district for more than 15 years. As a member of an elementary school building-based problem-solving team, she meets with the teachers, parents, and building principal of a first grader, Tim, who has been experiencing academic difficulties in reading. Together, the team considers the youngster's strengths and weaknesses and develops an intervention plan that includes Tim receiving small-group instruction (a Tier 2 intervention) in his areas of need designed to focus specifically on teaching him the basic reading skills that he appears to be lacking. Tim's parents and teachers and the building principal all agree this is an appropriate intervention. The meeting occurs during the first week in November, and it is agreed that Tim's progress will be monitored on an ongoing basis and that the group would meet again in January to evaluate his progress, unless there is a reason to meet sooner.

The following day when Jane arrives at school, she learns that the decision made by the building-based problem-solving team has been questioned by the assistant superintendent for instruction. Instead of beginning the intervention, the assistant superintendent is requesting that Tim be evaluated by the child study team. This message is delivered to Jane by her direct supervisor, the director of special services. Jane questions the need for Tim to be considered for evaluation by the child study team prior to determining whether he would respond satisfactorily to the planned intervention. When she requests that a meeting be scheduled with the assistant superintendent to discuss the situation, her supervisor becomes quite angry with her, shouting that the decision has been overruled; she is told directly, "You will evaluate this child." The building principal is also present during this verbal exchange between Jane and her supervisor but says nothing.

Jane is feeling personally and professionally astounded by her supervisor's demands.

Following district policy and state department of education regulations governing special education, Jane is aware that a child's parents or his/her building principal can request that the child study team *consider* evaluating a child. Since the building principal is now supporting the director of special service's edict that the child be evaluated, a meeting is scheduled with the Tim's parents, teachers, and child study team members to consider the possibility of a referral for evaluation. Both the director and principal attend the meeting, which is not typical but is nevertheless permitted. During the meeting, the parents appear confused, asking why the decision reached at the last meeting was being questioned, and so on. After considering all the information and lengthy discussion, the child study team, teachers, and parents again agree that instead of evaluating Tim immediately, they would like to see him receive small-group instruction in reading designed to address his weaknesses and monitor his progress. All of this is captured in writing and signed by the parent and members of the child study team.

This is when the fun really begins. Leaving the meeting, the director of special services (who in this case is not considered a member of the child study team) is furious and requests that the parents come to his office prior to leaving the building. The parents, more confused than ever, meet separately with the director and principal. At this meeting, the director convinces the parents to give consent for Tim to be evaluated, promising the parents that their son will be given a full child study team evaluation to gather additional information, along with a complete medical examination at a nearby hospital. An evaluation plan is developed, agreed upon, and signed only by the parents, director, and principal; it lacks the agreement or signatures of the child study team or teachers. The director adds insult to injury by informing Jane that he is placing a letter of reprimand in her employment file because of her behavior in this situation.

Applying the decision-making model to the case of Jane and the director

If we apply an ethical and legal decision-making model (see Table 7.1) to this situation, the process might go something like this:

1. Describe the problem situation. In attempting to objectively examine the situation, Jane outlines the issues as follows:
   (a) Initially, the building-based problem-solving team attempted to develop intervention strategies that would provide Tim with early instruction in the areas which he was struggling.
   (b) Tim's parents and teachers, who are most familiar with his achievement in first grade, along with the school psychologist,

collaborated in developing the interventions and agreed to monitor his progress.

(c) At a meeting to consider whether Tim should be evaluated by the child study team, all parties agreed that an immediate evaluation would be premature prior to determining whether the specifically focused instruction would be helpful.

(d) Despite the efforts outlined above, administrative directives were circumventing the problem-solving, response-to-intervention model.

2. Define the potential ethical and legal issues involved. Ethically, Jane believes that she and the others involved in the initial problem-solving phase of Tim's case were motivated to do what would be in his best interest. Legally, she believes that the rules and regulations that govern special education in her state were circumvented when the director, along with the principal, convinced the parent to sign permission for Tim to be evaluated by the child study team, in direct opposition to the child study team's decision. She is wondering whether the parents were coerced in any way in order to pressure them to grant permission.

3. Consult available ethical and legal guidelines. Jane consults NASP's *Principles for Professional Ethics*. As she recalls from graduate school and from a recent ethics workshop that she attended, school psychologists are obligated "to act as advocates for their students and, at the very least, school psychologists will do no harm" (NASP, 2000a, Introduction). She also consults the fifth edition of Jacob and Hartshorne's *Ethics and Law for School Psychologists* (2007) to be reminded that administrative pressure is one of the most common factors in attempting to influence school psychologists' decision making. In this case, if she succumbed to her director's edict to "just evaluate Tim," then the dilemma would end.

Jane also checked IDEA 2004 and the state rules and regulations governing special education, and just as she recalled, a decision as to whether or not to evaluate a child is made collaboratively by the child study team, the student's teacher, and the parent. She now believes even more strongly that her director had acted contrary to both ethical and legal regulations. She is questioning whether her supervisor has the right to override the referral team's decision on whether to evaluate Tim.

4. Consult with supervisors and colleagues. Jane consulted with a variety of sources. She spoke with the other members of the child study team (social worker and educational consultant), who shared her perspective on the situation. As a member of the local education association, Jane also consulted with the union leadership and grievance chairperson, particularly with regard to the letter

of reprimand being placed in her file. She telephoned the county level supervisor of special education, who informed her that he thought the director did not have the right to unilaterally make the decision about whether a child should or should not be evaluated. He also recommended that Jane contact the state department of education to get a further ruling. She did so and was told verbally that the district's supervisor's actions were illegal and she could file a complaint with the state department of education. Finally, Jane contacted her state school psychology association ethics committee chairperson to discuss the situation. Through this contact, an Office of Administrative Law (OAL) court decision was secured. Briefly, the OAL's decision in a similar case ruled that the administrator could not overrule the decision of the child study team.

5. Evaluate the rights, responsibilities, and welfare of all affected parties. Consider alternative solutions and consequences of making each decision. Reviewing all the information, Jane decided that she had a few choices: (a) pursue the complaint through state department of education; (b) file a grievance through her union; (c) meet with her supervisor to present the information she had gathered and hope he would admit his mistake; and (d) if that was not successful, meet with the superintendent to present the same information. Ultimately, she was most concerned with Tim's welfare. While all this has been occurring, Tim was not receiving any intervention to address his reading deficits.

6. Make the decision and take responsibility for it. Jane decided to take all the information she had gathered and request a meeting with the superintendent of schools. Once she presented copies of emails and the OAL court decision, the superintendent agreed to take action to provide the instruction for Tim that was originally requested by the building-level team and to have the director meet with the parents and explain his lapse in judgment. From that point, based upon the parents' wishes, the child study team, the director, and the superintendent would determine the next course of action.

Alternative pedagogical strategies applied to the case of Jane and the director

Role playing

Tryon (2001) identified that school psychology graduate students felt they were not prepared to deal with potential ethical violations by colleagues and suggested that students practice role playing in confronting colleagues. The case study presented above demonstrated how an experienced school psychologist was able to confront her superiors; however, a novice school psychologist may not feel as comfortable doing so. Using a case study like this, students can practice confronting ethical violations made by future colleagues.

Mock ethics committee

The mock ethics committee described by Johnson and Corser (1998) could also be used in conjunction with this case study to promote ethical decision-making skills in graduate classrooms. Jane enlisted the help of the state association's ethics committee chairperson. Class members could act as members of the state association's ethics committee and problem solve and gather the legal information Jane needed to confront her supervisors. Following the committee's ruling, the class could be presented with the information from the ethical decision-making model process above and compare and contrast results through class discussion.

Class discussion and reflection papers

This case study could also serve as a topic for a class discussion or reflection paper. Students could be presented with the case study and asked questions such as the following: Explain why or why not you think Jane handled the situation to the best of her ability. How would you have handled the situation differently? As a fellow school psychologist, what advice would you have given Jane if she had enlisted your help? Taking the perspective of the (a) assistant superintendent, (b) director of special services, and (c) building principal, what are the possible motivating factors for wanting a child study team evaluation for Tim?

SUMMARY AND CONCLUSIONS

Teaching school psychology candidates how to appropriately handle ethically and legally challenging situations is essential to their graduate training. We believe this objective can be accomplished only through the use of a variety of activities and rehearsals using dilemmas that represent real-life situations involving colleagues, students, parents, teachers, and others. While this is being done, the implications of diversity issues and the role and function of the school psychologist also must be considered. We have suggested the use of exposure to scenario-based case studies, combined with an ethical and legal decision-making model, as well as ethical diaries, ethical autobiographies, reflection papers, a mock ethics committee, "strengths and weaknesses" exercises, ethics rounds, and role playing. Below are several annotated resources that will be helpful to school psychology graduate educators and graduate students as they practice their ethical and legal decision making.

RESOURCES

Jacob, S., & Hartshorne, T. S. (2007). *Ethics and law for school psychologists* (5th ed.). Hoboken, NJ: John Wiley & Sons.

This text discusses four broad ethical principles (respect for the dignity of persons, welfare of the client, integrity in professional relationships, and responsibility to community and society), as well as NASP and APA codes of ethics. The topical discussions are strengthened by case vignettes. This text also provides a good introduction to educational law and discusses the legal and ethical issues associated with the specific roles of the school psychologist, with an emphasis on understanding the implications of legislation that protects children and families.

Osborne, A. G., & Russo, C. J. (2006). *Special education and the law: A guide for practitioners* (2nd ed.). Thousand Oaks, CA: Corwin Press.

This book provides information on many facets of special education law with in-depth explanations of IDEA 2004. It also includes an expanded list of case law, detailed information regarding student discipline, and advice on legal requirements for related services.

Tryon, G. S. (2000). Ethical transgressions of school psychology graduate students: A critical incidents survey. *Ethics and Behavior, 10*(3), 271–279.

This article investigates the difference between knowledge of ethics and actual ethical behavior. The author suggests that a formal ethics course should be offered early in the curriculum but must also be integrated in courses throughout the professional training program, including practica and internships. The goal is for students to view ethical decision making as an active, ongoing activity that applies to all aspects of a school psychologist's work.

Williams, B. B., Armistead, L., & Jacob, S. (2008). *Professional ethics for school psychologists: A problem-solving model casebook.* Bethesda, MD: NASP Publications.

Believing that school psychologists need preservice and ongoing training in the legal and ethical aspects of their practice, this book presents ethical training as a dynamic process. The authors advocate for the use of a problem-solving model to examine the legal and ethical dilemmas that school psychologists face in their school-based practice. Embedded within NASP's *Principles for Professional Ethics* are vignettes (provided to the authors by school psychology practitioners) that illustrate how school psychologists are confronted with ethical and legal issues on a daily basis. Many of these dilemmas are explicated by the authors, while others are offered for discussion and problem solving using the decision-making model. This book is the natural training companion to the gold standard Jacob and Hartshorne (2007) text, *Ethics and Law for School Psychologists.*

REFERENCES

Bashe, A., Anderson, S. K., Handelsman, M. M., & Klevansky, R. (2007). An acculturation model for ethics training: The ethics autobiography and beyond. *Professional Psychology: Research and Practice, 38*(1), 60–67.

Carlson, J. S., Thaler, C. L., & Hirsch, A. J. (2005). Psychotropic medication consultation in schools: An ethical and legal dilemma for school psychologists. *Journal of Applied School Psychology, 22*(1), 29–41.

Helton, G. B., & Ray, B. A. (2005). Strategies school practitioners report they would use to resist pressures to practice unethically. *Journal of Applied School Psychology, 22*(1), 43–65.

Hosp, J. L., & Reschly, D. J. (2004). Disproportionate representation of minority students in special education: Academic, demographic, and economic predictors. *Exceptional Children, 70*, 185–199.

Jacob, S., & Hartshorne, T. S. (2007). *Ethics and law for school psychologists* (5th ed.). Hoboken, NJ: John Wiley & Sons.

Jacob-Timm, S. (1999). Ethically challenging situations encountered by school psychologists. *Psychology in the Schools, 36*(3), 205–217.

Johnson, W. B., & Corser, R. (1998). Learning ethics the hard way: Facing the ethics committee. *Teaching of Psychology, 25*(1), 26–28.

McMinn, M. R. (1988). Ethics case-study simulation: A generic tool for psychology teachers. *Teaching of Psychology, 15*(2), 100–101.

National Association of School Psychologists. (2000a). Principles for professional ethics. In *Professional conduct manual* (pp. 13–62). Bethesda, MD: Author. Retreived from http://www.nasponline.org/standards/ProfessionalCond.pdf

National Association of School Psychologists. (2000b). *Standards for training and field placement programs in school in school psychology. Standards for the credentialing of school psychologists.* Retrieved from http://www.nasponline. org/standards/FinalStandards.pdf

National Association of School Psychologists. (2003). *Portraits of the children: Culturally competent assessment video/CD-ROM.* Bethesda, MD: Author.

National Association of School Psychologists. (2006). *School psychology: A blueprint for training and practice III.* Retrieved from http://www.nasponline.org/resources/blueprint/FinalBlueprintInteriors.pdf

National Research Council (2002). *Minority students in special education and gifted education.* Washington, DC: National Academic Press.

Oswald, D. P., Coutinho, M. J., Best, A. N. & Singh, N. N. (1999). Ethnic representation in special education: The influence of school-related economic and demographic variables. *Journal of Special Education, 32*, 194–206.

Plante, T. G. (1998). Teaching a course on psychology ethics to undergraduates: An experimental model. *Teaching of Psychology, 25*(4), 286–287.

Sattler, J. M. & Hoge, R. D. (2006). *Assessment of children: Behavioral, social and clinical foundations* (5th ed.). San Diego, CA: Jerome M. Sattler, Publisher, Inc.

Tryon, G. S. (2000). Ethical transgressions of school psychology graduate students: A critical incidents survey. *Ethics & Behavior, 10*(3), 271–279.

Tryon, G. S. (2001). School psychology students' beliefs about their preparation and concern with ethical issues. *Ethics & Behavior 11*(4), 375–394.

U.S. Department of Education (2004). *Fact sheet: NCLB provisions ensure flexibility and accountability for limited English proficient students*. Retrieved from http://www.ed.gov/print/nclb/accountability/schools/factsheet-english.html

Williams, B. B. (2007, March). Culturally competent mental health services in schools: Tips for teachers. In *Communiqué, 35*, 6. Retrieved from http://www.nasponline.org/resources/culturalcompetence/cultcompmhservices.pdf

Williams, B. B., Armistead, L., & Jacob, S. (2008). *Professional ethics for school psychologists: A problem-solving model casebook*. Bethesda, MD: National Association of School Psychologists.

8   Multiculturalism and diversity

Implications for the training of school psychologists

Elsa Arroyos-Jurado, Ivelisse Torres Fernández, and Rachel L. Navarro

In recent years, the United States has experienced significant changes in its demographic composition. These demographic trends have certainly changed the face of the population and, subsequently, our schools. According to the U.S. Census Bureau (2000), the population is composed of 70.7% White/Caucasian, 12.5% Hispanic/Latino, 12.3% Black/African American, and 3.6% Asian-American/Pacific-Islander. In 2007, it was estimated that about one in three U.S. residents was a minority (U.S. Census Bureau News, 2007). More specifically, Hispanics continue to be the fastest growing minority group, with a 3.4% increase noted between July 2005 and July 2006, accounting for almost half of the national population growth within this time frame, and the largest minority group, comprising 14.8% of the total population. Of particular importance to schools is that the Hispanic population in 2006 was much younger, with about a third of the population being younger than 18 years of age, compared with one fourth of the total population. Similar trends are noted with the African American population, as African Americans continue to be the second-largest minority group, with 31% of this group being younger than 18 years of age. Currently, four states and the District of Columbia are considered to be "majority-minority": Hawaii (75% minority), District of Columbia (68%), New Mexico (57%), California (57%), and Texas (52%). Given these trends, it is not surprising that school enrollment is projected to set new records every year from 2006 until at least 2014 (U.S. Department of Education, National Center for Education Statistics, 2006a). Although there continues to be a downward trend in the ratio of students to school psychologists (Curtis et al., 2008) it is logical to conclude, on the basis of these statistics, that the student–school psychologist ratio is likely to experience an increase as well in the near future.

In regards to linguistic diversity, 17.9% of the U.S. population speaks a language other than English at home, with 10.7% of the population speaking Spanish; of these populations, 8.1% and 5.2%, respectively, speak English less than *very well* (U.S. Census Bureau, 2000). In the 2003–2004 school year, 11% of all students received services in learning English as a second language (U.S. Department of Education, National Center for Education Statistics, 2006b). These statistics point to the importance of school psychologists attaining skills in working with linguistically diverse students and families. Unlike the U.S. population, the field of school psychology has seen very little shift in its population demographics. According to the 2004–2005 National Association of School Psychologists (NASP) membership survey, the field continues to be composed primarily of women (74%) over 50 years of age (47.5%) who are White/Caucasian (92.6%) working in public schools (83.1%; Curtis et al., 2008). The rest of the field is composed of 3.0% Hispanic/Latino, 1.9% Black/African American, 0.9% Asian American/Pacific Islander, 0.8% American Indian/Alaskan Native, and 0.8% "other" (Curtis et al., 2008). School psychologists who participated in the membership survey reported serving students from culturally and linguistically diverse backgrounds, with 47% serving 25% or more minority students and 28% serving more than 50% minority students, yet only 7.6% identified themselves as being members of a minority group (Curtis et al., 2008).

Based on these trends, the need to recruit and retain graduate students, trainers, and practitioners from diverse cultural and linguistic backgrounds is of the utmost importance in better meeting the needs of students and their families. It is likely that in the 21st century we will continue to experience these demographic trends and shifts in diversity. As such, "school psychology must be infused with the diverse and multiple perspectives of the populations the profession is supposed to be serving. This infusion, possible only with diversity among the practitioners and academicians of our profession, is fundamental in meeting the ethical imperative of competence" (Henning-Stout & Brown-Cheatham, 1999, p. 1049).

As such, in this chapter, we provide an introductory discussion of the relevant issues related to the training of school psychologists to serve culturally and linguistically diverse (CLD) students, families, and communities. We begin with a brief review of the multicultural competencies that guide the field, followed by specific recommendations related to the training for professional roles and functions. Attention is then given to pedagogy and supervision issues, followed by a case illustration.

MULTICULTURAL COMPETENCIES AND TRAINING

NASP and the American Psychological Association (APA) have developed standards for practice and training, guidelines, and position statements that inform the field and trainers about culturally competent practices (see Table 8.1 for a listing of these documents). These documents have certainly influenced the multicultural practice of school psychologists, as they provide guidelines and standards for ethical practice. However, it has been argued that perhaps of equal relevance to practice are the competencies that have

Table 8.1 NASP and APA Documents for Multicultural Practice and Training

National Association of School Psychologists

Guidelines for the Provision of School Psychological Services (2000a)

Principles for Professional Ethics (2000b)

Standards for Credentialing of School Psychologists (2000c)

Standards for the Training and Field Placement Programs in School Psychology (2000d)

Position Statement on Minority Recruitment (2003)

American Psychological Association

Ethical Principles of Psychologists and Code of Conduct (2002a)

Guidelines on Multicultural Education, Training, Research, Practice, and Organizational Change for Psychologists (2002b)

Guidelines and Principles for Accreditation of Programs in Professional Psychology (2002c)

been developed by researchers in the field. Furthermore, although NASP and the APA emphasize multicultural standards for practice, what they fail to do is provide precise recommendations for achieving them, thus giving more credence to researchers who can provide precision.

Sandoval (2007) suggested that guidelines and competencies developed within the field/divisions of counseling psychology have been generally applied for "work with children, youth and adults, and have not been formulated for the types of counseling and interventions conducted by school psychologists" (p. 37). He recommended the work of the Taskforce on Cross-Cultural School Psychology Competencies of the APA Division of School Psychology (Rogers et al., 1999) as "a set of possibly more relevant recommendations" (Sandoval, p. 37). Rogers et al. summarized the existing knowledge base, offered practical illustrations and applications of that knowledge base, and presented recommendations for providing psychological services (in six major domains of service delivery) in schools to diverse students and groups. The competencies were developed to "pertain specifically to children, their families and school personnel who, because of their status as diverse racial, ethnic, linguistic or cultural group members, may be at risk for receiving inadequate and/or inappropriate services" (p. 245). As such, it is the school psychologist's responsibility to determine whether problems presumed to reside within the child may actually be a result of institutional biases in the school (Rogers et al.).

Although these competencies provide some guidance to a field in need of continued professional development in cross-cultural competencies, Lopez and Rogers (2007) argued that in order to reach the goal of equipping school psychologists with these competencies we must first continue to investigate and validate cross-cultural competencies. Specifically, competencies for bilingual psychologists working with bilingual students and English language learners must be investigated and validated, and valid and reliable tools must be developed to assess the cross-cultural competencies of graduate students in training programs. Secondly, Lopez and Rogers argued that we must continue to meet training needs, i.e., meeting NASP and APA training standards, recruiting faculty with cross-cultural expertise, meeting recruitment challenges, recruiting culturally competent field experience supervisors, etc. The challenges described by these researchers are exacerbated by the shortage of culturally diverse and/ or bilingual school psychologists in the field. It is also difficult to recruit culturally and linguistically diverse graduate students who will then enter the field as practitioners and/or become trainers themselves; this perpetuates the shortage. It will certainly take much time before we see the shortage in the field diminish. In order to address the shortage there is a need to meet, and rectify, these challenges. The most logical place to begin is with training programs.

TRAINING MODELS

In reviewing both APA and NASP standards, Rogers (2005) outlined that these organizations advise training programs to establish three priorities in their commitment to diversity and multiculturalism, namely, (a) recruiting and retaining students and faculty of color, (b) integrating multicultural curricula and applied training with diverse clients, and (c) giving attention to the overall training environment; however, no specific recommendations are provided on how to implement these priorities, leaving trainers with little direction for how to achieve them (Rogers, 2005). In an effort to rectify the lack of guidance in how to achieve these priorities, Rogers identified four characteristics of the multicultural curricula and training environments found in exemplary programs:

1. Employment of an integration model of multicultural training (i.e., incorporation of multicultural themes, content, and perspectives into the curriculum)
2. Exposure of students to a diverse clientele during applied training via supervised practica and internship
3. Emphasis on diversity issues in research training (i.e., joined program with intrinsic interests in diversity issues or the development of such interests during their studies)
4. Assessment of cross-cultural knowledge on comprehensive examinations (i.e., assessing student cross-cultural competencies in courses, applied training, and comprehensive exams) (Rogers, 2005, pp. 1007–1009)

Furthermore, specific minority recruitment strategies should focus on faculty making contact with students, funding students, and maintaining a high percentage of CLD students who can also help with recruitment and programs seeking students from other universities. On the other hand, retention strategies should focus on faculty maintaining a supportive institutional climate, engaging in multicultural research and course work, engaging in campus-wide diversity initiatives, and schools providing support groups for CLD students (Rogers, 2005).

Similarly, Braden and Shah (2005) identified four major themes essential to multicultural training and practice in school psychology. These include the following:

1. Respect for ethnic, cultural, and linguistic diversity
2. A commitment to understanding and responding to such diversity in training programs
3. Recognition of one's own racial and cultural biases and their influence upon practice
4. Recognition of the limits of one's competence and expertise in working with diverse populations (Braden and Shah, 2005, p. 1024)

The authors further outlined specific program options to improve multicultural training and student outcomes. These include but are not limited to adding multicultural courses and practica, having students complete a multicultural self-study, and recruiting and retaining diverse students and faculty. Lastly, they stated that in order to advance multicultural training programs, language issues, training research, and training practice should also be taken into consideration.

Overall, training efforts should focus on achieving understanding and acceptance of diversity. This acceptance of diversity should not only be reflected in the student and faculty bodies, but should be supported by the institutions that house these training programs. Cultural competency is a quality that should be taught and possessed by the individuals providing and supporting training efforts.

TRAINING FOR PROFESSIONAL ROLES AND FUNCTIONS

It is evident from the brief overview of multicultural training models (Braden and Shah, 2005; Rogers, 2005) that the integration of a multicultural curriculum is a key component to teaching cultural competence. We would argue that the courses that comprise this curriculum go beyond pedagogy that centers only on acquiring multicultural awareness, knowledge, and skills. Although previous research has shown that multicultural courses are effective in increasing students' multicultural awareness, knowledge, and skills upon completion of the course, one course is not enough to guarantee cultural competence, but it can lay the foundation for future training (Keim, Warring, & Rau, 2001). There have even been discussions around the "essence" of cultural competence, and it was noted that it cannot be defined "simply as knowledge of the particular characteristic of a given cultural group... [and] does not automatically imbue practitioners with the necessary skills with which to effectively and appropriately serve multicultural populations or implement culturally appropriate interventions or treatments" (Ortiz, 2006, p. 164). In order for one course to have a significant impact on cultural competence it needs to take a nontraditional approach.

Many multicultural courses focus on what Vázquez and García-Vázquez (2003) called a *traditional* approach that centers on learning the characteristics of specific minority/majority groups (i.e., stereotypes) while keeping diversity issues at a superficial/intellectual level, and at the same time deflecting attention from issues of power and discrimination. A *nontraditional* approach focuses on a "multicultural critical pedagogical process" that includes fundamental elements of educating students in a self-reflective process of understanding power and discrimination regardless of ethnic/racial background (Vázquez & García-Vázquez, 2003, p. 551). Such a course is not based on teaching or endorsing stereotypes surrounding minority and majority cultures but instead focuses on social justice issues by adopting a philosophy of *justice for all*. This course takes a social justice focus and explores such variables as ethnicity/race, religion, sexual orientation, gender, and socioeconomic status, all within the context of understanding theories of worldview, acculturation, and ethnic identity. These theories form the foundation of understanding within and between group differences and similarities (Vázquez & García-Vázquez, 2003).

Furthermore, a successful multicultural course follows a developmental perspective and is experientially based and process oriented. Development occurs through this pedagogical method and applied work via journaling, completing a multicultural genogram, acculturation and identity awareness papers, and group experiential exercises. Interestingly, a course like this should not be taken lightly; it is strongly recommended that individuals enter such a course with their eyes wide open to a curriculum that will reflect a developmental and emotional learning succession with a powerful process orientation. This process orientation is critical to such a course as "individuals develop their emotional, psychological and behavioral reactions to their perceptions of diverse issues through experiential learning from the family of origin, personal critical incidents, and the projections from mass media" (Vázquez & García-Vázquez, 2003, p. 333). It is logical to conclude, then, that training culturally competent school psychologists would mirror the same process.

A course of this nature in the psychology of multiculturalism should serve as one of the first learning experiences in a school psychology program, as it will lay the necessary foundation in theories of acculturation, worldview, and identity development. These theories should then permeate the rest of the curriculum and skill development of a school psychologist, from consultation to assessment to research practices. As such, the following sections will describe how these theories can be integrated across the various roles and functions.

ASSESSMENT

There is a plethora of literature that has investigated multicultural issues in assessment, with recent foci on best practices in nondiscriminatory assessment (e.g., Ortiz, 2008); multicultural school psychology handbooks devote many contributions to this issue (e.g., Frisby & Reynolds, 2005; Esquivel, Lopez, & Nahari, 2007). As such, nondiscriminatory assessment practices are nothing new, especially in light of federal guidelines such as the Individuals with Disabilities Education Improvement Act (IDEIA, 2004), as well as NASP and APA ethics/standards on assessment. Aside from a psychology of multiculturalism course, students are required to take several assessment courses that hopefully integrate other relevant issues around assessment, such as test bias, selection of culturally appropriate tests, and interpretation that takes into account the cultural context of the individual being evaluated. Of critical importance to the latter is the ability to assess for language proficiency and acculturation while considering the client's worldview and ethnic identity in the impact these variables have on test scores/results.

An interesting outcome of training graduate students to consider and assess these variables thoroughly and concisely that has been observed is that many of these graduate students believe that tests, in particular those assessing cognitive functioning, are so biased that they should never be used. That is, they are ready to throw out the baby with the bath water, so to speak. They truly believe, because of the training that they have received in being aware of bias and sensitive to the cultural context of the client, that tests/results cannot be accurate because of cultural bias and, consequently, that they should not be used to make educational decisions about clients. On the one hand, as trainers, we are proud that students are keenly aware of the impact of culture on assessment practices, but, on the other hand, have come to realize that it is also important for our students, via our training methods, to also understand how to balance this cultural sensitivity with best practices that continue to advocate on behalf of our clients. That is, graduate students still need to be aware of the utility of our assessment practices and that tests can be useful tools when used in a culturally appropriate manner.

CONSULTATION

The integration of multicultural variables in the practice of consultation has received more attention in recent years, even warranting a miniseries in the *School Psychology Review* (2000) on multicultural and cross-cultural consultation. Overall, Ingraham (2000) and Rogers (2000) suggested that multicultural school consultation integrate diversity variables in all aspects (process, context, and interactions) and across all individuals (school psychologist, consultee, and client) involved in consultation. The three theories of multicultural psychology (acculturation, worldview, and ethnic identity) are of particular importance in consultation, as it will be necessary for a school psychologist to consider these concepts not only as they relate to those they are consulting with (teachers or parents) but as they relate to themselves via interactions with these individuals.

Individuals are inherently complex, and nowhere is this more salient than in the consultative process. Assessing for acculturation, worldview, and identity needs to be a multifaceted process, as it will be critical to assess these variables at different levels for the consultee. For example, in consulting with a teacher and assessing the impact of that individual's culture on the consultative process, a school psychologist will need to assess not only the teacher's personal worldview but how that worldview fits into the teaching culture and, subsequently, the school culture. In addition, ethnic identity will need to be assessed again at the individual level: how does that teacher identify, ethnically, and how does this integrate with his or her identity as a teacher? It is critical for a school psychologist to be able to understand these variables in a multifaceted manner, as well as the interaction and intersection of multiple variables at once. The same multifaceted process would need to be applied to students, parents, and so on.

Once this process is embraced, it will be easier for school psychologists to help their consultees develop skills and implement interventions that are consistent with the level of acculturation, worldview, or identity of the student. It is critical to the success of the consultation that targeted behavior changes are consistent with these variables and where the teacher, student, or family is.

PREVENTION AND INTERVENTION

The reauthorization of the IDEIA (2004), the No Child Left Behind Act (2002), and the inception of response to intervention have ignited the interest in prevention and intervention efforts as the primary focus of the role and functions of the school psychologists. Moreover, these changes have also shifted the focus toward empirically based or research-based interventions as central to prevention and intervention efforts at the individual and systemic levels. More work is needed in this area to determine the effectiveness of empirically based interventions (EBIs). Ortiz (2006) noted in a critical analysis of published works on multicultural issues in school psychology that there is almost no research regarding the effectiveness of a particular intervention program for use with individuals from

CLD backgrounds. Furthermore, he stated that until the research has been conducted on validating interventions on CLD populations, practitioners would have to rely on their best judgment to determine the degree to which any EBI is appropriate for use with such populations across diverse settings. In light of this information, it will be critical for training programs to teach students how to evaluate EBIs for their cultural appropriateness.

Graduate students will also need to acquire the ability to recognize how cultural factors impact prevention and intervention efforts, from development/identification and planning to implementation efforts. Understanding the impact of these variables on treatment will help to achieve better outcomes, as treatment is being considered in the cultural context of the student and/or his or her family. Understanding a student's or parent's level of acculturation and worldview may help with maintaining the integrity of the intervention, since it is being implemented with these factors in mind.

RESEARCH

Given the current emphasis on EBIs and acknowledging the lack of research in the area of CLD populations, training programs are in excellent positions to push through multicultural research agendas. Faculty and students alike can engage in research that supports efforts in validating prevention and intervention programs, as well as validating assessment techniques/strategies/tests that focuses on understanding the unique educational needs of CLD populations. These research efforts in turn will better inform practice and move the profession forward. Furthermore, training programs need to help graduate students achieve competencies in program evaluation in general. It is critical for graduate students to be informed consumers of research in order to evaluate existing programs for their soundness. It is more important for graduate students to achieve these practical research skills that are more easily translatable to actual practice. Although learning about research methods is important, of equal importance is being able to evaluate the quality of existing research in the field. Research efforts should therefore focus on linking research to practice.

USE OF INTERPRETERS

As stated at the beginning of this chapter, the U.S. population has changed dramatically in recent years. Some of the most salient changes include the increase in the number of minorities, particularly those who speak a language other than English (U.S. Census Bureau, 2000; U.S. Department of Education, National Center for Education Statistics, 2006). These changes in the demographic composition of our country not only have impacted the outlook of the U.S. public school system but also have prompted the need for the provision of relevant services to CLD students and families.

Because of the nature of our roles and functions, school psychologists are faced with additional challenges. Among the most salient ones we could mention is the pressing issue of the English barrier. In other words, how do monolingual English-speaking school psychologists best provide services to non-English speakers? This issue becomes more important when we analyze the results of the 2004–2005 NASP membership survey (Curtis et al., 2008). According to this survey, there is a strong need to both recruit and retain minorities, as well as a lack of individuals who are proficient in languages other than English.

Statistics show that school districts are experiencing an increase in students who are second language learners (U.S. Department of Education, National Center for Education Statistics, 2004), pointing to the significant role of interpreters in school psychology services. In New Mexico, a majority-minority state, there are multiple languages (English, Spanish, and several Native American languages) represented in the student population. It is not difficult to deduce from these statistics that it is very likely that school psychologists will at some point in their careers have to employ the services of translators. Because of this, it is becoming imperative that training programs provide training on the pros and cons of using interpreters in their practice. Furthermore, being bilingual or multilingual does not guarantee that you will never need to use an interpreter.

The current state of affairs in the school psychology practice has prompted an increase in the use of translators and interpreters for the provision of school psychological services. Currently, both the APA and the NASP have addressed those issues in their training and ethics standards. As a result many professional organizations have developed guidelines and recommendations for working with interpreters. Most recently, Lopez (2002, 2008) published a series of recommendations aimed to help school psychologists understand best practices when working with interpreters. Among them, she highlights the importance of interpreters being properly certified and trained. This has become an issue, particularly when some school districts still rely on close relatives for the provision of interpretation services; this constitutes a serious ethical violation and needs to be taken seriously.

Lopez (2002, 2008) also pointed out the importance of maintaining direct contact and communication with the interpreter. This allows the school psychologist the opportunity to provide the interpreter with background information relevant to the case, to address confidentiality issues, and to clarify any medical terminology or information provided. Another important consideration is that even though the school psychologist might not be able to communicate with the client and the family in their native language, he or she still needs to take time to build rapport with them. Other recommendations include the discussion of the outcomes of the translation session with the interpreter. Finally, Lopez also cautioned about the use of appropriate tools for the assessment of English language learners.

In sum, training in the use of interpreters needs to take into account how bringing a third party into the client–practitioner relationship has an impact on that relationship. There is a need to recognize that the interpreter's own identity, acculturation level, and worldview can have an impact on how information is communicated, either verbally or nonverbally. As such, understanding how to use interpreters goes beyond the mechanics (i.e., where one sits and how/with whom to make eye contact, etc.) to include these psychological aspects as well. It seems that trainers, supervisors, and graduate students alike would benefit from training in interpersonal processes (IP; e.g., Teyber, 2006) as a means to become keen observers of the intimate nature of this type of relationship. Understanding how the school psychologist, interpreter, and client influence each other in session via IP may serve to improve the dynamics of this triarchic relationship.

PEDAGOGY AND SUPERVISION
OF CULTURAL COMPETENCY

Directors of training programs endorse the philosophies and practices of culturally sensitive and responsive training (Arroyos-Jurado & Savage, 2006). Training directors strongly agree that sensitivity to culture and accurate assessments of similarities and differences are vital to preparing graduate students for life in a diverse setting. Furthermore, a culturally responsive education facilitates students' abilities to interact effectively and work cooperatively with diverse groups in society. Philosophically, it seems that training programs aspire to culturally responsive pedagogy. What is less known is how programs are translating these philosophies into practice beyond the teaching of a single course on multicultural issues (Rogers, 2005).

Although having a diverse faculty is important, of greater importance is being able to translate one's own cultural experience and knowledge into pedagogy that supports the training of others to be culturally competent. It is not enough just to be a faculty member of color and teach about multicultural issues; often, our effectiveness as faculty also stems from how we are perceived by our students in and out of the classroom through our actions and words. Graduate students need to see role models who are committed to social justice issues, who advocate for all issues of diversity, and who take into account their environment and the social justice concerns and issues that are in their immediate context. Students need to observe that our actions are consistent with the teaching of our courses outside of the classroom as well.

SUPERVISION

As was previously discussed, much of the field consists of practitioners who are nearing retirement. As such, many of these individuals were likely trained in a time before multicultural issues were incorporated into training programs. As Harvey and Struzziero (2008) stated, "supervisors are likely to be even less prepared to deal with multicultural situations than their supervisees because they attended graduate school prior to the infusion of multicultural issues into the curricula and/or completed their training and internship in homogeneous settings...[and] are very likely to need to address the development of their own multicultural competencies as well as that of their supervisees" (p. 70). Butler (2003) reiterated the importance of the supervisor being frank about his or her own multicultural competence, whether it is perceived as positive or negative, and being able to manage his or her anxiety, generally, or in relation to these particular skills. Furthermore, supervisors should be held accountable for their own use of culturally sensitive skills and techniques, as well as for the integration of discussions about the effects of societal and institutionalized racism within the context of the supervisory relationship (Butler, 2003). Overall, a culturally competent supervisor is one who can also integrate his or her own and the supervisee's worldviews, identity, and acculturation levels within the realm of the supervisory relationship.

The reality that supervisors may not perceive themselves to be as culturally competent because of lack of training highlights the importance of continued professional development and, once again, provides an opportunity for training programs to play a key role. Training programs can provide an invaluable service to the community, while at the same time meeting accreditation standards. A requirement of the NASP program approval guidelines (NASP, 2000d) is that programs provide training opportunities for practitioners in the field. Professional development activities can center on multicultural issues and competencies for supervising practitioners.

CASE ILLUSTRATION

At New Mexico State University (NMSU), we have been invested in developing a multicultural training program in school psychology for educational specialists since 1997. We understand that such an endeavor is a process that demands an ongoing evaluation of our program philosophy, content, and commitment to multiculturalism and diversity. That is, we recognize that a program never truly achieves multicultural competence and sensitivity. Instead, a multicultural training program is always striving to do better in this regard. Rogers (2006) investigated the key characteristics of exemplary multicultural training programs in school psychology. In this section, we use these key characteristics to illustrate our program's multicultural emphasis in training.

Rogers (2006) cited the climate of the university and department as an important aspect of exemplary multicultural school psychology training programs. NMSU is a Hispanic-serving institution that is located in the U.S./Mexico borderland. In Doña Ana County, where NMSU is located, 63.4% of the people are of Hispanic descent, 54.4% speak another language other than English in their homes, and 45.6% of individuals and families are living in poverty (U.S. Census Bureau, 2000). As a land grant university, NMSU has been committed to meeting the needs of its community, region, and state via education, research, extension education, and public service (NMSU Committee on Committees, 1990). For example, in combining two of its main missions—education and public service—NMSU has made pre-K-12 outreach a priority in hopes of helping local public schools address low student test scores and academic retention (Martin, 2006).

This pre-K-12 outreach initiative has resulted in greater support from the NMSU administration for campus programs and departments that train teachers and professionals who will work in the public school system. Hence, NMSU's School Psychology training program and its department—Counseling and Educational Psychology (CEP)—has found support for its multicultural emphasis. This support has manifested in a new faculty line for the School Psychology program and financial resources to recruit and retain CLD faculty (e.g., merit pay, research monies, travel funds, mentorship programs) and students (e.g., travel awards, assistantships, and fellowships). Currently, 100% of the School Psychology faculty and 66% of the School Psychology student body are from CLD backgrounds. Furthermore, 70% of the total counseling and educational faculty and 40% of the tenured faculty are CLD. These figures far outweigh the percentage of faculty (25%) and students (31%) in Rogers' (2006) investigation of exemplary multicultural school psychology training programs.

Beyond the numbers of CLD faculty and students and the administration's commitment of financial resources for the School Psychology program, the CEP and School Psychology faculty are committed to recruiting and retaining CLD students. Thus, we actively promote the multicultural focus of our program in our philosophy, recruitment brochures, and Web site. We also actively recruit CLD students by (a) asking our colleagues in the community and around the nation to refer CLD students to our program, (b) involving current students in our recruitment process, and (c) making personal contact with CLD recruits during the admissions process. In terms of retention, we actively mentor our CLD students by (a) providing helpful suggestions for navigating the university and professional school psychology organizations, (b) supporting the activities of the School Psychology Graduate Student Association, (c) encouraging students to attend and present at national and regional conferences related to school psychology, and (d) including one 1st-year and one 2nd-year student in our training committee to act as student–faculty liaisons. As documented by Rogers (2006), our recruitment and retention efforts have been used by other exemplary multicultural school psychology training programs.

We understand that recruiting and retaining CLD faculty and students alone does not make a school psychology training program multicultural. As suggested by Rogers (2006), the faculty expertise, course content, and the number of multicultural curriculum models used is a strong indicator of a program's commitment to multicultural issues. At NMSU, 70% of our faculty specializes in multicultural issues related to psychology. We use both the separate course and integration approaches to emphasize multicultural issues in our curriculum. We believe that striving for multicultural competence begins with self-exploration and self-reflection. Thus, we have school psychology students begin their program with a psychology of multiculturalism course in which they engage in such a process. Culturally relevant activities, such as a multicultural family genogram, cultural immersion activities, and cultural integrated discussion groups, assist students in understanding ways in which they have been oppressed and ways in which they have been privileged based on their multiple cultural identities (e.g., race, ethnicity, gender, sexual orientation, ability, religious affiliation, social class). These course activities also promote awareness of others' cultures. We believe that such self-awareness and awareness of others' cultures provides a base to begin an integrative understanding of school psychology practices in a multicultural society. Thus, as a program, we strive to infuse multicultural content into all graduate courses. This integration comes in the form of course readings, lectures, assignments, videos, case studies, and discussions. Also, in the school psychology research course and for their research project, we urge school psychology students to conduct research examining the multicultural contexts and identities of their participants.

Whereas our didactic courses infuse multiculturalism, we also make sure that the school psychology students have exposure to CLD clients in their practicum and internship experiences. Given our geographic location, all of the school's psychology students complete practica in school districts where the majority of the student bodies come from CLD backgrounds. In these practicum experiences, school psychology students begin to learn how to apply the multicultural knowledge learned from our curriculum in real-world diverse school settings with CLD students and families. Case presentations that include multicultural contexts and sensitive practices are required to successfully fulfill the requirements of practicum. Taken together, the didactic courses and practical experiences required by NMSU's School Psychology training program provide crucial training for those working with CLD populations.

We do not believe that our standard training alone is sufficient in producing school psychology professionals with expertise in working with CLD populations. Hence, Drs. Elsa Arroyos-Jurado and Enedina García-Vázquez secured funding from the U.S. Office of Special Programs to train school psychology students to work more effectively with CLD populations. In essence, this funding has created an area of concentration that emphasizes bilingual services.

Students participating in the grant training take additional course work to increase their Spanish language proficiency while also learning to use interpreters and/or translators as a means of providing services to students and families who are linguistically diverse. At the outset of the program, students complete a university sanctioned Spanish language proficiency exam. Based on the results of this exam, students follow recommended course work in one of two tracks: native speakers or nonnative speakers of Spanish. Students then take a minimum of two courses focusing on grammar/composition and oral proficiency in Spanish language development at the level they tested at. As such, the grant training opportunity is open to both monolingual English-speaking students and bilingual English/Spanish-speaking students. They are also required to take a course, Spanish for the mental health provider, which focuses specifically on the impact of culture, ethnicity, and language on the various roles/functions of school psychologists with particular emphasis placed on the use of interpreters and application of Spanish language skills to assessment, consultation, intervention, and so on. The goal of the grant is to train highly qualified school psychologists to provide services to students and families from diverse cultural and linguistic backgrounds.

CONCLUSION

The primary goal of this chapter was to provide an introductory discussion of the relevant issues related to the training of school psychologists to serve CLD students, families, and communities. It is our hope that the information provided will serve as a guide for trainers and, more importantly, a blueprint for the development of comprehensive school psychology training programs that incorporate multiculturalism and diversity as an essential component in the formation of future professionals in the field.

We cannot deny that society is changing. More than ever, population shifts characterized by an increase in the numbers of minorities and non-English-language speakers in our school systems highlight the need to train school psychologists to become culturally competent and responsive practitioners. As such, in order to meet these challenges, school psychology training programs must move beyond the more traditional training models and begin to embrace a nontraditional training model that focuses on a "multicultural critical pedagogical process" (Vázquez & García-Vázquez, 2003, p. 551). Regarding training programs, two points are of particular importance. First, training needs to focus on self-awareness followed by applied practice with CLD populations. Second, there is a need for trainers and supervisors who are self-aware and who are also able to teach these concepts and supervise the work in these areas.

On the other hand, the development and implementation of such nontraditional training programs represent both a challenge and an opportunity for training directors. One of the most salient challenges is that there is still no prescribed process on how to train and provide services to CLD populations. The challenge arises because of within-group differences. Therefore, there is a need to develop an approach that takes into consideration within-group differences (a case by case approach, taking into consideration multicultural variables, versus a single standardized approach to all children). Also, there seems to be confusion about specialist level versus doctoral level training. Furthermore, the current trends in the field stress the importance of acknowledging our multicultural limitations and seeking assistance (professional development, consultation with peers, etc.) when needed. Other challenges faced by training programs include the need to recruit and retain CLD faculty and students. An additional point to note is that being bilingual or of a diverse background does not automatically guarantee cultural competency.

Finally, becoming a culturally competent practitioner is both a summative and a formative process. This process starts with self-awareness and an understanding of one's own biases, values, and beliefs and how those aspects impact our work with CLD populations. The formative process includes formal instruction of multicultural competencies and infusion of these throughout the entire training experience. In other words, training programs not only should recruit and retain CLD faculty and students but must ensure that a multicultural philosophy of research and training becomes part of the culture of that program. In sum, we recognize that there are many challenges ahead and that there is much that needs to be done in this regard; however, we hope this information will motivate and inspire training directors to start considering and addressing these issues in their programs.

RESOURCES

National Association of School Psychologists (2007). *Programs with a focus on mul-
      ticulturalism and/or bilingualism.* Retrieved December 10, 2007 from http://
      www.nasponline.org/resources/culturalcompetence/multprograms.aspx
This Web site, sponsored by NASP, provides a listing of programs that were self-nominated as part of an NASP multicultural training program survey. A listing of each of the programs is provided, along with pertinent information related to mission statement, funding in the form of grants, and faculty research interests. Further descriptions of the programs are gleaned from the respective program Web sites. Special designation is provided for programs offering bilingual specializations, those that are considered to have a comprehensive model of training and financial support, student minority representation, multicultural curricular emphasis, faculty members involved in minority research and outreach, and recruitment and financial retention strategies in the form of research and training grants.

Rogers, M. R. (2006). Exemplary multicultural training in school psychology programs. *Cultural Diversity and Ethnic Minority Psychology, 12*(1), 115–133.
This study examined the characteristics of 17 programs noted for their emphasis on training students from a multicultural perspective via semi-structured interviews with faculty and students and review of application materials. A description of the multicultural curriculum, recruitment strategies, retention strategies, environment, and demographics of the student and faculty is synthesized and discussed.

Vázquez, E., Vázquez, L., & Ivey, M. B. (2002). *Counseling Latina/o children and adolescents: Cross-cultural issues* [Motion picture]. (Available from Microtraining and Multicultural Development, 141 Walnut Street, Hanover, MA 02339)
This video focuses how demonstrations showing how to work effectively, cross-culturally, with culturally and linguistically diverse children and their families. Demonstrations provide an ineffective model of cross-cultural service delivery followed by a more culturally sensitive approach. Particular emphasis is placed on how to work with acculturation issues and helping children build a cultural strength. Lastly, special attention is given to working with families effectively by providing effective translation for non-English-speaking students and their families.

REFERENCES

American Psychological Association (2002a). *Ethical principles of psychologists and code of conduct.* Washington, DC: Author.
American Psychological Association (2002b). *Guidelines on multicultural education, training, research, practice, and organizational change for psychologists.* Washington, DC: Author.
American Psychological Association (2002c). *Guidelines and principles for accreditation of programs in professional psychology.* Washington, DC: Author.
Arroyos-Jurado, E., & Savage, T. A. (2006, March). *School psychology training programs and issues of cultural sensitivity and responsivity.* Poster session presented at the National Association of School Psychologists Conference, Anaheim, CA.
Braden, J. P., & Shah, K. G. (2005). A critique of multicultural training in school psychology: Rationale, strategies, and tactics. In C. L. Frisby & C. R. Reynolds (Eds.), *Comprehensive handbook of multicultural school psychology* (pp. 1023–1047). Hoboken, NJ: John Wiley & Sons, Inc.
Butler, S. K. (2003). Multicultural sensitivity and competence in the clinical supervision of school counselors and school psychologists: A context for providing competent services in a multicultural society. *The Clinical Supervisor, 22*(1), 125–141.
Curtis, M. J., Lopez, A. D., Lopez, A. D., Castillo, J. M., Batsche, G. M., Minch, D., et al. (2008). The status of school psychology: Demographic characteristics, employment conditions, professional practices, and continuing professional development. *NASP Communiqué, 36*(5).

Esquivel, G. B., Lopez, E. C., & Nahari, S. (Eds.). (2007). *Handbook of multicultural school psychology: An interdisciplinary perspective.* Mahwah, NJ: Lawrence Erlbaum Associates, Publishers.

Frisby, C. L. & Reynolds (Eds.) (2005). *Comprehensive handbook of multicultural school psychology.* Hoboken, NJ: Wiley.

Harvey, V. S. & Struzziero, J. A. (2008). *Professional development and supervision of school psychologists: From intern to expert.* Thousand Oaks, CA: Corwin Press and National Association of School Psychologists.

Henning-Stout, M. & Brown-Cheatham, M. (1999). School psychology in a diverse world: Considerations for practice, research, and training (pp. 1041–1055). In C. R. Reynolds and T. B. Gutkin (Eds.), *The handbook of school psychology* (3rd ed.). New York: Wiley.

Ingraham, C. L. (2000). Consultation through a multicultural lens: Multicultural and cross-cultural consultation in schools. *School Psychology Review, 29*(3), 320–343.

Keim, J., Warring, D. F., & Rau, R. (2001). Impact of multicultural training on school psychology and education students. *Journal of Instructional Psychology, 28*(4), 249–252.

Lopez, E. C. (2002). Recommended practices in working with school interpreters to deliver psychological services to children and families. In A. Thomas and J. Grimes (Eds.), *Best practices in school psychology IV* (pp. 1419–1432). Bethesda, MD: National Association of School Psychologists.

Lopez, E. C. (2008). Best practices in working with school interpreters. In A. Thomas and J. Grimes (Eds.), *Best practices in school psychology V* (pp. 1751–1770). Bethesda, MD: National Association of School Psychologists.

Lopez, E. C., & Rogers, M. R. (2007). Multicultural competencies and training in school psychology: Issues, approaches, and future directions. In G. B. Esquivel, E. C. Lopez, & S. Nahari (Eds.), *Handbook of multicultural school psychology: An interdisciplinary perspective* (pp. 47–67). Mahwah, NJ: Lawrence Erlbaum Associates, Publishers.

Martin, M. V. (2006). *Outreach to public schools essential to state's future* [Bulletin]. Las Cruces, NM: New Mexico State University.

National Association of School Psychologists (2000a). *Guidelines for the provision of school psychological services.* Bethesda, MD: Author.

National Association of School Psychologists (2000b). *Principles for professional ethics.* Bethesda, MD: Author.

National Association of School Psychologists (2000c). *Standards for credentialing of school psychologists.* Bethesda, MD: Author.

National Association of School Psychologists (2000d). *Standards for the training and field placement programs in school psychology.* Bethesda, MD: Author.

National Association of School Psychologists (2003). *Position statement on minority recruitment.* Retrieved December 10, 2007, from http://www.nasponline.org/about_nasp/positionpapers/MinorityRecruitment.pdf

New Mexico State University Committee on Committees (1990). *New Mexico State University mission statement.* Retrieved March 31, 2008, from http://www.nmsu.edu/manual/documents/intro.pdf

Ortiz, S. O. (2006). Multicultural issues in school psychology practice: A critical analysis. *Journal of Applied School Psychology, 22*(2), 151–167.

Ortiz, S. O. (2008). Best practices in nondiscriminatory assessment. In A. Thomas & J. Grimes (Eds.), *Best practices in school psychology V* (pp. 661–678). Bethesda, MD: National Association of School Psychologists.

Rogers, M. (2005). Multicultural training in school psychology. In C. L. Frisby & C. R. Reynolds (Eds.), *Comprehensive handbook of multicultural school psychology* (pp. 993–1022). Hoboken, NJ: John Wiley & Sons, Inc.

Rogers, M. R. (2000). Examining the cross cultural context of consultation. *School Psychology Review, 29*(3), 414–417.

Rogers, M. R. (2006). Exemplary multicultural training in school psychology programs. *Cultural Diversity and Ethnic Minority Psychology, 12*(1), 115–133.

Rogers, M. R., Ingraham, C. L., Bursztyn, A., Cajigas-Segredo, N., Esquivel, G., Hess, R., et al. (1999). Providing psychological services to racially, ethnically, culturally, and linguistically diverse individuals in the schools. *School Psychology International, 20*(3), 243–264.

Sandoval, J. H. (2007). Professional standards, guidelines, and ethical issues within a multicultural context. In G. B. Esquivel, E. C. Lopez, and S. Nahari (Eds.), *Handbook of multicultural school psychology: An interdisciplinary perspective* (pp. 29–45). Mahwah, NJ: Lawrence Erlbaum Associates.

Teyber, E. (2006). *Interpersonal process in psychotherapy: A relational approach* (5th ed). Belmont, CA: Thomson Brooks/Cole.

U.S. Department of Education, National Center for Education Statistics (2004). *English language learner students in U.S. public schools: 1994 and 2000.* Retrieved September 15, 2008, from http://nces.ed.gov/pubs2004/2004035.pdf

U.S. Department of Education, National Center for Education Statistics (2006a). Digest of education statistics (2005). In *Fast facts, NCES 2006-030 (chapter 1)*. Retrieved December 17, 2007, from http://nces.ed.gov/fastfacts/display.asp?id=65

U.S. Department of Education, National Center for Education Statistics (2006b). *Public elementary and secondary students, staff, schools, and school districts: School year 2003-4 (NCES 2006-307)*. Retrieved December 17, 2007, from http://nces.ed.gov/fastfacts/display.asp?id=96

U.S. Census Bureau News (2007). *Minority population tops 100 million.* Retrieved December 17, 2007, from http://www.census.gov/Press-Release/www/releases/archives/population/010048.html

U.S. Census Bureau (2000). *Statistical abstract of the United States: 2000* (120th ed.). Washington, DC: U.S. Government Printing Office.

Vázquez, L. A. & García-Vázquez, E. (2003). Teaching multicultural competencies in the counseling curriculum. In D. B. Pope-Davis, H. L. K. Coleman, W. M. Lui, & R. L. Toporek (Eds.), *Handbook of multicultural competencies in counseling and psychology* (pp. 546–561). Thousand Oaks, CA: Sage Publications, Inc.

9 Preparing students for leadership roles

Clare N. Lowell, Robert J. Rimmer, and Roger D. Zeeman

INTRODUCTION

The focus of this chapter is the preparation of school psychologists for positions of leadership. These positions most commonly fall under the titles of chairperson of the individualized education program (IEP) team or committee on special education, director of pupil personnel services or pupil services, special services, or special education. Of course, school psychologists also become principals, guidance directors, and school superintendents.

When one coauthor gained his degree and certification as a school psychologist, he was well prepared through 75 graduate credits in psychoeducational and psychodynamic evaluation and diagnosis, counseling, statistics, research and experimental design, child psychopathology, education of exceptional children, consultation, and community resources. Barely competent as a beginning practitioner working with kindergarten through eighth grade, he was learning his craft when new state laws mandated an increase in services and the need to hire a learning specialist, social worker, supplementary instructor, additional teachers, speech therapists, and paraprofessionals. This meant understanding the development of job descriptions, the process of recruiting candidates, employment interviewing, contacting and interpreting references, analyzing an applicant's portfolio of experiences, assisting human resources in hiring practices and guide placement, providing guidance and supervision and subsequently performance evaluation for new employees, and overall leadership to a team of child study personnel. Which courses prepared the school psychologist for this challenge? All knowledge was acquired on the job with help from the central office and principals. Now, 40 years later, have there been courses added to graduate school psychology programs that address the requisite skills to become a team leader, or eventually, a director of special education or pupil services? This chapter addresses some of the essential proficiencies needed to perform as a colleague/chairperson or as a supervisor/director.

LITERATURE REVIEW

Along with the stated principles of school psychology (to promote adherence to high standards, ensure appropriate high quality services to children and youth, and provide appropriate evaluation of personnel), there must be an ongoing, positive, systematic, collaborative process that focuses on promoting personal growth and exemplary professional practice leading to improved performance of all concerned—the school psychologist, supervisor, students, and the entire school community (National Association of School Psychologists [NASP], 2004).

Oftentimes, the forces that unite a school psychologist and his or her team accompany a host of related problems, among them personnel issues, logistics of service delivery, and legal, contractual and organizational practices. An experienced school psychologist frequently assumes a supervisory relationship with interns or other school psychologists, but within the confines of the child study team, the position usually functions in a consultative manner, as team supervision often requires "metasupervision" that addresses the conceptual, interpersonal, and technical skills required in traditional supervisory roles (NASP, 2004).

Often, these organizational structures follow classic models that fall out along group lines: the vertical differentiation by authority (hierarchical) versus the horizontal dimension by specialization. In a very small organization such as a child study team, the most compelling source of conflict is often based in power, although the concept of power itself is a dynamic one that ebbs and flows with group purpose (Ullrich & Wieland, 1980).

In a team meeting, like any other meeting of professionals, the rules of discourse generally govern what is said and what remains unsaid in addition to identifying those who speak with authority and those who must listen. Professional educators like to be in control of what they say as well as what is said, but we are all subjected to the rules of appropriate discourse. Educational excellence is often touted as a worthy goal and one that each reform movement seeks to attain, and yet there is often doubt about what it means, simply because not everyone recognizes it when they see it—if they see it at all (Cherryholmes, 1988, pp. 35–39). Likewise, educational success for a special needs student may be similarly distorted, according to those who are evaluating the process as well as the product. It is the goal of the team leader, or school psychologist, to set the standards and lay the groundwork for the practical realization of the success. It is not sufficient for special services personnel to have substantive knowledge of the students themselves who require these services. The team members must make themselves personally and professionally available to the entire school community in sharing their expertise and bringing everyone onboard in the attainment of success. In doing so, there can be enhanced investment in the ultimate goal—the student's progress and achievement.

This shared vision is critical in enabling team members to view each other as colleagues in establishing a positive tone and thereby offsetting the vulnerability that dialogue brings. By seeing each other as colleagues who are working toward a common goal, team members can develop a dialogue and may discover emergent feelings of respect and even friendship with one another, even if, initially, they do not appear to have much in common. What is essential to this equation is the willingness of team members to consider each other as colleagues and, in doing so, to hold assumptions in abeyance. By treating each other as professionals, they acknowledge mutual risk and establish a stronger sense of safety in facing that risk (Senge, 1990).

This does not mean that everyone need share identical views—quite the contrary, as the true power of collegiality can only be revealed through differences of view. There may, on occasion, appear to be adversarial perspectives. This is the true test of supervisory capability, for the very hierarchy that puts the school psychologist in the position of team leader may squelch any benefit of differing dialogues under his or her leadership. This is where ego meets expostulation, for if one person assumes that his or her position will be the prevailing one in the discussion because of the privileges of rank, the dialogue is effectively ended and the team itself will be silenced into submission. It is in this situation where a team leader must fine tune his or her skills as "process facilitator," even if that means walking a fine line between being the acknowledged expert and being the team moderator (Senge, 1990).

The concept of trust—although elusive—is critical in putting together this delicate balance. By encouraging personal vision for what each individual views as essential to a student's growth, a powerful synergy emerges that creates the ultimate direction for that child. It is within this context that teams put aside personal self-interests in deference to the best interests of that youngster. For example, if a science teacher is fixated on strict classroom management compliance of a mainstreamed special needs child, even if that child is bewildered in note-taking and consequently disruptive in class, the other academic professionals on the team may suggest alternate ways of dealing with the issue (closer seat placement, class scribes for the student, visual cues between teacher and student, etc.). If there is sufficient trust around the table, the science teacher will welcome these suggestions without question or judgment as to his colleagues' motivation. In doing so, the child will be served more appropriately, the parent will glean a strong sense of professional commitment from the staff, and the school psychologist will be able to articulate an administrative vision that is both discipline-specific and educationally sound.

In reflecting upon the authority of the team leader, one must also consider the definition of *power* as it relates to his or her particular situation. Often, in providing leadership, school psychologists utilize whatever personal power they may have. This personal power is derived from the respect of their colleagues as well as the commitment of the team itself, but it also depends, in large part, on the perception of that leader as both an individual and a professional. A team leader who is highly regarded (and therefore considered powerful by his or her peers) is usually accepted as being fair and knowledgeable in his or her dealings with people. This individual's interpersonal skills, influence within the school community, and academic respect all add to a personal power that can be neither delegated nor bestowed—it must be earned (Tucker, 1981, pp. 29–32).

Blackbourn, Papasan, Vinson, and Blackbourn (2000) discussed the leadership lessons of Glasser (1990), as well as those of W. Edward Deming, upon whose pioneering ideas (e.g., "quality products ... quality people") Glasser based his teachings. They stated "The reality of today's schools, with respect to acts of change and the nature of the change process itself, requires a rethinking and redesigning of the concept of leadership" (p. 58). Glasser has had a profound effect on educational theory and its application to the quality school. Most school psychologists are familiar with his teachings on counseling (reality therapy, choice theory) but are less familiar with his concepts of leadership. Glasser's (1994) lead managers place the interests of their colleagues above all others. They are supportive and develop trusting relationships. Lead managers continually work on the system to create a noncoercive environment that encourages employees to self-evaluate and achieve quality work. Glasser's concepts are one of the foundations of the Leadership Project of the Canadian Coalition of Community-Based Employability Training (CCCBET). The CCCBET Web site (2008) extends Glasser's contribution by summarizing the principles of involved leadership of Kouzes and Posner (1995), as shown in Table 9.1.

Lead-managers use caring habits akin to those of William Purkey, described in the next section. They are the opposite of boss-managers, who

Table 9.1 Principles of Involved Leadership

Principle	Applications
Question the way things are done	Seek challenges that encourage change, growth, innovation, and progress.
	Experiment, take risks, and learn from mistakes.
Promote a shared vision	Envision a future that motivates and encourages people to give their best.
	Win your team's trust by appealing to their values, interests, hopes, and dreams.
Empower others to take action	Build a trusting environment and foster cooperation by promoting shared objectives.
	Support individuals by conferring power and choice, developing their skills, assigning important tasks, and showing support at all times.
Lead by example	Be an example to others by respecting the team's values.
	Celebrate minor victories to highlight the importance of continuing the struggle and to encourage individual commitment.
Recognize and reward success	Recognize individual contributions to the success of each project.
	Reward and celebrate team achievements regularly.

rely upon external rather than internal motivation and are coercive, narrow-minded, and rule-focused.

TRAINING FOR PROFESSIONAL ROLES AND FUNCTION

The literature is replete with discussions of two contrasting leadership styles, whether they are called technical/managerial and supportive/artistic (Deal & Peterson, 1994), *gesellschaft* and *gemeinschaft* (Sergiovanni, 2005), or other terms that describe similar paradigms. Leaders should remember that it is a false dichotomy that asserts that effective leaders employ one model or the other exclusively. Rather than being mutually exclusive, these two models are inextricably linked, and this is particularly important in any case when a psychologist assumes a leadership role in a school.

School leaders must be knowledgeable in a wide range of tasks, both organizational and educational (Jay & McGovern, 2007). He or she must be well versed in staff and student scheduling, state and federal laws, budgeting, department of education regulations, local board of education policies, the bargaining agreement, and a host of other areas that are necessary to function in a school bureaucracy. These tasks, although important, must take a secondary place behind the educational tasks that are at the core of the educator's mission. Since the bureaucratic requirements of leadership roles are generally clearly defined, one would think that training psychologists in these areas should be relatively straightforward in terms of graduate school courses. The reality serves in stark contrast, however. Most graduate school leadership programs fail in this seemingly simple challenge. The majority of courses are theoretically based, without practical instruction on the basics of the organizational skills necessary to function in today's schools. Too often educators are thrust into leadership roles, with few of the skills necessary to function effectively. Little of consequence can be accomplished if the day to day operational tasks are left unaddressed. These skills are prerequisites to focusing on the larger and more important issue of creating and maintaining an educational environment that meets the needs of students with disabilities. Donaldson (2001) asserted that school leaders engage in the three types of activities that are related to addressing both the management function and the educational function: they "articulate programs that staff and constituents view as morally good, mingle the practical, daily work with staff, students, and parents with the ideals of the school's purposes and seek out challenges by questioning incongruities in their work and asking, 'what can we do about this?'" (p. 50).

In terms of the educational tasks that school leaders in general face, the school psychologist has added pressures based on the uniqueness of the position and the population it serves. Flores (2004) described effective leadership "as being knowledgeable, strong and goal-oriented, but, at the same time, flexible, encouraging, supportive, helpful, and close to staff" (p. 299).

The second half of this description identifies many of the characteristics that are expected of the school psychologist, regardless of role. The school psychologist assumes a leadership role in a particular context, and that context and all that it entails are key to the individual and the group success in accomplishing the mission (Gordon & Patterson, 2006).

Rather than attempt to balance the roles of psychologist and school leader, the successful individual is one who learns to integrate them in the daily activities that constitute the job tasks of the specific position held. Although the managerial tasks will vary widely depending on the specific leadership position (i.e., supervisor, director, principal, or superintendent), the educational tasks should be relatively constant. It is in this area that authenticity and modeling become keys to maximizing performance in the role of leader.

The ideal school psychology program today should look to educational leadership programs at graduate institutions and incorporate at least one required course in administration of special education/pupil services. Typical graduate courses in educational leadership provide an in-depth understanding of the various contexts within which school leaders must evaluate and supervise support personnel and educational programs. School and board level policies, which define the role of school leaders within the context of these services, are examined. These typical courses encourage future leaders to examine their thinking about leadership and the change process, decision making, influencing people, and understanding relationships. Graduate courses in leadership teach about constructs of power, team building, communication, and conflict resolution. There are also fundamental courses in basic administrative procedure, finance, budget, and management. Role playing and the Socratic method help to develop personal and professional approaches to problem solving, including preparation for situations that may be contentious.

As a school psychologist, however, the team leader must himself or herself be aware of various methods of motivation that direct the actions of individual team members. A mastery of basic motivation theories is essential for any supervisor who is attempting to effectively lead his or her group to reasonable goals. The two primary approaches to these theories center around content and process—the most well known, of course, being Maslow's hierarchy of needs, which identifies five levels of needs that motivate people (MacNeil & Yelvington, 2005).

Maslow starts with the most basic of human needs (Level 1—physiological) and moves systematically to the most sophisticated category (Level 5—self-actualization), which challenges minds as well as engaging prior learning and natural aptitude. The levels of needs in the middle range from Level 2 (safety) to Level 3 (social) and Level 4 (esteem). A successful team leader may well recognize the necessity to meet various needs on various levels. For example, some members may demonstrate enhanced social needs by reaffirming the organization's concern for respecting and valuing the contributions of each person in the group. By doing so, he or she is reinforcing a sense of belonging and trust. This is closely related to those who are on Level 4, where the desire for self-respect, as well as recognition by others, is clearly tied to the skills and abilities of these individuals to do the job. The supervisor (team leader) can help fulfill these esteem needs by showing workers how much their input is appreciated. When this is done, many professionals are motivated to realize their full potential through the assignment of duties and tasks that challenge their minds and abilities while simultaneously drawing upon their training. It takes a clear understanding of interpersonal relationships in order to reach and maintain this delicate balance of power, but the attainment of a group goal is payment for whatever effort has been expended.

There are other theories of motivation that build upon Maslow that bear mentioning as well: Alderfer's existence, relatedness, and growth model (Alderfer & Guzzo, 1979) identifies three categories of needs (similar to Maslow's) and maintains that when individuals are frustrated in meeting higher level needs, the next lower level needs reemerge. His growth level need reiterates the group member's desire to be creative and to make useful and productive contributions to the group in order to satisfy his or her desire for personal development. Similarly, McClelland's learned needs (Walker, 1983) divide motivation into needs for power, affiliation, and achievement. Within this model and in the context of the group dynamic of a child study team situation, the need to control may supersede the need to conform. Consequently, the power-players may dominate and seize the opportunity to control others. Their need to influence the outcome—regardless of the necessity for such an action—is a reflection of an assertiveness that arises whenever a decision is to be made. Less confident members may find that their desire to cooperate and socialize compromises their innate sense of right and wrong (MacNeil & Yelvington, 2005). Therefore, it is the leader's role and responsibility to maintain equity, i.e., a sense of fairness. This must be perceived by each team member equally. The psychologist/leader not only motivates his or her colleagues but also sees that their opinions are being heard, respected, and considered. The overall outcomes of a child study team may be easily observable (an improvement in a child's attitude or an upward turn in his or her achievement level) or simply symbolic (a positive write-up that boosts a youngster's self-esteem). Either way, these results reflect the collective efforts of teachers, specialists, or parents who create partnerships that ultimately result in healthier school environments for children at risk.

What are essential skills for the school psychologist who takes on the role of director of special education, special services, or pupil services? First and foremost, the psychologist must create an inviting atmosphere. Some key tenets of invitational education (Purkey & Novak, 1996) include (a) creating a democratically oriented, positive approach to leadership; (b) educating in a collaborative and cooperative manner; (c) appreciating that all staff and students have untapped potential; and (d) being intentionally inviting, both personally and professionally. Purkey urges educational leaders to "visit the provinces." That is, the director should develop a schedule of frequent visits to as many self-contained or inclusive classes for students with disabilities as possible.

Administrative support goes beyond visits, policies, and procedures. It can include (a) support for in-service training for general and special education teachers, paraprofessionals, and other staff; (b) payment for time spent outside regular school hours; (c) credits toward district service requirements; (d) clerical support for IEPs and recordkeeping; and (e) direct intervention with students' aggressive behaviors (Yoon & Gilchrist, 2003).

The administrative psychologist may benefit from an open door policy. Teachers, paraprofessionals, and team members are confronted with difficult problems. Some require urgent intervention or decisions. Accessibility to a member of the administrative team demonstrates support, empathy, and help in problem solving. Support of common planning time for coteachers or collaborative teachers is critical. In addition, allowing staff input into scheduling and student grouping decisions boosts morale and effectiveness. Thorough planning for and preparation of substitute teachers and aides is also a critical role for the director. The psychologist should also attend to training of the secretarial staff in responsiveness to staff, students, and parents and in responses to crises. In addition, he or she can contribute to planning by being aware of the academic accommodations available and providing essential materials and resources. A director must be trained in significant levels of awareness of the effectiveness of computer hardware and software for management of IEPs, data, and reporting.

PEDAGOGICAL/SUPERVISORY ISSUES

Leading a child study team (CST) can present its own unique set of challenges and circumstances. In order to enhance its function and ensure its utmost success, the school psychologist should be armed with leadership strategies that enable him or her to analyze situations, receive feedback, and facilitate solutions in a manner that reflects his or her experience, expertise, and professionalism.

The school psychologist should be well versed in theories of classic management styles of formal organizational structures so as to allow for maximum participation of all of the organization's disparate members. Oftentimes, educational institutions may include both a CST—consisting of a full-time learning disabilities teacher, a school psychologist, school social worker, and/or speech/language specialist—and a resource center program for classified students. These special services personnel work in conjunction with mainstream academic teachers, as well as the child's parents and/or advocate (when appropriate).

When all these players are called into action to deal with a student who may be experiencing academic, emotional, social, or behavioral problems that impede his or her daily ability to function, the playing field can be very crowded and very chaotic. It is up to the team leader to sort out the various agenda intrinsic to each individual and to clear the path for educational opportunities that enable his or her staff members to share their expertise with the entire school community. In order to successfully enact such a scenario, however, the school psychologist must know the rules of the game or, at the very least, the various players that enable his or her team to achieve its goal.

Thomas J. Sergiovanni (1984), a renowned educational theorist known for his concept/practices approach for effective department leadership, starts with the most basic of premises: that all educational organizations are, essentially, human organizations that reflect a strong commitment to goals, as well as a confidence that is reflected in enhanced motivation and increased job satisfaction resulting from the quality of their work. Supervisory leadership, to his way of thinking, should be more concerned with action, change, and improvement than it is with control, order, and checking.

Unlike most educational leaders, however, the successful school psychologist must possess certain qualities that set him or her apart from other educational personnel within the institution. Although he or she should be armed with unimpeachable knowledge of subject matter, the strength and scope of his or her training must rest in specializations in both psychology and education. School psychologists are often called upon to use this training with teachers, parents, and other mental health professionals in identifying academic potential and behavior influences, as well as administering, analyzing, and interpreting tests in prescribing specific behavioral and educational strategies. Often, no other school professional on staff has such a commanding familiarity of the multifarious influences that affect learning and behavior. School psychologists are the resident professionals who enable others to better understand child development and counseling techniques in fostering an atmosphere of tolerance and understanding for the special needs student.

Preparation of school psychologists for administrative roles should include an introduction to two leading professional associations: the Council of Administrators of Special Education (CASE), a division of the Council for Exceptional Children, and the National Association of State Directors of Special Education (NASDSE). In fact, getting to know one's state director and key staff is one of the most valuable resource connections.

CASE is an international professional educational organization that provides many resources, leadership, and support to members by shaping policies and practices that impact the quality of education. The credo of CASE (n.d.) is that local administrators are critical change agents who affect the quality and future of special education and the education of students with exceptionalities. Four of the most important goals of the organization are (a) providing opportunities for professional growth through conferences and workshops, (b) affording opportunities for exchange and interaction with colleagues, (c) upholding high ethical and professional standards of practice, and (d) keeping current with federal, state, and local laws and regulations. Learning to maintain contact with a national organization like CASE, as well as state and local professional organizations for administrators of special education services and personnel, is a given.

NASDSE is a resource for all local directors, and therefore graduate students should become knowledgeable about the association. NASDE focuses on policies and practices and on the improvement of educational services and outcomes for students with disabilities (NASDE, n.d.). A novice director can benefit from NASDSE's knowledge base for current issues, technical assistance, policy analysis, research, publications, specialized Web sites, national initiatives, and collaborative partnerships. New IEP requirements have the potential of altering the nature of special education services and their purpose through provisions that require consideration of how a student will access and progress in the general education curriculum. Access to the general education curriculum is intended to ensure that students with disabilities have access to the same challenging standards that are at the core of national and state reforms. Legal requirements must be considered as part of the actual process of ensuring access to the general education curriculum for students with disabilities. Their data and recommendations are based upon a three-tier system: "(1) *Best practices* (also known as evidence-based practices) documented through a synthesis of research; (2) *Promising practices* which are interventions, administrative practices or approaches for which there is considerable evidence or expert consensus; and (3) *Emerging practices* which are new innovations that do not yet have scientific evidence or broad expert consensus support" NASDE (n.d.). Some examples of NASDE publication topics that are very useful for a trainer in leadership include amendments to the Individuals With Disabilities Education Act, access to the general education curriculum, accountability for students in out-of-district settings, transition, response to intervention, alternative assessment, certification for special educators, and alternative schools.

In addition to the resources of CASE and NASDE, training in leadership should include an introduction to the U.S. Department of Education and, in particular, the Office of Special Education Programs, which provides assistance to states for children from birth through age 21. Most helpful are their Regional Resource Centers. These centers offer consultation, information services, technical assistance, training, and product development, as well as other activities.

In the resource guide published by the New York City Task Force for Quality Inclusive Education, recommended practices for administrators are summarized as follows:

- Create an inviting, positive, accepting school climate.
- Visit and interact frequently in classrooms and around the school.

- Provide up-to-date information, resources, materials and current IEP data.
- Offer incentives and credits.
- Allow input into planning and scheduling.
- Provide common planning time for coteachers or collaborative teachers.
- Manage availability and training of substitutes.
- Schedule in-service training and encourage professional development.
- Recommend the selection of colleagues.
- Support the [child study] team or CSE (Committee of Special Education).
- Intervene personally in serious behavior situations.
- Be knowledgeable about education of students with disabilities (Zeeman, 2008, p. 28).

These are some of the skill areas that should be included in any graduate program preparing school psychologists for leadership roles. The extent to which the director of special services becomes personally involved in any of the aforementioned tasks, depends, in part, upon the size of the district and the population with IEPs. In large districts, the director must also learn to select, assign, and manage his or her assistants and area coordinators.

CASE ILLUSTRATIONS

In a suburban/urban school district in central New Jersey, a school psychologist had served the district for over 20 years, in different settings, including both elementary and high school. During that time he had established a reputation as a knowledgeable and caring individual who was supportive of his colleagues and enjoyed the affection and respect of students and parents. He was a model of collegiality in his interactions with teachers and other members of the child study team. And although the interests of the students are always paramount in reaching decisions, the opinions and feelings of his peers were also given significant weight. In his 21st year in the district, he applied for and was appointed to the position of supervisor of special education for Grades 6 through 12, and his supervisory responsibilities included both the special education faculty and the CST, one at the middle school and one at the high school. Since this was a newly created position, he soon discovered that the teachers were not complying with many school directives and even some board of education policies and that several of his former colleagues on the child study team were behind in their paperwork and therefore out of compliance in terms of a variety of responsibilities. Soon after assuming the position, this former school psychologist held a joint meeting with both the teachers and the CST members in which he outlined their responsibilities and informed them that everything needed to be in compliance with school directives and state guidelines. A deadline was issued.

The response of both teachers and team members was immediate. They felt betrayed and saw their new supervisor as someone who no longer valued them as professionals. They were angered by the lack of consultation and resented the fact that the issues of concern were addressed to a large group rather than to each person individually. This initial meeting set the adversarial tone that plagued the department for the next several years. During that time, there were numerous grievances filed through the education association, as well as both formal and informal complaints made to the supervisor's superiors. The situation ended only when the psychologist/ supervisor chose to retire.

The lesson here is clear. There was a demonstrated need to address management issues that had been neglected by the staff. The failure to address them in a way that was congruent with the belief system that had come to be shared among department members caused a backlash that ultimately was a detriment to the functioning of the group in offering the best possible services to students and their parents. The supervisor was seen as the quintessential bureaucrat for whom correctly completing paperwork was the ultimate goal, not the welfare of students. Although the characterization was unfair, it was the inevitable result of the psychologist's failure to realize that the behaviors that had been so successful in his former role were equally important in his new one.

When one coauthor, a school psychologist, served as director of pupil services in a suburban K-12 New Jersey district, he was appointed interim superintendent of schools for 8 months. The very first decision was how to address the faculty on the opening day of school that fall. Obvious traditional choices were preparation for the new state and district testing programs, curricular initiatives, building construction, college admissions, transportation issues, changes in board policies, and others. However, a school leader whose identity is as school psychologist should bring something different to the table. That entire first meeting was devoted to an introduction of the aforementioned invitational education. Audio-visual materials included a large chart on stage illustrating the basic principles taught by John M. Novak and William Watson Purkey (2001). This chart was designed so that it could be moved and circulated from one school lobby to another. The five assumptions of Invitational Education were presented: (a) respect: people are valuable, able, and responsible and should be treating accordingly; (b) trust: education is a cooperative, collaborative activity; (c) care: the personal needs for joy and fulfillment in the process of producing something of value; (d) optimism: people possess untapped potential in all areas of human endeavor; (e) intentionality: designing places, policies, processes, and programs by people who are personally and professionally inviting with themselves and others.

All district employees—instructional staff, as well as support staff, business staff, maintenance, and bus drivers—were included that day. They learned that everybody and anything adds to, or subtracts from, the educational process. Every environment, every person should be so "intentionally inviting" as to create a school in which each adult and each student develops intellectually, socially, physically, and emotionally. Feedback from the message of this opening presentation was genuinely positive. An atmosphere and tone were set that carried over to the first weeks and months of the semester.

A current, most relevant example of the need for leadership training is the movement in school psychology emphasizing response to intervention (RTI). RTI is a systems approach within schools to early identification of academic and behavioral difficulties, providing tiered levels of support and closely monitoring pupil progress. The four-phase model of Adelman and Taylor (1997) as described in Glover and DiPerna (2007) describes how RTI may be implemented in a school:

> Creating readiness refers to an increase in the motivation and capability of key stakeholders to develop an organizational climate that is receptive to change. Initial implementation refers to sequenced implementation of systemic changes and provision of necessary support to involved stakeholders. Institutionalizing new approaches refers to a change in system policies and practices to maintain and sustain the implemented reforms, and ongoing evaluation and renewal refers to the development of stakeholders' capacity to adapt and engage in problem solving to refine systematic changes needed. (p. 534)

The message is that the school psychologist in a leadership role must be trained to inspire a healthy organizational climate and system change, implement reforms, and evaluate results. The article goes on to state that a "leadership team assumes primary responsibility for coordinating the change process" (Glover and DiPerna, 2007, p. 531).

SUMMARY AND CONCLUSIONS

In summary, school psychology university faculty should include training in administration and leadership. This includes practical information about laws, regulations, rights, and practices; resources, local, state, and national professional associations, governmental agencies, reaching out to colleagues and both theoretical knowledge and experiential/practical training in dimensions of leadership. The latter includes, for example, how to use persuasive powers to guide a group, motivating others, responding to needs, gaining respect, communicating effectively, winning confidence, promoting shared vision, leading by example, recognizing and rewarding success, ethics, having a strategic vision, and being able to recognize one's own faults and plan for self-improvement.

As Sergiovanni (2005) stated, "the heartbeats of leadership in schools are strengthened when word and deed are one" (p. 112). Authenticity, which is so important to leadership in general, has an increased significance in terms of psychologists serving in leadership roles. In addition to the skill set that is essential in overseeing a program, or aspect of a program, that addresses students with special needs, the school psychologist/supervisor must model the behaviors that are intrinsic to his or her training.

RESOURCES

Donaldson, G. A. (2001). *Cultivating leadership in schools: Connecting people, purpose, and practice.* New York: Teachers College.
In this study Donaldson examined the relationship between transformational and instructional leadership. The sample consisted of 24 schools, 8 elementary, 8 middle, and 8 high schools. The study found that although transformational leadership is an essential component of effective instructional leadership, its effect on student achievement is greatly enhanced when combined with shared instructional leadership.

Novak, J. M., & Purkey, W. W. (2001). *Invitational education.* Bloomington, IN: Phi Delta Kappa Educational Foundation.
John Novak and William Watson Purkey have written an invaluable tool for school psychologists in their roles as systems managers, organizational change agents, and leaders. Invitational education enumerates practices to improve communication in schools and school districts and is based upon self-concept theory. This *fastback* is an ideal concise summary of the more extensive material in their many texts and journal publications. It teaches the principles of collaboration, cooperation, respect, optimism, strategies for change and managing conflict.

Senge, P. M. (1990). *The fifth discipline.* New York: Doubleday.
Peter Senge has introduced five disciplines as the basic means of building "learning organizations" (as opposed to traditional, authoritarian "controlling organizations"). Three of these disciplines deal with individuals, two are group-oriented. Senge himself states that these disciplines "might just as well be called the leadership disciplines" as "those who excel in these areas will be the natural leaders of learning organizations" (p. 359). In discussing the discipline of team learning, Senge stressed personal mastery, shared vision, dialogue, and discussion as being essential elements to the success of any organization.

Sergiovanni, T. J. (1984). *Handbook for effective department leadership* (2nd ed.). Boston: Allyn and Bacon.
Thomas Sergiovanni is an acknowledged leader in the field of supervision and best practice. His approach incorporates the thinking of Peter Drucker, Abraham Maslow, Max Weber, and other educational and business

management innovators in the field of educational leadership. By delving into the personal side of leadership, he demonstrates how to survive educational politics while incorporating compelling management ideas that address professional goals as well as personal ambitions. The strength of his work is evidenced by a comprehensive and definitive treatment of organizational as well as administrative leadership, particularly in the realm of understanding power and how to use it.

REFERENCES

Adelman, H. S., & Taylor, L. (1997). Toward a scale-up model for replicating new approaches to schooling. *Journal of Educational and Psychological Consultation, 8*, 197–230.

Alderfer, C. P. & Guzzo, R. A. (1979). Life experiences and adults' enduring strength of desires in organizations. *Administrative Science Quarterly, 24*(3), 347–361.

Blackbourn, J. M., Papasan, B., Vinson, T. & Blackbourn, R. (2000). Leadership of the new millennium: Lessons from Deming, Glasser, and Graves. *National Forum of Educational Administration and Supervision Journal, 17E*(4).

Canadian Coalition of Community-Based Employability Training. (2008) *Leadership.* Retrieved January 4, 2008, from http://cccbt-ccocde.savie.ca.

Cherryholmes, C. H. (1988). *Power and criticism.* New York: Teachers College Press.

Council of Administrators of Special Education. (n.d.) *About us.* Retrieved December 10, 2007 from http://www.casecec.org/about.htm

Deal, T. E. & Peterson, K. D. (1994). *The leadership paradox.* San Francisco: Jossey-Bass.

Donaldson, G. A. (2001). *Cultivating leadership in schools: Connecting people, purpose, and practice.* New York: Teachers College.

Flores, M. A. (2004). The impact of school culture and leadership on new teachers' learning in the workplace. *International Journal of Leadership in Education, 7*(4), 297–318.

Glasser, W. (1990). *The quality school: Managing students without coercion.* New York: Harper and Row.

Glasser, W. (1994). *The control theory manager.* New York: Harper and Row.

Glover, T. A. & DiPerna, J. C. (2007). Service delivery for response to intervention: Core components and directions for future research. *School Psychology Review, 36*(4), 526–540.

Gordon, J. & Patterson, J. A. (2006). School leadership in context: narratives of practice and possibility" *International Journal of Leadership in Education, 9*(3), 205–228.

Jay, A. B. & McGovern, J. (2007). Not just a manager anymore. *National Staff Development Council, 28*(4), 51–54.

Kouzes, J. M. & Posner, B. Z. (1995). *The leadership challenge: How to keep getting extraordinary things done in organizations.* New York: Jossey-Bass.

MacNeil, A. & Yelvington, M. (2005). *The principalship: Manager to leader.* Retrieved October 22, 2007, from http://cnx.org/content/m12924/1.2

National Association of State Directors of Special Education, Inc. (n.d.). *Mission Statement*. Retrieved December 10, 2007, from http://www.nasdse.org/AboutNASDSE/MissionStatement/tabid/405/Default.aspx

National Association of School Psychologists. (2004). *NASP position statement on supervision in school psychology*. Retrieved October 22, 2007, from http://www.NASPonline.org/about_NASP/pp_supervision.aspx

Novak, J. M., & Purkey, W. W. (2001). *Invitational education*. Bloomington, IN: Phi Delta Kappa Educational Foundation.

Purkey, W. W., & Novak, J. M. (1996). *Inviting school success: A self-concept approach to teaching, learning and democratic practice* (3rd ed.). Belmont, CA: Wadsworth.

Senge, P. M. (1990). *The fifth discipline*. New York: Doubleday.

Sergiovanni, T. J. (1984). *Handbook for effective leadership* (2nd ed.). Boston: Allyn and Bacon.

Sergiovanni, T. J. (2005). The virtues of leadership. *The Educational Forum, 69*(2), 112–123.

Tucker, A. (1981). *Chairing the academic department*. Washington, DC: American Council on Education.

Ullrich, R. A. & Wieland, G. F. (1980). *Organization theory and design*. Homewood, IL: Richard D. Irwin, Inc.

Waker, S. G. (1983). The motivational foundations of political belief systems: A re-analysis of operation code construct. *International Studies Quarterly, 27*(2), 179–202.

Yoon, J. S., & Gilchrist, J. (2003). Elementary teachers' perceptions of "administrative support" in working with disruptive and aggressive students. *Education, 123*, 564–569.

Zeeman, R. (2008) Administrative support of inclusive practices. In D. J. Connor (Ed.), *Supporting inclusive classrooms: A resource*. New York: NYC Task Force for Quality Inclusive Schooling.

Part III

Training for assessment and evidence-based practice

10 Culture and psychoeducational assessment

Cognition and achievement

Yuma I. Tomes

The accurate assessment of children's functioning continues to be a critical concern to educators and especially school psychologists. A National Association of School Psychologists (NASP) survey revealed that school psychologists spend as much as one half (or more) of their professional time on assessment (NASP, n.d.). School psychologists are considered the gatekeepers of special education. In order to gain admittance into the special programs, most school psychologists use a discrepancy model between a student's cognitive and achievement abilities, although changes are on the horizon, including response to intervention (RTI). Cognitive abilities were defined as the intellectual processing of students, whereas achievement abilities focused on academic skill sets; however, as the landscape of the United States is vastly changing, so is the significance (or lack thereof) of traditional psychoeducational assessment. Another reason for this shift is the growing realization that traditional norm-referenced assessment, despite early indication to the contrary, has limited utility for teachers and others involved in delivering instruction to children (Chittooran & Miller, 1998). Clearly, findings of studies (Dolan, 1999) suggest that the consideration of students, especially students of color, as a referral for a psychoeducational assessment should take into account that particular's child's cognitive style, family expectations, and background, as well as specific classroom behaviors. "An awareness of the attitudes of the child's family towards schooling, academic achievement, school attendance and school completion is necessary in order to account for factors outside the classroom that may be influencing the child's learning" (Dolan, 1999, p. 70).

INTRODUCTION

Although many advances have been made in the field of assessment, the fundamentals have remained the same. Assessment, regardless of cognitive or achievement, "is a process of gathering information used in screening, diagnosing, and determining eligibility, program planning and service delivery, and monitoring progress during treatment or intervention" (Vance &

Awadh, 1998, p. 1). At this juncture in the history of school psychology, it is difficult to say what constitutes best practices when conducting psycho-educational assessment with culturally and linguistically diverse students, because there are extreme varieties in presenting difficulties. This may be especially true for cases involving linguistic minority children who struggle to master the dominant language.

BACKGROUND

The social sciences illustrate, partially, one's set of philosophical premises or worldviews, on the basis of theory, methodology, and practice (Patton, 1992). Moreover, Patton (1992) states that the worldviews one possess help to shape a variety of areas, such as logic of inquiry, modes of knowledge, methods of organizing, and verification of knowledge. Nestled within these areas is the significance of culture. Since the worldviews of assessment share values with European and European American developers of intelligence tests, it is not surprising that this orientation assumes both a hierarchal understanding of ability within limited constructs of intelligence and also the notion that intelligence tests measure true intelligence.

A significant indicator of intelligence and cognitive abilities as measured by assessments is language. Language acquisition and development has been connected to intelligence and is assessed in numerous cognitive assessment measures, such as the Wechsler Intelligence Scale for Children IV (WISC-IV) and the Woodcock-Johnson III—Cognitive. Language, just like intelligence, is shaped by cultural experiences of the specific social group that uses it. Since language is typically used as a vehicle for securing information on a test, proficiency in standard English becomes a basic criterion (Gopaul-McNicol, Reid, & Wisdom, 1998).

The major goal of this chapter is to give school psychologists, trainers, and other professionals who work with students of color meaningful and technically sound information regarding psychoeducational assessments. School psychologists are frequently called on to provide valid and reliable assessment data for students who have not been progressing as minimally expected or on par with peers who receive similar classroom exposure to their school system's grade level curriculum. Standardized measures of intelligence continue to be frequently used by school psychologists in their effort to provide meaningful information to educators and parents (Flanagan & Ortiz, 2002). During meetings where school psychologists share results of their psychoeducational evaluations, they are often urged to provide only information regarding intellectual functioning in the form of a global score, such as the Full Scale Intelligence Quotient (IQ) score of the WISC-IV (Glutting, Watkins, Konold, & McDermott, 2006). Global score information is of limited value for those needed specific information, recommendations, and consultations about how to provide effective instructional support for referred students. Moreover, global scores do not provide information regarding referred students' individual strengths and needs (McCloskey & Maerlender, 2005).

Through the use of the psychoeducational assessments that yield global scores, it has been generally reported that as a group, Black students consistently score, on average, 15 points lower than White (Caucasian) students (Harris & Llorente, 2005). When adjusted for differences in socioeconomic status (SES), the trend is that Asian Americans score 3 points higher than White Americans on standardized tests of intelligence, and Hispanic Americans score somewhere within the 15 point differential between Whites and Blacks. The differences in global intelligence test scores among racially or ethnically different groups has led to rationalizations for minimizing equitable opportunities and interventions that could assist students in closing achievement gaps (Berliner, 1991). The disparity of scores and perceptions of unfairness pertaining to various ethnic groups of students has resulted in court actions to minimize the use of intelligence tests within the schools in some states (Wesson, 2000). Additional concerns regarding the practical utility of comprehensive intelligence tests in terms of time involved for administration, scoring, and interpretation, as well as efficacy for treatment outcomes, have also led to a decrease in reliance on intelligence tests in some school systems across the United States (Reschly & Grimes, 2002). This has raised voices of concern among school psychologist practitioners, researchers, and others who would also use the information garnered from psychological and educational testing to guide their instructional recommendations, consultations, and overall treatment efforts.

Influences on contemporary practices and the current concerns about intelligence testing across ethnic or racially different population groups have been present since the early 1900s, when the recently translated Stanford-Binet began to be used as a screening instrument to keep "mentally defective" persons out of the United States (Schultz & Schultz, 2004). During this time, it was believed that intelligence could be inherited, and some sought to limit immigrant populations that tested within the mentally defective range because of their perceived limited ability to contribute positively to the culture and society within the United States. The data amassed from non-English-speaking Russian, Jewish, Italian, and Hungarian immigrants led to federal legislation restricting the immigration of population groups assumed to be inferior in intelligence. It was already assumed that Black population groups were inferior in intelligence, and with the data from World War I testing, it appeared that Black, Mediterranean, and Latin American groups were intellectually inferior to Northern European immigrant and White population groups acculturated within the United States (Schultz & Schultz, 2004).

One well-known finding is that IQ scores have been increasing across the populations of Austria, Belgium, Britain, Canada, China, France, Germany, Japan, Norway, Denmark, and the United States for about 60 years

(Flynn, 1999). The sometimes sharp gains in scores have corresponded with the changes worldwide from an agriculture-based economy to one of industrialization. Restandardization or renorming of often-used intelligence tests such as the Stanford-Binet and Wechsler series has become necessary to address the phenomenon (Sattler, 2001). Mean scores and standard deviations of the contemporary standardization sample, reflected by the most recent data from the census bureau, often with oversampling of minority participants, must be reset to 100 and 15, respectively, for the entire test. IQ tests are particularly prone to schooling effects, as scores tend to improve with learning, including structured school and other environmental or ecological experiences (Kaufman, 1994).

PROFESSIONAL ROLES AND FUNCTIONS

Competency

According to Ogbu (1988), intelligence tests measure very distinct, Eurocentric cognitive skills, specific to Western culture. As a result, the more limited a cognitive assessment test is in its ability to take into consideration diversities of language, the more likely it will be inappropriate for test takers who are not part of the dominant culture in which it was normed. Several cognitive assessment measures have increased the ethnic and cultural norming group, but still many lack inclusivity when it comes to language diversity.

The competency necessary to sufficiently assess students coming from multicultural backgrounds goes beyond the actual test administration; more importantly, it extends to the test construction and the training of the practitioner. In 1988, The Joint Committee on Testing Practices created the Code of Fair Testing Practices in Education (Table 10.1) addressed the problems of test development and selection, but limited gains have been made in devising specific tests for specific populations (Vance & Awadh, 1998). As a result, tests still remain inherently biased to diverse population such as Blacks, Latinos, Laotians, Asian Americans, and others. Ponterotto and Alexander (1996) suggested that "a culture-bound (or biased) assessment device in the hands of a well-trained multicultural practitioner is preferred over a culture-fair instrument in the hands of a poorly trained (multicultural) practitioner" (p. 652). Examination of factor invariance is one of several different techniques to evaluate bias and determine whether tests measure the same constructs with similar fidelity across examinee subgroups (Watkins & Canivez, 2001).

Training standards

In order to develop the requisite cross-cultural competencies needed for administering and interpreting cognitive and academic measurements,

Table 10.1 Code of Fair Testing Practices in Education

Developing/selecting appropriate tests

1. Define the purpose for testing in the population to be tested. Then, select a test for that purpose and that population based on a thorough review of the available information.
2. Investigate potential useful sources of information, in addition to test scores, to corroborate the information provided by the tests.
3. Become familiar with how and when the test was developed, normed, and marketed.
4. Read independent evaluations of the test and if possible, alternative measures. Look for evidence to support the claims of test developers.
5. Select and use only those tests for which the skills needed to administer the test and interpret scores correctly are available.

Interpretation of test scores

1. Obtain information about the scale used for reporting scores, the characteristics of any norms or comparison group(s), and the limitation of these scores.
2. Interpret scores taking into account any major differences between the norms or comparison group(s) and the actual test takers. Also, take into account any differences in test administration practices of familiarity with specific questions in the test.
3. Avoid using tests for purposes not specifically recommended by the test developer unless evidence is obtained to support the alternate use.
4. Explain how any passing scores were set and gather evidence to support the appropriateness of the scores.
5. Obtain evidence to show the test is meeting its intended purpose(s).

Striving for fairness

1. Evaluate the procedures used by test developers to avoid potentially insensitive content or language.
2. Review the performance of test takers of different race, gender, and ethnic background when samples of sufficient size are available. Evaluate the extent to which performance differences may have been caused by inappropriate characteristics of the tests.
3. When necessary and feasible, use appropriately modified forms of tests or administration procedures for test takers with handicapping conditions. Interpret standard norms with care in the light of the modifications made.

Informing examinees

1. When a test is optional, provide test takers or their parents/guardians with information to help them judge whether the test should be taken or whether an available alternative should be used.
2. Provide test takers information about coverage of the test, types of question formats, directions, and appropriate test taking strategies. Strive to make such information equally available to all test takers.
3. Provide test takers or their parents/guardians with information describing rights test takers may have to obtain copies of tests and completed answer sheets, retake tests, or have tests rescored or scores canceled.
4. Tell test takers or their parents/guardians how long scores will be kept on file and indicate to whom and under what circumstances they will or will not be released.
5. Describe the procedures that test takers or their parents/guardians many use to register complaints and have problems resolved.

school psychologists need to be well informed about a range of topics, including, but not limited to, "language development, second-language acquisition, nonbiased assessment techniques, culturally sensitive environmental and individual evaluation procedures, and culturally appropriate intervention strategies" (Rogers, 1998, p. 365). Moreover, there are three distinct areas in which school psychology graduate students should be trained regarding the use of cognitive or academic achievement measures. School psychologist trainees should (a) have extensive course work and training in the construction, selection, use and interpretation of tests (especially as they relate to students of color or linguistically diverse students), (b) develop a knowledge base in cross-cultural psychology to be able to provide culturally sensitive and meaningful assessment service, and (c) have firsthand exposure to and supervised casework experience with racial, ethnic, and linguistic minority children during course work, practica, and internships—no exceptions.

Studies by Derr-Minneci and Shapiro (1992) have indicated that the conditions under which curriculum-based measurements (CBMs) are administered have an important influence on student outcomes, as do the conditions of administration of cognitive assessment. "Various discrepancies that occurred between the setting, tester, and task demand conditions across reading levels ... implies the conditions of curriculum-based measurement may affect oral reading rate data whether students are low, average, or high readers" (p. 13).

Although it is clear that no currently published cognitive or academic assessment instrument is appropriate for all students, there are methods to ensure that school psychologists employ the best professional judgment regarding assessment instrument selection. According to Rogers (1998), tests should be analyzed with respect to the following characteristics:

1. Does the test contain an adequate and representative standardized sample?
2. Have the test authors employed a minority review panel and/or statistical item analysis procedures to detect biased items?
3. Is the reliability and validity of the scale established and documented?
4. Are diverse racial/ethnic groups represented in the test materials through pictures and other illustrations?
5. Does the test contain sample or practice items?
6. Is a parallel or alternate form available?
7. Is there empirical evidence supporting the use of the instrument with English as a second language students?
8. Has a Spanish version of the test been developed and properly normed?

Once these areas have been sufficiently addressed, the assessment instrument may be deemed appropriate for use.

Another area, less researched and less well known by school psychologists but equally important, is when to test a student. A lot of training programs operate under the assumption the best time to test a student is in the morning. Given the difficulty that can be presented by finding the student or finding time to administer a cognitive or psychological measure, school psychologists desire to work with the student immediately, whenever he or she is available; however, Dunn, Griggs, and Price (1993) suggested that Mexican American elementary and secondary students preferred learning new and/or difficult material in the afternoon rather than early or late morning. This preference is complementary to when intellectual activities such as thinking, problem-solving, and debating are best performed: that is, in the afternoon. Moreover, other research (Tomes, 2009) has supported the idea that comprehension increases throughout the day as reading speeds decrease. Therefore, it is incumbent upon school psychologists to exhibit professional judgment as to when a psychoeducational assessment should be administered.

PEDAGOGICAL AND SUPERVISORY CONSIDERATIONS

Assessment process

Assessment practices are often poorly understood or confused with run-of-the-mill expectations. For a school psychologist, clinical skills require more than the ability to follow the appropriate directions when administering a test. Best practices mandate necessary skills such as rapport building, positive interactions, test interpretation, inference drawing, interviewing, and observation (Vance & Awadh, 1998).

School psychology students are taught that best practices in psychoeducational assessment include comprehensive and more than one set of valid evaluation measures. Out of a variety of measures, the school psychology student must choose an appropriate measure and administer it in a nondiscriminatory manner that is considerate of the elementary/middle/high school student's individual communication abilities. Prior to assessing a student, the school psychologist in training should identify the school-age student's specific disability and ensure that his or her physical condition and health status have been examined. According to Magyar, Pandolfi, and Peterson (2007), "this information guides the evaluator in the selection of tests, the process of assessment, and any special accommodations used to make the assessment results more meaningful and useful for developing interventions" (p. 334).

Tests once were thought to be biased if scores from one group were higher or lower than scores from other groups, even if the factors were invariant across examinee subgroups. This standard for judging test bias is seriously flawed and has been replaced by an examination of forms of error, especially two possible contributors: systematic error and random error (Edwards & Oakland, 2006, p. 358).

There is considerable variation in the reasons for carrying out psychoeducational evaluations. Regardless, there are psychometrically sound and valid assessment techniques that should be followed: (a) the most reliable, valid, and appropriate techniques should be selected for use during the evaluation; (b) bilingual students should be assessed separately in both languages with instruments that are technically sound in each language; (c) parents may be included in the evaluation process (through a two-way mirror); and (d) testing-of-limits procedures should be employed as necessary (Rogers, 1998).

Cognitive assessment measures

The Kaufman Assessment Battery for Children, Second Edition (KABC-II), is a test of cognitive ability designed for use with children between the ages of 3 and 18. The broader theoretical base, more inclusive standardization, and the ability to individualize the test make it an instrument of choice all cognitive assessment applications. Like the original Kaufman Assessment Battery for Children, but with more flexibility, the second edition more fairly assesses children of different backgrounds and with diverse problems, with small score differences between ethnic groups. The KABC-II subtests are designed to minimize verbal instructions and responses, giving the school psychologist in-depth data with less filtering due to language. Moreover, test items contain little cultural content, so children of diverse backgrounds are assessed more fairly; however, there is cultural unfairness.

With the KABC-II, the school psychologist can choose the Cattell-Horn-Carroll model for children from a mainstream cultural language background, or, if crystallized ability would not be a fair indicator of the child's cognitive ability, the school psychologist may choose the Luria model, which excludes verbal ability. Administering the same subtests on four or five ability scales and then interpreting the results on the basis of the chosen model yields global scores that are highly valid minimizes differences between ethnic group comparisons.

The WISC-IV is probably the most well known and commonly used intellectual measurement by school psychologists (Tomes, 2008). The WISC-IV, given to persons between the ages of 6:0 and 16:11, provides four index scores that reflect different abilities, important in the expression of cognitive behavior in the classroom and beyond. The profile of the four domains (verbal comprehension, perceptual reasoning, working memory, and processing speed) represents key clinical indicators of the cognitive strengths and weaknesses important to assessing learning disabilities and other cognitive abilities. Unlike the KABC-II, the WISC-IV is much more language based, but it also has a somewhat diversified normative sample, stratified on age, sex, parent education level, geographic region, and race/ethnicity. With a heavy emphasis on left-brain activity, the WISC-IV may underestimate the true cognitive ability of a student, especially from a nondominant culture background (Tomes, 2008). More empirical research is being conducted by neuropsychologists supporting the creativity of right brain functions in varied populations and how these functions are not being fairly assessed with traditional cognitive assessments. Moreover, current research is yielding results that language development may be more of a right brain function than initially thought (Bryan & Hale, 2001).

Other tests that are considered more culturally fair cognitive assessments are the Comprehensive Test of Nonverbal Intelligence; Differential Ability Scales, Second Edition; Test of Nonverbal Intelligence, Third Edition; Leiter International Performance Scale, Revised; Universal Nonverbal Intelligence Test; and Process Assessment of the Learner, Second Edition.

Academic achievement assessment

Depending on the reason for the referral and the characteristics of the referred individual, the school psychologist will need to make a decision about the scope and type of academic achievement measure should be conducted. As the primary purpose of many academic assessments is to gain meaningful information about the student's skills and abilities in order to inform instruction, norm-referenced test (often used by school psychologists) may not be the best choice for a given child in a particular situation. Research findings, as noted by Rogers (1998), suggest that standardized reading achievement tests and the actual curriculum may be seriously mismatched, in that the standardized tests do not cover material that students are taught in a classroom. Regardless, for situations that are better served by a standardized measure, here are some recommendations.

The Kaufman Test of Educational Achievement (KTEA), second edition, is an individually administered battery that provides the school psychologist with a flexible, thorough assessment of academic skills in reading, math, written language, and oral language. The KTEA is used with children, adolescents, and adults between the ages of 4 years 6 months and 25 (comprehensive form) and 4 years 6 months and 90+ (brief form). The standardization group for the first edition of the KTEA approximated the 1983–1984 U.S. Census Bureau data in terms of proportionately representing all groups. The second edition continues to proportionally include representation from Whites, Blacks, Latino(s), American Indians, Alaskan, Asians, and Pacific Islanders. The comprehensive form provides composite scores for students in Grade 1 and above in reading, math, written language, and oral language. A comprehensive achievement composite can be computed for all students. Also, six additional subtests assess reading related skills and give valuable diagnostic information; however, like its cognitive assessment predecessor, KABC-II, there is no complete Spanish version.

Culture and academic achievement

Although standardized psychoeducational achievement tests purport to measure the acquired knowledge of students throughout his/her formal education, paradoxically such test actually measure grammatical knowledge that has been usually been acquired through familial and community influences (Gopaul-McNicol et al., 1998). Ebonics, for example, offers a parody of how a student may perform poorly on a standardized measure but possess sufficient to excellent language and cognitive skills. Wolfram (1990) suggested that the distance between students' everyday dialect and the language system used on standardized psychoeducational assessments is directly proportional to the likelihood that task interference due to language differences will negatively affect those students' test performance. Students who use Ebonics, because of dialectal rules, may become confused in employing techniques to differentiate between words in their pronunciation: for example, "mild" and "mile" are pronounced the same because of the phonological rule in Ebonics that calls for the elimination of terminal consonants. As Gopaul-McNicol et al. found, "when children whose spoken dialect is Ebonics ... they are likely to confuse the Standard English form for the Ebonics one or vice-versa" (p. 18).

RTI

The reauthorization of the Individuals with Disabilities Educational Improvement Act of 2004 included provisions for alternative evidenced-based practices such as RTI. Wodrich, Spencer, and Daley (2006) proposed a series of assumptions that should guide the combining of RTI and psychoeducational assessment when determining the need for special education services for students. Moreover, Wodrich et al. felt that a thorough evaluation at Tier III includes an examination of personal skills and abilities with standardized instrument that yields information on how to educate a student. As it relates to working with students who are mentally retarded, some school psychologists may contend that specific learning disability (SLD) and mild mental retardation (MMR) are important; however, conducting a comprehensive evaluation on a mildly mentally retarded student is not necessary for MMR identification. This assumption may be less accurate, because information gathered from a cognitive assessment may yield the intellectual potential/ability of a student who has scored below the MMR range (Wodrich et al.).

Another assumption addressed by Wodrich et al. (2006) involves using RTI alone in differentiating slow learners from students with SLD. Individuals with an IQ score between 70 and 85 with concomitant academic levels define SLD (Oehler-Stinnett, Stinnett, Wesley, & Anderson, 1988). Although many school psychologist may feel that students who fall through the cracks are good candidates for a RTI approach, subsequently leading to a SLD classification, limited research has been conducted. Moreover, does the RTI system help or hurt students from minority backgrounds? Currently, students of color are overrepresented in the special education system, and allowing these students to receive services under the RTI model may exacerbate overrepresentation (Healy, Vanderwood, & Edelston, 2005). Caution is certainly expected with using RTI in isolation, as it purports to measure true response to intervention over a period of time yet may fail in being comparable to the information yielded by cognitive assessment.

According to Fuchs, Fuchs, and Compton (2004), a key assumption underlying RTI is that the assessment process used for the identification of disabilities is valid. CBM is heralded as being truly authentic and extremely valid, as it yields data that are directly relevant to classroom instruction. However, CBM is only effective as the curriculum it is based on. If a curriculum is culturally inappropriate, then inequitable outcomes will be obtained (Green, McIntosh, Cook-Morales, & Robinson-Zanartu, 2005). In addition, although there has been sufficient evidence to substantiate the validity and utility of CBM, potential methodological concerns in CBM administration are less conspicuous (Colon & Kranzler, 2006).

Alternative assessments

Despite the implementation of "nonbiased" assessment practices in many educational settings, students from culturally and linguistically diverse backgrounds are being misdiagnosed by school psychologists, speech pathologists, and other professionals in special education (Gersten & Woodward, 1994). The three major characteristics of the dynamic assessment model that are appealing to school psychologists are test, teach, and retest. The theoretical grounding for dynamic assessment is Vygotsky's notion of the "zone of proximal development" (Pena, Iglesias, & Lidz, 2001). Assumptions of dynamic assessment as suggested by Reschly and Robinson-Zanartu (2000) include the following: (a) the aptitude is not static, but modifiable; (b) the assessment can yield both targets and process of intervention; and (c) authentic assessment should be dynamic in nature and sensitive to modifiability. Like Vygotsky, school psychologists should not rely solely on estimation of the student's independent performance without attention to the student's ability to profit from instructional interaction with more experienced collaborators, which is directly aligned with RTI. A study conducted by Pena et al. (2001) yielded findings consistent with other dynamic assessment studies, in that children from nonmainsteam groups improve their standardized test scores when given short-term mediated learning experiences. Thus, the application of dynamic assessment to language assessment is promising for students from diverse language backgrounds.

PSYCHOEDUCATIONAL ASSESSMENT AND REPORT

School psychologists should be trained to assist their school systems in two important ways: by educating and upgrading the skills of those who provide services to minority children and by participating in school-based prereferral teams. When school psychologists are taught how to take an active role on prereferral teams, problem solving is emphasized, teachers expectations are researched, and psychoeducational assessments may be minimized. If a determination is made to continue with the assessment, the school psychologist will need to conduct record reviews, environmental assessments, and language proficiency assessment (for linguistically diverse students). When conducting a review of the records, particular attention should be given to school history, interruptions in schooling, language(s) used in former classrooms, history of retentions, and curricula the student has been exposed to over time (Rogers, 1998). A simple environmental assessment includes a systematic analysis of the characteristics of the classroom (e.g., seating arrangement), school, home, and community environments in which the student functions. Next, appropriate cognitive, academic, and/or alternative assessments are administered. After the necessary assessments have been administered, the multidisciplinary team will reconvene with the necessary participants and discuss the student's abilities according to the assessments.

The final component is a written document identifying the student's strengths and weaknesses based upon the measures used in the assessment and through observations conducted. Also, the school psychologists should include both successful and unsuccessful interventions attempted by the teacher. The psychoeducational assessment report should indicate aspects such as the language spoken at home/school/during assessment, any deviations in standardization during the administration of norm-referenced instruments, and any alternative assessment used with explanation.

CASE ILLUSTRATION

"Sally," a 7-year- and 3 months-old Mexican student with a suspected disability, has been struggling in her second grade classroom. She is a very verbal student and shows interest in other students. Moreover, she appears to enjoy all the subjects taught, but her conceptualization of topics covered is sketchy, at best. Although she understands numbers, she is not able to subtract well and often miss-adds with double digits. During language arts, she will read the first few words of a sentence and then immediately shut down, with little attempt to read the remainder of the sentence. She does possess word attack strategies but still struggles with spelling and recognizing similar words in other passages.

Sally's primary language is English, but Spanish is the dominant language spoken at home. She has good relationships with her two siblings, an older brother and younger sister. As a matter of fact, she often converses with her brother in English in an effort to understand the language better. Sally's parents attempt to help her with any homework, but their English is limited and at times their efforts are met with frustration by Sally. Her parents are concerned with her academic performance at school and have attended a few meetings.

Sally's teacher, Mr. Monroe, began a reading intervention 5 weeks ago, and there has been limited improvement. Concurrently, a math intervention has also begun, and there has been steady improvement. Mr. Monroe is concerned that Sally will fall further behind other same age students and her self-esteem will suffer if she does not receive the necessary supplemental education. He has returned to the prereferral intervention team meeting with his results and is asking the committee to proceed with a full psychoeducational assessment.

On the basis of this presenting information, how would you proceed with any additional data collection or psychoeducational evaluation? What questions do you have, and how would you go about answering them? What specific actions would you take to better understand and address Sally's educational needs? How would you involve the parents and other family members in assisting with Sally's needs? What should your role be on the prereferral team?

SUMMARY AND CONCLUSION

The school learning and performance of all children, and especially children of color, are influenced by complex social, economic, historical, and cultural factors. "Traditional psychoeducational assessments do not adequately consider, nor do they fully account for or adapt to, the nonstandard dialects and cultural experiences that certain test takers bring to the evaluation experience (Gopaul-McNicol et al., 1998, p. 16). Culturally competent practice as a school psychologist means to use culturally sensitive tests, multicultural consultations, appropriate individual/group counseling, and preventions/interventions (Tomes, 2009). Psychoeducational assessments play a major role in clinical and school settings. Moreover, the measurement of various psychological constructs from intelligence to academic achievement play a major role in the assessment of children from varying backgrounds in public and private school settings. As noted by Chittooran and Miller (1998), "The accurate assessment of children's functioning continues to be a critical concern to teachers and school psychologists" (p. 13). Although certain measures, such as the WISC-IV, Woodcock-Johnson III, and others, purport to fairly assess students of all racial/cultural/ethnic backgrounds, the measures still present items of bias, especially in the area of linguistic sensitivity. Psychoeducational evaluators such as school psychologists must be formally introduced to the most current research on areas such as bidialectism, neuropsychology, cognitive styles, and empirically validated taxonomies. Without exposure to these and other areas, it is difficult for school psychologists to accurately assess students beyond traditional psychoeducational methods that may yield more infallible results.

RESOURCES

Floyd, R. G., McCormack, A. C., Ingram, E. L., Davis, A. E., Bergeron, R., & Hamilton, G. (2006). Relations between the Woodcock-Johnson III clinical clusters and measures of executive functions from the Delis-Kaplan executive function system. *Journal of Psychoeducational Assessment, 24,* 303–317.
This empirical study examined the convergent relations between scores from different cluster areas of the Woodcock-Johnson III (WJ III) Test of Cognitive Abilities and measures of executive functions from sample of school-aged children and adults. The study yielded statistically significant results and moderate positive relations across both sampling groups with some measure of executive functioning. In particular, the executive processes cluster, when compared with the other WJ III clinical clusters, demonstrated the strongest relations with measure of executive functions.

Gopaul-McNicol, S., Reid, G., & Wisdom, C. (1998). The psychoeducational assessment of Ebonics speakers: Issues and challenges. *The Journal of Negro Education, 67*(1), 16–24.
This article discusses the traditional standardized assessments poor construct validity in adequately considering and fully accounting for nonstandard dialects and cultural experiences of test takers. In particular, Black Ebonics-speaking students present specific challenges. The authors highlight limitations of popular standardized measures and offer alternatives assessments that yield more accurate results of the student cognitive and academic abilities.

Wodrich, D. L., Spencer, M., & Daley, K. (2006). Combining RTI and psychoeducational assessment: What we must assume to do otherwise. *Psychology in the Schools, 43,* 797–806.
This article discusses joint need of RTI and psychoeducational assessment when determining specific learning disabilities. The dangers of just utilizing one measure places a student at a disadvantage of uncovering academic problems. The authors address assumptions of singular use of RTI and psychoeducational assessments. These assumptions have led to misuse and poor placement of students needing special education services. Moreover, these assumptions have continually led to misclassification of slow learners and ineffective interventions. The article concludes with assumptions regarding the opportunity to learn.

REFERENCES

Berliner, D. C. (1991). Education psychology and pedagogical expertise: New findings and new opportunities for thinking about training. *Educational Psychologist, 26*, 145–155.

Bryan, K. L., & Hale, J. B. (2001). Differential effects of left and right cerebral vascular accidents on language competency. *Journal of International Neuropsychological Society, 7*, 655–664.

Chittooran, M. M., & Miller, T. L. (1998). Informal assessment. In H. B. Vance (Ed.), *Psychological assessment of children: Best practices for school and clinical settings* (2nd ed.). New York: John Wiley & Sons, Inc.

Colon, E. P., & Kranzler, J. H. (2006). Effects of instructions on curriculum-based measurement of reading. *Journal of Psychoeducational Assessment, 24*, 318–328.

Derr-Minneci, T. F., & Shapiro, E. S. (1992). Validating curriculum-based measurement in reading from a behavioral perspective. *School Psychology Quarterly, 7*, 2–16.

Dolan, B. (1999). From the field: Cognitive profiles of First Nations and Caucasian children referred for psychoeducational assessment. *Canadian Journal of School Psychology, 15*, 63–71.

Dunn, R., Griggs, S., & Price, G. (1993). Learning styles of Mexican American and Anglo American elementary school students. *Journal of Multicultural Counseling and Development, 21*, 227–247.

Edwards, O. W., & Oakland, T. D. (2006). Factorial invariance of Woodcock-Johnson III scores for African Americans and Caucasian Americans. *Journal of Psychoeducational Assessment, 24*, 358–366.

Flanagan, D. P., & Ortiz, S. O. (2002). Best practices in intellectual assessment: Future directions. In A. Thomas and J. Grimes (Eds.), *Best practices in school psychology IV* (pp. 1351–1372). Washington, DC: National Association of School Psychologists.

Flynn, J. R. (1999). The discovery of IQ gains over time. *American Psychologist, 54*(1), 5–20.

Fuchs, D., Fuchs, L. S., & Compton, D. L. (2004). Identifying reading disabilities by responsiveness-to-instruction: Specifying measures and criteria. *Learning Disabilities Quarterly, 27*, 216–227.

Gersten, R., & Woodward, J. (1994). The language-minority student and special education: Issues, trends, and paradoxes. *Exceptional Children, 60*, 310–322.

Glutting, J., Watkins, M., Konold, T. R., & McDermott, P. A. (2006). Distinctions without a difference: The utility of observed versus latent factors from the WISC-IV in estimating reading and math achievement on the WIAT-II. *The Journal of Special Education, 40*(2), 103–114.

Gopaul-McNicol, S., Reid, G., & Wisdom, C. (1998). The psychoeducational assessment of Ebonics speakers: Issues and challenges. *The Journal of Negro Education, 67*, 16–20.

Green, T. D., McIntosh, A. S., Cook-Morales, V. J., & Robinson-Zanartu, C. (2005). From old schools to tomorrow's schools: Psychoeducational assessment of African American students. *Remedial and Special Education, 26*, 82–92.

Harris, J. G., & Llorente, A. M. (2005). Cultural considerations in the use of the Wechsler intelligence scale for children (4th ed.). In A. Prifitera, D. H., Saklofske, & L. G. Weiss (Eds.), *WISC-IV clinical use and interpretation: Scientist-practitioner perspectives* (pp. 381–413). San Diego, CA: Elsevier.

Healy, K., Vanderwood, M., & Edelston, D. (2005). Early literacy interventions for English language learners: Support for an RTI model. *California School Psychologist, 10*, 55–63.

Individuals With Disabilities Education Improvement Act of 2004. Pub. L. No. 108–446, 118 Stat. 2647 (2004).

Joint Committe on Testing Practices. (1988). *Code of Fair Testing Practices in Education*. Washington, DC: Author.

Kaufman, J. (1994). White-black and white-Hispanic differences on fluid and crystallized abilities by age across the 11- to 94-year range. *Psychological Reports, 75*, 1279–1288.

Magyar, C. I., Pandolfi, V., & Peterson, C. R. (2007). Psychoeducational assessment. In J. W. Jacobson, J. A. Mulick, & J. Rojahn (Eds.), *Handbook of intellectual and developmental disabilities* (pp. 334–351). New York: Springer.

McCloskey, G., & Maerlender, A. (2005). The WISC-IV integrated. In A. Prifitera, D. Saklofske, & L. Weiss (Eds.). *WISC-IV clinical use and interpretation: Scientist-practitioner perspectives* (pp. 101–149). San Diego, CA: Elsevier.

National Association of School Psychologists. (n.d.). *Home page*. Retrieved June 12, 2008, from http://www.nasponline.org

Oehler-Stinnett, J., Stinnett, T. A., Wesley, A. L., & Anderson, H. N. (1988). The Luria Nebraska Neuropsychological Battery-Children's Revision: Discrimination between learning-disabled and slow-learner children. *Journal of Psychoeducational Assessment, 6*, 24–34.

Ogbu, J. (1988). Human intelligence testing: A cultural-ecological perspective. *National Forum, 68*(2), 23–29.

Patton, J. M. (1992). Assessment and identification of African-American learners with gifts and talents. *Exceptional Children, 59*, 150–159.

Pena, E., Iglesias, A., & Lidz, C. S. (2001). Reducing test bias through dynamic assessment of children's word learning ability. *American Journal of Speech-Language Pathology, 10*, 138–154.

Ponterotto, J. G., & Alexander, C. M. (1996). Assessing the multicultural competence of counselors and clinicians. In L. A. Suzuki, P. Melle, and J. G. Ponterotto (Eds.), *Handbook of multicultural assessment: Clinical, psychological, and educational applications* (pp. 651–672). San Francisco: Jossey-Bass.

Reschly, D. J., & Grimes, J. P. (2002). Best practices in intellectual assessment. In A. Thomas & J. Grimes (Eds.) Best practices in school psychology IV (pp. 1337–1350). Washington, DC: National Association of School Psychologists.

Reschly, D. J., & Robinson-Zanartu, C. (2000). Aptitude tests in educational classification and placement. In G. Goldstein & M. Hersen (Eds.) *Handbook of psychological assessment* (3rd ed. pp. 183–201). Boston: Allyn & Bacon.

Rogers, M. R. (1998). Psychoeducational assessment of culturally and linguistically diverse children and youth. In H. B. Vance (Ed.), *Psychological assessment of children: Best practices for school and clinical settings* (2nd ed. pp. 355–384). New York: John Wiley & Sons.

Sattler, J. M. (2001). *Assessment of children: Cognitive applications* (4th ed.). La Mesa, CA: Jerome Sattler Publisher.

Schultz, D., & Schultz, W. (2004). Cultural competence in psychosocial and psychiatric care: A critical perspective with reference to research and clinical experiences in California, US, Germany. *Social Work in Health Care, 39*, 231–247.

Tomes, Y. I. (2009). Competency in cross-cultural school psychology. In T. Lionetti, E. Snyder, & R. Christner (Eds.) *Building professional competencies in school psychology* (pp. 117–141). New York: Springer.

Tomes, Y. I. (2008). Ethnicity, cognitive styles, and math achievement: Variability within African-American post-secondary students. *Multicultural Perspectives, 10*(1), 17–23.

Vance, H. B., & Awadh, A. M. (1998). Best practices in assessment of children: Issues and trends. In H. Booney Vance (Ed.), *Psychological assessment of children: Best practices for school and clinical settings* (pp. 1–10). New York: John Wiley & Sons, Inc.

Watkins, M. W., & Canivez, G. L. (2001). Longitudinal factor structure of the WISC-III among students with disabilities. *Psychology in the Schools, 38*, 291–298.

Wesson, C. (2000). Substance abuse. In B. Fogel (Ed.), *Synopsis of neuropsychiatry* (pp. 375–404). Philadelphia, PA: Lippincott Williams & Williams Publishers.

Wodrich, D. L., Spencer, M. L., & Daley, K. B. (2006). Combining RTI and psycho-educational assessment: What we must assume to do otherwise. *Psychology in the Schools, 43*(7), 797–806.

Wolfram, W. (1990). *Dialectal differences and testing*. Washington, DC: Center for Applied Linguistics.

Woodcock-Johnson III—Test of Achievement. (n.d.). Retrieved June 18, 2008, from http://www.cps.nova.edu/~cpphelp/WJIII-ACH.html

11 The importance of personality assessment in school psychology training programs

Tammy L. Hughes, Kara E. McGoey, and Patrick Owen

Teaching personality assessment to graduate students is an important part of school psychology training programs and serves to prepare and empower the future school psychologist with valuable skills. When grounded in the normative context of child and adolescent development, personality assessment can help in unique ways to identify delayed or disordered child development for the purpose of providing effective interventions (Knoff, 2003). Skillfully conducted and well-conceived assessment of a child's personality provides important information regarding the child's functioning and can assist in the optimum selection and tailoring of evidence-based interventions (Hughes, Gacono, & Owen, 2007). In a broader context, Dana (2007), Flanagan (2007), and Steadman, Hatch, and Schoenfeld (2001) have pointed out that the school psychology graduate programs that successfully integrate personality assessment skills with behavioral intervention strategies, and do so within the overall context of ecological assessments, will be better equipped to prepare the next generation of school psychologists to provide culturally competent full-service delivery systems.

The purpose of this chapter is to discuss the value of teaching personality assessment in school psychology programs and some of the critical challenges. A brief review of certain historical issues and theoretical debates will be presented, together with some evidence-based research associated with personality assessment measures. A suggested teaching approach and curriculum sequence for personality assessment training will also be provided, as well as two integrated case examples highlighting the usefulness of personality assessment for children in the schools.

OVERVIEW AND HISTORY

In the effort to promote positive development in children, school systems, teachers, parents, mental health professionals, and community members routinely engage in informal evaluations of children's emotional, social, and cognitive functioning (Knoff, 2003). This informal, naturalistic process mirrors in important ways the scope and purpose of the formal assessment of personality; the assessment is typically initiated when a child shows adjustment difficulties that are significant and not readily remedied with the support systems available to the child in his or her school, community, or family.

Although an understanding of the individual through personality assessment practices was formally highlighted during the 1949 Boulder Conference (Childs & Eyde, 2002) and remains integral to comprehensive assessment in current school psychology practice (Steadman, Hatch, & Schoenfeld, 2001), school psychology graduate programs do not consistently provide personality assessment training to their students (Crespi & Politikos, 2008). This lack of training proves unfortunate, as the type of information that can be gathered from an assessment of a child's psychological organization can reveal the quality and nature of the child's thinking and information processing, capacity to handle stress and emotionally arousing situations, perception of self and others, handling of affect and degree of emotional control, and the nature and competency of the child's social skills (see Handler & Hilsonroth, 1998, for a comprehensive review). This type of data, seen within the context of the child's current stressors and historical experiences, can provide substantial and unique insight into the child's decision making and reasoning contributing to his current behavioral adjustment (Exner & Erdberg 2005; Hughes, Gacono, & Owen, 2007).

Possessing the skills to access such important features of a child's personality would empower school psychologists and add to their professional competence. Personality assessment provides the tools to measure and understand the internal psychological functioning of the child and allows the school psychologist to utilize that information to assist and advocate for that child. Such assessment tools, when skillfully handled, tap unique kinds of information that is not already provided by other individualized education program (IEP) team members. This places the school psychologist in a unique position to provide important descriptions of a child's psychological organization and social and emotional functioning for consideration with teachers, school administrators, parents, IEP teams, and others interested in maximizing the child's educational experience and school adjustment. In general, the type of information and insight provided by a competent personality assessment helps school personnel develop greater sensitivity toward the child's needs and decision making that serves to create a positive intervention climate (Knoff, 1983), in which interventions can be selected on the basis of social validity (Bihlar & Carlsson, 2000; Teglasi, 1998), consistent with the child's individual education programs (Pierce & Penman, 1998; Socket, 1998). Such data would also clearly be of utility in weighing and monitoring the effectiveness of intervention outcomes (Stokes et al., 2003).

Although the importance of the social and emotional assessment of children is accepted by school systems, there is less consensus on when a formal personality assessment should be initiated, which techniques should be used as part of this assessment, and how results can be used to inform interventions. In this regard, it is unfortunate but clear that many current school psychology programs reflect (or create) a trend in which course work in behavioral assessment is more common than training in personality assessment (Prout, 1983; Shapiro & Heick, 2004; Stinnett, Havey, & Oehler-Stinnett, 1994). This emphasis is true at both the specialist and doctoral levels of graduate training (Culross & Nelson, 1997) and is one converse to American Psychological Association-accredited clinical psychology programs, in which training in personality assessment is found to be more common than behavioral assessment (Piotroski & Zalewski, 1993). Not surprisingly, surveys of practitioners conducting social–emotional assessments in schools report that they rely on behavioral rating scales more often than personality measures (Shapiro & Heick, 2004; Stinnett et al., 1994), and both assessment strategies are secondary to the use of interviews, family/developmental histories, and classroom observations (Shapiro & Heick, 2004; Stinnett et al., 1994).

This de-emphasis of training in personality assessment in school psychology programs rests on a number of factors and the lack of consensus about the usefulness of personality assessments. From a philosophical perspective, the importance of qualitative descriptions versus quantitative scores (Hunt, 1946; Groth-Marnat, 2000) and clinical versus statistical data (Ægisdóttir, Spengler, & White, 2006; Meehl, 1954) remains unresolved, and the ramifications of these debates still influence how all assessment data, including personality assessment, are regarded. In addition, theoretical perspectives where the clinician acknowledges personality variables and seeks to understand the connections between these personality variables and behavioral outcomes vie with contrary theoretical positions such as radical behaviorism where personality, per se, is not even acknowledged or, if acknowledged, is thought to be immeasurable (Exner, 2003). From a school-practitioner perspective, it is also common for school districts to request or require the school psychologist to start the problem-solving process with intervention (Reynolds & Shaywitz, 2009) before first allowing an appropriate interval of time for at least a preliminary assessment of the child's psychological status (Knoff, 2003), even if a trial and error approach is less time and cost effective (Ervin, Ehrhardt, & Poling, 2001). Also of note are empirical studies considering the usefulness of personality assessment, where comparative analyses of varying quality yield mixed outcomes. Each of the above competing approaches bears a literature base where if one wished, one could select manuscripts to highlight fatal-flaw arguments for any bias (Masling, 2006). When considered holistically, however, the usefulness of personality assessment has been demonstrated (Flanagan, 2007; Knoff, 2003; Weiner, 2000).

Understanding a child's social and emotional needs has long been required as part of a comprehensive school assessment when a child's school functioning is being negatively influenced by learning, socialization, and family problems (Knoff, 2003). In terms of special education eligibility, the enactment of P.L. 94-142 legally mandates that a child's social and emotional functioning be assessed when a question of emotional disturbance in the child is suspected. Further, in 2004 IDEIA required assessment of a child's social and emotional status if suspected to be related to a child's disability.

In regard to school practice in particular, there have been some authors to suggest that behavioral assessment alone is sufficient in and of itself for determining special education eligibility (Shapiro & Kratochwill, 2000) and for designing behavioral interventions in the schools (Watson & Steege, 2003). These authors question the genuine usefulness of personality assessment in school evaluations (Merrell, 2008; Shapiro & Kratochwill) and are supported by the positions of some (e.g., Lilienfeld, Wood, & Garb, 2001) who oppose personality assessment regardless of supporting data (Gacono, Evans, & Viglione, 2002). The use of behavioral strategies as part of social–emotional assessment, however, neither negates nor hinders the importance of gaining an appreciation of the child's internal experience (Stage et al., 2006). Self-report and performance measure data provide information about different aspects of a given construct (e.g., emotional regulation) that are used to clarify how conscious reports (e.g., "I can control myself") are related to actual behavioral performance (Teglasi, 2007). Rather than artificially presenting behavioral and personality assessment procedures as competitive, it is much more useful to highlight their complementary nature (Bardos, Politikos, & Gallagher, 2002) and seek to fully appreciate the different kinds of information that can be made available to enrich the assessment yield. That said, the spirited debate that has often mischaracterized these different strategies as incompatible has no doubt also lead to more refined research studies all around. Indeed, the path of scientific progress is often marked by warring camps that eventually integrate (Groth-Marnat, 2000).

LITERATURE REVIEW

Personality assessment has a rich history in which both forced choice self-report tests (e.g., the Minnesota Multiphasic Personality Inventory [MMPI]) and performance-based measures (e.g., Rorschach) have had an important influence across a 50-year period (Groth-Marnat, 2000), including school assessment (Hughes, Gacono, & Owen, 2007; Knauss, 2001; Stinnett et al., 1994; Teglasi, 1998). This category of assessment encompasses a wide range of techniques that are similar in their purpose (e.g., contextualizing, describing, and anticipating the mechanisms that contribute to observed behaviors) but vary widely in their psychometric properties. Measures with good psychometric properties code responses and allow for sample comparisons. Strong psychometric support has been documented for the Behavior Assessment Scale for Children, Second Edition (BASC-2; Reynolds & Kamphaus, 2004); Minnesota Multiphasic Personality Inventory-Adolescent (MMPI-A; Butcher et al., 1992); Rorschach, when using Exner's *Comprehensive System* (cf., Society for Personality Assessment, 2005); Thematic Apperception Test (TAT; Murray, 1943), when using Teglasi's (2001) coding system; and figure drawings when using Naglieri, McNiesh, and Bardos's (1991) Draw-a-Person system, among others. Researchers have reported that Rorschach and MMPI reliability and validity (Meyer & Archer, 2001) data are similar to intelligence quotient measures and fare better than some common medical tests (Meyer et al., 2001). In contrast, direct observation, the cornerstone of behavioral assessment, often lacks traditional psychometric properties of reliability and validity and instead relies on rater agreement. Of course, not all conclusions drawn from these assessments are equal, as some are more speculative than others (Exner & Wiener, 1982). Thus, general conclusions about the usefulness of personality tests are less useful than the efforts to document which measures are reliable and valid for which decisions about specific populations (Meyer, 2004; Meyer et al., 2001). See Table 11.1 for a summary.

School psychologists face similar decisions daily when choosing psycho-educational and behavioral assessment measures; thus, they are familiar with the process for selecting personality assessment protocols, as the same considerations apply to all testing measures. As described by Jacob and Hartshorne (2003) legal and ethical standards are met when (a) tests are selected based on psychometric properties and demonstrated applicability (e.g., validity) for answering the referral question, (b) examiners have adequate training and are well versed with the current literature base, and (c) data are used as part of a multimethod comprehensive strategy in which cross-validation is employed for decision making. Embedded in this list is the requirement for evaluators to consider cultural and linguistic differences, a responsibility that should be explicitly stated, as it is often overlooked (Dana, 2007).

Culturally competent assessment corrects for bias in test scores; it is informed by a diverse world view that is often the result of direct training in self-awareness and cultural sensitization and is demonstrated by clinicians when making conclusions based on comparisons to cultural relevant norms. Performance-based personality measures (normed on relevant populations) are useful because they provide context to forced-choice scores (Dana, 2007). In fact, performance-based measures provide the type of data that cue clinicians to adjust their world view. For example, narrative assessments such as TAT describe important relationships and motivations in an individual's context that can point the examiner to cultural influences. Dana suggests that Rorschach, TAT, and creative drawings are likely to increase their prominence as clinicians continue to improve their skills in conducting assessment research with diverse populations.

Table 11.1 Examples of Performance-Based Measures and Outcomes

Technique	Information Provided	Population	Study
Rorschach[a]	Aggressive behaviors	Conduct-disordered children with and without psychopathic traits	Gacono & Meloy, 1994; Loving & Russel, 2000; Smith, Gacono, & Kaufman, 1997
	Attachment and anxiety	Conduct or dysthymic adolescents	Weber, Meloy, & Gacono, 1992
	Delinquency	Childhood predictors to adolescent and adulthood delinquency	Janson & Stattin, 2003
	Negative affectivity	Children diagnosed as emotionally disturbed	Hughes, Miller, & Morine, 2005
TAT[b]	Self-regulation	Children with high levels of negative emotionality	Bassan-Diamond, Teglasi, & Schmitt, 1995
	Organization, logic, judgment, affect modulation, and perception of personal adequacy	Emotionally disturbed and well-adjusted boys	McGrew & Teglasi, 1990
	Characterizations of others, investment in relationships, affect, and attribution tendencies	Sexually abused girls and clinical, nonabused girls	Ornduff, Freedenfeld, Kelsey, & Critelli, 1994
	Sexual preoccupation, guilt	Sexually abused girls and clinical, nonabused girls	Pistole & Ornduff, 1994
Drawings[c]	Disturbed emotional functioning	Regular and special education students; children with and without ODD/CD diagnoses	McNeish & Naglieri, 1993; Naglieri & Pfeiffer, 1992
	Internalizing behavior problems	Children receiving counseling at outpatient or residential facilities	Matto (2002)
	Self-image (e.g., sex role identification)	Male and female undergraduates	Aronoff & McCormick, 1990

[a] Rorschach is a perceptual problem-solving task providing information about an individual's stress tolerance, affect, interpersonal, and self-perceptions and cognitive processes.
[b] Thematic Apperception Test (TAT) provides information about perceptions of significant others, motivations, needs, and threats.
[c] Draw-a-Person provides information about self-image and general psychological adjustment.

TRAINING FOR PROFESSIONAL ROLES AND FUNCTION

With the combination of behavioral assessment and personality assessment techniques, the whole child is assessed. As each piece of the puzzle falls into place, a hypothesis about the child's behavior is formed and tested. As each hypothesis is tested and evaluated, another, more complex level of assessment may be warranted. Thus, each step of the assessment is linked to the level of need of the child, intervention, and outcomes.

FUNCTION AND CAUSE OF BEHAVIOR

In this comprehensive approach to evaluating social–emotional functioning, behavior is seen as multifaceted. Behavior is observable and well-defined, and it may be maintained by a function in the environment but is often caused (generated) by a life experience that impacts (emotional, social, or cognitive) development. Therefore, behavior can be modified by changing the variables in the environment but may not be eliminated until the impact on development has been addressed.

Without awareness and assessment of both aspects of behavior, a school psychologist may misdiagnose, mistreat, and inadvertently increase psychopathology in children and young adults. This misguided practice can be compared to the unethical action of implementing an intervention without first conducting an functional behavior assessment (FBA) to determine the function of the behavior and an appropriate replacement behavior. Within this view of behavior, an integrated view of intervention emerges. For example, a behavior problem may lead to a behavior management intervention, a skill deficit to a teaching intervention, a performance deficit to generalization training and a production deficit to therapy aimed at changing the obstacle preventing the production of the behavior. To identify each of the possible intervention targets, assessment must examine all aspects of behavior.

INTEGRATED SOCIAL–EMOTIONAL ASSESSMENT

Assessment of problem behavior, therefore, must take a multidimensional, multitiered approach (see Figure 11.1). At referral, the school psychologist would first hypothesize whether the problem was a classroom management or individual issue. If the referral was thought to be a classroom management issue, the school psychologist would provide consultation to the teacher and recommend general class-wide strategies to decrease the problem behavior. However, if the referral was centered on one individual student, the school psychologist would conduct a complete FBA to define the target behavior, the patterns of the behavior, and the environmental factors impacting the behavior (see Watson & Steege, 2003, for a review).

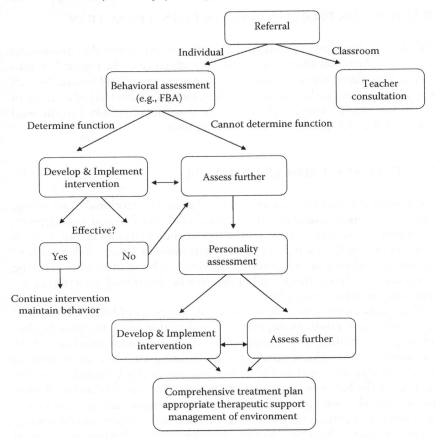

Figure 11.1 Social–emotional assessment decision diagram.

While gathering the data to complete the FBA, the school psychologist would approach the task with a problem-solving orientation by constantly evaluating the data collected for missing pieces. If the data converged to create a pattern and a hypothesized function, the school psychologist would implement an intervention and test the hypothesis. If the data were not converging or the intervention was not successful, the school psychologist might elect to assess the student using forced choice measures (e.g., BASC-2 or MMPI-A) or performance-based measures (e.g., Rorschach or TAT) depending on the type of variables needed to be considered (see Table 11.1 for summary).

Personality assessment findings also generate a hypothesis that can once again be presented and tested. This second level hypothesis may help explain persistent behaviors, those behaviors without proximal antecedents, and ineffective problem-solving strategies created through a life history experience. In addition, by examining hypotheses around both the environmental variables influencing problem behavior and the underlying psychological processes causing the behavior, a comprehensive treatment plan that intervenes in the natural environment and with the individual child (when that level of intervention is required) can be developed for school success.

LINKING ASSESSMENT AND INTERVENTION

Although behavior and personality assessments provide different information and can lead to different interventions, they are both aimed at relevant pieces of the problem behavior. By completing behavior and personality assessments, both overlapping supportive data and nonoverlapping unique data can be gathered. This helps to identify the incremental variance from the shared results, giving greater certitude to the hypothesis. Likewise, completing both forms of assessment may clarify inconsistencies in the assessment data and offer alternative hypotheses. Ultimately, a comprehensive, multitiered, multimethod approach to assessment will lead to a comprehensive, multitiered, multimethod intervention aimed at getting the child back on the appropriate developmental track.

Practitioners who are competent in personality assessment have likely gained these skills through graduate training programs. Teaching comprehensive social–emotional assessment skills requires a sequenced, coordinated, and integrated curriculum in which the goals of instruction are comprehensive and teach students considered test selection, multimodal assessment, for the purpose of selecting evidence-based interventions that match individual needs. Course work will need to highlight typical child development and cultural considerations as the backdrop for interpreting data, and applied exercises will focus on how developmental trajectories serve to highlight the complexity and opportunity in treating children.

Although there are a variety of courses in which these skills could be delivered to graduate students, the following is a suggested a course sequence:

- Child and adolescent development course is foundational and thus needs to be comprehensive, addressing the dynamic factors of temperament; personality; and emotional, social, and cognitive development.
- Psychological testing course work should encourage students to grapple with error variance in test scores and diversity issues, such as test score bias and predictive bias and how each impacts test score interpretation.
- Grounded in theory, the behavior assessment course should focus on assessment, interpretation, and intervention skills.
- A developmental psychopathology course should include the dynamic systems that contribute to the manifestation of maladjustment.

- The personality assessment course must be comprehensive in nature, addressing competing view points (e.g., forced-choice and performance-based measures, clinical versus statistical data, etc.). Instructors should directly link behavioral and personality assessment to behavioral intervention and psychotherapy course content goals.
- The psychotherapy course should address the individual assets and liabilities identified by multimodal assessment as it relates to selecting and implementing interventions. Although beyond the scope of this chapter, the work of Shirk and Russell (1996) describing how to select evidence-based interventions for the individual is a foundational part of this class.
- Practicum opportunities, beyond laboratory practice, in which students can use their skills in an applied setting with close supervision is important.
- Of course, advanced course work in personality and behavioral assessment would aid in moving students beyond the advanced beginner skill level.

FACULTY COMPLEMENT

The faculty members in an integrated training program do not have to have the same theoretical orientation, similar training, or professional experiences or even agree on how to assess and treat children. Rather, the members of a program faculty that provides a comprehensive view of training for both specialist and doctoral students need a commitment to retaining their expertise, as well as allowing multimethod assessment and delivery options in student training. Of course, a commitment to child-focused, school-based considerations is maintained as an essential priority for school practice. That is, personality assessment for children does not simply mean clinical psychology training that is portable to school.

PEDAGOGICAL ISSUES

Psychological assessment is one of the defining areas of practice for psychologists (Piotrowski & Zalewski, 1993) and provides stakeholders with a permanent product resulting from an effective evaluation process. A psychological evaluation report with sophisticated conclusions, written by an informed and thoughtful psychologist, can meaningfully improve a child's social and academic experiences. The graduate school instructor therefore must transmit through the teaching process to school psychology students the essential skills of psychological testing, data interpretation, and test report writing.

Writing psychological reports is a complex process and entails a careful integration of information from multiple sources in order to arrive at appropriate conclusions and to form effective interventions. Although students often demonstrate technically accurate test administration and data interpretation skills, many students' interpretations tend to be simplistic, cookbook lists of basic level interpretations. Simplistic approaches such as these invariably result in psychological reports that are of limited utility and resemble more a list of problems rather than a meaningful assessment of a child's unique psychological organization and functioning. Test reports should be clear and well-written documents to make important points to address direct ways to help children.

In my (T.L.H.) 4th year of teaching personality assessment, student and site supervisor feedback suggested that students needed additional support with test data integration upon starting practicum. I had previously used a traditional teaching approach for test score interpretation and psychological report writing that included a lecture–write–read–edit sequence. I modeled how to think about cases, provided interpretation templates, and engaged in a read–edit–return report-writing cycle. Each year, with the traditional approach, my skill in this teaching method improved, but students' applied skills, as observed in practicum settings, in most cases had not. Thus, I became motivated to develop a teaching technique to improve student learning needs in test score interpretation and psychological report writing that would ultimately translate into better interventions for my students' child constituency.

The goal of the teaching technique was to remedy conceptual problems in student thinking such as limited ability to generate diverse interpretations for a single psychological test score, poor integration of scores across different types of tests (forced-choice and performance-based tests) and different informants (parent, teachers, self), difficulty integrating contradictory test scores, and unsophisticated interpretation of test scores in the context of normal child development. Learning to write psychological reports requires aspects of creative and critical thinking ("Interview with Dr. Leonard Handler," 2003). Divergent and convergent thought processes emulate the interpretative routine needed for generating conclusions from many sources of data in a psychological evaluation. Once students learn creative and critical thinking processes, these processes can be applied to understanding psychological data and report writing ("Interview with Dr. Leonard Handler," 2003).

School psychologists use aspects of creative and critical thinking to process data and arrive at useful conclusions in their reports. Specifically, divergent thinking generates multiple hypotheses regarding assessment data, and convergent thinking narrows the hypotheses, resulting in well-reasoned conclusions. Aspects of critical thinking, such as gathering information, testing hypotheses, and communicating with school professionals and parents further facilitate this report-writing process. Thus, the process of report writing and the final report is equally important.

The first author hypothesized that if students could change their inflexible and narrow thinking about test score interpretation, then report-writing skills would also improve. The instructor evaluated these goals through students' (a) knowledge of data interpretation and psychological report writing, (b) skill in divergent and convergent thinking strategies and psychological data interpretive routines, and (c) qualitative changes in psychological report writing. The following is an exemplar for teaching comprehensive integrated test score interpretation and measuring graduate students learning.

Participants

This sample of convenience included 10 graduate level school psychology students (7 women and 3 men; mean age = 26.3 years) who completed the questionnaires, provided psychological report interpretations, and participated in the teaching strategy as part of their required course in personality assessment.

Description of the teaching strategy

There are two aspects to the teaching strategy presented: (a) a unique data analysis process and (b) an innovative instructional technique using a sequence of coordinated divergent and convergent thinking exercises conducted throughout the course. After students established requisite skills for test administration and basic level interpretations, the instructor introduced the instructional technique. Figure 11.2 illustrates the data analysis process that was explained in detail to the students as a model for interpreting multiple sources of test data. Students then began a sequence of coordinated in- and out-of-class exercises in divergent and convergent thinking.

The divergent thinking exercises included generating as many potential interpretations from a single score (see Figure 11.2, panels 1.1–1.4). First test scores must result in multiple hypotheses (Figure 11.2, panel 1.1). Next, interpretations across multiple tests (e.g., Test A and Test B) were generated (Figure 11.2, panel 1.2). Next, interpretations across multiple informants (parent, teacher, and self) were included in higher order interpretations (Figure 11.2, panel 1.3). Finally, developmental histories (Figure 11.2, panel 1.4) were considered. Over the course, students practiced each level of divergent thinking (Figure 11.2, panels 1.1–1.4) during class sessions in a large group format, as well as individually for required homework assignments. In class, students helped clarify the divergent thinking of classmates—often identifying connections their student colleagues had not considered. Throughout this data analysis process, students charted their thinking on a visual graphic provided by the instructor, which is provided in Figure 11.2. The use of this visualization technique incorporates both sequential and holistic encoding of information that will ensure transfer of

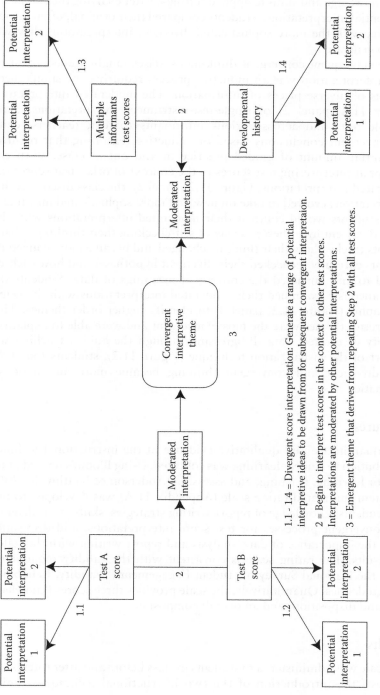

Figure 11.2 Divergent–convergent interpretive routine for psychological report writing.

1.1 – 1.4 = Divergent score interpretation: Generate a range of potential interpretive ideas to be drawn from for subsequent convergent interpretaion.

2 = Begin to interpret test scores in the context of other test scores. Interpretations are moderated by other potential interpretations.

3 = Emergent theme that derives from repeating Step 2 with all test scores.

both knowledge and skills to applied settings. After charting the complexity of potential interpretations, students compared their original, often myopic, thinking with the more sophisticated divergent interpretations they were able to generate.

The subsequent convergent thinking exercises taught students that test score interpretation was an inductive process requiring the simultaneous analysis of diverse pieces of information. The moderated interpretations (Figure 11.2, panel 2) of single-test-instrument interpretations, across multiple tests and across various informants (parent, teachers, child), are convergent conclusions based on inductive reasoning that require a substantial amount of guided practice in and out of class. With each attempt at interpreting test scores in the context of other test scores (i.e., moderated interpretations; Figure 11.2, panel 2), the class discovered how interpretations evolved to take on new and more sophisticated meaning. In class, students would contrast their moderated interpretations with their initial divergent hypotheses as way of self-checking their thinking. That is, students tracked how their thinking changed and became more convergent. Students carefully rechecked their divergent hypotheses and how each was related to and impacted the convergent meanings of data. Students then simultaneously examined their moderated interpretations with the help of the graphic (Figure 11.2, panel 3) to identify higher order themes. These interpretive themes were the most convergent and were able to explain the majority of the test data. Progressing through the guided teaching with support of the visualization technique (Figure 11.2), students found that their divergent and convergent thinking became more automatic and systematic.

Measures

Both quantitative and qualitative evidence of the instructional technique contribution to student learning was collected. Using Bloom's revised taxonomy for learning, teaching, and assessing (Anderson & Krathwohl, 2001), a 20-item summated rating scale (Appendix 11.A) was developed to measure students' knowledge of report-writing strategies, skills at the divergent and convergent processes for test score interpretations, and dispositions about the importance of data analysis and report writing with the following results. The rating scale is consistent with the validity requirements set by the National Survey of Student Engagement ("Validity, Reliability," n.d.) guidelines. Quantitatively, the scale provides three scores (knowledge, skill, and disposition) and an overall composite.

Results

The scale was administered to students in class before and after (pretest and posttest) the introduction of the two instructional techniques (unique

Table 11.2 Student Mean Performance Scores of Report-Writing Strategies

Score	Pretest (Mean)	Posttest (Mean)	F(1,17)
Knowledge	3.46	4.15	26.67*
Skill	3.31	3.65	6.04**
Disposition	3.74	3.87	.49
Overall composite	3.45	3.77	10.42***

* $p < .001$; ** $p < .05$; *** $p < .01$.

graphical data analysis process and teaching technique). The results of the rating scale and statistical analysis are summarized in Table 11.2.

Results of the analysis of variance indicated that students reported statistically significant overall improvement in psychological test data interpretation [$F(1, 17) = 10.42$, $p < .01$] as a result of the instructional technique. The instructional technique significantly [$F(1, 17) = 26.67$, $p < .001$] increased student knowledge of how to interpret psychological test data using divergent and convergent strategies. Students reported a statistically significant increase [$F(1, 17) = 6.04$, $p < .05$] in skill at divergent and convergent thinking strategies and interpretive routines as a result of the instructional technique. Dispositions were not significantly different after the instructional technique. Student disposition scores were high at pretest and were slightly higher after the instructional technique, suggesting that students already held the belief they needed to conduct sophisticated interpretations and that report-writing skills were important.

Qualitatively, psychological report-writing skills improved. Independent raters compared pre- and postinstructional technique reports. Qualitative comparisons were important because students hold various levels of practical experience when they begin the course. Novice and more experienced report writers showed improvements in moving from basic level, cookbook interpretations to integrated interpretive conclusions.

Conclusions

Results of this classroom study provided initial evidence for the effectiveness of the instructional technique to improve school psychology students' comprehension of strategies for data interpretation related to personality assessment. Students in the personality assessment class showed significant improvement in interpreting psychological assessment results, as well as using convergent and divergent thought to interpret data and qualitative change in their report-writing skills. Teaching students to think flexibly, using divergent and convergent skills during the assessment process, clearly impacts the teaching of personality assessment at the graduate level (Halpern, 2003; "Interview with Dr. Leonard Handler," 2003). It is possible to measure instructor level teaching outcomes in graduate course work.

Limitations

Of course, there are several limitations to this study, including the sample of convenience, no control group, and the one-time application of this teaching strategy; thus, these results should be replicated before strong statements about generalizability can be made. Although the sample size was small, there was enough power to detect meaningful differences.

OBSTACLES AND OPPORTUNITIES

Likely the biggest obstacle to teaching personality assessment to school psychology students is finding qualified school psychologists. Second, comprehensive training requires graduate students to be able to shift their thinking and jargon across various courses. Although this can be conceptually challenging (to say the least), it provides the student important opportunities for enhanced skill development (e.g., flexibility, increased problem solving). As students increase their repertoire of skills, so too will they increase their ability to engage in more diverse roles.

PROFESSIONAL DECISION MAKING: CASE EXEMPLARS ADDING PERSONALITY ASSESSMENT

The decision to add personality performance-based measures to an assessment battery can arise for various reasons. A parent, school administrator, or teacher, for example, may seek a deeper understanding of a child's functioning and a better appreciation of what possible internal factors may be contributing to the child's problematic behaviors. It is possible that despite best efforts a pattern of antecedents and consequences identified around a child's behavior through an FBA has failed to provide effective interventions. Figure 11.1 provides a decision tree for adding personality assessment.

In light of the above, consider the following two case examples. In the first case, Ms. Downy, a school psychologist, has spent 2 weeks conducting an FBA of Phil, a 14-year-old ninth-grade student in Mr. Crane's class. Phil is reported to be attention seeking during class and resentful of his teachers' authority. There are also reports that Phil may have been involved in some destruction of school property, which Mr. Crane suspects happened on the same day that Phil had been corrected in class and referred to the assistant principal for disruption.

Ms. Downy has followed best practices procedures in this assessment and has observed Phil on numerous occasions and at various times of the day. She has also conducted a teacher and parent interview, and she has personally interviewed Phil. After a careful analysis of her findings, however, Ms. Downy has concluded that unfortunately she has not been able to identify a clear pattern in Phil's disruptive classroom behavior, nor has she been able to uncover or isolate any unusual setting events or circumstances that may be germane to Phil's behavior problems.

Although still unclear about the function of Phil's behavior, Ms. Downy does feel that she needs to assist Mr. Crane. In an effort to help the classroom situation, Ms. Downy suggests that perhaps Phil's disruptive behavior during class is being reinforced to some degree by a pattern through which greater teacher attention is awarded Phil when he is misbehaving and much less attention is given to Phil when he is behaving appropriately. To address this difference, Mr. Crane is instructed to frequently reward Phil when Phil is following the rules and exhibiting positive social behavior. Following 2 weeks of this intervention, however, Phil's classroom behavior is reported to have only worsened. Frustrated and increasingly concerned, Mrs. Downy consults with her school psychologist colleague, Mr. Frank, who in turn recommends that a series of performance-based measures be conducted with Phil (with the appropriate permissions) in an effort to uncover what other factors might be contributing to Phil's misbehavior.

Mr. Frank is thoroughly trained in various personality assessment techniques. First, Mr. Frank administers the TAT to Phil in an effort to gather some thematic narrative information. He then administers the Rorschach to Phil following the guidelines provided by Exner's *Comprehensive System* and notes comparisons with Exner's age reference data for other 14-year-olds. Through this assessment data, Mr. Frank discovers that Phil's level of distress is exceeding Phil's current coping skills and that he is clearly more vulnerable than other children his age to experience emotional dysregulation in unpredictable or changing situations. Phil also appears to be very strongly suppressing his feelings, which most likely contributes in some measure to his current emotional discomfort. Phil's very tight emotional control also likely contributes to his tendency to emotionally withdraw around others and/or to display passive-aggressive behaviors. From an information processing perspective, Phil demonstrates a tendency to screen out complexity and the nuance of events in an effort to make his decision making more manageable. When overwhelmed by stress, however, this narrow, simplistic approach in decision making likely contributes to Phil's tendency to make premature, erroneous decisions (observed by the teacher as attention seeking). In addition, it is also clear that Phil anticipates limited support from others, which serves only to add to his sense of interpersonal isolation and further compromises his ability to express his emotions appropriately (observed by the teacher being as resentful of teacher authority).

Based on this more elaborated picture of Phil's internal psychological functioning and in combination with other (e.g., observational, interview) assessment information, Ms. Downy and Mr. Frank are now in a much better position to create a comprehensive intervention plan to better structure Phil's environment in a supportive manner in an effort to help decrease and manage his stress (so that his coping resources are not chronically overtaxed) while providing Phil with the therapeutic support he needs to expand his problem-solving strategies (increase breath and flexibility when making decisions that inform his actions) and increase appropriate expression of emotion (express needs with words and replace "attention seeking" behavior) so that he increases his ability to benefit from the social support (positive praise in natural setting) provided by peers and teachers.

In the second example, John's case illustrates the value of seeking personality assessment information in developing effective intervention strategies to foster a child's successful adjustment to school, as well as placement decisions around alternative education settings. John is a 12-year-old seventh-grade student who is classified as a student with an emotional disturbance. After numerous FBAs and implementation of evidence-based interventions, he has not responded consistently to the interventions delineated in his behavior intervention plan and his continuing aggressive behavior raises the possibility of transferring him to an alternative education school. His teachers describe him as detached and uncaring; he is defiant in the classroom, showing volatile, extreme behaviors. In order to attain a better picture of John's emotional and behavioral strengths and weaknesses, as well as insight into how to best support John's school adjustment a battery of clinical interviews, forced-choice (e.g., parent, teacher, and self-report versions of the BASC-2), and performance-based measures (TAT and Rorschach) were administered.

Behavior rating scales describe a boy with an overall behavioral symptom index in the clinically significant range, with marked elevations in the area of externalizing problems (hyperactivity, aggression, and conduct problems). Teacher and parent BASC-2 scores showed clinically significant elevations across multiple areas of functioning, with marked emphasis in the area of aggression and conduct problems. John's mother also rated John as showing symptoms of depression and anxiety. He endorsed several scales in the clinically significant range and admitted to feeling marked discomfort in school, dissatisfaction with teachers, and a propensity to engage in risk-taking behaviors (also punctuated in his interview). In addition, a sense of feeling inadequate academically heightened social stress and a general feeling of helplessness emerged in John's rating scale. His positive endorsement of such items as "I just don't care anymore" and "I feel like my life is getting worse and worse," were of special concern.

The data from John's personality assessment measures provided additional information regarding how his problem-solving strategies and personality strengths and vulnerabilities result in the reported and observed behaviors. John's Rorschach and TAT results reveal an emotionally guarded but potentially quite labile boy who lacks a consistent, well-defined coping style. John clearly appears to be under considerable emotional stress and susceptible to periods of marked unhappiness. Test indications of dysphoria augur ominously for the development of a significant depression and further highlight John's emotional distress (consistent with the BASC-2 report). Test data also reveal that John appears to be preoccupied with his own needs beyond what is typical for his age, and a sense of entitlement may be serving to further alienate him from others (he was observed by the teacher as cool and uncaring). Most likely, this combination of factors is contributing to John's vulnerability to becoming easily insulted and challenged, and increasingly unhappy when he does not feel his needs are being appropriately responded to by other people. Not surprisingly, John's social skills appear to be quite poor, and he does not demonstrate an adequate (a *Mister Rogers' Neighborhood*) understanding of people. Findings show that his interpersonal relationships tend to be superficial (observed by the teacher as detached and uncaring). Authority conflicts repeatedly emerged in John's narrative test material (consistent with BASC-2 reports), together with themes suggesting feelings of helplessness and of being misunderstood when he tries to convey his needs or to articulate his emotions.

The assessment data in John's case provided by personality measures highlight multiple levels of this boy's psychological organization and show that John is experiencing considerable emotional trouble, rather than simple defiance and aggression. The frequency and intensity of John's emotional and behavioral difficulties indicate his need for careful monitoring and close academic support during the school day. Alternative education placement is appropriate only if there is a substantial therapeutic component to this environment. Specifically, he requires a classroom in which positive behavioral support is used consistently. That is, rather than punishing inappropriate behaviors, the teacher should help John to identify (and put into words) his emotions as they are occurring, together with providing instruction and role modeling on how he can appropriately express his feelings (e.g., anger, helplessness, and feelings of being misunderstood). This type of school setting is in contrast to a response cost behavioral system sometimes used in alternative education environments. Curricular activities could also focus on helping John to take the perspective of others (e.g., persuasive writing), and reading assignments that include stories of successful problem-solving protagonists can support behavioral needs. A cognitive-behavioral approach could help John to identify the triggers that lead to his feelings of helplessness and think through alternative interpretations to his conclusions that others are not responding to him adequately, and metacognitive techniques to improve his self-management strategies could help him better handle his easily stirred volatility. In addition, social skills instruction and group activities that emphasize assertiveness to get needs met balanced with the development of reciprocal friendships may prove helpful to enhance John's peer and authority relations. In summary, the type, nature, and depth of information made available by personality assessment measures in this boy's case can provide important insight to better inform and guide his teachers, parents, and school administrators in their understanding of his behavior and to increase their appreciation of his unique strengths and special areas of weaknesses with the goal of guiding and developing an effective and uniquely tailored intervention strategy.

SUMMARY AND CONCLUSIONS

Personality assessment instruction can flourish when competent professionals work in an inclusive rather than a prescriptive environment. Personality assessment serves a unique purpose and has a legitimate place in the practice of school psychology in providing a way for school psychologists to understand the psychological process of decision making that contributes to behavior. The information such assessment can provide to an IEP team, for example, can serve to enhance the IEP team's understanding of the child's functioning useful for selecting evidence-based interventions that match the child's needs. Particularly in refractory and difficult to treat cases, school psychologists need to understand the personality characteristics of the child and how those characteristics impact the child's social and emotional functioning in schools (Hughes, Gacono, Owen, 2007).

There are many opportunities to focus on integrating behavioral and personality assessments in school practice. Increasing the dialogue and research opportunities among behavioral and personality assessment groups can serve to increase skill level for practitioners serving diverse students in schools. Future research should address how personality assessment can assist in measuring student outcomes in a manner that is time efficient in schools. School psychologists need to measure how personality assessment outcomes are related to decision making by IEP teams particularly in cases in which the students are culturally diverse or do not respond to evidence-based interventions as expected. Educating both graduate and undergraduate institutions that create and perpetuate the appearance of controversy and a negative view of personality measures (Gacono, Evans, & Viglione, 2002; Masling, 1997) remains an important task. Ongoing dialogues and the seeking of better ways to help children should always be encouraged.

APPENDIX 11.A: SUMMATED RATING SCALE

---

1. I understand the methods of interpreting the results of assessment.

   Strongly disagree · Disagree · Not sure · Agree · Strongly agree

2. I understand how to integrate the background information, observations, and results of assessment.

   Strongly disagree · Disagree · Not sure · Agree · Strongly agree

3. I understand how to generate interventions based on assessment results.

   Strongly disagree · Disagree · Not sure · Agree · Strongly agree

4. I use a systematic method of data interpretation.

   Rarely · Infrequently · Sometimes · Often · Very often

5. I generate divergent hypotheses of the problem based on test data.

   Rarely · Infrequently · Sometimes · Often · Very often

6. I generate a variety of potential interventions based on test data.

   Rarely · Infrequently · Sometimes · Often · Very often

7. I integrate assessment data across settings and informants.

   Rarely · Infrequently · Sometimes · Often · Very often

8. I integrate contradictory information in assessment data.

   Rarely · Infrequently · Sometimes · Often · Very often

9. I integrate comorbid, preexisting conditions and developmental information in assessment.

   Rarely · Infrequently · Sometimes · Often · Very often

10. I recognize contradictory statements in written reports.

    Rarely · Infrequently · Sometimes · Often · Very often

11. I recognize contradictory conclusions in written reports.

    Rarely · Infrequently · Sometimes · Often · Very often

12. I recognize contradictory recommendations for intervention in written reports.

    Rarely · Infrequently · Sometimes · Often · Very often

13. It is easy for me to write integrated psychological reports.

    Rarely · Infrequently · Sometimes · Often · Very often

(Continued)

Appendix 11.A (*Continued*)

14. Accuracy in report writing is important.

    Strongly   Disagree   Not sure   Agree   Strongly agree
    disagree

15. Integrating test data is important.

    Strongly   Disagree   Not sure   Agree   Strongly agree
    disagree

16. Generating divergent hypotheses of the problem is important.

    Strongly   Disagree   Not sure   Agree   Strongly agree
    disagree

17. I tend to interpret test data in a pollyanish manner.

    Strongly   Disagree   Not sure   Agree   Strongly agree
    disagree

18. I tend to interpret test data in a morbid manner.

    Strongly   Disagree   Not sure   Agree   Strongly agree
    disagree

19. I am prepared to interpret assessment data under supervision in a practicum setting.

    Strongly   Disagree   Not sure   Agree   Strongly agree
    disagree

20. I am prepared to interpret assessment data independently.

    Strongly   Disagree   Not sure   Agree   Strongly agree
    disagree

RESOURCES

Handler, L., & Hilsenroth, M. J. (1998). *Teaching and learning personality assessment*. Mahwah, NJ: Lawrence Earlbaum.
This book provides a comprehensive overview of techniques for teaching assessment as detailed by resident experts in the field. In an attempt to bridge the gap between theory and practice, the editors have selected clinicians whose skills and expertise in the fields of assessment and instruction grant students access to esoteric information, providing practical assistance for its application. Numerous examples used to illustrate key concepts are included.

Knoff, H. M. (2003). *The assessment of child and adolescent personality*. New York: Guilford Press.
This book provides an inclusive review of theory, research, and practice in child and adolescent personality assessment. The book is composed of four

sections and can serve as a well-organized reference volume. Basic information regarding theories, issues, and concepts is presented in section 1 in order to provide a framework for assessment as a "hypothesis-generating, problem-solving process." Section 2 reviews and evaluates a range of approaches, tests, and techniques, including the administration, scoring, and interpretation of each. Intervention generation and implementation based on the findings of personality assessment are reviewed in section 3. Lastly, section 4 provides a summary of perspectives and recommended practices, as well as suggested future directions for the field.

Society for Personality Assessment. (2005). The status of the Rorschach in clinical and forensic practice: An official statement by the Board of Trustees of
   the Society for Personality Assessment. *Journal of Personality Assessment, 85,*
   219–237.
The intended audience of this official statement includes psychologists, other mental health professionals, educators, attorneys, judges, and administrators. This statement presents an overview of issues and empirical evidence regarding the Rorschach, resulting in an affirmation of the reliability and validity of this instrument. The statement asserts the psychometric properties (i.e., reliability and validity) of the Rorschach are comparable to that of other personality assessment instruments. In all, the Board of Trustees of the Society for Personality Assessment conclude that use of the Rorschach within personality assessment is appropriate and justifiable when done in a responsible manner.

Teglasi, H. (2001). *Essentials of TAT and other story telling instruments assessment.*
   New York: Wiley.
This book provides comprehensive instruction in test administration, scoring, and interpretation in order for practitioners to develop the knowledge and skills needed to utilize a variety of storytelling techniques effectively. In addition, Teglasi provides the reader with an overview of relevant strengths and weaknesses, as well as advice on clinical applications. Numerous features are embedded within each concise chapter to ensure mastery of the information presented (e.g., key concept callout boxes, bulleted points, illustrative material, etc.). Case studies illustrating effective implementation of a storytelling approach to personality assessment using best practices are included.

Teglasi, H., & Flanagan, R. (Eds.). (2007). Personality assessment [Special issue].
   Psychology in the Schools, 44(3).
This issue of *Psychology in the Schools* provides an updated comprehensive review of information regarding the assessment of children's personalities; specifically, the authors discuss the many socioemotional variables that comprise the construct of personality. The role that personality variables play in one's daily functioning, as well as the relationship between these and other types of variables in determining one's ability to function in

diverse contexts, is examined. Individual articles focus on the importance of integrating multiple variables within a personality assessment battery by utilizing multiple measures, frameworks for utilizing multiple measures, the role of sociocultural context, details of specific performance measures of personality, and the development of assessment procedures that lend themselves to generating therapeutic goals.

REFERENCES

Ægisdóttir, S., Spengler, P. M., & White, M. J. (2006). Should I pack my umbrella? Clinical versus statistical prediction of mental health. *Counseling Psychologist, 34*, 410–419.

Anderson, L. W., & Krathwohl, D. R. (2001). *A taxonomy for learning, teaching, and assessing.* New York: Longman.

Aronoff, D. N., & McCormick, N. B. (1990). Sex, sex role identification, and college students' projective drawings. *Journal of Clinical Psychology, 46*, 460–466.

Bardos, A. N., Politikos, N., & Gallagher, S. L. (2002). Use of projective techniques with school aged children. In J. F. Carlson & B. B. Waterman (Eds.), *Social and personality assessment of school aged children: Developing interventions for educational and clinical use* (pp. 123–140). Boston: Allyn & Bacon.

Bassan-Diamond, L. E., Teglasi, H., & Schmitt, P. V. (1995). Temperament and a story-telling measure of self-regulation. *Journal of Research in Personality, 29*, 109–120.

Bihlar, B., & Carlsson, A. (2000). An exploratory study of agreement between therapists' goals and patients' problems revealed by Rorschach. *Psychotherapy Research, 10*, 196–205.

Butcher, J. N., Williams, C. L., Graham, J. R., Archer, R. P., Tellegen, A., & Ben-Porath, Y. S. (1992). *MMPI: A manual for administration, scoring and interpretation.* Minneapolis, MN: University of Minnesota Press.

Crespi, T. D., & Politikos, N. N. (2008). Personality assessment in school-based practice: Considerations, challenges and competence. *The School Psychologist, 62*, 12–15.

Culross, R. R., & Nelson, S. (1997). Training in personality assessment in specialist-level school psychology programs. *Psychological Reports, 81*, 119–124.

Dana, R. (2007). Culturally competent school assessment: Performance measures of personality. *Psychology in the Schools, 44*, 229–241.

Education of all Handicapped Children Act of 1975 P.L. 94-142. § 20 U.S.C. 1401 et seq.

Ervin, R. A., Ehrhardt, K. E., & Poling, A. (2001). Functional assessment: Old wine in new bottles. *School Psychology Review, 30*, 173–179.

Exner, J. E. (2003). *The Rorschach: A comprehensive system. Basic foundations and principles of interpretation* (Vol. 1, 4th ed.). New York: John Wiley & Sons.

Exner, J. E., & Erdberg, P. (2005). *The Rorschach: A comprehensive system. Advanced interpretation* (3rd ed.). New York: John Wiley & Sons.

Exner, J. E., & Weiner, I. B. (1982). *The Rorschach: A comprehensive system. Assessment of children and adolescents* (Vol. 3). New York: John Wiley & Sons.

Flanagan, R. (2007). Comments on the miniseries: Personality assessment in school psychology. *Psychology in the Schools, 44,* 311–318.

Gacono, C. B., Evans, F. B., & Viglione, D. J. (2002). The Rorschach in forensic practice. *Journal of Forensic Psychology Practice, 2,* 33–53.

Gacono, C. B., & Meloy, J. R. (1994). *The Rorschach assessment of aggressive and psychopathic personalities.* Lawrence Erlbaum.

Groth-Marnat, G. (2000). Visions of clinical assessment: Then, now and a brief history of the future. *Journal of Clinical Psychology, 56,* 349–365.

Handler, L., & Hilsenroth, M. J. (1998). *Teaching and learning personality assessment.* Mahwah, NJ: Lawrence Earlbaum.

Halpern, D. F. (2003). Thinking critically about creative thinking. In M. A. Runco (Ed.), *Critical Creative Processes* (pp.189–207). Creskill, NJ: Hampton Press.

Hughes, T. L., Gacono, C. G., & Owen, P. F. (2007). Current status of Rorschach assessment: Implications for the school psychologist. *Psychology in the Schools, 44,* 281–291

Hughes, T. L., Miller, J. A., & Morine, K. A. (2005). Indicators of negative affectivity in children's Rorschach responses. *South African Rorschach Journal, 2,* 45–52.

Hunt, W. A. (1946). The future of diagnostic testing in clinical psychology. *Journal of Clinical Psychology, 2,* 311–317.

Individuals with Disabilities Education Improvement Act of 2004. (2003). In GovTrack.us (database of federal legislation). Retrieved July 1, 2009, from http://www.govtrack.us/congress/bill.xpd?bill=h108-1350

Interview with Dr. Leonard Handler. (2003, Summer). *SPA Exchange, 15,* 18–19.

Jacob, S., & Hartshorne, T. S. (2003). *Ethics and law for school psychologists* (4th ed.). Hoboken, NJ: John Wiley & Sons.

Janson, H., & Stattin, H. (2003). Prediction of adolescent and adult delinquency from childhood Rorschach ratings. *Journal of Personality Assessment, 8,* 51–63.

Knauss, L. K. (2001). Ethical issues in psychological assessment in school settings. *Journal of Personality Assessment, 77,* 231–244.

Knoff, H. M. (1983). Justifying projective /personality assessment in school psychology: A response to Batsche and Peterson. *School Psychology Review, 12,* 446–451.

Knoff, H. M. (2003). *The assessment of child and adolescent personality.* New York: Guilford Press.

Lilienfeld, S. O., Wood, J. N., & Garb, H. N. (2001). The scientific status of projective techniques. *Psychological Science in the Public Interest, 1,* 27–66.

Loving, J., & Russell, W. F. (2000). Selected Rorschach variables of psychopathic juvenile offenders. *Journal of Personality Assessment, 75,* 126–142.

Masling, J. M. (1997). On the nature and utility of projective tests and objective tests. *Journal of Personality Assessment, 69,* 257–270.

Masling, J. M. (2006). When Homer nods: An examination of some systematic errors in Rorschach scholarship. *Journal of Personality Assessment, 87,* 62–73.

Matto, H. C. (2002). Investigating the validity of the Draw-a-Person: Screening Procedure for Emotional Disturbance: A measurement validation study with high-risk youth. *Psychological Assessment, 14,* 221–225.

McGrew, M. W., & Teglasi, H. (1990). Formal characteristics of Thematic Apperception Test stories as indices of emotional disturbance in children. *Journal of Personality Assessment, 54,* 639–655.

McNeish, T. J., & Naglieri, J. A. (1993). Identification of individuals with serious emotional disturbance using the Draw a Person: Screening Procedure for Emotional Disturbance. *The Journal of Special Education, 27*, 115–121.

Meehl, P. A. (1954). *Clinical versus statistical prediction: A theoretical analysis and a review of the evidence.* Minneapolis: University of Minnesota.

Merrell, K. W. (2008). *Behavioral, social, and emotional assessment of children and adolescents* (3rd ed.). New York: Lawrence Erlbaum.

Meyer, G. J. (2004). The reliability and validity of the Rorschach and Thematic Apperception Test (TAT) compared to other psychological and medical procedures: An analysis of systematic gathered evidence. In M. J. Hilsenroth, D. L. Segal, & M. Hirshen (Eds.), *Comprehensive handbook of psychological assessment: Personality assessment.* New York: Wiley.

Meyer, G. J., & Archer, R. P. (2001). The hard science of Rorschach research: What do we know and where do we go? *Psychological Assessment, 13*, 486–502.

Meyer, G. J., Finn, S. E., Eyde, L., Kay, G. G., Moreland, K. L., Dies, R. R., et al. (2001). Psychological testing and psychological assessment: A review of evidence and issues. *American Psychologist, 56*, 128–165.

Murray, H. A. (1943). *Thematic Apperception Test manual.* Cambridge, MA: Harvard University Press.

Naglieri, J. A., McNiesh, R. J., & Bardos, A. N. (1991). *Draw-a-Person: Screening procedures for emotional disturbance.* Austin, TX: ProEd.

Naglieri, J. A., & Pfeiffer, S. I. (1992). Performance of disruptive behavior disordered and normal samples on the Draw-a-Person: Screening Procedure for Emotional Disturbance. *Psychological Assessment, 4*, 156–159.

Ornduff, S. R., Freedenfeld, R. N., Kelsey, R. M., & Critelli, J. W. (1994). Object relations of sexually abused female subjects: A TAT analysis. *Journal of Personality Assessment, 63*, 223–238.

Pierce, G. E., & Penman, P. (1998). Rorschach psychological characteristics of students with serious emotional disturbance. *California School Psychologist, 3*, 35–42.

Piotrowski, C., & Zalewski, C. (1993). Training in psychodiagnostic testing in APA-approved PsyD and PhD clinical psychology programs. *Journal of Personality Assessment, 61*, 394–405.

Pistole, D. R., & Ornduff, S. R. (1994). TAT assessment of sexually abused girls: An analysis of manifest content. *Journal of Personality Assessment, 63*, 211–222.

Prout, H. T. (1983). School psychologists and social-emotional assessment techniques: Patterns in training and use. *School Psychology Review, 12*, 377–383.

Reynolds, C. R., & Kamphaus, R. W. (2004). *Behavior assessment scale for children* (2nd ed.). Circle Pines, MN: American Guidance Service, Inc.

Reynolds, D. R., & Shaywitz, S. E. (2009). Response to intervention: Ready or not? Or wait-to-fail to watch-them-fail. *School Psychology Quarterly, 24*, 130–145.

Shapiro, E. S., & Heick, P. F. (2004). School psychologist assessment practices in the evaluation of students referred for social/behavioral/emotional problems. *Psychology in the Schools, 41*, 551–561.

Shapiro, E. S., & Kratochwill, T. R. (2000). *Behavioral assessment in schools* (2nd ed.). New York: Guilford Press.

Shirk, S. R., & Russell, R. L. (1996). *Change processes in child psychotherapy.* New York: Guilford Press.

Smith, A. M., Gacono, C. B., & Kaufman, L. (1997). A Rorschach comparison of psychopathic and non-psychopathic conduct disordered adolescents. *Journal of Clinical Psychology, 53,* 239–300.

Society for Personality Assessment. (2005). The status of the Rorschach in clinical and forensic practice: An official statement by the Board of Trustees of the Society for Personality Assessment. *Journal of Personality Assessment, 85,* 219–237.

Socket, B. (1998, March). *The Rorschach and the traditional psychoeducational battery.* Paper presented at the midwinter meeting of the Society for Personality Assessment, Boston, MA.

Stage, S. A., Jackson, H. G., Moscovitz, K., Erickson, M. J., Thurman, S. O., Jessee, W., et al. (2006). Using multimethod-multisource functional behavioral assessment for students with behavioral disabilities. *School Psychology Review, 35,* 451–471.

Stokes, J. M., Pogge, D. L., Powell-Lunder, J., Ward, A. W., Bilginer, L., & DeLuca, V. (2003). The Rorschach ego impairment index: Prediction of treatment outcomes in a child psychiatric population. *Journal of Personality Assessment, 81,* 11–19.

Steadman, J. M., Hatch, J. P., & Schoenfeld, L. S. (2001). Internship directors' valuation of preinternship preparation of test-based assessment and psychotherapy. *Professional Psychology: Research and Practice, 32,* 421–424.

Stinnett, T. A., Havey, J. M., & Oehler-Stinnett, J. (1994). Current test usage by practicing school psychologists: A national survey. *Journal of Psychoeducational Assessment, 12,* 331.

Teglasi, H. (1998). Assessment of schema and problem solving strategies with projective techniques. In C. R. Reynolds (Ed.), *Handbook of clinical psychology: Vol. 4. Assessment.* New York: Elsevier.

Teglasi, H. (2001). *Essentials of TAT and other story telling instruments assessment.* New York: Wiley.

Teglasi, H. (2007). Introduction to the series-personality assessment: The whole and its parts. *Psychology in the Schools, 44,* 209–214

Validity, reliability, and credibility of self-reported data. (n.d.). Retrieved August 15, 2003, from http://nsse.iub.edu/2002_annual_report/html/conceptual_validity.htm

Watson, T. S., & Steege, M. W. (2003). *Conducting school-based functional behavioral assessments.* New York: Guilford Press.

Weber, C. A., Meloy, J. R., Gacono, C. B. (1992). A Rorschach study of attachment and anxiety in inpatient conduct disordered and dysthymic adolescents. *Journal of Personality Assessment, 58,* 16–26.

Weiner, I. (2000). Making Rorschach interpretation as good as it can be. *Journal of Personality Assessment, 74,* 164–17

12 Neuropsychology in school psychology

Catherine A. Fiorello, James B. Hale, Scott L. Decker, and Schehera Coleman

IMPORTANCE OF NEUROPSYCHOLOGY FOR SCHOOL PSYCHOLOGY

Neuropsychology has traditionally been defined as the study of brain–behavior relationships in patient populations. It has flourished as a profession because of an accumulated body of knowledge of brain functions in relation to cognition (Fiorello, Hale, Snyder, Forrest, & Teodori, 2008) and real world outcomes (Hale & Fiorello, 2004). From its beginning in the prediction of behavioral deficits based on localization of brain injury to modern methods of brain scanning and imaging to predict outcomes and inform intervention, neuropsychology has been enriched by a long history of empirical investigation, making it the quintessential science in psychological practice.

Although school neuropsychology as a specialty area is relatively new (Hale & Fiorello, 2004), neuropsychology has a long history of school and educational applications (Hynd & Reynolds, 2005). Unfortunately, and perhaps because of the definition of neuropsychology as the study of brain–behavior relationships, some have suggested that neuropsychology is only applicable for children with frank neurological trauma, such as brain injury. However, as the science of neuropsychology has emerged, it is clear that neuropsychological principles and practices are relevant for almost every Individuals with Disabilities Education Improvement Act (2004) eligibility category (Davis, 2006; Hale & Fiorello, 2004; Peterson & Panksepp, 2004; Schaer & Eliez, 2007; Semrud-Clikeman & Pliszka, 2005).

For example, specific learning disabilities (SLDs) are known to have empirical correlates with numerous biological variables, such as genetics (Decker & Vanderberg, 1985), neurological development (Gaddes & Edgell, 1994; Hynd, Semrud-Clikeman, & Lyytinen, 1991; National Joint Committee on Learning Disabilities, 2005; Torgesen, 1991), and functional brain activation patterns (Shaywitz et al., 2004). Children with SLDs differ from typical children in the cognitive processing contributions to reading and math (e.g., Hale et al., 2008), consistent with longitudinal findings that they have developmental *deficits*—not delays (Francis, Shaywitz, Stuebing,

Shaywitz, & Fletcher, 1996). Similar findings support the biological basis of attention-deficit/hyperactivity disorder (Barkley, 1997; Hale, Fiorello, & Brown, 2005), autism (Allen, Robins, & Decker, 2008) and other pervasive developmental disorders (Smalley & Collins, 1996), seizure disorders (Clark & Christiansen, 2005), depression and anxiety (Lichter & Cummings, 2001), and many other conditions, such as fetal alcohol syndrome, cerebral palsy, Tourette syndrome, and schizophrenia. Understanding a biopsychosocial perspective will become increasingly important for distinguishing typical from atypical neuropsychological development (Miller, 2007), especially given that reduced federal funding for children with disabilities requires schools to provide more intense levels of care (Fletcher-Janzen, 2005). In addition, school neuropsychologists are perhaps the best prepared to rapidly incorporate advances in medical, genetic, neuroscience, neurology, and psychopharmacology disciplines to foster application of neuropsychological principles within the educational context (Davis, 2006).

NEUROPSYCHOLOGY TRAINING IN SCHOOL PSYCHOLOGY

It is typical for school psychology programs to have only one course in the "biological bases of behavior," sometimes taught by professors with little training in child neuropsychology or school psychology. We would recommend that practical training in child neuropsychological assessment be a part of training programs at the doctoral level and that at least some familiarity with the concepts and procedures be given at the specialist level. Including neuropsychological, cognitive, and psychometric approaches to data interpretation not only fosters identification of learning and behavior problems for more accurate differential diagnosis, but it can also be used to inform intervention development, implementation, monitoring, and evaluation.

We conceptualize training in school neuropsychological theory and practice as occurring in multiple stages, with each stage adding a layer of knowledge and skill competency. We initially present our students a basic version of a neuropsychological model, recommending a two-axis interpretation method. The first axis of interpretation is the posterior–anterior axis. The posterior, or back, of the brain is Luria's (1973) second functional unit, where information processing begins and is integrated for comprehension. Information is received here and analyzed at a preliminary level. The primary cortex receives auditory, visual, and somatosensory input. Most childhood learning disorders are not caused by sensory problems located in this primary cortex or input area, despite the popularity of interventions that focus on multisensory instruction and "learning styles." Information from the second functional unit is instead integrated in the secondary and tertiary cortical areas, which make up Luria's *zones of overlapping* (see Figure 12.1).

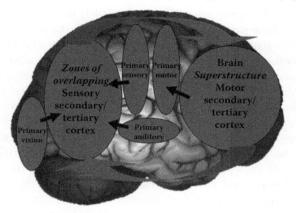

Figure 12.1 Luria's working brain. (From Luria, A. R., *The Working Brain*, Penguin Books, New York, 1973.)

This area of the brain coordinates, integrates, and comprehends information passed from the primary sensory cortex. This is also the place where many receptive learning disabilities are found—not at the basic input level of processing, but at the level of integration and comprehension (Hale & Fiorello, 2004).

Whereas input is located in the back of the brain, output is located in the frontal lobes. The primary motor area, or output region, is also found in Luria's third functional unit. The most anterior (behind the forehead and eyes) frontal brain area is considered the prefrontal cortex. Luria called this the brain's *superstructure*, responsible for the executive functions of planning and coordinating all brain activity. So information moves from the posterior of the brain to the anterior as it enters, is processed and integrated, and is acted upon by the frontal lobes. As depicted in Figure 12.1, input begins in the primary cortex and is interpreted in the tertiary cortex (1→2→3), but output begins with planning in the tertiary cortex and the action is carried out by the primary cortex (3→2→1). In addition, the tertiary regions communicate with each other, so these highest levels of comprehension and action communicate with each other.

The second axis of interpretation is the left–right axis. Early conceptualizations of hemisphere function were based on patient populations and were found to be inaccurate. Early theories, dominating neuropsychology for nearly 100 years, suggested that the left hemisphere was the dominant verbal hemisphere, and the right hemisphere was the nondominant nonverbal one, but subsequent neuroimaging and neuropsychological studies have revealed that content dichotomy to be incorrect. Instead of content, *process* is the important difference between the hemispheres (Reynolds, Kamphaus, Rosenthal, & Hiemenz, 1997). The left hemisphere handles routinized, crystallized, and detail processing, whereas the right handles novel, fluid, and global processing (Goldberg, 2001; Bryan & Hale, 2001). As the left hemisphere processes known information and is specialized for concordant/convergent thought, it is dominant after material is learned and mastered. However, the right hemisphere, specializing in novel problem solving and discordant/divergent thought, is dominant when processing complex or ambiguous information and learning new material (Bryan & Hale, 2001). The left hemisphere prefers facts, details, and correct responding (a little like the obsessive-compulsive part of our brain), whereas the right hemisphere likes multiple ideas, complex problem solving situations, and the global, holistic big picture. This is consistent with Cattell–Horn–Carroll theory, with crystallized processing (Gc) occurring in the left hemisphere and fluid reasoning (Gf) occurring in the right (Hale & Fiorello, 2004). Taken together, the posterior–anterior and left–right axes form the basis of school neuropsychological interpretation (see Figure 12.2).

This basic school neuropsychological model necessitates idiographic as opposed to nomothetic interpretation, as any given task might be novel or routinized for a given student. Valuation of individual differences in cognition and brain function must be of paramount importance when conducting any school neuropsychological evaluation. Any given student may use different cognitive processes to complete a particular task, especially on multifactorial intellectual measures (Hale, Fiorello, Kavanagh, Holdnack, & Aloe, 2007). Few tasks are designed to preclude the use of different strategies or processes to solve them, and children who wish to perform well will

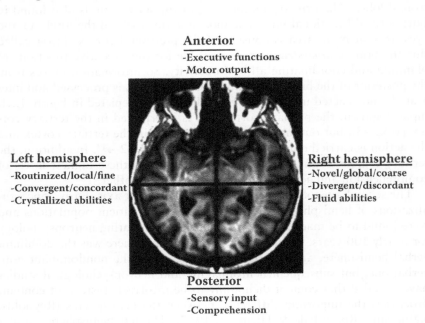

Anterior
-Executive functions
-Motor output

Left hemisphere
-Routinized/local/fine
-Convergent/concordant
-Crystallized abilities

Right hemisphere
-Novel/global/coarse
-Divergent/discordant
-Fluid abilities

Posterior
-Sensory input
-Comprehension

Figure 12.2 The two-axis interpretation.

use compensatory approaches when they have difficulty on a particular task. Exploration of a student's processing skills, through observation, further testing, and formal demands analysis may be necessary, and precludes the use of "cookbook" (i.e., "one interpretation fits all") approaches to interpretation (Fiorello et al., 2008; Hale & Fiorello, 2004).

In addition, neuroimaging research also reveals that many brain areas are involved in any given task, but processing demands will determine which areas are dominant for solving the problem (Goldberg, 2001). Understanding basic brain structures and functions can provide information about how students think, learn, and behave, but lesion localization is not the task of the school neuropsychologist. Instead, hypotheses about individual strengths and weaknesses should be tested iteratively, with test data evaluated and interventions recycled until concurrent, ecological, and treatment validity is established.

IDENTIFICATION OF LEARNING DISORDERS

Historically, one of the criteria used to identify individuals with learning disabilities was the presence of a severe discrepancy between the individual's intelligence quotient (IQ) score and score on a test of academic achievement. The discrepancy model assumes that IQ and achievement measures are independent of each other (Siegel, 2003), when clearly there is a great deal of overlap (Fiorello et al., 2008; Hale & Fiorello, 2004; Hale et al., 2007). Different methods of determining a discrepancy have been devised to minimize this difficulty, but even regression methods rather arbitrarily determine which students will be considered eligible or not, despite equal academic needs. In addition, severe discrepancy methods have been called a "wait to fail" model, as most students must experience a great deal of school failure before exhibiting a numerical discrepancy (Reschly, 2005). Other explanations for the inherent problems in traditional psychoeducational evaluation include inappropriate use of psychometric instruments and overreliance on simplistic criteria for differential diagnosis of complex clinical conditions (Hale & Fiorello, 2004; Mather & Gregg, 2006; Mather & Kaufman, 2006). These problems may be more generally summarized as problems in decision-making procedures (Decker, 2008), not problems with the assessment tools. It makes no sense to eliminate some of the best psychological tools available to practitioners just because they have not been used effectively (Hale et al., 2006, 2008).

In order to address these concerns, an alternative model called response to intervention (RTI) has been proposed and included as an alternative in the reauthorization of the Individuals with Disabilities Education Act (IDEA, 2004). Reynolds (2008) identifies RTI as a way of screening children who may not be responding to instruction. Although there is no uniform definition of RTI and there is much debate regarding its scientific credibility, many have suggested that it is preferred practice over standard-ized psychological assessment (e.g., Reschly, 2005). Certainly, using ongo-ing progress monitoring of student achievement, and providing preventive academic interventions for those who are struggling, is a positive con-tribution (Fiorello, Hale, & Snyder, 2006; Hale, Kaufman, Naglieri, & Kavale, 2006), with some even suggesting it should be mandated and funded (Hale, 2006).

Certainly, RTI can help struggling children, but the assumption that failure to respond is due to an SLD is not scientifically defensible (Hale et al., 2008). Unless an underlying causative explanation is entertained and evaluated using comprehensive evaluation, no one can be sure why the child did not respond (Hale et al., 2006). Students who do not progress at an appropriate rate may be identified as learning disabled, even though the slow rate of development may be due to lack of background, English lan-guage learner status, or an overall slow rate of development. In addition, the RTI assumption that effective, research-based teaching and interven-tions will occur is unlikely to be met in high-need districts. RTI depends on assessment of a student's progress based on local norms rather than the population at large, making the definition of a learning disability depen-dent on the makeup of a classroom or neighborhood (Reynolds, 2008). RTI also ignores the processing deficit component of the definition of a learn-ing disability in IDEA (Hale et al., 2006; Reynolds, 2008). These prob-lems illustrate how simplistic decision-making and conclusions made from an RTI methodology, in isolation from other methods, may have as many problems as (or even more than) the traditional psychometric approaches RTI was meant to resolve.

Does clarifying the attribution or explanation of SLD really matter? We believe it does. First, the current controversy about SLD seems to present a (false) dichotomy between those who see value in psychological testing and those who see the value in alternative behavioral approaches. This does not take into consideration many who see the value in both procedures (Berninger, 2006; Fiorello et al., 2006; 2007; Flanagan, Ortiz, Alfonso, & Dynda, 2006; Hale et al., 2006, 2007, 2008; Mather & Gregg, 2006; Ofiesh, 2006; Schrank, Miller, Caterino, & Desrochers, 2006; Semrud-Clikeman, 2005; Willis & Dumont, 2006; Wodrich, Spencer, & Daley, 2006). These models have in common an emphasis on individual clinical evaluation of cognitive strengths and weaknesses and a link of assessment to intervention. According to Flanagan, Ortiz, and Alfonso (2008), "use of one approach need not exclude use of the other and it is unlikely that children with SLDs will be served well by any approach that represents an extreme position" (p. 17).

Second, viewing the problem as one of poor operationalization and decision-making (e.g., Reschly & Hosp, 2004), rather than philosophical orientation, reveals problems with both traditional and alternative sys-tems (Flanagan et al., 2006; Hale et al., 2006; Willis & Dumont, 2006).

Although there is legitimacy to the accusation that diagnostic categorical systems are often loosely defined and do not represent a homogeneous groups of students (Reschly & Hosp, 2004), there is little reason to believe using an RTI approach in its current conceptualization will provide a more valid or more discriminating procedure (Gerber, 2005; Fuchs & Deshler, 2007; Hale, 2006; Kavale, Holdnack, & Mostert, 2005). In fact, many indicators suggest that attempting to label children as *responders* versus *nonresponders* will result in problems similar to those caused by using traditional discrepancy criteria (Decker, 2008; Gerber, 2005). Often, what intervention should be used for what problem for what length of time and why is left unspecified in an RTI approach (Mather & Kaufman, 2006). Despite school psychologists' support for RTI, numerous methodological issues remain unsolved, and there is already sufficient evidence to suggest that RTI strictly defined and in isolation may not provide all of the benefits for which it was intended (Fuchs, 2003; Fuchs & Deshler, 2007; Hale et al., 2006; Kavale, Holdnack, & Mostert, 2006; Naglieri & Crockett, 2005).

Viewed from this perspective, specification of a decision-making, problem-solving model that adequately represents the multivariate nature of the problems faced by school psychologists is crucial. Such models indicate that the ultimate problem faced by school psychologists is not simply how to select the right test, procedure, or methodology, but how to make decisions for optimizing child outcomes under conditions of uncertainty. Not every child needs a psychological evaluation; not every child needs an intervention. The psychologist must use a variety of methods, always evaluating hypotheses against empirical evidence, while acting in the best interest of the child. This is the true definition of scientist–practitioner.

CONDUCTING SCHOOL NEUROPSYCHOLOGICAL EVALUATIONS USING COGNITIVE HYPOTHESIS TESTING

Unlike traditional school psychology evaluations that solely address entitlement decisions (Gresham et al., 2005), school neuropsychological evaluations should be comprehensive enough to address both diagnosis and intervention (Hale & Fiorello, 2004). Determining whether a child has a significant reading problem or attention problem may be enough to qualify him or her for IDEA (2004) SLD or Other Health Impaired (OHI) services, respectively, but good school neuropsychological evaluations need to inform intervention because there are so many different subtypes of disorders, even within a specific disability category (Hale et al., 2008). For instance, children with reading disabilities can have phonemic, orthographic, phoneme–grapheme correspondence, reading fluency, automaticity, lexical-semantic, language comprehension, sequencing, syntactic, working memory, or oral expression problems (Fiorello, Hale, & Snyder, 2006). Children diagnosed with attention deficit/hyperactivity disorder (ADHD) may respond to medication because they have executive deficits in response inhibition, working memory, mental flexibility, and sustained attention, whereas others diagnosed with ADHD may have other disorders that do not respond (Hale et al., 2005; Reddy & Hale, 2007). It is an understanding of these psychological processes and how they interfere with reading achievement and classroom behavior that matters for intervention, yet all these deficits would qualify a child for IDEA services.

Traditional school psychological evaluations are also limited because conclusions are typically based on limited data. As a result, more parents are requesting a "neuropsychological evaluation," because as informed consumers they know that most childhood disorders have a brain–behavior basis (Davis, 2006; Hale & Fiorello, 2004; Peterson & Panksepp, 2004; Schaer & Eliez, 2007; Semrud-Clikeman & Pliszka, 2005) and that these types of evaluations are often comprehensive enough to integrate cognitive, academic, and behavioral functioning of their child and can inform intervention (Fiorello, Hale, Snyder, Forrest, & Teodori, 2008). In Table 12.1, we present some useful instruments

Table 12.1 Useful Measures for Neuropsychological Assessment

Major neuropsychological test batteries for use in schools

	Cognitive Assessment System
	Comprehensive Test of Nonverbal Intelligence, 2nd ed.
	Differential Abilities Scale, 2nd ed.
	Kaufman Assessment Battery for Children, 2nd ed.
	Kaufman Tests of Educational Achievement, 2nd ed.
	NEPSY-II, 2nd ed.
	Raven's Progressive Matrices
	Stanford-Binet Intelligence Scales, 5th ed.
	Universal Nonverbal Intelligence Test
	Wechsler Individual Achievement Test, 3rd ed.
	Wechsler Preschool and Primary Scale of Intelligence, 3rd ed.
	Wechsler Intelligence Scale for Children, 4th ed.
	Wechsler Intelligence Scale for Children, 4th ed.—Integrated
	Woodcock Johnson, 3rd ed., Tests of Academic Achievement
	Woodcock Johnson, 3rd ed., Tests of Cognitive Abilities

Supplemental neuropsychological tests by area of concentration

Sensory–motor function	Beery-Buktenica Developmental Test of Visual Motor Integration, 5th ed.
	Bender Visual-Motor Gestalt Test, 2nd ed.
	Dean-Woodcock Sensory Motor Battery
	Full Range Test of Visual-Motor Integration

Table 12.1 (Continued)

	Motor-Free Visual Perception Test, Revised
	Quick Neuropsychological Screening Test, 2nd ed.
	Test of Visual-Motor Skills, Revised
Attention	Delis-Kaplan Executive Function System
	Conners' Continuous Performance Test, 2nd ed.
	Gordon Diagnostic System
	Test of Everyday Attention for Children
	Wide Range Assessment of Memory and Learning, 2nd ed.
	Wisconsin Card Sorting Test
Visual–spatial processes	Developmental Test of Visual Perception
	Benton Facial Recognition Test
	Delis-Kaplan Executive Function System
	Motor-Free Visual Perception Test, 3rd ed.
	Test of Visual Perceptual Skills, 3rd ed.
Language	Comprehensive Test of Phonological Processing
	Auditory Processing Abilities Test
	Boehm Test of Basic Concepts, 3rd ed.
	Boston Naming Test
	Clinical Evaluation of Language Fundamentals, 4th ed.
	Comprehensive Assessment of Spoken Language
	Comprehensive Receptive and Expressive Vocabulary Test
	Expressive One-Word Picture Vocabulary Test
	Expressive Vocabulary Test, 2nd ed.
	Kaufman Survey of Early Academic and Language Skills
	Oral and Written Language Scales
	Peabody Picture Vocabulary Test, 4th ed.
	Process Assessment of the Learner
	Receptive One-Word Picture Vocabulary Test
	Test for Auditory Comprehension of Language
	Test of Auditory Processing Skills, 3rd ed.
	Test of Language Development
	Wepman's Auditory Discrimination Test
	WORD Test 2nd ed.
Memory and learning	Children's Memory Scale
	California Verbal Learning Test—Children's Version
	Test of Memory and Learning
	Wechsler Memory Scale, 3rd ed.
	Wide Range Assessment of Memory and Learning, 2nd ed.
Executive functioning	Delis-Kaplan Executive Function System
	Stroop Color–Word Test
	Wisconsin Card Sorting Test

for school neuropsychologi-cal evaluations. It is not uncommon for a "comprehensive" school psychology evaluation to include only an intellectual measure, an achievement measure, a measure of visual–motor integration, and a behavior rating scale. Clinical interviews and classroom observations are sometimes included, but it is not uncommon to have other multidisciplinary team members complete those parts of the evaluation, and in some states, a special educator administers the achievement test. This compartmentalization of a child's psychological functioning limits inferences drawn from the data. It is extremely difficult to make recommendations for a child with a math reasoning disorder if the school psychologist has not assessed his or her math skills.

Another problem has to do with the number of evaluations required in most schools and time to complete them (Sheridan & Gutkin, 2000). We could advocate hiring more and more school psychologists to reduce caseloads, and this would be a laudable goal. But the reality is that we have limited resources in the schools, and so we must use our time more effectively. Readers may be surprised that in a chapter focused on neuropsychology we will argue that practitioners need to spend *more* time on intervention and *less* time on comprehensive evaluations. Even before RTI became law, we argued that practitioners must *intervene to assess* (Hale & Fiorello, 2004). Unless comprehensive evaluation caseloads decrease through an RTI approach in general education, we will never be able to provide the comprehensive school neuropsychological evaluations needed to provide the accurate diagnostic pictures of children necessary to inform classroom intervention. As we have stated elsewhere (e.g., Fiorello et al., 2006; Hale, 2006; Hale et al., 2006), comprehensive evaluations are needed for children who do not respond to standard interventions, and if RTI is implemented well, we will need to do fewer evaluations but do a more thorough job when they are necessary for nonresponders.

Our cognitive hypothesis testing (CHT) model (Hale & Fiorello, 2004; see Figure 12.3) provides a framework for integrating multiple data sources for children who do not respond to standard interventions and may have a brain-based learning or behavior disorder requiring special education services. Based on scientific method principles, the CHT approach to comprehensive cognitive and neuropsychological assessment is used for identification and intervention within the context of the problem-solving paradigm. Although some would argue that nonresponsiveness is sufficient for classification of childhood disorders (e.g., Reschly, 2005), there are many reasons why a child might not respond, only one of which may be a disability (e.g., Mather & Gregg, 2006). We argue that a comprehensive CHT evaluation is necessary prior to any entitlement decision, not only to ensure diagnostic accuracy but also to inform subsequent intervention efforts (Fiorello et al., 2006; Hale, 2006; Hale & Fiorello, 2004; Hale et al., 2006).

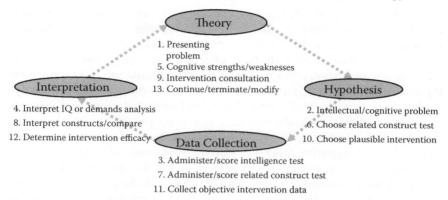

Figure 12.3 Cognitive hypothesis testing model. (From Hale, J. B., & Fiorello, C. A., *School Neuropsychology: A Practitioner's Handbook*, Guilford Press, New York, 2004.)

In the CHT model, some diagnostic impressions can be formed using profile analysis of intellectual subtest scores, a frequently used interpretive strategy in school psychology practice (Pfeiffer, Reddy, Kletzel, Schmelzer, & Boyer, 2000). However, a child's performance on the multifactorial subtests vary for reasons not easily identified in group studies (Baron, 2005), and the clinical utility of such profiles is extremely limited (e.g., Watkins, Glutting, & Youngstrom, 2005), especially if additional data sources are not considered to establish concurrent, ecological, and treatment validity of findings (Hale & Fiorello, 2004). As a result, we argue that any hypotheses or impressions derived from intellectual measures must be confirmed or refuted using additional standardized cognitive/neuropsychological testing and other data sources using the CHT model, not only for more accurate diagnoses but also for developing informed interventions sensitive to child needs (Hale & Fiorello, 2004). Children with brain-based disorders experience developmental deficits (e.g., Castellanos et al., 2002; Francis et al., 1996)—not delays—which suggests that simply using similar instructional strategies at greater intensities (e.g., Barnett, Daly, Jones, & Lentz, 2004) will not meet their unique needs (Hale et al., 2008). The goal of CHT is to develop individualized single-subject interventions that are subsequently monitored to determine their effectiveness within the context of the problem-solving model (Hale & Fiorello, 2004).

The CHT model helps practitioners overcome the limitations of traditional profile analysis, not only to ensure accurate diagnosis (i.e., reducing false positives or negatives) but also to link assessment data to empirically supported interventions. It begins with an examination of referral question, historical data, observational data, interviews of the teacher, parent, and child, and previous intervention attempts (i.e., Tiers 1 and 2 RTI data).

If the presenting problem (Step 1) appears to be related to one or more cognitive problems (Step 2), an intellectual/cognitive measure is administered and scored (Step 3). Careful recording of all child behavior and item responses is critical during all data collection, especially during this step. Next, practitioners must evaluate whether they should interpret the global IQ score or conduct a demands analysis, which is similar to a profile analysis but examines the input, processing, and output demands of subtests in understanding the child's cognitive and neuropsychological assets and deficits (Hale & Fiorello, 2004). Unfortunately, most of our initial conceptualizations of cognitive processes were derived from our examination of input (e.g., auditory, visual) or output (e.g., verbal, fine motor), but with the advent of neuroimaging we have realized that it is the psychological processes that must be interpreted, not the observable input or output (Fiorello et al., 2006; 2007; 2008; Hale et al., 2006, 2007, 2008).

Demands analysis is a core component of the cognitive hypothesis testing model and looks at individual differences in processing, both for diagnostic purposes and to develop individualized interventions. Demands analysis was derived from two strands of assessment research. The "intelligent testing" and cross-battery approaches depend on psychometric and quantitative research into test demands (e.g., Flanagan, Ortiz, & Alfonso, 2007; Kamphaus, 2001; Kaufman, 1994; McGrew & Flanagan, 1997; Sattler, 2008). The second strand is the process approach to neuropsychological assessment, which involves more idiopathic interpretation (e.g., Holmes-Bernstein, 2000; Kaplan, 1988; Lezak, 1995; Luria, 1973). To conduct a demands analysis, one must draw on the psychometric literature as well as the neuropsychological processing literature to identify the input, processing, and output demands of each task. Although identifying the input and output demands is relatively straightforward, identifying the processing demands goes beyond the typical versions of profile analysis taught to school psychologists (e.g., Kaufman, 1994).

To conduct a demands analysis, tasks (tests and subtests) that are strengths and weaknesses for the student should be identified using appropriate clinical and statistical criteria (Fiorello et al., 2008; Hale & Fiorello, 2004; Hale et al., 2006, 2007, 2008). For each task, the input, processing, and output demands should be determined. Although input and output may be important for students with sensory or motor disabilities, or English language learners, processing demands are the most important for identifying learning disabilities and most neuropsychologically based disorders (Fiorello et al., 2007; Hale & Fiorello, 2004; Hale et al., 2006). Identifying processing demands should start with a review of technical manuals and other sources of group data about what tasks measure (e.g., Flanagan, Ortiz, & Alfonso, 2007; Sattler, 2008). However, secondary requirements may include such constructs as attention, working memory, and executive functions necessary to attend to and mentally manipulate stimuli. In CHT, any demands analysis patterns of strengths and weaknesses are merely hypotheses that must be confirmed or refuted using observations of the student, input from teachers and parents, work samples, and other cognitive, academic, or behavioral data.

Although some academics claim that intellectual/cognitive profile analysis should be avoided and global IQ is the only score worth interpreting (Watkins, Glutting, & Lei, 2007), our own research suggests global IQ is of limited utility in predicting achievement and neuropsychological outcomes, because it is composed of disparate parts that have adequate interpretive specificity, not a single construct (Fiorello, Hale, McGrath, Ryan, & Quinn, 2001; 2007; Hale et al., 2002, 2007, 2008). This research shows that profile variability is common in typical and clinical populations, which suggests to some that it has limited diagnostic relevance (Glutting, McDermott, Watkins, Kush, & Konold, 1997), but profile differences are being found for clinical populations (Fiorello et al., 2006; 2007; Hale et al., 2007, 2008; Mayes & Calhoun, 2004; 2006; Mayes, Calhoun, & Crowell, 1998). Although we recognize that profile analysis without supportive evidence is of limited diagnostic value, we do not concur with the position that its prominence in both clinical and typical populations is without meaning. Profile variability is not just measurement "noise" or error, because this would be reflected in the standardization reliability and validity studies. Instead, it *could* reflect meaningful individual differences in cognition during the particular test administration for a particular child at that specific time. Whether it is an enduring pattern is another question, one that can be answered—substantiated or refuted—during the second phase of the CHT evaluation.

Although level of performance is considered during these first four steps, we suggest that profile variability should preclude global IQ interpretation and instead demands analysis of factors and/or subtests should be conducted. On the basis of these initial findings (including all data collected up to this point), a theory of what the cognitive assets and deficits is developed (Step 5), and other cognitive and/or neuropsychological measures are chosen to test that theory (Step 6) and administered/scored (Step 7). For instance, if the pattern of performance suggests graphomotor skills might be impaired, a child would be administered a measure of spatial processing without motor demands, a visual–sequential task without motor demands, a somatosensory task that requires perception of touch without visual or motor demands, and a fine motor task that requires minimal visual processing or graphomotor skills. There are not cognitive or neuropsychological tests/subtests that allow examination of single skills, so this "leave one construct out" principle allows the clinician to confirm or refute initial hypotheses (Step 8).

Integrating all the data sources collected up to this point allows the practitioner to write a comprehensive evaluation report detailing the child's cognitive/neuropsychological assets and needs, draw conclusions about the impact these processes have on academic and behavioral functioning, and provide multiple recommendations for intervention. During the feed-back session and/or multidisciplinary team meeting, intervention ideas are shared and a plan of action is developed. A critical first step includes meeting with the teacher to develop an intervention plan (Step 9). The process then follows the problem solving model of developing (Step 10), implementing (Step 11), evaluating (Step 12), and modifying (Step 13) the intervention as necessary until treatment efficacy is achieved.

The CHT model intervention phase requires use of single-subject methodologies to determine treatment efficacy. Our experience in the Student Neuropsychological Assessment Profiles for Innovative Teaching project, which uses CHT methodology, is that interventions often need recycling during the problem-solving process. Each intervention is individually tailored to child needs on the basis of all data sources, but each must be carefully monitored, evaluated, and recycled until treatment efficacy is obtained (Hale & Fiorello, 2004). Rather than trying to make a child fit a subtype and a specific intervention, each child is an "*n* of 1" case study, which appears to be the most effective approach for these types of specialized interventions (e.g., Fiorello et al., 2006; Hale et al., 2006; Reddy & Hale, 2007). More specialized interventions that are labor intensive may require direct services by the school psychologist or another specialist, but if possible, the interventions and data collection should be completed by those who have direct, regular access to the child (e.g., teacher, parent) and/or the child.

Although similar approaches for differential diagnosis are offered in the cross-battery approach (e.g., Flanagan et al., 2006) and neuropsychological process approaches (e.g., Kaplan, 1988), what is innovative about CHT is the use of cognitive and neuropsychological data to guide subsequent development of individualized single-subject interventions sensitive to individual needs within the context of a flexible problem-solving model, thereby effectively linking assessment results to intervention in an iterative process that ensures ecological and treatment validity. This approach exemplifies the integration of normative/psychometric methods with ideographic/single-subject methods.

Combining knowledge and skills in school neuropsychology with an adaptive problem-solving model and single-subject designs may seem antithetical to some readers. However, the literature on both approaches reveals one commonality—they are both empirically based. As the school neuropsychology knowledge base expands to address the educational arena, practitioners will need to keep abreast of the literature to advance their clinical assessment and intervention skills. Studies in the last 10 years have demonstrated the importance of understanding neuropsychological profiles for developing targeted interventions and differentiated classroom instruction (see Hale et al., 2008). We predict that these findings will soon become commonplace as practitioners become more effective in using this knowledge base and advancing their skills for differential diagnosis and intervention development, progress monitoring, and evaluation. These advances can be facilitated by trainers and training programs that incorporate school neuropsychological principles and practices in the classroom, training clinic, and field.

REFERENCES

Allen, R., Robins, D., & Decker, S. L. (2008). Neuropsychology of autism and response to intervention models. *Psychology in the Schools, 45,* 905–917.
Barkley, R. A. (1997). Behavioral inhibition, sustained attention, and executive functions: Constructing a unifying theory of ADHD. *Psychological Bulletin, 121,* 65–94.
Barnett, D. W., Daly, E. J., Jones, K. M., & Lentz, F. E. (2004). Response to intervention: Empirically based special service decisions from single-case designs of increasing and decreasing intensity. *The Journal of Special Education, 38,* 66–79.
Baron, I. S. (2005). Test review: Wechsler intelligence scale for children-fourth edition (WISC-IV). *Child Neuropsychology, 11,* 471–475.
Berninger, V. W. (2006). Research-supported ideas for implementing reauthorized IDEA with intelligent professional psychological services. *Psychology in the Schools, 43,* 781–796.
Bryan, K. L., & Hale, J. B. (2001). Differential effects of left and right cerebral vascular accidents on language competency. *Journal of the International Neuropsychological Society, 7,* 655–664.
Castellanos, F. X., Lee, P. P., Sharp, W., Jeffries, N. O., Greenstein, D. K., Clasen, L. S., et al. (2002). Developmental trajectories of brain volume abnormalities in children and adolescents with attention-deficit/hyperactivity disorder. *Journal of the American Medical Association, 288,* 1740–1748.
Clark, E., & Christiansen, E. (2005). Neurological and psychological issues for learners with seizures. In R. C. D'Amato, E. Fletcher-Janzen, & C. R. Reynolds (Eds.), *Handbook of school neuropsychology.* Hoboken, NJ: John Wiley & Sons.
Davis, A. S. (2006). The neuropsychological basis of childhood psychopathology. *Psychology in the Schools, 43,* 503–512.
Decker, S. L. (2008). Intervention psychometrics: Using norm-referenced methods for treatment planning and monitoring. *Assessment for Effective Interventions, 34,* 52–61.
Decker, S. N., & Vanderberg, S. G. (1985). Colorado twin study of reading disability. In D. B. Gray & J. F. Kavanaugh (Eds.), *Biobehavioral measures of dyslexia.* Parkton, MD: York Press.
Fiorello, C. A., Hale, J. B., Holdnack, J. A., Kavanagh, J. A., Terrell, J., & Long, L. (2007). Interpreting intelligence test results for children with disabilities: Is global intelligence relevant? *Applied Neuropsychology, 14,* 2–12.
Fiorello, C. A., Hale, J. B., McGrath, M., Ryan, K., & Quinn, S. (2001). IQ interpretation for children with flat and variable test profiles. *Learning and Individual Differences, 13,* 115–125.
Fiorello, C. A., Hale, J. B., & Snyder, L. E. (2006). Cognitive hypothesis testing and response to intervention for children with reading disabilities. *Psychology in the Schools, 43*(8), 835–853.

Fiorello, C. A., Hale, J. B., Snyder, L. E., Forrest, E., & Teodori, A. (2008). Validating individual differences through examination of converging psychometric and neuropsychological models of cognitive functioning. In S. K. Thurman & C. A. Fiorello (Eds.), *Applied Cognitive Research in K-3 Classrooms*. New York: Routledge.

Flanagan, D. P., Ortiz, S. O., & Alfonso, V. C. (2007). *Essentials of Cross Battery Assessment* (2nd ed.). Hoboken, NJ: John Wiley & Sons, Inc.

Flanagan, D. P., Ortiz, S. O., & Alfonso, V. C. (2008). Response to Intervention (RTI) and cognitive testing approaches provide different but complementary data sources that inform SLD identification. *Communiqué, 36,* 16–17.

Flanagan, D. P., Ortiz, S. O., Alfonso, V. C., & Dynda, A. M. (2006). Integration of response to intervention and norm-referenced tests in learning disability identification: Learning from the tower of Babel. *Psychology in the Schools, 43*(7), 807–825.

Fletcher-Janzen, E. (2005). The school neuropsychological examination. In R. C. D'Amato, E. Fletcher-Janzen, & C. R. Reynolds (Eds.), *Handbook of school neuropsychology* (pp. 172–212). Hoboken, NJ: Wiley.

Francis, D. J., Shaywitz, S. E., Stuebing, K. K., Shaywitz, B. A., & Fletcher, J. M. (1996). Developmental delay versus deficit models of reading disability: A longitudinal, individual growth curve analysis. *Journal of Educational Psychology, 88,* 3–17.

Fuchs, L. S. (2003). Assessing intervention responsiveness: Conceptual and technical issues. *Learning and Disability Research & Practice, 18,* 172–186.

Fuchs, D., & Deshler, D. D. (2007). What we need to know about responsiveness to intervention (and shouldn't be afraid to ask). *Learning Disabilities Research & Practice, 22,* 129–136.

Gaddes, W. H., & Edgell, D. (1994). *Learning disabilities and brain function: A neuropsychological approach*. New York: Springer.

Gerber, M. M. (2005). Teachers are still the test: Limitations of response to instruction strategies for identifying children with learning disabilities. *Journal of Learning Disabilities, 38,* 516–523.

Glutting, J. J., McDermott, P. A., Watkins, M. M., Kush, J. C., & Konold, T. R. (1997). The base-rate problem and its consequences for interpreting children's ability profiles. *School Psychology Review, 26,* 176–188.

Goldberg, E. (2001). *The executive brain: Frontal lobes and the civilized mind*. New York: Oxford University Press.

Gresham, F. M., Reschly, D. J., Tilly, D. W., Fletcher, J., Burns, M., Crist, T., et al. (2005). Comprehensive evaluation of learning disabilities: A response to intervention perspective. *The School Psychologist, 59*(1), 26–29.

Hale, J. B. (2006). Implementing IDEA with a three-tier model that includes response to intervention and cognitive assessment methods. *School Psychology Forum: Research and Practice, 1,* 16–27.

Hale, J. B., & Fiorello, C. A. (2004). *School neuropsychology: A practitioner's handbook*. New York: Guilford Publications, Inc.

Hale, J. B., Fiorello, C. A., & Brown, L. (2005). Determining medication treatment effects using teacher ratings and classroom observations of children with ADHD: Does neuropsychological impairment matter? *Educational and Child Psychology, 22,* 39–61.

Hale, J. B., Fiorello, C. A., Kavanagh, J. A., Holdnack, J. A., & Aloe, A. M. (2007). Is the demise of IQ interpretation justified? A response to special issue authors. *Applied Neuropsychology, 14,* 37–51.

Hale, J. B., Fiorello, C. A., Miller, J. A., Wenrich, K., Teodori, A. M., & Henzel, J. (2008). WISC-IV assessment and intervention strategies for children with specific learning disabilities. In A. Prifitera, D. H. Saklofske, & L. G. Weiss (Eds.), *WISC-IV clinical use and interpretation: Scientist-practitioner perspectives* (2nd ed, pp. 111–171). New York: Elsevier Science.

Hale, J. B., Hoeppner, J. B., & Fiorello, C. A. (2002). Analyzing Digit Span components for assessment of attention processes. *Journal of Psychoeducational Assessment, 20,* 128–143.

Hale, J. B., Kaufman, A. S., Naglieri, J. A., & Kavale, K. A. (2006). Implementation of IDEA: Integrating response to intervention and cognitive assessment methods. *Psychology in the Schools, 43,* 753–770.

Holmes-Bernstein, J. (2000). Developmental neuropsychological assessment. In K. O. Yeates, M. D. Ris, & H. G. Taylor (Eds.), *Pediatric neuropsychology: Research, theory, and practice* (pp. 405–438). New York: Guilford.

Hynd, G. W., & Reynolds, C. R. (2005). School neuropsychology: The evolution of a specialty in school psychology. In R. C. D'Amato, E. Fletcher-Janzen, & C. R. Reynolds (Eds.), *Handbook of school neuropsychology* (pp. 3–14). Hoboken, NJ: Wiley.

Hynd, G. W., Semrud-Clikeman, M., & Lyytinen, H. (1991). Brain imaging in learning disabilities. In J. E. Obrzut & G. W. Hynd (Eds.), *Neuropsychological foundations of learning disabilities: A handbook of issues, methods and practice* (pp. 475–518). San Diego, CA: Academic Press.

Individuals with Disabilities Education Improvement Act, H.R. 1350. (2004).

Kaplan, E. (1988). A process approach to neuropsychological assessment. In T. Boll & B. K. Bryant (Eds.), *Clinical neuropsychology and brain function: Research, measurement, and practice* (pp. 129–231). Washington, DC: American Psychological Association.

Kaufman, A. S. (1994). *Intelligent testing with the WISC-III.* Hoboken, NJ: Wiley.

Kavale, K. A., Holdnack, J. A., & Mostert, M. P. (2006). Responsiveness to intervention and the identification of specific learning disability: A critique and alternative proposal. *Learning and Disability Research & Practice, 29,* 113–127.

Lezak, M. D. (1995). *Neuropsychological assessment* (3rd ed.). New York: Oxford University Press.

Lichter, D. G., & Cummings, J. L. (Eds.). (2001). *Frontal-subcortical circuits in psychiatric and neurological disorders.* New York: Guilford Press.

Luria, A. R. (1973). *The working brain.* Baltimore, MD: Penguin Books.

Mather, N., & Gregg, N. (2006). Specific learning disabilities: Clarifying, not eliminating, a construct. *Professional Psychology: Research and Practice, 37,* 99–106.

Mather, N., & Kaufman, N. (2006). Introduction to the special issue, part one: It's about the what, the how well, and the why. *Psychology in the Schools, 43,* 747–752.

Mayes, S. D., & Calhoun, S. L. (2004). Similarities and differences in WISC-III profiles: Support for subtest analysis in clinical referrals. *Clinical Neuropsychologist, 18,* 559–572.

Mayes, S. D., & Calhoun, S. L. (2006). WISC-IV and WISC-III profiles in children with ADHD. *Journal of Attention Disorders, 9,* 486–493.

Mayes, S. D., Calhoun, S. L., & Crowell, E. W. (1998). WISC-III profiles for children with and without learning disabilities. *Psychology in the Schools, 35,* 309–316.

McGrew, K. S., & Flanagan, D. (1997). *The intelligence test desk reference: The Gf-Gc cross-battery assessment.* Upper Saddle River, NJ: Pearson Education.

Miller, D. C. (2007). *Essentials of school neuropsychological assessment.* New York: John Wiley & Sons, Inc.

Naglieri, J. A., & Crockett, D. P. (2005). Response to intervention (RTI): Is it a scientifically proven method? *Communiqué, 34,* 38–39.

National Joint Committee on Learning Disabilities. (2005). Responsiveness to intervention and learning disabilities. Report available online at http://www.ncld. org/resources1/njcld-position-papers/index-and-summaries-of-njcld-reports

Ofiesh, N. (2006). Response to intervention and the identification of specific learning disabilities: Why we need comprehensive evaluations as part of the process. *Psychology in the Schools, 43,* 883–888.

Peterson, B. S., & Panksepp, J. (2004). Biological basis of childhood neuropsychiatric disorders. In: Panksepp, J. (Ed.), *Textbook of biological psychiatry* (pp. 393–436). Wilmington, DE: Wiley-Liss.

Pfeiffer, S. I., Reddy, L. A., Kletzel, J. E., Schmelzer, E. R., & Boyer, L. M. (2000). The practitioner's view of IQ testing and profile analysis. *School Psychology Quarterly, 15,* 376–385.

Reddy, L. A., & Hale, J. B. (2007). Inattentiveness. In A. R. Eisen (Ed.), *Clinical handbook of childhood behavior problems: Case formulation and step-by-step treatment programs* (pp. 156–211). New York: Guilford Press.

Reschly, D. J. (2005). Learning disabilities identification: Primary intervention, secondary intervention, and then what? *Journal of Learning Disabilities, 38,* 510–515.

Reschly, D. J., & Hosp, J. L. (2004). State SLD policies and practices. *Learning Disability Quarterly, 27,* 197–213.

Reynolds, C. R. (2008). RTI, neuroscience, and sense: Chaos in the diagnosis and treatment of learning disabilities. In: E. Fletcher-Janzen & C. R. Reynolds (Eds.), *Neuropsychological perspectives on learning disabilities in the era of RTI: Recommendations for diagnosis and intervention* (pp. 14–27). New York: Wiley.

Reynolds, C. R., Kamphaus, R. W., Rosenthal, B. L., & Hiemenz, J. R. (1997). Applications of the Kaufman Assessment Battery for Children (K-ABC) in neuropsychological assessment. In: C. R. Reynolds & E. Fletcher-Janzen (Eds.), *Handbook of clinical child neuropsychology* (2nd ed., pp. 252–269). New York: Plenum.

Sattler, J. M. (2008). *Assessment of children: Cognitive foundations* (5th ed.) San Diego, CA: Jerome M. Sattler, Publisher.

Schaer, M., & Eliez, S. (2007). From genes to brain: Understanding brain development in neurogenetic disorders using neuroimaging techniques. *Child and Adolescent Psychiatric Clinics of North America, 16,* 557–579.

Schrank, F. A., Miller, J. A., Caterino, L., & Desrochers, J. (2006). American Academy of School Psychology survey on the independent educational evaluation for a specific learning disability: Results and discussion. *Psychology in the Schools, 43,* 771–780.

Semrud-Clikeman, M. (2005). Neuropsychological aspects for evaluating learning disabilities. *Journal of Learning Disabilities, 38*, 563–568.

Semrud-Clikeman, M., & Pliszka, S. R. (2005). Neuroimaging and psychopharmacology. *School Psychology Quarterly, 20*, 172–186.

Shaywitz, B. A., Shaywitz, S. E., Blachman, B. A., Pugh, K. R., Fulbright, R. K., Skudlarski, P., et al. (2004). Development of left occipitotemporal systems for skilled reading in children after a phonologically-based intervention. *Biological Psychiatry, 55*, 926–933.

Sheridan, S. M., & Gutkin, T. B. (2000). The ecology of school psychology: Examining and changing our paradigm for the 21st century. *School Psychology Review, 29*, 485–502.

Siegel, L. S. (2003). Learning disabilities. *Handbook of psychology, educational psychology, 7*, 457–460.

Smalley, S. L., & Collins, F. (1996). Genetic, prenatal and immunological factors. *Journal of Autism and Developmental Disorders, 26*, 195–198.

Torgesen, J. K. (1991). Learning disabilities: Historical and conceptual issues. In B. Y. Wong (Ed.), *Learning about learning disabilities* (pp. 3–37). San Diego, CA: Academic Press.

Watkins, M. W., Glutting, J. J., & Lei, P. W. (2007). Validity of the full-scale IQ when there is significant variability among WISC-III and WISC-IV factor scores. *Applied Neuropsychology, 14*, 13–20.

Watkins, M. W., Glutting, J. J., & Youngstrom, E. A. (2005). Issues in subtest profile analysis. In D. P. Flanagan & P. L. Harrison, (Eds.), *Contemporary intellectual assessment* (2nd ed.). New York: Guilford.

Willis, J. O., & Dumont, R. (2006). And never the twain shall meet: Can response to intervention and cognitive assessment be reconciled? *Psychology in the Schools, 43*, 901–908.

Wodrich, D. L., Spencer, M. L., & Daley, K. B. (2006). Combining RTI and psychoeducational assessment: What we must assume to do otherwise. *Psychology in the Schools, 43*, 797–806.

Part IV

Training for intervention

Systems, settings, and
special populations

13 School-based mental health

Training school psychologists for comprehensive service delivery

Rosemary B. Mennuti and
Ray W. Christner

Schools and educators have a prominent and important role in the lives of children and adolescents. Each day, approximately 50 million students attend public schools in the United States (National Center for Education Statistics, 2005), with an unspecified number attending private or parochial educational programs. Although many students enter school ready, willing, and able to learn and participate in the education process, a number of students enter schools struggling with emotional, behavioral, and family problems that can notably affect their learning, as well as the learning of others. Given this, the need for schools and school systems to provide interventions to help these students overcome the emotional and behavioral barriers to learning is becoming more and more prominent.

Supporting the social and emotional growth of youth to enhance their educational success is not a new idea, though many questions remain. How do we effectively deliver mental health services in a school setting? What programs and approaches have the potential to overcome social and emotional barriers? What types of training would be the most beneficial for school psychologists to enhance their skills the delivery of mental health services? In this chapter, we offer information regarding school-based mental health services and discuss issues of training school psychologists to be efficient and effective within a comprehensive service delivery system.

REVIEW OF LITERATURE

Mental health and school systems

Incidences of social, emotional, and behavioral difficulties often emerge in childhood. In addition, when proper attention and intervention is not provided, it is likely that these problems will become more serious and prolonged. Kessler, Berglund, Demler, Jin, and Walters (2005) reported that when these issues occur in childhood and adolescence and are not addressed, they lead to more extensive problems later in life. The number of children and adolescents with unmet mental health needs is a notable concern in the United States. Researchers have estimated that between 20% and 38% of children and adolescents have emotional and behavioral difficulties severe enough to warrant intervention, though less than 20% of these individuals actually receive mental health services (Power, 2003; Prodente, Sander, & Weist, 2002; Paternite, 2005). There are a number of negative outcomes related to being nonresponsive to the mental health needs of youth, including increased rates of teen pregnancy, substance abuse, criminal offenses, psychiatric hospitalization, and even early death (Prodente et al.), as well as academic problems and school dropout. To prevent the detrimental and long-term effects of these untreated problems facing our society, it is necessary to enhance prevention and early intervention approaches to influence prosocial development, resilience, and emotional well-being.

Schools are a natural entry point for the delivery of mental health services (Christner, Forrest, Morley, & Weinstein, 2007; Mennuti & Christner, 2005; Mennuti, Freeman, & Christner, 2006), as they offer access to children at a point of engagement for addressing educational, emotional, and behavioral needs (Paternite, 2005). For youth, schools are considered the major providers of mental health services, as the majority children and adolescents (70–80%) receiving mental health services do so within the school environment (Rones & Hoagwood, 2000). Given the ongoing stigma related to the need for mental health services, receiving services within an alternative setting, such as schools, is often more acceptable. Prodente et al. (2002) noted that 96% of families offered school-based mental health services engaged in interventions, whereas only 13% referred to community-based services followed through on the recommendation.

Given this information, it is logical to see the benefit and need for the provisions of school-based mental health services. It is necessary that we caution that school systems are not in a position to meet all the needs of their students, though they are responsible and must meet the challenge of addressing these needs when they directly affect learning (Adelman & Taylor, 2006). This call to provide and implement school-based mental health programs is crucial, though it does not come without difficulties, such as obtaining funding, trained personnel, space, time, and resources. Additionally, many school psychologists continue to struggle with the model, approach, or orientation to take when delivering such services (Christner & Mennuti, 2008). Each of these barriers, as well as others that exist, must be considered as schools and school psychologists work toward meeting the mental health needs of students.

Legislation and school-based mental health initiatives

The Education of All Handicapped Children Act that was passed in 1975, later revised in 1997 as the Individuals with Disabilities Education Act and most recently in 2004 as the Individuals with Disabilities Education Improvement Act, embraced a national policy requiring schools to address the social emotional problems of children and provide mental health services to children as needed. The original act placed responsibility on the education system to meet the mental health needs of students with an "emotional disturbance," and it required the education system to supply all support services needed to help educate students with disabilities (Kutash, Duchnowski, & Lynn, 2007). This federal mandate prompted questions about the "who, what, and how" that would be needed to provide mental health services to children in the school setting.

In 2002, President George W. Bush signed additional mandates into law, particularly No Child Left Behind (NCLB). NCLB included language aimed at ensuring the emotional well-being of youth (Kutash et al., 2007). Examples of programs were identified, including character education, safe schools, drug free school initiatives, violence prevention programs, and specific programs for at-risk students. Yet again, NCLB does not offer guidelines on how to implement these services.

The Department of Health and Human Services funded two centers for school-based mental health in 1995: (a) University of California, Los Angeles, and (b) University of Maryland. These programs remain available and provide a wealth of information to those interested in the implementation of school-based mental health, including research data and practical approaches for various mental health services for children through collaborative partnerships between school and community. Information on each of these centers can be found on their respective Web sites—University of California, Los Angeles (UCLA), at http://smhp.psych.ucla.edu and University of Maryland at http://csmh.umaryland.edu.

The *President's New Freedom Commission on Mental Health*: *Achieving the Promise: Transforming the Mental Health Care in America* (2003) highlights the need for early identification of mental health issues through screening, assessment, and referral. In addition, it sets forth the following recommendations:

- Promote the mental health of young children
- Improve and expand school mental health programs
- Screen for co-occurring mental and substance use disorders
- Link with integrated treatment strategies
- Screen for mental disorders and connect children to treatment and supports

As stated earlier, each of these directives offers support for serving mental health issues in children, yet questions remain: Who should provide the service, how it is to be accomplished, and how is it to be funded?

Models of school-based mental health

There are various perspectives regarding the delivery model for school-based mental health services. Kutash et al. (2007) discuss three prevailing models of implementing mental health services in the schools, which they discuss in *School-Based Mental Health: An Empirical Guide for Decision-Makers*.

Mrazek and Haggerty (1994) and Weisz et al. (2005) used the phrase "spectrum of mental health interventions and treatments," which can be viewed as regarding the implementation of traditional mental health interventions in a school setting. The methods used in this model have their roots in the psychological and mental health literature. Prevention and treatment services focus on identifying diagnostic categories and selecting intervention methods that are designed for specific problems.

The second model is one supported by the UCLA and University of Maryland federally funded programs mentioned previously. This model is referred to as the interconnected systems model, and it is guided by a public health strategy and based on collaboration between systems (Adelman & Taylor, 2008). This model reflects the idea that schools must address the mental health needs of students, yet it acknowledges the effectiveness of combining resources from the school and the community. This model involves three levels: (a) systems of prevention—universal interventions that encourage parent and community involvement; (b) systems of early intervention—at-risk and moderate needs targeted; and (c) systems of care—framework of an integrated and collaborative continuum of services provided by the various child-serving agencies, aimed at children with the most intensive needs (Adelmen & Taylor, 2004). Finally, this system of care model is a comprehensive approach addressing both the internal (specific to child) and external (environmental) causes of psychosocial barriers to learning (Kutash et al., 2007).

Another model is the positive behavioral supports (PBS) model, which has theoretical underpinnings in applied behavior analysis (Farrell, 2008; Sugai & Horner, 2002). Its application has expanded to include students with a wide range of academic, social, and behavior challenges in the home, school, and community. PBS uses educational and environmental redesign to enhance quality of life and minimize problem behavior (Kutash et al., 2007). PBS is a three-tiered model, with 80–90% of students requiring only universal preventions. The middle tier consists of 5–15% of students who are at risk for emotional or behavior problems, and the top tier consists of the remaining 1–7% of students with chronic and intense problem behavior that require intensive prevention (Sugai & Horner, 2002). The percentages conceptually being served at each level correspond to the children's mental health epidemiological findings that 20% of children, at a point in time, have a diagnosable disorder that meets *Diagnostic and Statistical Manual of Mental Disorders* criteria, and about 5% have a more serious and persistent disorder.

Elements of effective programs

Many of the current models of school-based mental health offer services at different levels; however, program selection at each level of intervention involves consideration of several elements. Regardless of the level of intervention, integration of theory, research, and practice should be evident. Moreover, programs used should include an ecological framework, be collaborative, and provide for opportunities for program evaluation (Pluymert, 2002). Within the school context, a collaborative approach would entail participation opportunities for students, teachers, guidance counselors, school administration, support staff, parents, and community agencies. A key to effective programs is ease of program evaluation. To ensure effectiveness, programs must explore ways to collect data, monitor progress, and modify the program as needed.

Professional roles and functions

A multitiered approach that includes both prevention and intervention is the most efficient and effective way to provide services in school for students with mental health concerns (Christner, Forrest, Morley, & Weinstein, 2008; Smallwood, Christner, & Brill, 2007). Traditionally, we have focused on a delivery service model, which was designed for special education children only and reacted to pathology. A contemporary delivery approach is a tiered model that varies the intensity of intervention depending on the severity of student need. Therefore, services move along a continuum from working with all students in a school or school district to providing services to an individual child who has a severe need.

Schools should seek to offer assessment and treatment across four facets of intervention: universal, targeted, intensive, and crisis. In addition, some children will present with needs that require more care than a school can provide, and thus, collaboration and referral to outside professionals and agencies is imperative. It is important for school psychologists to recognize that the delivery of services in this model should not be hierarchical and rigid, but instead fluid and dynamic, so that we intervene at a time and in a manner that constitute a thoughtful and effective approach to the identified issues. This method integrates the basic components that make up a systematic approach to understanding, conceptualizing, assessing, intervening, and monitoring problems of students and systems across all levels of the multitiered model.

Figure 13.1 illustrates a process that can be employed by school psychologists when providing mental health services in schools. This approach highlights the need to plan the approach, as well as to monitor progress and outcomes to determine whether interventions are working and, if not, to reconceptualize the presenting problem and modify the interventions as needed. The next sections will offer a brief overview of each level of

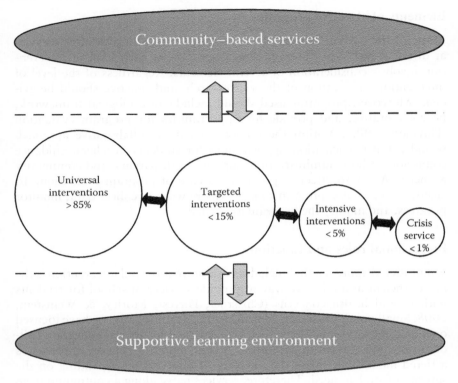

Figure 13.1 Multilevel design of school-based mental health services. (Copyright Christner, R.W., & Mennuti, R.B.)

intervention, including the process of assessment and case conceptualization, consistent with Figure 13.1.

Universal interventions

Overview of universal interventions

Universal interventions encompass a framework designed to improve the well-being of all students in a school district or a specific school. Key aspects include building protective factors to ensure that the vulnerability of all students is minimized and styles of coping are adaptive, preventing mental health problems, creating overall supportive environments, and creating global resources for students who are at risk. Thus, in general, services are aimed toward building resiliency and prevention. When protective factors are built, there is the potential to prevent the onset of social and emotional problems and learning difficulties. Examples of services include psycho-educational programs around critical issues for a specific age group, such as drug and alcohol, violence prevention, physical well-being, and social problem solving. Although universal interventions are generally aimed at all students, some individuals may be at higher risk and thus be in need of more specific services. Our aim is to impact approximately 85% of students through prevention and early intervention mental health programming.

Assessment for universal intervention

To begin the implementation of universal interventions, it is important to know where to focus attention. This requires an assessment of the needs of the entire school district or school where interventions are being developed. To begin this process, key school personnel (e.g., administrators, teachers, guidance counselors, support staff, and parents) should join together to develop an extensive list of problems that take into account school-wide and systemic issues. The identified issues and the context in which they occur must be looked at closely in terms of frequency, intensity, and duration. Next, themes and the underlying mechanism can be identified and thoroughly assessed by using a variety of strategies and methods of data collection. The specific methods employed depend on factors such as the specific nature of the issue, district policies, and monetary funds. General assessment practices suggested by Christner and Mennuti (2008) are included for review in Table 13.1. These, together with other practices, offer a way to appraise the situation and to make the necessary for program selection for effective outcomes.

Table 13.1 Assessment for Universal Interventions

Focus group data	Focus groups can be conducted with students, faculty, administrators, and/or parents to determine issues that are present within the schools. For information on conducting focus groups, see Krueger and Casey (2000).
Survey data	Surveys can be developed and used with students, faculty, administrators, and/or parents to identify specific needs within the school community.
Pre-existing school data	Schools maintain many sources of data that can be used to identify areas of need, as well as to monitor changes following an intervention (e.g., discipline referrals, dropout rate, truancy, or grades). These data typically exist and do not require additional work, other than analyzing the information that has been previously collected.
Pre-existing community data	Local government and community agencies often gather and maintain data on various community issues that also have relevance to school-based intervention (e.g., drug use and youth crime).

Source: Adapted from Christner, R. W., & Mennuti, R. B. (Eds.). (2008). *School-based mental health: A practitioner's guide to comparative practices.* New York: Routledge.

Table 13.2 Sample of Universal Intervention Programs

I Can Problem Solve (Shure, 2001)
Positive Alternative for Thinking Strategies (Kusch & Greenberg, 1994)
School-wide Positive Behavior Support (Sugai & Horn, 1999)
Resilient Classrooms (Doll & Brehm, 2004)
PREPARE (Goldstein, 1998)
Social Decision Making (Elias & Butler, 2005)

Universal intervention program selection

Using the data collected from the needs assessment allows for district- or school-wide mental health promotion as a way to promote change and prevent future problems. Readers are encouraged to see the work of Simonsen and Sugai (2007), who offer an excellent discussion of using school-wide assessment data. There are approaches to service delivery at the universal level (see Barbarasch & Elias, 2008; Brehm & Doll, 2008; Farrell, 2008), and there are numerous programs. It is beyond the scope of this book to offer information on all available programs, although Table 13.2 provides a sample of programs that school psychologists may consider when implementing service at this level.

Outcome evaluation of universal interventions

Assessment to monitor the effectiveness of universal interventions can offer information about the program efficiency and treatment success for the identified needs. These data allow evaluation of the process of program implementation as well. Ongoing monitoring of program implementation and progress allows for assessment of the identified goals and provides the opportunity to make changes or adapt the approach, as needed. Postintervention assessment will produce outcome data that focus on the impact on students and school climate, which may be useful in justifying program costs and continuation. Decisions about how to measure progress should be discussed prior to implementation and most often will include methods similar to those described in Table 13.1.

Targeted interventions

Overview of targeted interventions

Interventions offered at the targeted level are designed for children who did not respond at the universal level and/or who are at risk for developing an emotional or behavioral disorder. These students may be showing some initial signs or symptoms of problems and showing the need for early intervention. It should be noted that student's with identified psychiatric, psychological, and learning issues are also targeted at this stage to minimize the impact of their difficulties on the students' learning and educational success. Thus, intervention at this stage may eliminate presenting issues and reduce the influence of the barriers and stressors that could lead to greater mental health concerns. Targeted interventions are more specialized and intensive than school-wide interventions, though these are not used as a substitute individualized treatment for students with a high level of need. For example, students who are struggling with anger issues may need support and exposure to additional interventions, despite the district-wide violence and bullying prevention efforts. This service is provided in small groups with interventions strategies targeted to the specific problem. In addition, some children displaying emotional or behavioral difficulties may be children with specific risk factors, such as demographic conditions, physical health and general well-being, and family dysfunction. These factors may increase the chance that a problem will develop. Coie et al. (1993) identified a number of risk factors that are thought to increase the risk of poor outcome in children and adolescents and may lead to difficulty functioning in adulthood. There are several domains of risk factors to consider, including constitutional handicaps, skill development delays, emotional difficulties, family circumstances, interpersonal problems, school problems, and ecological risks (Coie et al., 1993). Other research (see Doll & Lyons, 1998) also discussed risk factors such as poverty, minimal parent education, marital discord or family dysfunction, ineffective parenting, child maltreatment, poor physical health of the child or parents, parent mental illness or inadequacy, and large family size. Although schools cannot directly modify many of these factors, through targeted interventions they may help students build protective or resilience factors that could moderate and compensate for the impact of adversity.

Assessment for targeted intervention

In order to receive services at the targeted level, students risk level should be assessed on the basis of the presence of numerous risk factors, early signs of mental health concerns, or lack of response at the universal level. Best practices to assess children in need of targeted interventions may include some of the same tools employed at the universal level, though the focus now must remain on the specific presenting issues and problems. For instance, data on students who have frequent peer difficulties can be used to identify students for inclusion in a social skills group intervention. Internalizing disorders, such as depression, are more difficult to identify and are easily overlooked. Assessment will require input from school personnel who have direct contact with the identified child or children. For example, the district's standardized testing program or benchmark assessments may cause competent students to demonstrate high levels of anxiety and interfere with performance. Teacher identification of these students based on past experience can be utilized to develop a group on stress reduction and skills to cope with test or performance anxiety.

In addition, the use of formal and informal screening instruments or programs is a way to identify students at risk. The Columbia University (2003) TeenScreen program, a national screening program used to help identify students who are at risk for mental health issues and suicide, is an example. This voluntary program offers youth the opportunity for mental health check-ups. Furthermore, schools can develop an informal screening process by implementing the use of rating scales and questionnaires that are applicable to their situation.

Assessment of the targeted interventions is a necessary part of obtaining information about individual student progress and gaining knowledge about the overall response to intervention. Assessment is completed on an ongoing basis and may be utilized before, during, and after implementation of targeted interventions. Since targeted interventions are developed to focus on particular skill deficits or specific undesired behavior, the assessment methods must also be specific and directed at the specific goal. Targeted assessments can also include rating scales addressing a set of symptoms (e.g., Beck Youth Depression Scales, Beck, Beck, & Jolly, 2003) or there may be informal measures developed to facilitate this process. Table 13.3 also offers examples of assessment data that can be used at the targeted level.

Table 13.3 Targeted Assessment Considerations

Pre-existing school data	The pre-existing school data described above can be used to identify students who may require more intensive services (e.g., discipline referrals by specific student, specific students demonstrating certain risk factors, or students who are frequently tardy or truant).
Prereferral data	This would include a review of response to school-wide interventions (e.g., Tier I or universal interventions), based on monitoring the progress that students make toward school-wide goals.
Screening programs	This may include screening instruments that are developed by a school or district or a screening measure that is commercially available.
Student referrals	It is essential that schools have a safe and accessible method for students to self-refer or to refer other students. This process needs to be done in a confidential manner for those referring themselves and in an anonymous way for those referring peers.
Staff and parent referrals	There should be a mechanism in place for teachers and parents to initiate a referral for a specific student to be screened. This can be part of the district's student assistance program or other prereferral process.

Source: Adapted from Christner, R. W., & Mennuti, R. B. (Eds.). (2008). *School-based mental health: A practitioner's guide to comparative practices.* New York: Routledge.

These, together with other practices, offer a way to appraise the situation and to make the necessary program selection for effective outcomes.

Targeted intervention program selection

Programs at the targeted level of intervention can be implemented with individual students; however, we recommend utilizing group interventions at this level whenever possible. The type of targeted intervention utilized will depend on the developmental level of the students, nature of the target behaviors, and the organizational climate of the school, which may support or impede the application of different strategies. A variety of manualized interventions or programs are available for use at this level (see Christner, Stewart, & Freeman, 2007, for a review), or school psychologists and other staff members may develop their own programs. Table 13.4 offers a sample of some of the commercially available manualized programs that school psychologists may consider for use.

Outcome evaluation of targeted interventions

It is vital for school systems to evaluate and monitor progress of students participating in targeted level interventions to determine growth and benefit from a given intervention. In addition, this information

Table 13.4 Sample of Manualized Programs for Use at the Targeted Level

Anxiety
Coping Cat (Kendall, 1993)
Social Effectiveness Therapy for Children (Beidel & Turner, 1998)
Cognitive-Behavior Group Therapy—Adolescent (Albano, 2000)
Friends for Life

Anger and aggression
Coping Power Program (Larson & Lochman, 2002)
Chill Out Program (Feindler & Ecton, 1986; Feindler & Gutman, 1994)
"Keeping Cool" (Dwivedi & Gupta, 2000).
Aggression Replacement Training (Goldstein, Glick, & Gibbs, 1998)

Depression
Coping with Depression (Clarke, Lewinsohn, & Hops, 1990)
ACTION Program (Stark & Kendall, 1996)

Social problem solving
I Can Problem Solve (Shure, 2001)
The Stop and Think Social Skills Program (Knoff, 2001)
The Equip Program (Gibbs, Potter, & Goldstein, 1995)
PREPARE Curriculum (Goldstein, 1999)

provides an evaluation of the program and monitors the integrity of program implementation. Practitioners can use this information to re-evaluate identified goals and to make changes or adaptations, as needed. Postintervention assessment will produce outcome data on individual student progress within the specific area of focus. For instance, following a targeted intervention for anxiety, school psychologists may wish to conduct postintervention assessment using a self-report rating scale (e.g., the Beck Youth Inventory for Anxiety) at a 1-month and 6-month follow-ups. This information can then be used to determine the need for "booster" sessions or other interventions to maintain the students' progress.

Intensive interventions

Overview of intensive intervention

Intensive interventions are developed for the small number of students who have extensive difficulties or who have not responded to interventions offered at the universal and targeted level. These students are often in need of more intensive support and individualized interventions. For many of these students, intensive support can occur within the school-based mental health program alone or in conjunction with services provided in community-based programs. In some cases, services may go beyond what can be provided in the school mental health programs and require a higher level of care that includes partial hospitalization programs, inpatient programs, or even alternative education. The goal of intensive interventions is to decrease the level of emotional or behavioral impairment and to enhance a student's level of functioning and ability to learn. The interventions at this level can be provided in a group intervention format; however, in most cases, students in need of services at this level will require individualized intervention or treatment plans (Smallwood et al., 2007).

Assessment for intensive intervention

Interventions at this level are individualized and based on the student's areas of need. The intervention is determined by the assessment and should be guided by the case conceptualization (Mennuti et al., 2006). Assessment can include gathering previous evaluations completed on the student, reviewing records, and obtaining new data (e.g., rating scales, observations, and functional behavior assessment). Special note of the frequency and severity of the student's symptoms is necessary so that operational intervention goals can be developed and appropriately monitored. School psychologists not familiar with a case conceptualization model are referred to Murphy and Christner (2006), who have developed a framework and worksheet to assist practitioners in reviewing information necessary to develop a specific plan. Although Murphy and Christner's framework was designed from a

Table 13.5 Examples of Assessment Data at the Intensive Level

Response to intervention	Students who are part of a prereferral process or who receive Tier I and Tier II interventions should be monitored, and those not responding to interventions should be considered for interventions at the Intensive level.
Rating scales	Both broad-band and narrow-band rating scales can be used to collect information from observers, such as parents or teachers, as well as students.
Observations	Observations should occur in various environments, including classrooms, playgrounds, cafeterias, etc.
Functional behavioral assessment (FBA)	Information gathered as part of an FBA can provide details to help identify targets of behaviors, as well as specific positive behavioral interventions.

Source: Adapted from Christner, R. W., & Mennuti, R. B. (Eds.). (2008). *School-based mental health: A practitioner's guide to comparative practices.* New York: Routledge.

cognitive-behavioral orientation, it can be extended and modified for use with any theoretical model. Various types of intensive level assessments are provided in Table 13.5

Intensive intervention selection

Intensive interventions are typically delivered by someone with formal training and experience in treatment of emotional and behavioral disorders. In the schools, the school psychologists, school counselors, social workers, or other mental health specialists are often the service providers. At times, school districts contract with community-based providers, who provide mental health treatment in the school or at a community-based mental health center. Intensive interventions are typically delivered on an individual basis, and they often take on a more traditional psychotherapy format. The focus is more than on skill building and involves goals such as reducing symptoms, increasing coping skills, reducing risk factors, and building protective factors. The specific strategies used in intensive interventions will depend on the clinician's theoretical orientation and training. Christner and Mennuti (2008) offered several key points for intensive interventions, which are noted in Table 13.6.

Crisis services

Overview of crisis intervention

Crisis intervention is essential in any comprehensive school-based mental health service model that attempts to meet the emotional needs of children. Crisis intervention services involve planning for crises, as well as preventing and intervening with crises as they occur. Therefore, crisis prevention and

Table 13.6 Key Points and Examples of Orientations Used at the Intensive
Intervention Level

Key points	Examples of treatment orientations
• Focuses on direct and ongoing interventions on the individualized needs of specific students • Uses data on each individual to conceptualize his or her needs, to identify detailed goals, and to monitor progress • Utilizes individual, group, and/or family treatments designed to address individual goals and need • Provides opportunities and supports for practice of skills aimed at stabilizing and treating a student with a specific disorder • Offers individual and/or group therapy to foster growth and enhance functioning	Cognitive-behavior therapy (CBT) Rational emotive behavior therapy (REBT) Behavior therapy or modification Reality therapy Client-centered therapy Family systems therapy Algerian therapy Psychodynamic therapy

Source: Christner, R. W., & Mennuti, R. B. (Eds.). (2008). *School-based mental health: A practitioner's guide to comparative practices.* New York: Routledge.

intervention services can be implemented at all levels—universal, targeted, and intensive levels of service.

In the school-based mental health framework offered in Figure 13.1, crisis services refer to brief counseling for students who are at-risk for harm to self or others or who are experiencing some other personal crisis (e.g., death of a parent). The focus of crisis services is stabilization and not behavioral change. The interventions at this level emphasize identifying student strengths and existing coping resources. In addition, Brock and Jimerson (2004) identify the need for interventions to reduce the severity and incidence of stress reactions and maladaptive coping responses, as well as identifying students who are at risk for developing a stress-related mental health problem (e.g., post-traumatic stress disorder). There are a number of excellent school crisis intervention resources available, and we refer the reader to Heath and Sheen (2005) and Brock, Lazarus, and Jimerson (2004).

Building professional competency

With current legislation and the critical need for mental health services that are comprehensive, high quality, efficient, and effective, it is imperative that school psychologists have the necessary training and skills to be key players in school-based mental health services. By building competence in school-based mental health service delivery, school psychologists will be able assist in the prevention of emotional and behavioral problems, intervene to reduce the impact of risk factors on students, promote resiliency and protective factors, and increase collaborative and consultative relationships with parents and school staff members.

In 2006, the National Association of School Psychologists (NASP) published a revised edition of *School Psychology: A Blueprint for Training and Practice* (*Blueprint III*; Ysseldyke et al., 2006). This document offers suggested guidelines for the training and practice of school psychology, and it promotes a shift to a service delivery model that addresses varying the intensity of intervention depending on the severity of student need. The model we described above is in line with this shift in focus from individual intervention to a continuum of services from district-wide (or school-wide) services to those focusing on a specific student's needs.

Blueprint III outlines eight basic domains of competence, all of which are interrelated and require school psychologists to engage in lifelong learning. Although these domains are designed to encompass all roles and functions of school psychologists, there is a direct call for school psychologists to enhance "the development of wellness, social skills, mental health, and life competencies" in students (Ysseldyke et al., 2006, p. 19). Ysseldyke et al. also note that school psychologist should be considered leading mental health experts within schools. To be competent in delivery of such services, school psychologists need education, supervision, and ongoing training in the following content areas:

- Professional, legal, and ethical responsibility
- Consultation and collaborative skills
- Program design and evaluation
- Systems level prevention and intervention (e.g., school climate)
- Group and individual counseling skills
- Behavioral interventions
- Service delivery models
- Data-based decision making

Enhancing knowledge and competency

According to the ethical principles set forth by NASP and the American Psychological Association, school psychologists must work within the bounds of their professional competency. This requires school psychologists to engage in appropriate training and supervision; however, many school psychologists enter the field with only basic knowledge and experience necessary to undertake the challenge of creating systems change and implementing mental health services at a system-wide level. Thus, it is necessary for school psychology training programs, as well as individual school psychologists, to seek out opportunities for training, support, and practical resources.

Coursework

An entry level means to develop competency is through coursework or workshops. This coursework can be in any of the content areas noted previously; however, coursework should not simply focus on didactic training, as it is important for skill practice to occur at this level. This may include role-play consultation or therapy sessions, the development of a social skills intervention program, the development of a plan for databased decision making using school-wide data, and/or a role-play of a school-wide meeting to determine the best way to monitor progress of current programs.

Practicum/intern supervision

Practicum and internship experiences offer school psychologists in training an ideal opportunity for enhancing their mental health skills. It is important for students and programs to explore internship sites that will offer diverse opportunities in these areas. Time in supervision should be dedicated to mental health services, including program evaluation, individual and group interventions, and program development.

Peer consultation

Oftentimes, school psychologists work in settings in which they are the only psychologist in their district, and they are supervised by nonpsychologists. Thus, it is important to seek alternate sources of supervision and support, such as peer supervision. Peer supervision is an excellent avenue through which professionals can connect, share ideas, gain experience, and problem solve. Established peer groups can be accessed through local professional organizations, such as state associations or local trainings, or school psychologists may directly contact peers in their area.

In addition to direct means of peer consultation, NASP and other organizations (e.g., the American Psychological Association and Association for Behavioral and Cognitive Therapies) provides a wide range of interest groups via the Internet, in which members can interact and engage in meaningful conversations. Currently, NASP offers an interest group for members, called Character Education and Social Emotional Learning. This group aims to provide a forum for members to converse and build a knowledge base grounded in research-supported strategies. The interest group also seeks to explore the role of the school psychologist in initiative development and program implementation.

Additional resources

In addition to connecting with other professionals, it is incumbent upon the individual to stay current regarding programming, best practices, and legislation and policy. A plethora of information is accessible via the Internet, as well as through professional organizations, publications and texts. A sample of online resources for school-based mental health is offered at the end of this chapter.

CASE ILLUSTRATION: A TRAINING MODEL IN SCHOOL-BASED MENTAL HEALTH

In the spirit of the guidelines for training for best practice, the Philadelphia College of Osteopathic Medicine (PCOM) has developed a comprehensive training model inclusive of both knowledge and skills for delivery of service in the suggested NASP standard domains. This includes a module in school-based mental health practice, with a specific focus on the use of a cognitive-behavioral theoretical model. The program is multileveled in sequence, beginning with a master's degree in school psychology (MS), followed by the educational specialist degree in school psychology (EdS), and ending with an option to continue on to a doctorate of psychology in school psychology (PsyD).

Coursework and field placements

The school-based mental health module begins with a 3-credit foundations of psychotherapy course at the MS level, which provides a broad overview of school-based mental health services, an introduction of different theoretical orientations to use in practice, evidence based practices, and basic skills and techniques in counseling. In addition to formal didactic presentations, students experience skill involvement through role-plays, demonstrations, in-class videotaping, and case discussions. The theoretical introduction is supplemented at the EdS level by several courses, including academic and behavioral interventions in schools, prevention and crisis intervention: home, school, & community, cognitive behavior therapy (CBT) in schools, and program evaluation, as well as a practicum and internship experiences that are inclusive of school-based mental health programming and supervision, along with the other domain competencies. The cognitive-behavior therapy in schools course is fully dedicated to well-being, social skill development, and mental health of children and families. This course addresses not only the basic set of CBT skills, but also reviews and discusses their applications within a multileveled or tiered model of service delivery.

The PsyD in school psychology curriculum further builds on the competencies of the practicing school psychologist and includes an additional coursework and supervised practice. A three-course sequence is taken during the 1st year of doctoral training. The first course in the area of concentration includes advanced techniques and strategies of CBT, as well as case conferencing with leaders in the field of CBT, including Dr. Arthur Freeman and Dr. Aaron Beck. Next, students take a course that is specific to the implementation of CBT in school-based mental health. In the third course, students are enrolled in a required CBT practicum, which includes discussion and consultation on delivery of service, supervision, and video and audio case presentation and review. The training ends with a required course in family and group psychotherapy, though many students go on to take additional electives that will further enhance their knowledge and skills (e.g., behavior therapy, substance abuse intervention). Final field training experiences include a traditional 2,000-hour doctoral level internship at sites that offer varied opportunities, including exposure to the implementation of mental health interventions and services.

Assessment of competencies

The PsyD student at PCOM is assessed utilizing a multisource, multimethod approach to ensuring that students have necessary skills and competencies for practicing school-based mental health in the schools and are able to demonstrate their skills and knowledge in daily practice. Through frequent progress assessment, a student's strengths and challenges can be well documented, identified, and remediated, if necessary.

In addition to the standard methods of exams (e.g., papers, logs, case notes, program development and evaluation projects, supervisor evaluations, field-based observations, portfolios, and data from those working with the students), PCOM has a unique opportunity to have a standardized skills review program in place, which is referred to as the Standardized Training Evaluation of Psychologists and Psychotherapists (STEPPS) program. All students in the PsyD program in school psychology must participate each year in STEPPS, which includes initial interviews and treatment sessions with a parent-child dyad.

Each student conducts an intake interview with the tasks of establishing a therapeutic or working alliance with parents and students and formulating an initial conceptualization and intervention plan. The student completes a form following each interview, which provides a means for him or her to document his or her case conceptualization and to begin development of the initial treatment or intervention plan discussed with the parent and child. The STEPPS tape of each student is reviewed and evaluated by trained external reviewers using the Psychotherapy Skills Inventory (PSI). The student will receive feedback from his or her advisor, who reviews the tape, the PSI ratings, the case conceptualization, and the treatment plan in a face-to-face conference. STEPPS interviews occur three times over the course of training—prior to beginning the doctoral program, upon completion of the 1st year of coursework, and upon the completion of the 2nd year of coursework. This provides the student and faculty another way to evaluate skills and student progress over time in the program and prior to entering internship.

SUMMARY AND CONCLUSIONS

Current trends in education, as well as existing national statistics and federal mandates, highlight the need for schools to have a unified system of mental health services. Schools are in a unique position to identify risk factors and future mental health problems in their early stages and to provide early intervention. School psychologists have the opportunity to expand their roles and function in this area and to be experts within their school systems. By integrating their research and consultative skills, they can help schools identify needs, choose and implement evidence-based interventions, and monitor progress to determine effectiveness.

Central to the mission of increasing school-based mental health services will be increasing the dialogue and collaboration between researchers and educators in order for the fields to be unified and to work toward providing the best services for children. Training programs are in an ideal position to facilitate this discussion through the training of school psychologists in the best practices of school-based mental health services. This training must go beyond traditional courses in psychotherapy, and there should be a focus on building professional competencies in all aspects of mental health work, including assessment, case conceptualization, program development and evaluation, and evidence-based intervention programs and counseling techniques.

RESOURCES

Collaborative for Academic, Social, and Emotional Learning. (n.d.). *Home page.* Retrieved May 12, 2009, from http://www.casel.org
The Collaborative for Academic, Social, and Emotional Learning (CASEL) focuses on enhancing social and emotional learning (SEL) in education settings. CASEL offers a number of resources, including newsletters, searchable databases, and a list of publications. In addition, this site provides a list of programs and lessons, guidance on implementation of SEL, and guidelines and tools for assessment.

Massachusetts General Hospital School Psychiatry Program and Madi Resource Center. (n.d.). *School-based interventions.* Retrieved May 12, 2009, from http://www2.massgeneral.org/schoolpsychiatry/classroom_interventions.asp
This site provides a list of interventions and/or strategies that can be used to help students with various mental conditions be successful in school. For each condition, suggestions are offered for accommodations, modifications, specially designed instruction, and behavioral planning.

University of California, Los Angeles, Center for Mental Health in Schools. (n.d.). *UCLA School Mental Health Project.* Retrieved May 12, 2009, from http://smhp.psych.ucla.edu

The Center for Mental Health in Schools provides a comprehensive Web site that offers a number of resources to be used by school-based mental health providers, including guides for practice and a number of links to a variety of resources.

University of Maryland School of Medicine. (n.d.). *Center for School Mental Health*. Retrieved May 12, 2009, from http://csmh.umaryland.edu

The Center for School Mental Health site provides a number of resources on school-based mental health including a list of related conferences, articles, and newsletters. This site also provides a summary of recognized evidence-based programs.

University of Maryland School of Medicine. (n.d.). *SchoolMentalHealth.org*. Retrieved May 12, 2009, from http://www.schoolmentalhealth.org

This site offers school-based mental health resources for educators, administrators, parents/caregivers, families, and students, as well as for clinicians. The resources available on this site provide practical information consistent with current research.

REFERENCES

Adelman, H. S., & Taylor, L. (2004). Mental health in schools: A shared agenda. *Report on Emotional & Behavioral Disorder in Youth, 4*(3), 59–62, 76–78.

Adelman, H., & Taylor, L. (2006). *The current status of mental health in schools: A policy and practice analysis*. University of California at Los Angeles, Los Angeles, CA: The Center for Mental Health in Schools.

Adelman, H., & Taylor, L. (2008). Ending the marginalization of mental health in schools: A comprehensive approach. In R. W. Christner & R. B. Mennuti (Eds.), *School-based mental health: A practitioner's guide to comparative practices*. New York: Routledge.

Albano, A. M. (2000). Treatment of social phobia in adolescents. Cognitive and Behavioral program focused intervention and prevention. *Journal of Cognitive Psychotherapy, 14*, 67–76.

Barbarasch, B., & Elias, M. (2008). Fostering social competence in schools. In R. W. Christner & R. B. Mennuti (Eds.), *School-based mental health: A practitioner's guide to comparative practices*. New York: Routledge.

Beck, J. S., Beck, A. T., Jolly, J., & Steer, R. (2003). *Beck youth inventories, second edition for children and adolescents*. San Antonio, TX: Harcourt.

Beidel, D. C. & Turner, S. M. (1998). *Shy children, phobic adults*. Washington, DC: APA.

Brehm, K., & Doll, B. (2008). Building resilience in schools: A focus on population-based prevention. In R. W. Christner & R. B. Mennuti (Eds.), *School-based mental health: A practitioner's guide to comparative practices* (pp. 55–85). New York: Routledge.

Brock, S. E., & Jimerson, S. R. (2004). School crisis interventions: Strategies for addressing the consequences of crisis events. In E. R. Gerler (Ed.), *The handbook of school violence* (pp. 285–332). Binghamton, NY: Haworth.

Brock, S., Lazarus, P., & Jimerson, S. (Eds.) (2004). *Best practices in school crisis prevention and intervention.* Bethesda, MD: National Association of School Psychologists.

Christner, R. W., Forrest, E., Morley, J., & Weinstein, E. (2007). Taking cognitive-behavior therapy to school: A school-based mental health approach. *Journal of Contemporary Psychotherapy, 37*(3), 175–183.

Christner, R. W., & Mennuti, R. B. (Eds.). (2008). *School-based mental health: A practitioner's guide to comparative practices.* New York: Routledge.

Christner, R. W., Stewart, J. L., & Freeman, A. (Eds.). (2007). *Handbook of cognitive behavior group therapy for children and adolescents: Specific settings and presenting problems.* New York: Routledge.

Clarke, G. N., Lewinsohn, P. M., & Hops, H. (1990). *Instructor's Manual for the Adolescent Coping with Depression Course.* Eugene, OR: Castalia Press.

Coie, J. D., Watt, J. F., West, S. G., Hawkins, J. D., Asarnow, J. R., Markman, H. J., et al. (1993). The science of prevention: A conceptual framework and some direction for a national research program. *American Psychologist, 48*, 1013–1022.

Doll, B., & Lyons, M. A. (1998). Risk and resilience: Implications for the delivery of educational and mental health services in the schools. *School Psychology Review, 27*, 348–363.

Doll, B., Zucker, S., & Brehm, K. (2004). *Resilient classroom: Creating healthy environments for learning.* New York: Guilford Press.

Dwivedi, K. N. and Gupta, A. (2000). Keeping cool: Anger management through group work. *Support for Learning, 15*(2): 76–81.

Elias, M. J., & Butler, L. B. (2005). *Social decision making/social problem solving: A curriculum for academic, social, and emotional learning.* Champaign, IL: Research Press.

Farrell, A. F. (2008). Building school wide positive behavior supports. In R. W. Christner & R. B. Mennuti (Eds.), *School-based mental health: A practitioner's guide to comparative practices.* New York: Routledge.

Feindler, E. L. & Ecton, R. B. (1986). *Adolescent anger control.* New York: Pergamon.

Feindler, E. L. & Guttman, J. (1994). Cognitive-behavioral anger control training. In C. W. LeCroy (Ed.), *Handbook of child and adolescent treatment manuals* (pp. 170–199). New York: Lexington Books.

Gibbs, J. C., Potter, G., & Goldstein, A. (1995). *EQUIP: Teaching youth to think and act responsibly through a peer-helping approach.* Champaign, IL: Research Press.

Goldstein, A. (1999). *The PREPARE Curriculum: Teaching prosocial competencies* (Rev. ed.). Champaign, IL: Research Press.

Goldstein, A. P., Glick B., & Gibbs, J. (1998). *Aggression replacement training: A comprehensive intervention for aggressive youth* (2nd ed.). Champaign, IL: Research Press.

Heath, M., & Sheen, D. (2005). *School-based crisis intervention: Preparing all personnel to assist.* New York: Guilford Press.

Kendall, P. C. (1993). *A coping cat workbook.* Ardmore, PA: Workbook Publishing.

Kessler, R. C., Berglund, P., Demler, O., Jin, R., & Walters, E. E. (2005). Lifetime prevalence and age-of-onset distributions of DSM-IV disorders in the national comorbidity survey replication. *Archive of General Psychiatry, 62*, 593–602.

Knoff, H. M. (2001). *The stop & think social skills program: Preschool–grade 1, grades 2/3, grades 4/5, Middle School 6–8.* Longmont, CO: Sopris West.

Kusche, C. A., & Greenberg, M. T. (1994). *The PATHS (promoting alternative thinking strategies) curriculum.* Seattle, WA: Developmental Research and Programs.

Kutash, K., Duchnowski, A. J., & Lynn, N. (2007). *School-based mental health: An empirical guide for decision-makers.* Tampa, FL: University of Southern Florida, The Louis de la Parte Florida Mental Health Institute, Department of Child & Family Studies, Research and Training Center for Children's Mental Health.

Larson, J., & Lochman, J. E. (2002). *Helping schoolchildren cope with anger: A cognitive-behavioral intervention.* New York: Guilford Press.

Mennuti, R. B., Freeman, A., & Christner, R. W. (Eds.) (2006). *Cognitive-behavioral interventions in educational settings: A handbook for practice.* New York: Routledge.

Mennuti, R., & Christner, R. W. (2005). School-based cognitive-behavioral therapy (CBT). In A. Freeman (Ed.), *International encyclopedia of cognitive behavior therapy* (pp. 343–347). New York: Springer/Kluwer.

Mrazek, P. J., & Haggerty, R. J. (Eds.). (1994). *Reducing risks for mental disorders: Frontiers for preventative intervention research.* Washington, DC: National Academy Press.

Murphy, V. B., & Christner, R. W. (2006). A cognitive-behavioral case conceptualization approach for working with children and adolescents. In R. B. Mennuti, A. Freeman, & R. W. Christner (Eds.), *Cognitive-behavioral interventions in educational settings: A handbook for practice.* New York: Routledge Publishing.

National Center for Education Statistics. (2005). *Digest of Education Statistics, 2004.* Publication NCES 2006005. Retrieved May 16, 2006, from http://nces.ed.gov/programs/digest/d04

New Freedom Commission on Mental Health: Achieving the promise: Transforming the mental health care in America. (2003). *Final report to the President: Full version.* Washington, DC: Author.

Paternite, C. E. (2005). School-based mental health programs and services: Overview and introduction to the special issue. *Journal of Abnormal Child Psychology, 33*, 657–663.

Pluymert, K. (2002). Best practices in developing exemplary mental health programs in schools. In A. Thomas & J. Grimes (Eds.), *Best practices in school psychology IV* (pp. 963–975). Bethesda, MD: National Association of School Psychologists.

Power, T. J. (2003). Promoting children's mental health: Reform through interdisciplinary and community partnerships. *School Psychology Review, 32*, 3–16.

Prodente, C. A., Sander, M.A., & Weist, M. D. (2002). Furthering support for expanded school mental health programs. *Children's Services: Social Policy, Research, and Practice, 5*, 173–188.

Rones, M., & Hoagwood, K. (2000). School-based mental health services: A research review. *Clinical Child and Family Psychology Review, 3*, 223–241.

Shure, M. B. (2001). I can problem solve (ICPS): An interpersonal cognitive problem solving program for children. In L. A. Reddy & S. Pfeiffer (Eds.), *Innovative mental health programs for children: Programs that work* (pp. 2–14). Binghamton, NY: Haworth Press.

Simonsen, B., & Sugai, G. (2007). Using school-wide data systems to make decisions efficiently and effectively. *School Psychology Forum: Research in Practice, 1*(2), 46–58.

Smallwood, D. L., Christner, R. W., & Brill, L. (2007). Applying cognitive-behavior therapy groups in school settings. In R. W. Christner, J. L., Stewart, & A. Freeman (Eds.), *Handbook of cognitive-behavior group therapy: Specific settings and presenting problems* (pp. 89–105). New York: Routledge.

Stark, K., Kendall, P. C., McCarthy, M., Stafford, M., Barron, R., & Thomeer, M. (1996). *Taking action: A workbook for overcoming depression*. Ardmore, PA: Workbook Publishing.

Sugai, G., & Horner, R. H. (1999). Discipline and behavioral support: Preferred processes and practices. *Effective School Practices, 17*(4), 10–22.

Sugai, G., & Horner, R. H. (2002). Introduction to the special series on positive behavior supports in schools. *Journal of Emotional and Behavioral Disorders, 10*, 130–135.

Weisz, J. R., Jensen, A. L., & McLeod, B. D. (2005). Development and dissemination of child and adolescent psychotherapies: Milestones, methods, and a new development-focused model. In E. D. Hibbs & P. S. Jensen (Eds.), *Psychosocial treatments for child and adolescent disorders: Empirically based strategies for clinical practice* (2nd ed., pp. 9–39). Washington, DC: American Psychological Association.

Ysseldyke, J., Burns, M., Dawson, M., Kelley, B., Morrison, D., Ortiz, S., et al. (2006). *School psychology: A blueprint for training and practice III*. Bethesda, MD: National Association of School Psychologists.

14 Educating consultants for practice in the schools

Sylvia Rosenfield,
Mary Levinsohn-Klyap,
and Katurah Cramer

Consultation and indirect service delivery models have evolved as integral to school psychology practice since the last quarter of the 20th century (Erchul & Sheridan, 2008). The recommendation that consultation be a primary role for school psychologists can be found in most of the major conferences, from Spring Hill (Ysseldyke & Weinberg, 1981) to the more recent Futures Conference (Cummings et al., 2004), and has been incorporated into major documents including the first *School Psychology: A Blueprint for Training and Practice* (Ysseldyke, Reynolds, & Weinberg) in 1984 to *Blueprint III* (Ysseldyke et al.) in 2006.

However, in spite of the call for increasing practice as well as research (e.g., Sheridan & Erchul, 2008) in consultation, there is a relative silence about consultation training. Yet Gutkin and Conoley (1990) explicitly stated that it should not be assumed "that psychologists who are adequately prepared to provide direct service are also adequately prepared to provide indirect service" (p. 205). The purpose of this chapter is to trace the history of consultation training and to recommend critical, often ignored, components of the education required to develop effective consultants.

LITERATURE REVIEW

Consultation, as other similar practice domains, can be described as "an art, science, craft and profession" (Thomas, 2004, p. 136). We begin with the assumption that effective consultation is neither a rote dissemination system for science-based interventions nor a mechanistic problem-solving series of steps. Rather, the development of school psychologists as skilled consultants needs to be viewed as a complex interpersonal process that unfolds over time (Rosenfield, 2002).

In the early 1980s, Alpert and Meyers (1983) published a series of papers based on a conference they convened on consultation training. However, two decades later, in the introduction to a special issue on training, Alpert and Taufique (2002) reflect on "the lack of research and writing in consultation training" (p. 8) and the need to evaluate and describe consultation training.

They raised a number of questions about consultation training that date back to the earlier conference: (a) in which orientation (e.g., mental health, problem-solving/behavioral, instructional, organizational, or some combination) should individuals be trained, (b) when in the education of school psychologists should training occur, and (c) how best to provide supervision.

For school psychologists and other applied psychologists, relatively little about systematic training on consultation has been reported over the decades. Concern about training in consulting extends beyond school psychology. Crego (1985) was concerned about the quality of consultation training in applied psychology, particularly the lack of education and training standards. Hellkamp, Zins, Ferguson, and Hodge (1998), recognizing the importance of competency in the process of consultation, surveyed faculty responsible for consultation training in doctoral graduate programs in clinical, counseling, school, and industrial/organizational psychology. They concluded that the programs did not offer "many courses, practicum experiences, or workshops on consulting" (p. 233).

A series of surveys have been conducted about consultation training in school psychology programs. Meyers, Wurtz, and Flanagan (1981), in their survey found that 60% of the responding school psychology programs, particularly specialist level programs, did not have a course on consultation. In a later survey, with a return rate of 48% of the 217 programs contacted, Anton-Lahart and Rosenfield (2004) found that, in comparison to the Meyers et al. (1981) study, a consultation course was offered by 87% of the specialist level programs and all of the doctoral programs that responded. The behavioral consultation model was taught most frequently (91% of responding programs), followed by mental health (59%), instructional (53%), and organizational (52%) consultation. Most programs taught more than one model, indicating a focus on breadth rather than depth. In addition, little time was devoted to communication and process skills during training and more time was spent teaching theory and intervention development skills. Even when two courses were offered, it appeared that the second course also focused largely on theoretical skills and intervention development. Although students in the majority of the courses were required to take one or more consultation cases, supervision was reported as minimal. Only a quarter of the programs that had responded returned the requested course syllabi, but evaluation of the syllabi found that they were not always congruent with the survey data.

Hazel and Laviolette (2008) conducted a more recent study of consultation course syllabi from American Psychological Association (APA)-accredited school psychology training programs. They received course syllabi from 25 of the 63 doctoral programs, a response rate of 40%. Although the majority of the responding programs offered one course, 16% did not have a dedicated consultation course and 32% did not require a field experience consultation. However, even for those requiring a field experience, it was often limited: In 12% of programs, only one interview was required and in 8%, three to five interviews were required; in 36% of the programs, only one case was required (Hazel & Laviolette). In sum, of the 25 programs, students in only 14 programs had a consultation experience beyond one interview and in 9 of those, only one case was required. As in Anton-Lahart and Rosenfield (2004), the supervision of consultation cases was limited. While audio or video recording was required in 13 of the 17 programs, the amount and type of supervision was difficult to determine from the syllabi. Apparently, only 10 of the 17 programs provided supervision at all and 10 programs required students to write a case report. Building competent consultation skills under those conditions would be extremely problematic. Hazel and Laviolette, on the basis of a content analysis of the course syllabi, noted the wide spread of content in many of the courses. In all of the surveys described thus far, however, response rates were problematic, suggesting that the surveys may over-report how much consultation training is actually occurring. Moreover, Hazel and Laviolette also noted that while some of the programs offer multiple courses, those programs do not require that students take more than one. In one program, for example, the required course field experience was limited to one problem-identification interview (Hazel, personal communication).

The state of training has left practitioners reliant on sources other than their preservice training for development of consultation skills. For example, Stewart (1985) reported that 20% of school psychology practitioners relied on skills they learned in their training programs, while 49% used techniques that were self-developed. Hughes (1992) also found that school psychologists relied heavily on professional articles and work experiences for acquiring consultation knowledge, even though 40% had completed a course during their preservice training.

The lack of training is particularly critical since school psychologists consistently indicate that they would like to do more consultation, intervention and research and less assessment (Hosp & Reschly, 2002). In fact, school psychology practitioners report feeling inadequately prepared to function as consultants (see, e.g., Costenbader, Swartz, & Petrix, 1992; Guest, 2000). When students were surveyed after completing a single consultation course, most shared that they did not yet feel confident in their consultation skills and still had many questions (Cramer, Rosenfield, Mewborn, Anton & Schulmeyer, 2001). In a study of school psychology students' practicum experiences (Tarquin & Truscott, 2006), 71% reported that they spent 0–25% of their time in consultation activities; only 6% spent 50% or more time in consulting activities. Their supervisors spend little time engaged in consultation activities, and consequently, may deter the practicum students from viewing consultation as a viable activity in the real world of practice.

CONSULTATION TRAINING

Core competencies: a set of guidelines

A critical question is what the core of consultation training should be. In 2007, the APA published guidelines for education and training at the doctoral and postdoctoral levels in consulting psychology. The Guidelines, applicable to individual, group, or systems level work, specify sets of competencies, including the overarching competencies of self-awareness/self-management and relationship development. Assessment, broadly defined, is considered a pivotal competency to assist in decision-making and in the change process. Process skills (Schein, 1999) are a third basic general competency. Additional competency areas include: interventions; knowledge of consulting psychology theory and practice; multicultural, international, gender, and life span competencies; and professional ethics and standards, many of which overlap with other domains of practice. It should be noted that the Guidelines have a specific definition of intervention, namely "activities both the consultant and the client agree have a high probability for solving the problem at hand" (APA, p. 982). It appears that many consultation courses incorporate study of interventions, such as behavioral strategies, but achieving consultee and consultant agreement requires additional skills. A large portion of time spent learning about interventions in consultation courses diminishes even further the attention to consultation specific skills (Hazel & Laviolette, 2008).

Consultation courses in school psychology typically focus on behavioral, mental health, instructional, and organizational models, or some combination of those models, so the approach and content may differ across programs depending upon the faculty instructor's orientation. The Guidelines (APA, 2007) provide a set of competencies generic enough to be useful for school psychology preservice programs, regardless of the consultation model selected. However, the surveys of program courses suggest that theory and concepts are taught more often than skills, particularly at the application level. Fullan (2008) emphasizes that people need to learn "in the specific context in which the work is being done" or they will be "inevitably learning superficially" (p. 89). The remainder of this chapter will be devoted to key concepts and strategies to facilitate the development of competent consultants, including a focus on supervision, which a review of course syllabi and surveys suggests is not well-structured in consultation courses. The structures and examples here are based on the experiences of the authors, who all have taught and supervised consultants at the pre-service and inservice levels. While the structures described in this chapter reflect one program's training model, we hope that the reader will take away the fundamental concepts presented and adapt them to their own unique contexts.

A framework for training skills: awareness to competence

The purpose of graduate level consultation course work should be to help students not only to gain and organize the central knowledge base of consultation and its role in school psychology practice but also to develop consultation skills. Professional education in any domain requires the individual to move through the stages of (a) acclimation or awareness, (b) early competence, (c) full competence, and finally, for some individuals, (d) expertise (Alexander, 1997). To move along that continuum, students require different activities and strategies. Joyce and Showers (1980) provided a framework for that process that has been adapted to consultation training (Rosenfield, 2002) Table 14.1 reflects the components taken from that framework.

Acclimation

During the acclimation, or awareness, stage, students begin with little knowledge or skills in the domain. Lecture and readings build knowledge, which is typically fragmented at this stage, and students are highly dependent upon external support in their practice activities. Instructors need to help students separate the essential information and "engage them actively in strategic processing and self-regulation" (Rosenfield, 2002, p. 98). The surveys of programs suggest that many school psychology programs focus on this theoretical and conceptual understanding of the knowledge base in consultation. However, course work on theory and conceptual understanding, while necessary at the acclimation stage, is not sufficient to move students to skilled consultation, even at the early competence level.

Skill acquisition does begin at the acclimation stage, as the student builds awareness and conceptual understanding of the consultation

Table 14.1 Training Methods and Levels of Impact

Training Method	Level of Impact	Evidence of Impact
Didactic presentation of theory and concepts	Awareness	Participant can articulate general concepts and identify problem
Modeling and demonstration (i.e., live, video, etc.)	Conceptual understanding	Participant can articulate concepts clearly and describe appropriate actions required
Practice in simulated situations with feedback (i.e., role-play, written exercises, etc.)	Skill acquisition	Participant can begin to use skills in structured or simulated situations
Coaching and supervision during application	Application of skills	Participants can use skills flexibly in actual situation

relationship, communication skills, and problem-solving structures. Role-playing and simulations in classroom settings with peers provide practice prior to application in school settings. For example, Jones (1999) developed a consultation simulation in which students can role-play the initial problem identification meeting with a trained individual acting in a prescribed manner as the teacher. In the authors' training program, all students are videotaped conducting this 20-minute simulation. After viewing their videotape, students evaluate their performance using a structured set of questions, based on the skill concepts being taught, thus enabling the student to get feedback before starting an actual case in the schools and to feel some comfort during their early problem identification sessions. While the questions for the students in this activity focus on instructional consultation, trainers using other models of consultation could develop their own simulations and structured question sets. (For more information about the simulation, see Jones.)

However, if skill training stops at the acclimation stage, preservice students may view consultation as a set of formulaic problem-solving steps or as an intuitive process conducted without much structure. Indeed, many school psychology practitioners report that their consultation practice follows no particular orientation (e.g., see Panahon, Hill-Panahon, Codding, & Lannie, 2008, who report that school psychologists most frequently use a behavioral model, followed by no specific approach to consultation services). Without sufficient support to move from awareness to competence, it is possible for consultant trainees to rely on a series of mechanical sequential stages learned in courses, leading "to inflexible reactions rather than to flexible and informed responses to problematic situations" (Mason, 2002, p. 55).

Competence

Given the limited amount of supervision and feedback that students typically receive in consultation at the internship and inservice levels (Cramer et al., 2001), it is essential for preservice training to guide the students to at least an early competence level of skill development during their preservice training. Students need the opportunity to consolidate their knowledge and skills by applying them in actual cases in the schools, under conditions where they can engage in reflection and receive supervision. According to Rosenfield (2002), such training is critical for facilitating competence in practice:

> Strategic processing around routine problems becomes more automatic, and novel problems can be addressed more intelligently. … it is important to diminish the amount of scaffolding and direction, provide more interesting and complex problems, and use performance-based tasks to permit the student to explore a variety of solutions. (p. 99)

During this early application phase, students should be supervised by consultants with expertise. Often, the on-site school psychology practicum supervisor may have only limited consultation expertise, either because of the limited training that most practitioners receive or because their schedules do not allow the time for intensive supervision. The more cases that can be supervised intensively, the more likely it is that the novice consultant can become more competent. In the authors' two-semester course, the student consultants complete three to five cases.

Furthermore, to the extent possible, consultation faculty should provide students the opportunity to observe and do their practicum in settings in which school psychologists practice from an indirect service delivery model for a considerable portion of their work; otherwise, students are unable to see how consultation can be integrated into service delivery. Newman and Burkhouse (2008), in describing their instructional consultation training at the University of Maryland from a student perspective, discuss the importance of the match between student training and fieldwork setting. To that end, the first author found it useful to provide inservice opportunities for local psychologists who wanted to do more consulting, in order to develop practicum sites conducive to consultation fieldwork.

Expertise

Alexander's (1997) third stage of development, expertise, is obtained during practice in the field following graduate school. This is the stage in which some consultants can actually make changes that reshape the domain itself (Alexander, 1997). Even as consultants reach this high level, they should be encouraged to continue professional development in order to maintain and develop their skills further. Continued learning can be accomplished through a variety of opportunities such as consulting with other professionals, studying material on their own, engaging in research and program evaluation activities, and providing professional development in consultation to colleagues. While developing expertise is beyond the focus of this chapter, those teaching consultation should be individuals with some degree of expertise beyond the knowledge level in this domain.

Consultation supervision to build consultation skills

Since surveys consistently find little supervision of consultation at the preservice level, this section describes a structured supervision plan. It is based on a developmental framework that has been implemented throughout a two-semester consultation sequence. The purpose of this supervision plan is to help students develop a level of knowledge and experience in consultation that will allow them to move from acclimation to at least early competence in executing these skills in the field. This plan includes audiotaping, reflection, and additional methods, such as role-playing, and is described as it is conducted in our training program. While the plan is based on developing competence in instructional consultation (Rosenfield, 1987; Rosenfield & Gravois, 1996), general principles for supervising consultation skills are embedded in the description.

In the first consultation course of the sequence, students complete one consultation case with a teacher in a school setting. Each consultation session with the teacher is audiotaped, and students are required to listen to the tape and write process notes about the session prior to supervision. Although this supervision structure remains the same throughout the student's learning experience, the substance of the sessions varies based on the student's level of experience and the case at hand, as Alexander's model of domain learning would suggest.

In the novice stage, students have limited and disjointed knowledge and need the supervisor to provide direct information and to prioritize the importance of information (Alexander, 1997). This stage is where all new consultation students begin and generally remain for the semester. Therefore the beginning of consultation supervision should help students to gain the knowledge they need in order to engage in the consultation process, as well as build students' independence by encouraging them to access resources to answer their own questions (Cramer & Rosenfield, 2003). It is also important to encourage novice students to engage in self-reflection and to build self-motivation and curiosity (Alexander, 1997).

Process notes

Process notes, also called logs, include what the students believe happened during the session, what communication and relationship issues were noted, what went well or not, what questions they would like to address in supervision, and how they plan to approach the next session. Students may also select a portion of the session tape, significant in some way to them, to play during the supervision session or transcribe it as part of their process notes. It may be something they did very well or would like to do better next time, a miscommunication segment that needs clarification, or a content issue related to the problem being addressed.

With respect to the process logs, Mason (2002) points out the importance of describing and reflecting on professional experiences and how essential reflection is to intentional learning. The process notes provide a rich opportunity for students to specify what happened based on listening to the tape and to reflect on their skills. It is often surprising to novice consultants to see how fragmented and unreliable their memory of the session is when they listen to the tape. By writing these reflections using a structured format, the session incidents are captured "for further analysis and preparation for the future" (Mason, p. 34).

The supervisor receives a copy of the process notes and the tape prior to the supervision session. This is important so that both supervisor and consultant come in with a full and accurate picture of what transpired during the meeting. During the actual supervision session, both the process skills, such as relationship and communication skills, and content, such as how understanding and resolving the problem are proceeding, are discussed. Supervisor and consultant may listen to the portion of tape previously identified, use role-playing to illustrate how something could have been done differently, or discuss how to engage in an anticipated interaction.

Audiotaping

According to Mason (2002), "the more you probe what happens ... by listening to audio-tapes of yourself ..., the more you realize that so many decisions are made on the fly with incomplete, even erroneous information" (p. 27). The use of audiotaping is particularly useful at the novice stage as it gives the supervisor a full and accurate picture of what was said during the consultation session and how it was said (see, e.g., Rosenfield, 2004, for the importance of language in consultation). Since at this stage the student does not always recognize key elements of the session, taping gives the supervisor important information. For example, in the context of an instructional consultation session, a consultant trainee asked a teacher whether the student was being taught at his instructional level without explaining what she meant by instructional level. The teacher said yes and the consultant accepted the answer without clarifying how the teacher made that judgment, such as what data she had already collected. The supervisor therefore needed to address the issues of instructional assessment and communication skills with the consultation student.

There are also times when a novice student may have inaccurate or insufficient information about a teacher's concern (Cramer & Rosenfield, 2003). For example, one consultant was looking for an experience working with a teacher on a behavior concern. She thought the student's needs were clear-cut and purely behavioral when she began the case and that she could therefore rule out academic concerns without conducting any instructional assessments. The supervisor needed to explain the importance of instructional assessments to ensure that there are no academic concerns before focusing on behavior, as many behavioral referrals are rooted in academic issues.

Many school psychology students also become concerned that they have less knowledge and experience than their consultees, and doubt the value of the consultation process as students. Through supervision, students gain the perspective that while others in the building may have more content knowledge, using collaborative and reflective communication skills are powerful tools to help consultees reflect on and resolve their own problems. Supervision helps students recognize that developing a collaborative relationship and following a process with the consultee is a powerful tool in problem solving, and understand that the consultant does not need to have "the answer."

Lastly, through the use of the data provided by recorded sessions, supervisors can help consultants to compare what they felt happened in the meeting with what actually occurred (Cramer & Rosenfield, 2003). In one case, the consultant told the supervisor that the session was a "nightmare," yet when listening to the tape, the supervisor heard the teacher expressing a mild degree of frustration. The supervisor was able to help the consultation student understand the teacher's behavior and develop a more objective perspective on the session. The student consultant then used collaborative communication skills to process the frustration the teacher was expressing, which ended up being very productive in building their relationship. In another case, the consultant believed she was being too aggressive in the session, yet when listening to the tape, it was difficult to even hear the consultant's soft voice. Again, a more objective perspective needed to be developed.

Sometimes the case requires more skill that a novice consultant can recognize. In another case, the supervisor was able to hear on the tape the teacher's lack of objectivity as she talked about a child's behavior, and then helped the student consultant understand the importance of the relationship between the child's behavior and the teacher's feeling about it. In that case, the teacher was unable to collaborate on a behavioral intervention because of her intense response to the child's behavior. Without the tape and the supervision, it is likely that the novice consultant would have continued to misinterpret the situation or view the teacher as simply resistant to a behavioral intervention. Addressing the teacher's lack of objectivity was a necessary step in the consultation process.

The use of audiotaping at the novice stage can also allow the supervisor to address communication skills (Cramer & Rosenfield, 2003). Communication skills are an important element of effective consultation (Rosenfield, 2004) but one that is especially hard for consultants-in-training to apply effectively, as they are typically caught up in trying to solve the problem. For example, clarification of the consultee's statements is a critical skill for an accurate understanding of the problem (Benn, Jones, & Rosenfield, 2008), but novice consultants more often are prone to barrage teachers with their own questions. Through audiotaping in combination with process logs, consultants can often hear the communication skills they need to work on and actually provide self-corrective feedback. The supervisor can help catch issues with communication skills that the student might miss.

Students may also transcribe a portion of tape to take a closer look at some aspect of the consultation session. In listening to her tape, one student discovered that she did not give the teacher the opportunity to reflect or share during the session and transcribed part of the tape to identify where she missed opportunities to involve the teacher. She was then able to think about how she would change this behavior for the next session.

Lastly, the use of audiotaping can help to increase consultant motivation and achievement. Cramer and Rosenfield (2003) found that consultation students spent more time planning the session when they knew that it was going to be taped. The taping process also made them a bit nervous, so they tended to be more alert and focused during the meeting.

There are some disadvantages of audiotaping that are most evident at the beginning of the supervision process. Cramer and Rosenfield (2003) found that taping could be stressful for students at first. It is a common phenomenon for students to have taping problems initially in which the recorder does not work, tapes are forgotten, or other errors are made. These seem to be avoidance techniques for nervous new consultants. However, the advantages of audiotaping seem to far outweigh these initial jitters.

One additional method to consider is videotaping. This method is helpful in supervision, as it captures all elements of communication, both verbal and nonverbal. However, videotaping can provide a lot of information to process at once, which can be overwhelming (Bernard & Goodyear, 2004). It can also be harder to arrange in the school setting than having a new consultant audiotape their sessions (Cramer & Rosenfield, 2003).

Role-playing

The use of role-playing can also be particularly useful at the early competence stage. Role-playing can be helpful to prepare consultant trainees for future interactions that are anticipated to be uncomfortable or challenging and can give them the opportunity to practice sharing certain information or ideas confidently and/or clearly and to prepare for various teacher responses (Cramer & Rosenfield, 2003). Finally, role-playing can help in refining students' communication skills.

Increasing student independence

As students enter Alexander's (1997) second stage of competence, they not only have more knowledge, but can also organize case information more effectively and can automatically execute some basic skills. During this stage, the instructor modifies the focus to provide more opportunities for the students' own reflection. Rather than the instructor choosing on what issues to focus, more independence and responsibility can fall on the student. There is less structure during supervision at this stage, and issues that are more difficult and less concrete are addressed (Cramer and Rosenfield, 2003).

In addition to having a systematic, structured supervision plan in place to help develop novice consultant's skills during their first case, it is necessary for them to have an opportunity to practice their emerging skills across multiple cases, with a variety of consultees, and with a diversity of concerns. The use of process notes in combination with audiotaping is even more useful as consultants-in-training work on additional cases. While beginning consultants are less able to pull out key points, as the trainees gain experience, they are better able to identify important points on their own. The use of process notes in combination with audiotaping helps them to reflect and make plans for change. When trainees do a thorough job with their reflections at this stage, sometimes the supervisor has little to add.

SUMMARY

A structured supervision plan has been described here, in which consultation students can move from the novice to the competence stage over the course of a two-semester consultation course sequence. Suggestions were made for meeting students' specific needs at each stage of development. The main foci of this plan are (a) to move students from fairly structured and supervisor-driven sessions to ones in which the consultation student gains more responsibility and (b) to shift from the discussion of structured content topics to more complex process issues. The use of audiotaping and process notes was recommended throughout the supervision process, although the focus of supervision changes as students gain experience.

However, not all school psychology programs have devoted, or can devote, sufficient resources for supervision in the consultation domain. Recognizing that skillful consultation is a goal for programs and that supervision of practice in context is critical for skill building are the first steps however. Supervising students in small groups may be an interim solution, as is building a cadre of advanced students in the program who can supervise novice consultants. Use of distance-based coaching as a professional developments strategy, as is done in the instructional consultation model (Gravois, Knotek, & Babinski, 2002; Vail, 2004) may be one additional way to build skills not developed at the preservice level. However, practitioners would have to recognize their need for additional competence in order for them to seek such intensive professional development.

Multicultural competencies

Surveys also have found a conspicuous lack of training in multicultural aspects of consultation, as rarely are students asked to analyze the consultation case using their own cultural lens and determine how that perspective might play a role in the consultation relationship. Sirmans (2004) surveyed practicing school psychologists on their multicultural consultation practices and found that (a) their training to address culture in consultation is limited; (b) their provision of consultation is limited and even more limited for culturally relevant consultation; and (c) based on their responses, many school psychologists' understanding of culture appears to be superficial at best and not nearly reflective of the existing literature on culturally relevant practices and consultation. An examination of how culture may impact the consultative relationship is an important component to include for new consultants.

Thus, another requirement for consultation training is developing cultural competence in consultation. It is useful for students to select at least one case where the consultee or client is of a culture that is different from their own. The students can then analyze the consultation relationship in terms of the cultural issues that arise. The multicultural school consultation framework (Ingraham, 2000) can serve as a guide for the student's analysis.

In one case, the student noted that the consultee's relationship with the child was impacting the case. The (Caucasian) teacher appeared to have low expectations for the (African American) student, was conceptualizing the concerns in behavioral terms, and was resistant to exploring a lack of academic skill as a possible root of the behavioral concerns. Earlier in the semester, the class had read Hamre and Pianta (2004), and through supervision, the difficult conversation about how culture and attitudes were affecting the consultative relationship was discussed. The concept explored in Hamre and Pianta was the "reciprocal association" that occurs between student and teacher. Specifically, if the student is engaged and displays motivation to learn, the teacher in turn becomes more engaged in the student and motivated to teach that student, which in turn results in the student feeling more accepted by the teacher and more engaged and motivated to engage. The impact of race and culture on the powerful positive (or negative) spiral of reciprocal association in this relationship became an important focus of the consultation. Considering sensitive issues, such as culture and attitudes, should be addressed with new consultants by the early competence level and is most often easily absorbed when they have already completed at least one full case with supervision and support.

Systems consultation training

One area with which many new consultants have little structured experience is systems-level consultation. *Blueprint III* (Ysseldyke et al., 2006) specifically addresses the need to build competencies so that school psychologists will be "proficient at helping systems build capacity" (p. 13). In this framework, the consultant not only collaborates with one teacher concerning instruction or behavior for one student within the classroom but can also use the problem-solving process for multiple students in the same classroom or staff members within the school. Thus, a specific course objective is for students to develop knowledge and basic skill in applying the consultation process to a systems level consultation. In the application of system-level consultation, new consultants are responsible for engaging in a consultation that is focused on multiple students or staff. The student consultant is required to conduct a needs assessment to uncover an issue and consult with an identified member(s) of the school staff. Expectations for supervision are the same for the system-level case as with the individual cases (e.g., weekly supervision, audio taping with consultee(s), process logs, or transcription of tapes).

The systems-level cases span the spectrum of concerns from academic to behavior to organizational. Despite the diversity of concerns identified, consultant-trainees use a structured process to work through the systems-level issue. The problem-solving steps for a systems level case are essentially the same as with an individual consultee-centered case, with some variations. Issues of who is the consultee are often more complex, and students refer frequently to Schein's (1999) structure for types of clients in process consultation.

To begin the systems case, students engage in contracting, where the consultant clarifies with the consultee(s) the problem-solving process, consultee(s) expectations of the process, time frame, and the collaborative nature of the relationship. Once the consultee(s) agrees to engage in the process, problem identification and analysis began. A needs assessment is conducted to help identify the concern. Once the concern has been identified, baseline data collected and goals set, intervention or strategy ideas are generated and implemented. Once the strategy or intervention is implemented, the intervention is evaluated to determine if the goals are met and the concern addressed. Closure is the final step in the process and is initiated when the data suggest that the goals are met and the consultee(s) no longer needs support with the intervention implementation.

Some examples will provide a picture of these cases. In one systems-level case, the student consulted with the on-site school psychologist and reading specialist regarding the vocabulary scores of students in the fifth grade. The concern was initially identified when the school's problem-solving team was reviewing grade level data. Through engaging in the problem-solving process, the student consultant and two consultees were able to narrow down the focus of the vocabulary concern and decided to implement a strategy to enhance the vocabulary knowledge of all the students within one classroom. The problem identification focused on determining if all students in the one classroom had similar vocabulary concerns or if the instruction should be differentiated based on students' patterns of strengths and needs within the area of vocabulary. Also, part of the process involved determining the appropriate goals to set and how to monitor progress toward the goals. Because the consultees and the classroom teacher were all on the school's problem-solving team, the process went relatively smoothly and they were able to apply what they already knew about consultee-centered consultation and problem-solving to the systems-level case.

An additional outcome of the case was that both consultees as well as the classroom teacher had a better understanding of how to apply the problem-solving process beyond one identified student and indicated comfort with engaging in such a process in the future. In this case, the student learned valuable skills of how to efficiently utilize grade-wide assessment data to identify systems level concerns and to link those data with instructional interventions within the classroom. The student consultant also collaborated with others in the building who were considered to be "experts" (e.g., the reading specialist), which further reinforced the power of the collaborative process and helped the student to internalize that she did not have to have "the answer" when consulting.

Another example of a systems-level case occurred in an elementary school where a positive behavioral supports program was being implemented. The school psychologist was the consultee. After agreeing to collaborate in the problem-solving process during contracting, the student consultant and school psychologist decided to conduct a needs assessment to help facilitate the problem identification process. They reviewed office referrals and found that the most common source of office referral was aggressive behavior. They narrowed the focus of office referrals to the behavior in the hallways during arrival time. Through observations, they found that running in the hallways during arrival time often led to physical aggression in the hallways, which contributed to the high rate of office referrals for aggressive behavior. They also found that a variety of school factors led to inappropriate hallway behavior, such as the students not receiving reminders of hallway rules since the beginning of the school year, rules not being posted in the hallway, and inconsistent staff responses to student behavior. For their intervention plan, they decided to have teachers engage each class in a refresher lesson about appropriate hallway behavior and model appropriate hallway behavior with students. Students' responses to the classroom lessons were used to create posters that hung in the hallways.

Through supervision, the student consultant reflected that concerns that arose in the case stemmed from not properly identifying all types of clients. Multiple types of clients are often a common feature of a systems-level consultation case; since more individuals are involved, consequently, there are potentially more clients/stakeholders. For example, while the primary client in the case was the school psychologist, other people who also had a role in the intervention included the teachers (unwitting clients) and administrators (primary stakeholders). Recognizing the impact of those clients on the success of the systems-level case was analyzed using Schein's model (1999). What was revealed during supervision was that some of the teachers had not been fully compliant with the intervention. The student consultant reflected that a teacher survey prior to implementing the systems-level intervention could have more effectively elicited teachers' input on the problems and might have been used to increase teachers' buy-in. Another learning experience from this case was the importance of including all the stakeholders; in this case, the assistant principal was not initially included until it was found that she was implementing her own behavioral intervention to address hallway behavior. Once this was realized, it became clear that the assistant principal needed to be included as a consultee. Understanding the different clients when addressing a systems level problem provides an important learning experience for the consultant-in-training.

Training school psychologists for team leadership and organizational change

There is not space in this chapter to describe training in two other areas, that of team facilitation and organizational change. School psychologists spend a considerable amount of time working with teams, and the skills required have not been sufficiently taught or researched. Thomas (2004) provides a conceptual overview of types of team facilitation. Forman (in press) provides a more elaborated view of doctoral school psychology training for innovation implementation in a chapter describing her course, which addresses theory, research, and skills needed for implementing evidence-based innovations in schools and other organizational settings.

SUMMARY AND CONCLUSIONS

Nearly two decades ago Gutkin and Conoley (1990) urged graduate programs in school psychology to address the "critical value of interpersonal influence with adults ... in considerable depth and detail" (p. 212). Moving from a child-centered approach to one that emphasizes interpersonal influence with adults requires more attention, yet training programs, especially at the specialist level, have traditionally emphasized individual assessment and the direct intervention process.

We have made the case here that one course in the theories and concepts of consultation, with limited application of skills under supervision, will not suffice to bring school psychology students to a level of early competence as they approach internship. Internship itself is unlikely, except in exceptional circumstances, to move the preservice student to early competence in consultation if the program did not provide essential supervision in critical skills.

In this chapter, we have reviewed some of the literature surveying school psychology programs on their consultation training, described the new guidelines on consultation published by the APA, and presented some practices that we have found productive in training consultation skills, particularly strategies related to supervision, multicultural skills, and systems-level practice within an adult-learning, developmental perspective. As Mason (2002) reminds us, "one thing we seem not to learn from experience, is that we rarely learn from experience alone" (p. 64). Without explicit attention, reflection, and supervision, consultation skills will remain elusive in practice.

Multiple questions remain. If school psychologists have not been trained well previously in consultation, how can the trainers who have limited expertise provide training for the next generation of practitioners? The question is how can we help school psychology faculty teaching consultation to become experts in their consultation training skills? Furthermore, there is a dearth of research on training. Sadly, the recent *Handbook of Research in School Consultation* (Erchul & Sheridan, 2008) has no chapter on consultation training, and training rarely appears, even in the index. In 1980, a conference on consultation training was convened, but progress since then has been slow. While interest in consultation research and practice has grown, training has not caught up as yet. It is well past time for school psychology trainers to seriously address this major domain in our programs.

RESOURCES

Alpert, J. L., & Taufique, S. R. (Eds.). (2002). Training in consultation: State of the field [Special issue]. *Journal of Educational and Psychological Consultation, 13* (1 & 2).
This special issue contains the most recent compendium of material on consultation training. The articles are written by individuals with considerable experience in teaching consultation across mental health, behavioral, and instructional consultation models.

American Psychological Association. (2007). Guidelines for education and training at the doctoral and postdoctoral levels in consulting psychology/organizational consulting psychology. *American Psychologist, 62,* 980–992.
These guidelines were developed by a task force from the Division of Consulting Psychology and approved by the APA. Although more focused on consulting in settings other than schools, they provide a useful roadmap for considering what to include in a course in consultation, no matter what the model of the instructor.

Anton-Lahart, J., & Rosenfield, S. (2004). A survey of preservice consultation training in school psychology programs. *Journal of Educational and Psychological Consultation, 15,* 41–62.
This survey provides a view of current consultation training along a number of important dimensions, against which instructors can compare their courses with others in the field. A more recent and intensive syllabus study will soon be available (Hazel & Laviolette, 2008).

REFERENCES

Alexander, P. A. (1997). Mapping the multidimensional nature of domain learning: The interplay of cognitive, motivational and strategic forces. *Advances in Motivation and Achievement, 10,* 213–250.
Alpert, J. L., & Taufique, S. R. (Eds.). (2002). Training in consultation: State of the field [Special issue]. *Journal of Educational and Psychological Consultation, 13*(1 & 2).

American Psychological Association. (2007). Guidelines for education and training at the doctoral and postdoctoral levels in consulting psychology/organizational consulting psychology. *American Psychologist, 62,* 980–992.

Anton-Lahart, J., & Rosenfield, S. (2004). A survey of preservice consultation training in school psychology programs. *Journal of Educational and Psychological Consultation, 15,* 41–62.

Benn, A. E., Jones, G., & Rosenfield, S. (2008). Analysis of instructional consultants' questions and alternatives to questions during the problem identification interview. *Journal of Educational and Psychological Consultation, 19,* 54–80.

Bernard, J. M., & Goodyear, R. K. (2004). *Fundamentals of clinical supervision* (3rd ed.). Boston: Pearson.

Costenbader, V., Swartz, J., & Petrix, L. (1992). Consultation in the schools: The relationship between preservice training, perception of consultative skills, and actual time spent in consultation. *School Psychology Review, 21,* 95–108.

Cramer, K., Rosenfield, S., Mewborn, K., Anton, J., & Schulmeyer, C. (2001, April). *The process of supervision in consultation for everyone involved.* Mini-skill workshop presented at the meeting of the National Association of School Psychologists, Washington, DC.

Cramer, K., & Rosenfield, S. (2003). Clinical supervision of consultation. *The Clinical Supervisor, 22*(1), 111–124.

Crego, C. A. (1985). Ethics: The need for improved consultation training. *The Counseling Psychologist, 13,* 473–476.

Cummings, J. A., Harrison, P. L., Dawson, M. M., Short, R. J., Gorin, S., & Palomares, R. S. (2004). The 2002 conference on the future of school psychology: Implications for consultation, intervention, and prevention services. *Journal of Educational and Psychological Consultation, 15,* 239–256.

Erchul, W. P., & Sheridan, S. M. (Eds.) (2008). *Handbook of research in school consultation.* NY: Erlbaum.

Forman, S. G. (in press). Innovation implementation: Developing leadership for evidence-based practice. In S. Rosenfield & V. Berninger (Eds.), *Translating science-supported instruction into evidence-based practices: Understanding and applying the implementation process.* New York: Oxford University Press.

Guest, K. E. (2000). Career development of school psychologists. *Journal of School Psychology, 38,* 237–257.

Gutkin, T. B., & Conoley, J. C. (1990). Reconceptualizing school psychology from a service delivery perspective: Implications for practice, training, and research. *Journal of School Psychology, 28,* 203–223.

Hamre, B. K., & Pianta, R. C. (2008). Student-teacher relationships as a source of support and risk in schools. In G. G. Bear & K. M. Minke (Eds.), *Children's Needs III* (pp. 59–71). Bethesda, MD: National Association of School Psychologists.

Hazel, C., & Laviolette, G. (2008). *Training school psychology students in consultation: What the syllabi tell us.* Unpublished manuscript.

Hellkamp, D. T., Zins, J. E, Ferguson, K., & Hodge, M. (1998). Training practices in consultation: A national survey of clinical, counseling, industrial/organizational, and school psychology faculty. *Consulting Psychology Journal: Practice and Research, 50,* 228–236.

Hosp, J. L., & Reschly, D. J. (2002). Regional differences in school psychology practice. *School Psychology Review, 31*, 11–29.

Hughes, C. (1992). A knowledge utilization investigation of the adoption and implementation of a consultation-based indirect service delivery model by multidisciplinary teams. Unpublished doctoral dissertation, Fordham University, New York.

Ingraham, C. L. (2000). Consultation through a multicultural lens: Multicultural and cross-cultural consultation in schools. *School Psychology Review, 29*, 320–343.

Jones, G. (1999). *Validation of a simulation to evaluate instructional consultation problem identification skill competence.* Unpublished doctoral dissertation, University of Maryland, College Park.

Joyce, B., & Showers, B. (1980). Improving inservice training: The messages of research. *Educational Leadership, 37*, 379–386.

Mason, J. (2002). *Researching your own practice: The discipline of noticing.* New York: Routledge/Falmer.

Meyers, J., Wurtz, R., & Flanagan, D. (1981). A national survey investigating consultation training occurring in school psychology programs. *Psychology in the Schools, 18*, 297–302.

Newman, D. S., & Burkhouse, K. S. (2008). Consultation training at the University of Maryland: A different perspective on consultation within graduate student practicum settings. *The School Psychologist, 62*, 67–69.

Panahon, C. J., Hill-Panahon, A., Codding, R. S., & Lannie, A. L. (2008, February). *Surveying school psychologists about consultation practices to inform pre-service training.* Poster presented at the meeting of the National Association of School Psychologists, New Orleans, LA.

Rosenfield, S. (1987). *Instructional consultation.* NY: Erlbaum.

Rosenfield, S. (2002). Developing instructional consultants: From novice to competent to expert. *Journal of Educational and Psychological Consultation, 13*, 93–107.

Rosenfield, S. (2004). Consultation as dialogue: The right words at the right time. In N. Lambert, I. Hylander, & J. Sandoval (Eds.), *Consultee-centered consultation: Improving the quality of professional services in schools and community organizations* (pp. 337–347). Hillsdale, NJ: Lawrence Erlbaum Associates.

Rosenfield, S., & Gravois, T. A. (1996). *Instructional consultation teams: Collaborating for change.* New York: Guilford.

Schein, E. H. (1999). *Process consultation revisited: Building the helping relationship.* Reading, MA: Addison-Wesley.

Sirmans, M. (2004). *Culturally relevant consultation among school psychology practitioners: A nation-wide study of training and practice.* Unpublished doctoral dissertation, University of Maryland, College Park.

Stewart, K. J. (1985, August). *Academic consultation: Differences in doctoral and non-doctoral training and practice.* Paper presented at the annual meeting of the American Psychological Association, Los Angeles, CA.

Tarquin, K. M., & Truscott, S. D. (2006). School psychology students' perceptions of their practicum experiences. *Psychology in the Schools, 43*, 727–738.

Thomas, G. (2004). A typology of approaches to facilitator education. *Journal of Experiential Education, 27*, 123–140.

Ysseldyke, J. E., Burns, M. K., Dawson, M., Kelly, B., Morrison, D., Ortiz, S., et al. (2006). *School psychology: A blueprint for training and practice III.* Bethesda, MD: National Association of School Psychologists.

Ysseldyke, J. E., Reynolds, M., & Weinberg, R. A. (1984). *School psychology: A blueprint for training and practice.* Minneapolis: University of Minnesota National School Psychology Inservice Training Network.

Ysseldyke, J. E., & Weinberg, R. A. (Eds.). (1981). The future of psychology in the schools: Proceedings of the Spring Hill symposium [Special issue]. *School Psychology Review, 10.*

15 Adolescent incarceration and children's psychiatric hospitalization

Training school psychologists for nontraditional settings

Tony D. Crespi and
Jeffrey R. Lovelace

Child psychopathology, adolescent suicide, adolescent violence, juvenile arson, juvenile delinquency, and child and adolescent homicide all illustrate a growing spectrum of problems demonstrated by children and adolescents. In point of fact, Duchnowski, Kutash, & Friedman (2002) note in the United States 10% of adolescents have severe to moderate mental health needs, but not all children in need of psychological services actually receive services. Broadly speaking, although potentially dangerous behavioral, adjustment, and psychological disorders are widespread in children and youth, many youth do not receive assistance, and a growing number of children have been placed in highly secure programs ranging from psychiatric hospitals to maximum security prisons. Fortunately, many programs provide a blend of mental health and educational services. Within this context, a number of school psychologists have accepted employment within these settings, often providing classically traditional school psychological services, albeit within very nontraditional settings. This chapter considers the issues.

INTRODUCTION

The depth and breadth of psychological issues in children and adolescents is notable. Mash and Wolfe (1999) observed that approximately 3 million children and adolescents receive mental health services in a given year. More specifically, Crespi (2002) indicated that juvenile delinquent and violent behavior has steadily increased, with more than 3 million youth arrested annually, and with crime statistics for youth ranging from arson to murder. Indeed, children and adolescents are demonstrating seriously maladaptive behavior requiring interventions from schools to psychiatric hospitals to correctional settings.

Today, the frequency of serious psychological and psychiatric disorders in children and adolescents has reached high levels, and it is still rising.

D'Eramo, Prinstein, Feeman, Grapentine, and Spirito (2004) noted, for example, that approximately 21% of children in schools consider suicide annually. Brener, Lowry, and Barrios (2005) indicated that 1 in 16 high school students carries a weapon to school, and approximately 10% of students have reported being threatened with a weapon. Looking at psychiatric disorders in children in a broad sense, Dalton, Muller, and Forman (1989) noted that psychiatric hospitalization for children is a critical focus in child psychiatry, with Hussey and Guo (2005) suggesting that residential treatment of children in a general framework covers a population of more than 223,000 youth.

Looking at the justice system, the involvement of juveniles in the nation's corrections system is noteworthy. Heide (1996) pointed out, as example, that 1 in 6 individuals arrested for homicide is a juvenile, and Hammett, Gaiter, and Crawford (1998) estimated more than 900,000 youth are incarcerated in approximately 600 facilities. With more than 3,000 jails in the United States housing 500,000 inmates and 1,000 prisons housing more than 1 million inmates, and with approximately 600 facilities dedicated to approximately 1 million youthful offenders, there is understandable concern about the trajectory of youthful aggression and violence.

Crespi (2002) reported that there has been a steady increase in correctional programs serving youthful offenders. With adult psychopathology having its genesis in childhood behavior and with clear indications that adult offenders and psychiatric patients classically experienced trauma in childhood, the issues are noteworthy. In point of fact, though, deeply troubled children are not confined solely to correctional and psychiatric settings. In a larger context, children are facing highly challenging problems, with the most disturbed children placed in a range of correctional (i.e., juvenile justice) and inpatient psychiatric facilities. Still, in a larger context, Robertson et al. (1998) noted that some youth move from regular education to special education to residential to juvenile justice settings. Such movement is notable as schools and school psychologists work with this population, both from within public school settings to positions within nontraditional settings, and this continuum provides a view from which to see the widespread nature of the issues.

Within this climate, school psychologists are in key positions to offer assistance. Although their work is not widely examined nor discussed, school psychologists are working actively within a range of nontraditional settings. In an earlier work, for instance, Crespi (2002) described the impact and roles of school psychologists within nontraditional settings serving dangerous and highly disturbed youth. The intention of this chapter is to examine the context of issues impacting both hospitalized and incarcerated youth, discuss the roles and functions of school psychologists within these nontraditional settings, and consider clinical supervision issues relevant to this work.

BACKGROUND

Children and adolescents are struggling, arriving at school from homes marked by a deep array of troubling familial problems. From spousal abuse, witnessed by approximately 80% of children, to drug abuse, sexual abuse, and aggression, families are increasingly in crisis (Crespi & Howe, 2002). Looking at the issues broadly, Fergusson, Horwood, and Lynskey (1994) noted that children who display problems seem to come from families with problems. This factor alone suggests that school psychologists in both traditional and nontraditional settings have ample issues and topics from which to develop individual, group, and family counseling programs. As an illustration, aggressive and violent youth often come from aggressive and violent homes, with violence begetting violence, and with children learning aggression from aggressive parents (Crespi, 1996). With 1 in 7 children having been punched, kicked, or choked by a parent (Moore, 1994), with children from violent homes demonstrating violent behavior at school (Crespi & Howe, 2002), and with the knowledge that school professionals can socialize children to different behaviors to decrease the chances of emulating aggressive and violent behavior learned at home (Dworetzky, 1996), both traditional and nontraditional employment opportunities are of increasing importance.

Sadly, the new millennium has found families marked by an increasing range and depth of problems. Crespi (1997) noted that marital dissolution, parental alcoholism, depression, suicide, and physical, sexual, and emotional abuse represent a sampling of contemporary problems faced in the home. Riddle and Bergin (1997) noted, for example, that in the United States some 28.6 million children live in an alcoholic family; Pope and Hudson (1992) estimate that as many as 67% of children may experience sexual abuse; and, in a more global way, the Carnegie Council on Adolescent Development (1996) reported that there are more than 8 million children in the United States in need of psychological services, with the majority not receiving intervention. More recently, Huang et al. (2005) noted that 1 in 5 children has a diagnosable mental disorder. Tragically, correctional and psychiatric settings serve as one point of intervention for youth who have demonstrated highly disturbed, illegal, violent, and aggressive acts, with a pressing need for mental health professionals with specific expertise in children's psychological issues.

With the average child spending approximately 6 hr each day in school, and given that academic performance and behavioral adjustment are correlated with parental conflict, the repercussions of family difficulties on school performance alone are notable. School psychologists can assist with the class socialization of children to different behaviors to decrease the chances of emulating aggressive and violent behavior learned at home (Dworetzky, 1996); counseling programs targeted at child and family issues are of increasing importance. Clearly, the range of issues and topics that can be addressed is broad.

Relative to nontraditional roles, and keeping in mind the continuum of placements—from general education to special education to day-treatment to residential schools to psychiatric hospitals to correctional prisons and jails—Murray (1997) noted that approximately 1,000 school-based health clinics operate throughout the United States. Fortunately, this suggests a growing awareness of the importance of less restrictive placements than hospitals and prisons. Of course, in addition to these 1,000 placements, Crespi (2002) noted that that there are also approximately 600 correctional facilities dedicated to youth. The range of inpatient and outpatient psychiatric facilities suggests that school psychologists, overall, have an assortment of nontraditional settings in which to seek employment and assist children.

Still, what are the problems? Crespi and Hughes (2003) reported that although institutionalized youth represent a large, and growing, population of children in need of mental health services, the recognition that this population possesses mental health, educational, and vocational needs must not be overlooked and is one reason why so many families are turning to school professionals for assistance. Kemph, Braley, and Ciotola (1997) found that approximately one half of the sample in their study of youthful offenders demonstrated special education problems, and the majority evidenced psychological problems. School psychologists are well placed to offer assistance and can be invaluable both in these individual settings in consulting roles between and across settings.

PROFESSIONAL ROLES AND FUNCTIONS

In both traditional and nontraditional settings, school psychologists can provide a diverse range of services. Classically, services fall under three broad domains: (a) assessment and diagnosis, (b) counseling and psychotherapy, and (c) consultation and collaboration.

Assessment and diagnosis

One of the hallmarks of school psychological services involves assessment and diagnosis. Cognitive, personality, behavioral, and neuropsychological assessments remain a key component to the work of school psychologists in traditional schools, as well as in nontraditional settings. In fact, looking at assessment globally, Mash and Wolfe (1999) observed that assessment is important in psychology as it can (a) pinpoint problem areas, (b) lead to formal diagnoses, and (c) guide treatment.

Just as assessment and diagnosis are critical in public schools, with issues of eligibility for special education and related services often involving attention deficit/hyperactivity disorder, learning disabilities, depression, suicidality, and conduct disorders, so too, school psychologists working in psychiatric and correctional settings are asked to provide comprehensive psychological evaluations with clarifying diagnoses. Often referred to as clinical assessment, assessments in institutional settings can be vital in addressing three broad categories: diagnostic classification, description, and prediction (Nietzel, Bernstein, & Milich, 1998).

Within correctional and psychiatric settings, a sampling of assessment questions follow that may be addressed by a school psychologist:

- What are individual intellectual strengths and weaknesses?
- What learning strengths and deficits are noted?
- What specific processing deficits exist?
- What personality strengths and weaknesses are notable?
- Is the child dangerous and/or posing a threat to self or others?
- What comorbid disorders might be demonstrated?
- Is the child competent to stand trial?
- What conclusions and recommendations can be provided?

School psychologists working in nontraditional settings provide diverse services, including psychological assessment services for children and consultation with clinical staff and institutional teachers, as well as consultation with community schools and agencies. In addition to uses within institutional settings, evaluations may be sent to public schools upon discharge from hospitals; assessments may be used by psychiatrists, clinical psychologists, and clinical social workers in formulating treatment decisions and discharge plans. In a basic way, just as assessments in public schools guide special education identification, classification, and intervention decisions, so too, assessments in institutional settings address similar questions while also providing clinical staff with psychological data useful for classification, diagnostic, and placement decisions.

Particular skill with personality assessment instrumentation, including both objective and projective tools, neuropsychological assessments, threat assessments, suicide assessments, and use of the *Diagnostic and Statistical Manual* (American Psychiatric Association, 2000), is often highly valued. Merrell (1999) observed that psychologists within psychiatric settings, for instance, will likely require a more comprehensive network of assessment tools than school and child clinical psychologists in more general settings. Truly, for school psychologists within psychiatric and correctional settings, strong assessment skills are an area of need and importance.

Overall, then, psychological assessment skills are a critical component of nontraditional service, requiring traditional assessment skills while also demanding additional specialty skills relevant to a highly at-risk and/or dangerous population. Skill sets involving personality assessment, assessment of suicide potential, and threat assessment illustrate skill sets of importance in addition to traditional assessment skills involving cognitive assessment, learning, and information processing.

Counseling and psychotherapy

Certainly one of the hallmarks of psychology involves the provision of individual and group counseling services. Within nontraditional settings, hospitalized and incarcerated youth also may require counseling and/or psychotherapy, and a school psychologist up-to-date on psychotherapy with dangerous, hospitalized, and incarcerated youth can be valuable with institutionalized youth. Thompson and Rudolph (2000) observed that counseling and psychotherapy have similar techniques, and counseling and psychotherapy can offer assistance to children with a wide spectrum of disorders. With behaviors ranging from coping with learning disabilities to the display of extreme violence inside and outside school settings, the set of challenges is wide for school psychologists working with institutionalized youth. Crespi and Fischetti (1997) noted that fortunately, most school psychologists have received training in counseling and psychotherapy and are in a unique and critical position from which to provide assistance to all children.

Broadly considered, counseling services within institutional settings can be demanding. Issues including transference and countertransference, resistance, and defense mechanisms, as well as an understanding of the implications of involuntary treatment in hospital and correctional settings, are important for school psychologists working within such settings. Overall, individual, group, and family counseling and psychotherapy can be beneficial to institutionalized children. Nietzel, Bernstein, and Milich (1998) reported that therapy can be beneficial to clients, and children and adolescents in hospitals and correctional settings may find multimodel models helpful in changing their developmental trajectory.

School psychologists in these settings, then, should possess refined skills in counseling and psychotherapy, understand the distinctions between these areas, and recognize the differences relating to working with children in public schools as opposed to children requiring hospitalization or incarceration. At the same time, specific knowledge of psychopathology, group counseling, and group psychotherapy, as well as advanced techniques for individual and family therapy with youth with various issues, including paranoia, schizophrenia, and violence disorders, is critical to successfully providing psychotherapy with this population. School psychologists within psychiatric and correctional settings, though, need to understand the complexity of psychiatric issues impacting psychotherapy, possess training in working with involuntary clients, and understand the ethical and legal issues involved in working with such a highly disturbed population. Furthermore, institutionalized youth represent a highly challenging population that may require more intensive clinical supervision (Crespi, 2003).

Consultation and collaboration

Consultation and collaboration are critical in the practice of school psychology within both traditional and nontraditional settings. Dougherty (2000) noted that, in fact, consultation and collaboration are practiced by most mental health professionals, in and out of schools, and have become key to working with children. Brown, Pryzwansky, and Schulte (2001) observed that consultation has roots in psychiatry, beginning with community psychiatry and psychiatric initiatives, and is rising in importance relative to community mental health. Within this multifaceted context of community-linked services for children, school psychologists working within both traditional and nontraditional settings must continually consult and collaborate with a wide array of individuals. Within nontraditional settings, this includes the following individuals.

- Institutional teachers
- Institutional child care staff
- Institutional administrators
- Staff psychiatrists
- Clinical social workers
- Guards
- Child care staff in hospitals
- Nursing staff
- Paraprofessional staff
- Discharge agencies
- Families
- Court personnel

Given that one goal of both hospitalization and incarceration involves the ultimate discharge or release of the child to a less restrictive setting, and because hospitals and correctional settings use a diverse array of staff, school psychologists need to be trained in contemporary models of consultation and collaboration. In a basic way, this includes knowledge of major models of mental health consultation (e.g., client-centered case consultation, consultee-centered case consultation, program-centered administrative consultation, and consultee-administrative consultation). In addition, knowledge of contemporary approaches can guide intervention and continued collaboration as children enter and leave facilities and as school psychologists work internally with staff and externally with receiving agencies. In a broad stroke, then, consultation and collaboration, and training in these models, are especially vital to nontraditional practice, as school psychologists in a correctional or psychiatric setting will continually consult both internally with diverse staff, as well as externally with agencies involved in the discharge placement and follow-up of children who have been institutionalized.

CONSIDERATIONS FOR CLINICAL SUPERVISION

Clinical supervision serves as a valuable continuing education tool that can upgrade knowledge, enhance skills, and expand breadth and depth of expertise for all school psychologists. More than three decades have passed since three critical advantages of clinical supervision were noted (Johnstone & Rivera, 1965). These advantages include becoming better informed, preparing for new jobs, and learning more about the job one already possesses.

Within nontraditional settings, clinical supervision can provide invaluable assistance for school psychologists. Supervision can accomplish the following:

1. Provide information on characteristics of the client population
2. Refine and expand psychological assessment skills
3. Refine and expand psychotherapy skills
4. Refine and expand consulting skills
5. Refine multicultural awareness and competence
6. Target skills for new and expanding roles and functions
7. Address limitations of skills sets
8. Monitor effects of working in psychiatric and correctional settings
9. Promote acquisition of new skills as roles change and evolve
10. Upgrade ethical and legal knowledge base

Clearly, a minority of school psychologists pursue employment within psychiatric and correctional settings. In fact, at present, data on the number of practitioners within these settings are sorely lacking. Still, it is clear that a subset of school psychologists, from interns seeking this training to seasoned professionals (Crespi, 2002), are employed in these settings. More to the point, the population served is significant relative to their problems. For these practitioners, clinical supervision is invaluable on both a preservice and in-service level.

Of note, one important aspect of supervision involves the *inappropriate* use of school psychological reports within these settings. Without specialty training, for instance, a school psychologist might conduct an evaluation that is inadvertently sent to a parole board. Or, as an evaluation to determine competency to stand trial requires specialty skills, a school psychologist lacking such expertise whose evaluation is inadvertently used in this process may pose harm to a child. Clinical supervisors must continually attend to competence, as nontraditional settings may request or use evaluations for purposes in which a school psychologist may lack expertise. Selected areas of high competency might include issues such as the following:

1. Competency to stand trial
2. Forensic profiling

3. Determination of violence potential
4. Parole recommendations
5. Potential for future violence
6. Determination of a thought disorder
7. Identification of neuropsychological deficits
8. Identification of suicidality
9. Identification of depression
10. Identification of organic deficits

Because clinical supervision can serve as a vehicle to enhance competence while safeguarding client/patient/inmate rights for evaluations and intervention within established areas of competence, clinical supervision is highly valuable for all school psychologists working within nontraditional settings. These points, although not inclusive, highlight broad areas school psychologists might address during supervision and include the broad areas of (a) psychological assessment, (b) counseling and psychotherapy, and (c) consultation and collaboration. In addition, clinical supervision can attend to broader areas of role and function and serve as an invaluable learning mechanism as roles evolve and change.

CASE ILLUSTRATION: CORRECTIONS
TRAINING FOR SCHOOL PSYCHOLOGISTS

Where or how might a school psychology student interested in nontraditional employment in a corrections setting seek appropriate training? The University of Hartford School Psychology Program is one program that has trained several graduates to work within correctional settings. In a 66-credit, 3-year, National Association of School Psychologists-approved school psychology program, the University of Hartford awards the MS degree in school psychology with a specialization in clinical child counseling at the end of the 2nd year of study and a 6th-year certificate in school psychology at the conclusion of the 3rd year. The program requires a year-long half-time practicum placement during the 2nd year of training followed by a year-long, full-time internship during the 3rd year. The internship has been viewed as a critical tool for developing beginning competency for working with incarcerated youth and has served as the vehicle for training students interested in working with correctional settings.

As background, this training option was initiated during the late 1990s and continued uninterrupted for approximately 5 years. During this time the program offered students the opportunity to complete internship training within the State of Connecticut Department of Correction's Unified School District (USD). As a school district operating within a department of correction, the USD employed approximately 300 permanent educational staff, as well as 70 grant-funded employees. This included approximately

12 school psychologists, 6 school counselors, 40 special education teachers, and 17 teachers of English as a second language, as well as school administrators at each of 19 correctional facilities scattered throughout Connecticut.

All interns were assigned to a full-time, permanent school psychologist and received 2 hr of weekly, site-based, individual, face-to-face clinical supervision. The primary role was to work in consort with educational and prison staff serving approximately 4,000 inmates in school out of a total population of approximately 17,000 inmates. In addition, all interns participated in 2.5 hr of university-based group supervision with a faculty member possessing credentials as a licensed psychologist, certified school psychologist, and nationally certified school psychologist who also has background experiences including service with hospitalized and adjudicated youth. The university supervisor also possessed ancillary credentials as a licensed marriage and family therapist and as a certified school counselor.

From 1998 to 1999, the 1st year of the training partnership, through the early part of the millennium, 7 interns elected to take this training opportunity. All were assigned to a site-based certified school psychologist within the Department of Correction, and all were assigned to a prison-based school serving youthful offenders, with one intern also assigned to a women's facility.

The training partnership required that interns conduct psychological assessments; provide counseling/psychotherapy; facilitate teacher, parent, and local school consultation; and participate in individualized education program meetings. All worked entirely with incarcerated offenders and complete appropriate, institution-based, security and safety training. Two interns attended and graduated from the Department of Correction Training Academy, completing a full-time 6-week training regime that included such components as hostage negotiation, pepper spray training room hardening, and security interventions.

As was done with all interns, this group of trainees was continually evaluated by both university and site-based supervisors and completed weekly training logs. Input and feedback on professional skills was continually provided. The overall goal was to foster skill sets while facilitating personal and professional development. Relative to education and training, several issues emerged:

1. Assessment skills: Prison-based school psychologists were not always up-to-date on contemporary psychological assessment tools. Training school psychologists for broad practice, for work both within and outside correctional settings, supported the notion that the year-long, half-time practicum should always be completed within a traditional school. Furthermore, institution administrators needed to agree to continuing education initiatives intended to provide school psychology supervisors with contemporary assessment expertise.

2. Counseling and psychotherapy: Prison-based school psychologists were not always up-to-date on a broad array of emerging models of counseling and psychotherapy; students were often not aware of the unique nature of psychotherapy within a correctional environment. Joint meetings intended to link supervisors with university faculty were helpful in melding such disparities, but this area was viewed as a skill set of concern relative to the need for continuing education on emerging models.

3. Clinical supervision: Prison-based clinical supervisors were tentative to address new skill sets feeling a lack of familiarity with contemporary tools and models of clinical supervision. Similarly, supervisors were routinely not aware of emerging theories on clinical supervision. Clinical supervision within corrections increasingly crystallized as a highly complex area of work.

4. Professional credentialing: Unique to the University of Hartford, graduates are also eligible, with appropriate post-MS supervision, to sit for credentialing as a nationally certified counselor (NCC) and licensed professional counselor (LPC). None of the supervisors held credentialing as a nationally certified counselor, licensed professional counselor, licensed psychologist, or nationally certified school psychologist. Students viewed this as a weakness, as the LPC and NCC credentials could not be pursued within this training context.

5. Professional affiliations: None of the supervisors were members of either the state school psychological association or the national association. It was felt that a strong identification with school psychological associations was lacking, and that a sense of connection to the broader profession was needed.

6. Professional continuity: The training partnership was initially developed through a close relationship with the State Department of Correction Director of Special Education, who was a former school psychologist. On his retirement, the partnership dissolved. As is typical of many training partnerships, and particularly true in this case, relationships can build programs, and that retirement created a chasm and brought an unfortunate end to a highly unique training opportunity.

Outcomes

Of the seven individuals who completed internship training within the Department of Correction, only two are presently employed within the juvenile justice system. On the other hand, the other five individuals are employed as school psychologists and using those skill sets within the larger context of public education. Overall, graduates felt that the intensive, full-time, year-long correctional internship provided beginning exposure to a highly demanding specialty, and all felt the training provided unusual skill sets with applicability both within and outside corrections. As a downside, not all site-based supervisors were able to maximally mentor and educate students on differences between traditional and nontraditional practices. Certainly, not all school psychologists, nor all clinical psychologists who seek or accept employment in such settings, have received specialty training, and this deficit was viewed within this perspective. Still, the graduates who completed this training felt the experience provided a unique exposure to a highly important area of practice and enhanced employability for all future work.

Personal reflections

Reflecting on my training in the Department of Correction it certainly helped my employablility and it clearly opened doors. It also helped in developing skills for dealing with those behavioral issues that all schools must handle. It forced me, as a professional, to face the decision as to whether to become stagnant or to become committed to continuing education and continual skill development. The first area, stagnancy, was something sometimes seen in institutional staff and the second, continuing learning, was an outgrowth I embraced. The other piece was that professional isolation urged me to become a self-starter and pushed me to continue learning. And, the Department of Correction exposed me to clinical syndromes and situations that I later experienced in schools. If I think of suicide, drug use, or violence, for instance, I was exposed to these components quickly and when I had a clinical supervisor. These syndromes and cases test schools but not always within a structured context with available clinical supervision. The Department of Correction and the Unified School District was a powerful learning opportunity and one which I certainly would not want to trade.

Richard F. Gallini, MS
Certified School Psychologist (Crespi, 2002)

SUMMARY AND CONCLUSIONS

Tragically, significant behavioral, adjustment, and psychological problems have increased in children. Issues including family discord, parental neglect and abuse, sexual abuse, attention disorders, and violence in the home all impact children's adjustment (American Psychiatric Association, 2000). The Carnegie Council on Adolescent Development (1996) reported that more than 8 million children are in need of psychological services. Unfortunately, large numbers of children exhibit multiple disorders, and an increasingly large population of children possess psychological and behavioral difficulties significantly severe as to require psychiatric placements or juvenile justice/correctional incarceration.

Within this context, school psychologists working within psychiatric and correctional settings can be said to apply traditional skills in nontraditional settings. That is, practitioners apply (a) assessment and diagnosis, (b) counseling and psychotherapy, and (c) consultation and collaboration skills. At the same time, working within nontraditional settings brings unique demands and challenges.

It is particularly notable that although such highly disturbed youth would typically represent a small sample of the service population, in public schools this group represents the entire population for these practitioners. Critical distinctions for this work includes the following:

1. Most youth are involuntarily placed in these settings.
2. Children in hospitals and correctional facilities, by definition, are dangerous to either themselves or others or have committed a societal act resulting in confinement.
3. This population can routinely possess comorbid, co-occurring disorders.
4. Whereas the mission of schools is education, psychiatric and correctional settings view education as an ancillary service.
5. Whereas consulting with psychiatric and juvenile justice authorities is not common in public schools, it is routine in these settings.

Most decidedly, a small cadre of school psychologists seek employment in psychiatric and/or correctional settings. At the same time, an increasingly large population of youth placed in these settings and a growing number of youth in traditional settings displaying highly dangerous and/or self-destructive behaviors suggest growing opportunities. For all school psychologists interested in helping this population of youth, a growing body of knowledge of the specific challenges of this work can be instructive. This chapter was intended to provide a beginning glimpse into this work arena.

RESOURCES

American Psychiatric Association. (2000). *Diagnostic and statistical manual of mental disorders* (4th ed., text revision). Washington, DC: Author.
The *DSM-IV-TR* represents a critical resource for school psychologists working within psychiatric settings. Its value cannot be underestimated as both a reference and resource.

Crespi, T. D. (2002). Training school psychologists in prison schools: Implications for training special service providers with delinquent adolescents. *Special Services in the Schools, 18,* 151–163.

This article provides an important glimpse into the work with most challenging populations. Students considering institutional work should find this a useful read.

Dalton, R., Muller, B., & Forman, M. A. (1989). The psychiatric hospitalization of children: An overview. *Child Psychiatry and Human Development, 19,* 231–244.

This overview on psychiatric hospitalization of children can serve as a helpful primer for students.

Fergusson, D. M., Horwood, L. L., & Lynskey, M. (1994). The childhoods of multiple-problem adolescents: A 15-year longitudinal study. *Journal of Child Psychology and Psychiatry, 35,* 1123–1140.

This article can provide a glimpse into the childhood backgrounds of deeply disturbed youth. For those considering working with this population this can be insightful.

Hussey, D. L., & Guo, S. G. (2005). Forecasting length of stay in child residential treatment. *Child Psychiatry and Human Development, 36,* 95–111.

Unlike public schools, hospitalized children are often in placements for extended periods of time. This article can serve to illuminate the important considerations of length of stay.

REFERENCES

American Psychiatric Association. (2000). *Diagnostic and statistical manual of mental disorders* (4th ed). Washington, DC: Author.
Brener, N., Lowry, R., & Barrios. (2005). Violence related behaviors among high school students—United States, 1991–2003. *Journal of School Health, 75,* 81–85.
Brown, D., Pryzwansky, W. B., & Schulte, A. C. (2001). *Psychological consultation: Introduction to theory and practice* (5th ed.). Boston, MA: Allyn & Bacon.
Carnegie Council on Adolescent Development. (1996). *Great transitions: Preparing adolescents for a new century.* New York: Author.
Crespi, T. D. (1996). Violent children and adolescents: Facing the treatment crisis in child and family interaction. *Family Therapy, 23,* 43–50.
Crespi, T. D. (1997). Bridging the home-school connection: Family therapy and the school psychologist. *Family Therapy, 24,* 209–215.
Crespi, T. D. (2002). Training school psychologists in prison schools: Implications for training special service providers with delinquent adolescents. *Special Services in the Schools, 18,* 151–163.
Crespi, T. D. (2003). Clinical supervision in the schools: Challenges, opportunities, and lost horizons. *The Clinical Supervisor, 22,* 59–71.
Crespi, T. D., & Fischetti, B. A. (1997, September). Counseling and psychotherapy in the schools: Rationale and considerations for professional practice. *NASP Communique,* pp. 18, 20.
Crespi, T. D., & Howe, E. A. (2002). Families in crisis: Considerations for special service providers in the schools. *Special Services in the Schools, 18,* 43–54.

Crespi, T. D., Hughes, T. L. (2003). School-based mental health services for adolescents: School psychology in contemporary society. *Journal of Applied School Psychology, 20*, 67–78.

Dalton, R., Muller, B., & Forman, M. A. (1989). The psychiatric hospitalization of children: An overview. *Child Psychiatry and Human Development, 19*, 231–244.

D'Eramo, K. S., Prinstein, M. J., Freeman, J., Grapentine, W. L., & Spirito, A. (2004). Psychiatric diagnoses and comorbidity in relation to suicidal behavior and psychiatrically hospitalized adolescents. *Child Psychiatry and Human Development, 35*, 21–35.

Dougherty, A. M. (2000). *Psychological consultation and collaboration* (3rd ed.). Belmont, CA: Wadsworth.

Duchnowski, A. J., Kutash, J., & Friedman, R. M. (2002). Community-based interventions in a system of care and outcomes framework. In B. J. Burns & K. Hoagwood (Eds.), *Community treatment for youth: Evidenced-based interventions for severe emotional and behavioral disorders* (pp. 16–37). New York: Oxford.

Dworetzky, J. P. (1996). *Introduction to child development* (6th ed.). St. Paul, MN: West Publishing.

Fergusson, D. M., Horwood, L. L., & Lynskey, M. (1994). The childhoods of multiple-problem adolescents: A 15-year longitudinal study. *Journal of Child Psychology and Psychiatry, 35*, 1123–1140.

Hammett, T. M., Gaiter, J. L., & Crawford, C. (1998). Reaching seriously at-risk populations: Health interventions in criminal justice settings. *Health Education & Behavior, 25*, 99–120.

Heide, K. M. (1996). Why kids keep killing: The correlates, causes, and challenges of juvenile homicide. *Stanford Law and Policy Review, 7*, 43–49.

Huang, L., Stroul, B., Friedman, R., Mrazek, P., Friesen, B., Pires, S., & Mayberg, S. (2005). Transforming mental health care for children and their families. *American Psychologist, 60*, 615–627.

Hussey, D. L., & Guo, S. G. (2005). Forecasting length of stay in child residential treatment. *Child Psychiatry and Human Development, 36*, 95–111.

Johnstone, J. C., & Rivera, R. J. (1965). *Volunteers for learning.* Chicago, IL: Aldine.

Kemph, J. P., Braley, R. O., & Ciotola, P. V. (1997). Description of an outpatient psychiatric population in a youthful offender's prison. *American Academy of Psychiatry and the Law, 25*, 149–160.

Mash, E. J., & Wolfe, D. A. (1999). *Abnormal child psychology.* Boston, MA: Wadsworth.

Merrell, K. W. (1999). *Behavioral, social, and emotional assessment of children.* Mahwah, NJ: Lawrence Erlbaum.

Moore, D. W. (1994, March). One in seven Americans are victims of child abuse. *The Gallup Poll Monthly*, pp. 18–22.

Murray, N. (1997, June). School-based health care gaining in popularity. *APA Monitor, 28*, 7.

Nietzel, M. T., Bernstein, D. A, & Milich, R. (1998). *Introduction to clinical psychology* (5th ed.). Upper Saddle River, NJ: Prentice Hall.

Pope, H. G., & Hudson, J. I. (1992). Is childhood sexual abuse a risk factor for bulimia nervosa? *American Journal of Psychiatry, 4*, 455–463.

Riddle, J., & Bergin, J. J. (1997). Effects of group counseling on the self-concept of children of alcoholics. *Elementary School Guidance & Counseling, 31*, 192–204.

Robertson, L. M., Bates, M. P., Wood, M., Rosenblatt, J. A., Furlong, M. J., & Casas, J. M. (1998). Educational placements of students with emotional and behavioral disorders served by probation, mental health, public health, and social services. *Psychology in the Schools, 35*, 333–345.

Thompson, C. L., & Rudolph, L. B. (2000). *Counseling children* (5th ed.). Belmont, CA: Wadsworth.

16 A framework for working with emotional and behavioral disorders

Considerations for trainers

Anita Sohn McCormick and Constance J. Fournier

OVERVIEW

Children with emotional and behavioral disorders (ED/BD) experience difficulties that interfere with their learning and social development and affect their ability to develop positive relationships with adults and peers. They constitute a largely diverse group of children whose difficulties vary in intensity, duration, and frequency, and yet they all constitute an educational, interpersonal, and disciplinary challenge for teachers and parents (NASP, 2005). Consequently, there are a number of conditions that have to be met in order to diagnose children with ED/BD. The official definition of severe emotional disturbance has been laid out by the Individuals with Disabilities Education Improvement Act 2004 (IDEIA 2004), which established a set of defining criteria or conditions that have to be met in order to categorize a child with an ED/BD.

In addition, three criteria regarding the impact of the child's behavior in an educational setting were established by the National Mental Health and Special Education Coalition (Forness & Knitzer, 1992). These criteria determine that the behavior of children who exhibit an emotional or behavioral disorder has to differ significantly from those behaviors generally accepted for age, ethnic, and cultural norms. Second, this behavior has to affect their performance in such areas as social relationships, personal adjustment, and classroom behavior. And finally, it establishes that the condition cannot be transient and will continue even after an individual intervention has been put in place. Furthermore, it states that these behaviors can coexist with other conditions.

When considering the incidence of different special education eligibility categories, children with ED/BD are under-identified within the educational system (NASP, 2005; Walker & Gresham, 2003). Using the IDEIA 2004 criteria for eligibility, the U.S. Department of Education's National Center for Education Statistics (2006) reported that approximately 489,000 students received services in public schools. This represents about 1% of the school-age population, a number that has remained fairly stable over the last 8 years.

Students with ED/BD may exhibit a number of different behaviors or characteristics such as aggression, withdrawal, inappropriate interactions with peers or adults, anxiety, and more serious disturbances, such as distorted thinking or abnormal mood swings, all of which affect the child's ability to learn and interact appropriately within the educational environment. Since children with ED/BD can exhibit a wide spectrum of behavioral difficulties, it becomes important for the school psychologist not only to be proficient at assessing this specific area of concern but also to become familiar with appropriate evidence-based interventions designed to address each area.

In order for school psychologists to address the needs of children with ED/BD, their difficulties have to be considered from two different yet related domains: the clinical dimension and the educational aspect. School psychologists are in a privileged position to identify and respond to these children's emotional and educational needs, because their clinical training provides them with the skills to address the assessment and diagnosis dimension, while at the same time being intimately familiar with the school system and the educational process. There is also a need for students to be familiar with evidence-based practices for both prevention and intervention, as this is another component that school psychologists can offer across settings.

PRACTICE DOMAINS AND ESSENTIAL TRAINING REQUIREMENTS

School psychologists have several areas of knowledge that are essential in working well with children with emotional and behavioral disorders; these include nosology, assessment, intervention, and ethics and pertinent laws. Because school psychologists may work with children in school settings as well as other settings, their training must have both a school focus as well as a traditional clinical focus. In this chapter, *clinical setting* will refer to any nonschool setting. These settings can include but are not limited to private practice, community mental health services, juvenile detention services, hospitals, and other related areas. Although the skills and knowledge needed for schools and clinical settings often overlap, there are some areas of difference that are important for the school psychologist trainee to understand and differentiate, especially for those trainees who may practice in nonschool settings.

How we describe children with mental health challenges often depends on the setting. The title of this chapter refers to emotional and behavioral disorders, which is more generic educational terminology. By law, in order to receive educational services in the schools, children with emotional or behavioral disorders must meet the following criteria:

A condition exhibiting one or more of the following characteristics over a long period of time and to a marked degree that adversely affects a child's educational performance—

1. An inability to learn that cannot be explained by intellectual, sensory, or health factors.
2. An inability to build or maintain satisfactory interpersonal relationships with peers and teachers.
3. Inappropriate types of behavior or feelings under normal circumstances.
4. A general pervasive mood of unhappiness or depression.
5. A tendency to develop physical symptoms or fears associated with personal or school problems. [Code of Federal Regulations, Title 34, §300.7(c)(4)(i)]

As defined by the IDEIA 2004 emotional disturbance includes schizophrenia but does not apply to children who are socially maladjusted, unless it is determined that they have an emotional disturbance as well [Code of Federal Regulation, Title 34, §300.7(c)(4)(ii)]. Furthermore, autism is a separate eligibility with specific criteria as well.

In contrast to the school setting, the clinical setting will typically utilize the *Diagnostic and Statistical Manual of Mental Disorders* (4th ed., text revision; *DSM-IV-TR*; American Psychiatric Association, 2000) designations for diagnosis. In the clinical setting, the child may be viewed as having an emotional or behavioral disorder; however, the specific type of disorder would be determined by the clinician using the *DSM-IV-TR* criteria. The school psychologist must be skilled at conducting both structured and unstructured clinical interviews. They must also be able to determine possible diagnoses in both the educational and *DSM-IV-TR* nosologies. The use of different methods of diagnosing an emotional or behavior disorder often can lead to confusion among professionals, as the criteria may differ depending on the setting. In particular, the *DSM-IV-TR* criteria are based on a medical model that looks at specific symptomatology, length of time, and intensity of symptoms to make a diagnosis, whereas educational eligibility criteria for ED/BD relates the symptoms specifically to the students' functioning within an educational setting and their ability to learn.

ASSESSMENT

The assessment skills needed in both the clinical and school setting are similar. The school psychologist must be familiar with academic, cognitive, socioemotional, and other measures that are appropriate for children no matter the setting. Protection in evaluation procedures (PEP) must be followed in school settings (American Educational Research Association, American Psychological Association, National Council on Measurement in Education [AERA], 1999). PEP includes concepts such as the use of racially and culturally nondiscriminatory assessment tools, assessment in the student's native language or primary mode of communication, and the selection of assessment tools that are valid for the purposes used. PEP and IDEIA 2004 also include the provision that the student must be assessed in all areas related to the potential disability, including health, vision and hearing social and emotional status, general intelligence, academic performance, communication skills, and motor skills. In a school district, a multidisciplinary decision team that includes at least one member with special knowledge of the potential disability is required by law.

In the school setting, there is also a set of rule-outs that must be considered. These are conditions such as intellectual, sensory (e.g., vision and hearing), and health factors that may influence the child's behavior. These factors must be assessed in order to obtain a clearer picture of the child's behavior and emotional functioning, and to rule out that the child's behavior is a result of these conditions. Furthermore, the child's previous schooling must be reviewed to determine whether lack of educational opportunity or lack of English language proficiency could be an alternative explanation for the behavior observed. When working in a school setting, it is essential for the ED/BD eligibility diagnosis that the child's condition directly interfere with his/her educational performance. In addition, IDEIA 2004 requires that the identification of this disorder be based on multiple sources of data, such as observations, teacher interviews, and rating questionnaires obtained in at least two different settings.

In the clinical setting, there are not the same legal requirements as in the educational setting; however, many of the same conditions have to be met based on the Standards of Educational and Psychological Testing developed by the American Education and Research Association and best practices (AERA, 1999; McConaughy, 2007). PEP criteria are legally required only in school settings, yet they can be used in clinical settings. Use of multiple sources of information and documentation of the degree of impairment is also best practices in other settings. Although there are similarities in the assessment process, there are some differences. For example, the school psychologist in the clinical setting may not require the same level of assessment for an honor student who is experiencing test anxiety in order to design a treatment intervention. Other conditions required for assessment in school settings may not be possible in a clinical setting, such as having access to a multidisciplinary team for decision making. Alternatively, school psychologists in a clinical setting may have access to medical resources that are not available in the schools, and if a multidisciplinary team is available, its composition may differ, resulting in potentially different conclusions.

Regardless of the setting, most of the legal conditions reflect ethical and best practices that should be part of the training of any psychologist.

PREVENTION/INTERVENTION

The implementation of appropriate prevention and intervention programs is another key area where there is overlap between the skills needed in different placement settings. In both settings, the intervention must be based on best practices and should be empirically supported for the specific condition of the child. For the most part, the school psychologist in the clinical practice will make recommendations that are related specifically to the diagnosed problem or disorder. Although these recommendations could extend to family members and even teachers, the clinical setting school psychologist can create and implement the intervention independently. In this setting, it is more likely that the interventions implemented respond directly to a current diagnosis rather than being designed as a preventative measure.

In contrast, given that the eligibility criteria in a school setting is less dictated by the medical model and therefore, more related to the child's functioning in the school setting, students who are at risk for ED/BD eligibility often are able to receive the same interventions as a prevention effort. However, for those students determined to be eligible for special education due to ED/BD, the school setting has specific conditions for interventions that must be fulfilled. The overall intervention is determined and approved by the multidisciplinary committee, and all aspects of the intervention must be accounted for in the student's individualized education plan (IEP) as determined in IDEIA 2004. The IEP has to clearly state such issues as the personnel providing the intervention service (such as the school psychologist), the amount of time the service will be provided, and the evaluation of progress. In practice, it is not likely that the multidisciplinary IEP committee will interfere with the school psychologist's recommendations for specific psychological interventions; however, interventions must be tied to the educational need and the specific problematic behaviors. Training in working on teams and team leadership would be helpful for all school psychologists regardless of the setting. It should be noted that students with ED/BD can receive counseling that is typically provided to any student in the school, usually by a school counselor or a school psychologist, without an IEP. Most typically, students diagnosed with ED/BD all have an IEP and will receive services as indicated in that document.

In a school setting, the school psychologist has the opportunity to promote and design interventions that foster social and emotional learning in a school-wide effort. These programs or school-wide interventions serve as prevention initiatives to address the needs of those students who are at risk for developing social and emotional difficulties that will affect their learning and progress in school. In addition, school psychologists are key in developing a primary prevention model for mental health services. In fostering prevention programs, as well as early identification of behavioral and educational difficulties, the school psychologist can offer their services effectively at different intensity levels.

Documentation of the intervention process will depend on the setting, local and state requirements, and, particularly for clinical settings, the Health Insurance Portability and Accountability Act (HIPAA). This act has specific requirements to protect client information that must be followed by personnel in hospital and clinical settings. In particular, there are provisions in HIPAA concerning note-keeping for the mental health professional. The Family Education and Rights Privacy Act (FERPA), which determines the accessibility of records in a school setting, also has provisions for protection of information. Because of FERPA, the child's academic and clinical information must be protected and can be viewed on an educational need-to-know basis only. Psychological reports will require greater security as the educational need to know is more limited. Specific recommendations, which would have a larger need-to-know audience, would be more accessible. The school psychologist must be trained in what constitutes both ethical and legal documentation for both school and clinical placements (Jacob & Hartshorne, 2007). This set of knowledge and skills for documentation is particularly crucial, as some schools have Medicaid reimbursement and therefore are subject to HIPAA, as well as school-related requirements (Rae & Fournier, 2004).

Ethical practices as applied to either school or clinical placement will be the same, as most school psychologists will practice according to the American Psychological Association (APA) or National Association of School Psychologists (NASP) ethical and professional guidelines (APA, 2002; NASP, 2000a, 2000c). In the case of school psychologists, both sets of guidelines would apply (Jacob & Hartshorne, 2007). In terms of laws, the school psychologist in the clinical setting will most likely need to follow HIPAA guidelines. For school psychologists in school settings, IDEIA 2004, No Child Left Behind (NCLB), and FERPA will all be followed (Rae & Fournier, 2004).

CONSIDERATIONS FOR PRACTICA DEVELOPMENT

Training needs to include mastery of theory and research, as well as specific skill sets (e.g., interviewing, manualized treatments, standardized testing, and consultation skills). Once the skills in assessment, intervention, and consultation have been attained in the classroom or laboratory setting, they must be transferred with appropriate scaffolding to the field. In order for school psychology students to develop the clinical skills necessary to assess, diagnose, and work with students with ED/BDs, it is essential for them to obtain practical experience under the supervision of a school psychologist with experience. Therefore, the availability of supervised practica is critical. In order for the practica to offer the richest experience, there are several issues that need consideration.

The number and variety of activities that the student is involved in while completing the practicum will depend on the expectations of both the training program and the field site. These expectations have to be clearly defined and agreed upon. Then, both entities can collaboratively develop the practicum. These interactions should culminate in a written agreement that stipulates the expected outcomes for the students, the commitment of staff and resources, and experience opportunities offered by the field site. The experiences and/or responsibilities directly related to serving students with ED/BD can include but are not limited to classroom observations; psychological assessment and diagnosis; design and implementation of specific interventions; behavior management and monitoring; and individual, group, and family counseling.

Expectations for students' performance and professional behaviors have to be clearly defined and communicated. Issues such as punctuality, attire, personal appearance (e.g., no visible tattoos or piercing other than ears), and expectations for overall performance will likely be dictated by the sited. University personnel have the responsibility of ensuring practicum students' compliance.

Given that students and trainees will participate in their field practica while working with children in either a school or clinical setting, it is expected that they obtain student malpractice insurance and undergo a background check. These requirements are especially important given the diversity and the sensitive nature of the needs of students with an ED/BD.

Another important dimension of the field practice for trainees working with children with ED/BD is the need for supervision by both the field-based mentor and the training supervisor. Although it is fair to assume that trainees who are eligible to participate in a field practicum experience have already had formal training in the skills that are required to assess and serve students with ED/BD, they still require guidance and supervision. Therefore, an appropriate field practicum should include a licensed school psychologist or other appropriate personnel who can provide on-site support and feedback. This supervision should include face-to-face meetings during which the trainee presents specific cases, articulates case formulations, and determines progress. The trainee is encouraged to ask questions and request guidance. Site supervisors, by being familiar with the practicum site, help trainees orient themselves in the practicum setting. Therefore, training the mentors and supervisors at the site is crucial to good training of practicum students. Site personnel must be educated about practica students' abilities and degree of independence, as well as university requirements that may be associated with the practica. This knowledge will assist site supervisors in offering an appropriate level of guidance, as well as appropriate experiences.

The degree and type of university supervision must also be addressed. It is recommended that the trainee also meet with a training or university supervisor to monitor progress during the practicum, attainment of additional skills, and evaluation of the experience. The training supervisor's responsibility is to ensure that by participating in the practicum, students continue to meet their training goals in terms of practicing the skills necessary to serve students with ED/BD. In order to design and deliver a practicum experience that enhances students' skills, both the training site and the university program have to commit to strong collaboration and regular communication.

Student progress will be measured against the explicit expectations developed at the beginning of the practica, based on NASP and APA training guidelines (NASP, 2000b). The success of any practicum student working with ED/BD students hinges on a thorough and clear evaluation of performance and experiences. The congruence between these experiences and the training expectations should reflect the articulation agreement. Evaluations should be conducted by supervisors and other personnel, such as teachers, principals, or other professionals who have had close or direct contact with the trainee and can give evidence of their clinical and professional behavior. To remain a viable experience for trainees, the practicum site has to be reviewed every year by university personnel. Mentor/supervisors, students, and others at the university can provide valuable information to evaluate the experience to determine whether the initial goals for the practicum were met, whether the breadth and depth of experiences offered were representative of the needs of ED/BD students, whether the setting was conducive to working with ED/BD students, and whether the supervision and support were adequate to meet both the children's and the practica students' needs. Only through continued and open communication and feedback can practica be designed that offer a trainee the opportunity to work with a wide range of ED/BD students and their needs.

EXEMPLAR OF EVIDENCE-BASED PRACTICE AND PROFESSIONAL TRAINING FOR ED/BD

Curriculum scope and sequence and specific courses required

In this section, the scope and sequence of courses specific to assessment and interventions are discussed. This is based on the assumption that the school psychology student has foundational knowledge of child development, as well as basic understanding of statistical concepts such as norms, reliability, and validity. In addition, school psychology students need to develop a solid understanding of child and adolescent psychopathology and acquire knowledge about the social and emotional development of children. Overarching all this specific knowledge, students have to be cognizant of the impact that social, cultural, and linguistic factors have on the development of risk and resiliency in children. Students should develop enough cultural competence to be able to work with children from backgrounds different from their own.

Laws and ethics are integral to the practice of the school psychology. The school psychologist can practice in a variety of settings and with a variety of age groups, including students at age 18 who are legally adults yet are not independent. A course in law is needed because there are federal, state, and even local district laws that must be followed. The same is true for ethics. Both NASP and APA guidelines have to be followed. Depending on how certification or licensure works at the state level, there may also be state ethical standards to follow. Once the basics of laws and ethics are addressed, these must be covered again with application to assessment and intervention in all specific courses. Although there is overlap with other disorders such as learning disabilities, it should be noted that the discussion below is geared toward the assessment and intervention of the student with possible ED/BD.

Assessment

Assessment is essential to both the identification of and intervention with students who potentially have an ED/BD. A reasonable sequence of training for assessment would be the following: academic, cognitive, emotional and behavioral, and integrated assessment. In academic assessment, the curriculum not only addresses typical formal and informal measures utilized to assess the achievement and academic progress of children, but pertinent laws such as IDEIA 2004, NCLB, and FERPA should also be addressed. The graduate student would begin the process of report writing and making recommendations based on academic assessment results. This course includes knowledge about working within and understanding the school organization so that the recommendations are reasonable, legal, and doable in the setting.

Cognitive assessment should build on the skills developed with academic assessment, focusing specifically on the accurate and standardized administration and interpretation of cognitive measures. In this course, it is particularly important to incorporate legal and ethical requirements with special emphasis on instrument reliability, validity, and appropriateness for diverse populations. Furthermore, observations during the assessment process and the integration of background information lead to more comprehensive report writing, along with recommendations for program intervention.

The assessment of emotional and behavioral difficulties would follow as the next step in the sequence, and it frequently requires two separate courses.

In this sequence of courses students will learn the process of completing a functional behavior assessment within the school setting, which is a critical element in the determination of an ED/BD eligibility process. Furthermore, during the behavior assessment component of this sequence, the student should learn to complete structured observations; determine antecedents and consequences to behaviors; examine the frequency, duration, and intensity of difficulties; and interpret time series data.

The emotional assessment component should have a larger emphasis on the clinical interview, as well as the formal and projective assessment tools used in the determination of an ED/BD. By now the school psychology student will have a strong foundation in the administration of standardized techniques, as well as recording testing and field observations. During this course, the student also should understand the value of integrating information obtained from a variety of sources and the importance of tailoring the evaluation tools and processes to the particular student's needs. Finally, this course allows the trainee to integrate the different assessments (academic, cognitive, and sociobehavioral), together with the clinical interview in order to develop a comprehensive report with general, as well as specific educational and behavioral recommendations.

The integrated assessment course, which can be associated with a practicum, allows the graduate student to put all the pieces together with referred cases. The trainee should have sufficient training to be able to select, administer, and interpret assessment tools germane to the case. The assessment tools used should be culturally and racially nondiscriminatory. Assessment results will be combined with observations and clinical interviews to provide a greater understanding of the child and the diagnosis. Report writing should reflect understanding of the whole child and the circumstances that may be contributing to the referral difficulties. The recommendations will reflect individual interventions, academic interventions, and program interventions needed to help the child, family, and school personnel.

Intervention

Intervention is another strand in the curriculum. The courses that address this area are most likely taken in tandem with the assessment courses. The foundation of any intervention should be knowledge of typical child development. Without this knowledge, the trainee would not be able to understand when a set of behaviors is typical in a particular stage of development, rather than an ED/BD diagnosis. There is also the assumption of understanding of statistical concepts such as reliability, and validity as applied to the research on interventions. Additionally, the trainee must also become a critical consumer of the literature and be able to judge the strength of evidence on effectiveness and efficiency of any potential intervention. Understanding of how cultural and ethnic diversity influences interventions must be addressed in every course.

The child psychopathology course work provides a framework for an understanding of diagnostic issues, as well as the springboard for determining the best possible evidence-based interventions. Behavioral assessment and interventions course work is vital, as many evidence-based interventions have a behavioral base and can translate well into the school environment. This type of course also provides the student with an understanding of basic behavior patterns, types of behavior recording techniques, and different strategies to affect behavior that can be translated into specific behavioral interventions in the school setting. Furthermore, the course should emphasize the importance of recording the level of success of all behavioral interventions previously utilized with a student who is being evaluated for an emotional or behavioral disorder. This documentation is essential in the process of determining eligibility for students with an ED/BD.

Behavioral assessment would be followed by a course that addresses the implementation of individual interventions geared toward specific diagnoses in both clinical and school settings. This includes learning about available manualized treatments, delivery of manualized treatments, and other interventions that are common to specific disorders (e.g., depression or encopresis). Other specific courses about intervention, such as family therapy and group therapy, would also be included. In all intervention courses, the importance of connecting with the child and family in a therapeutic manner has to be emphasized and practiced (Thompson Prout, 2007). In the case of school psychologists, the skills needed to establish rapport will also extend to the relationship with teachers and school administrators. Evaluation of the interventions utilized should also be addressed. This can include overall effectiveness, impact on the child, and impact in the environment (e.g., home and school). Evaluation can be supplemented with courses such as single-case design.

Course work in consultation is another essential piece in the delivery of interventions, particularly since intervention by school psychologists is not limited to the individual child or family. Often the classroom and the overall school environment are an integral part of the overall treatment plan, and thus the school psychologist must know how to work within a system. The trainee must become adept at providing both direct and indirect interventions and knowing when each type is needed to best serve the child. The trainee must also be able to address issues of diversity within the consultation process.

Practicum

One of the best methods to help students develop the interpretative and integrative skills needed for appropriate diagnosis and intervention of ED/BD is through a planned sequence of events that moves from analog to in vivo practice. Case studies, which contain information about a child or adolescent, allow the student to integrate formal and informal assessment information. Case studies also encourage the use of knowledge acquired through intervention courses to develop appropriate intervention plans. This process is completed with close guidance by the instructor, and it will eventually enable the student to develop the skills necessary to engage in the assessment process independently.

In addition to the case studies and practice assessments completed during the training courses, it is important for the students to take part in a course or training opportunity that allows them to complete an assessment in an educational environment with supervision. Assessment should be completed in a school or clinical practicum, and the results should be used for educational decisions. During the process of assessment, interpretation, and report writing, every student should be closely supervised by a licensed psychologist or a school psychologist. This type of practicum allows the students the opportunity to experience the assessment process, and it also allows them to write clinical and educationally sound recommendations that have real-life implications. After successfully completing this closely monitored experience, students should be sufficiently competent to engage in a school practicum where they not only complete the psychological assessment and write recommendations but are required to put some of the recommendations in place and monitor their effectiveness. The same process for developing assessment skills can be used in clinical settings.

Throughout the process of practicum training in assessment, the students have to be continuously evaluated to determine the level of their skill attainment and the areas of training need. Some of the areas in which the students should be evaluated include the following: timeliness and compliance with legal timelines, appropriate use of assessment tools, appropriate use of supervision and response to feedback, thoroughness and thoughtfulness in the assessment process, conclusions and recommendations that are useful, appropriate case formulation and diagnosis, ethical behaviors, legal compliance, and self-evaluation of performance. Evaluations are critical and should be conducted with the trainee throughout each experience. The evaluation will provide the supervisor with enough information to assign a grade and information critical to the positive developmental trajectory of the trainee.

The same process of case studies and analog practice moving to in vivo practice should be used for developing intervention skills. The case study provides the opportunity for determining appropriate interventions that can be checked and discussed with the university supervisor. The next step is assignment of screened cases in the practicum sites. Although it is not always possible to predict what may happen once a case unfolds, it is helpful to the emerging practitioner to start with more clear-cut diagnoses and manualized interventions before confronting more complex cases. At the end of this sequence of application of intervention to actual cases, the trainee should be able to do the following: integrate the information obtained through formal assessment procedures with information from other sources, select interventions with the best research-based evidence of success, and implement interventions effectively. Supervision is critical and should follow what is described in the assessment supervision, including timeliness or compliance with legal timelines, appropriate use of supervision and response to feedback, thoroughness and thoughtfulness in the intervention process, appropriate case formulation, and consideration of ethical behaviors and legal compliance. Fostering self-evaluation is also a critical part of the supervision process. The goal is for trainees to move into the next step of training well-armed with knowledge and skills. In addition, trainees need to have an accurate appraisal of their own abilities, as well as recognition about what skills they need to develop.

Internship

As a final, culminating experience in working with children with emotional and behavioral difficulties, the trainee participates in a full-year internship. During this internship, the trainee will have the opportunity to integrate all the assessment, intervention, and consultation skills obtained during the training program and provide services to school children while still being supervised by a licensed school psychologist. The importance of this internship experience is that trainees are immersed in a school setting and are directly involved in the complete process of identifying and diagnosing students with an ED/BD, as well as designing and monitoring interventions to help both teachers and the students. Their daily involvement in a school also allows them to engage in school-wide prevention and intervention activities in order to address potential areas of need. Finally, the internship experience allows the trainee to gain confidence in his or her skills and abilities to serve students with an ED/BD while still relying on the support of supervision.

CONCLUSION

The curriculum scope and sequence in an exemplary program is not static. A well-designed program to train school psychologists to assess, diagnose, and intervene with children with an ED/BD has to engage in frequent program evaluation. This evaluation is geared toward improving the training experience of the student and should include review of the course work, supervision, and practicum experiences provided by the program.

The program faculty should periodically review the sequence and content of the courses included in the training to ensure inclusion of up-to-date legal information and the most current research related to the field. Legal information, such as new federal laws and court decisions pertaining to children with emotional or behavioral disorders, must be included as soon as it is available. Incorporating the latest assessment tools and techniques and the most current knowledge and research about evidence-based treatments for each of the disorders included in the emotional and behavioral disability category is crucial. Evaluation of practicum sites and supervisors from both the trainee and university perspectives is required and should be a two-way process. Furthermore, the observations of supervisors in practicum sites regarding trainees' performance and knowledge base can provide valuable information that can assist in program review. These observations provide university faculty critical insight into how students are able to apply learning in the practicum setting and areas for further training within the university program. Since it is critical for the program to recognize how other courses support and augment the student's understanding of issues related to the assessment, diagnosis, and treatment of students with ED/BD, this evaluation from the outside is essential to any program's ongoing success. The program faculty must strive to ensure that graduate students receive the best and most current knowledge and skills to address the needs of all students, especially those with emotional and behavioral issues.

RESOURCES

American Psychological Association. (n.d.). *Home page*. Retrieved May 15, 2009, from http://www.apa.org
This Web site provides school psychologists and other mental health professionals with the most up-to-date information about training issues, standards of practice, ethics, and professional development, as well as specific issues on the diagnosis and treatment of mental health disorders in both children and adults.

Council for Exceptional Children. (n.d.). *Home page*. Retrieved May 15, 2009, from http://www.cec.sped.org
This Web site offers school psychologists, teachers, and other professionals who work with children with disabilities information and resources to help students succeed in academic settings. This site also offers updates on legal and governmental policies affecting the education of and delivery of services to children with exceptionalities.

National Association of School Psychologists. (n.d.). *Home page*. Retrieved May 15, 2009, from http://www.nasponline.org
This Web site is specifically focused on the needs of school psychologists and provides information on professional issues, legal updates, and resources for professionals delivering mental health services in school settings.

National Dissemination Center for Children with Disabilities. (n.d.). *Home page*. Retrieved May 15, 2009, from http://www.nichcy.org

This Web site provides information to families, educators and other professionals who interact and work with children with disabilities from birth to age 22. It provides information on specific disabilities, offers interpretations of legal and governmental policies, and supplies links to the most recent research-based information on effective interventions for children with exceptionalities.

Office of Civil Rights. (n.d.). *Health information privacy.* Retrieved May 15, 2009, from http://www.hhs.gov/ocr/hipaa
This link provides information specific to the National Standards to Protect the Privacy of Personal Health Information. This law provides information about how to handle, keep, and disseminate medical and clinical information, as well as information about confidentiality.

U.S. Department of Education. (n.d.). *Home page.* Retrieved May 15, 2009, from http://www.ed.gov
This Web site provides a wealth of resources on legal and governmental policies related to education.

U.S. Department of Education. (n.d.). *Individuals with Disabilities Education Act.* Retrieved from http://idea.ed.gov
This link leads directly to the Individuals with Disabilities Education Act, which is the law ensuring services to children with disabilities throughout the nation.

REFERENCES

American Educational Research Association, American Psychological Association, National Council on Measurement in Education. (1999). *Standards for educational and psychological testing.* Washington, DC: American Psychological Association.
American Psychiatric Association. (2000). *Diagnostic and Statistical Manual of Mental Disorders* (4th ed.). Washington, DC: Author.
American Psychological Association. (2002). *Ethical principles of psychologists and code of conduct.* Retrieved October 1, 2008, from http://www.apa.org/ethics/code2002.pdf
Code of Federal Regulations, Title 34, § 300.7 (2004).
Forness, S. R., & Knitzer, J. (1992). A new proposed definition and terminology to replace 'serious emotional disturbance' in individuals with disabilities education act. *School Psychology Review, 21,* 12–21.
Jacob, S., & Hartshorne, T. S. (2007). *Ethics and law for school psychologists* (5th ed.). Hoboken, NJ: Wiley & Sons.
McConaughy, S. (2007). Best practices in multimethod assessment of emotional and behavioral disorders. In A. Thomas & J. Grimes (Eds.), *Best Practices in School Psychology V* (Vol. 2, pp. 697–715). Bethesda, MD: NASP.

National Association of School Psychologists. (2000a). *Guidelines for the provision of school psychological services.* Washington, DC: Author.

National Association of School Psychologists. (2000b). *Standards for training and field placement programs in school psychology.* Bethesda, MD: Author.

National Association of School Psychologists. (2000c). *Professional conduct manual: Principles for professional ethics guidelines for the provision of school psychological services.* Bethesda, MD: Author.

National Association of School Psychologists. (2005). *Position statement on students with emotional and behavioral disorders.* Retrieved September 18, 2008, from http://www.nasponline.org/about_nasp/pospaper_sebd.aspx

Rae, W. A., & Fournier, C. J. (2004). Ethical and legal issues for pediatric psychology and school psychology. In R. Brown (Ed.), *Handbook of pediatric psychology in school settings.* (pp. 721–728). New York: Erlbaum.

Thompson Prout, H. (2007). Counseling and psychotherapy with children and adolescents: Historical developmental, integrative, and effectiveness perspectives. In H. Thompson Prout & F. T. Brown (Eds.), *Counseling and psychotherapy with children and adolescents* (pp. 1–31). Hoboken, NJ: Wiley.

U.S. Department of Education, National Center for Education Statistics. (2006). *Digest of Education Statistics, 2005* (NCES 2006-030, chapter 2). Retrieved September 18, 2008, from http://www.nces.ed.gov/fastfacts/display.asp?id=64

Walker, H. M., & Gresham, F. (2003). School related behavior disorders. In W. M. Reynolds & G. E. Miller (Eds.), *Handbook of psychology: Educational psychology* (Vol. 7, pp. 511–530). New York: John Wiley & Sons.

17 Training for work with special populations
Children with chronic illness

LeAdelle Phelps

It has been estimated that at least one in five youth have developmental, physical, or mental disabilities (U.S. Department of Health and Human Services, 2005a). This results in approximately 1 million children in this country who have a chronic illness that affects their daily functioning. The identification and treatment of children and adolescents with such disorders is a major health incentive in the United States. For example, the *Surgeon General's Call to Action to Improve the Health and Wellness of Persons with Disabilities* was released on July 26, 2005 (U.S. Department of Health and Human Services, 2005b). One of the goals of this initiative was to increase the knowledge of health care professionals for the improvement of services for this population.

In direct alignment with this goal, both Division 16 (School Psychology) of the American Psychological Association (APA) and the National Association of School Psychologists (NASP) advocate that school psychologists play a primary role in consulting and collaborating with other professionals for the health and wellness of children (APA, n.d.; NASP, n.d.). Not only can school psychologists interact with medical personnel to better link home and school health care services, they can also provide school-based personnel with much-needed information about the etiology, diagnostic indicators, and biopsychosocial outcomes of specific disorders. By increasing knowledge and facilitating the coordination of medical treatments, educational services, and social–emotional interventions, school psychologists are responding to the Surgeon General's initiative.

CHRONIC ILLNESSES IN CHILDREN

Chronic conditions are those that have a protracted course of treatment and often result in compromised physical, cognitive, and psychosocial functioning (Phelps, 2006). The prevalence of chronic medical conditions in children has nearly doubled in the last several decades (U.S. Department of Health and Human Services, 2005a). This increased prevalence has been attributed to improved medical care and early diagnosis, resulting in a significant decrease in infant mortality, as well as the amplified incidence of more recent diseases, such as acquired immune deficiency syndrome (AIDS). In addition, children from low-income and ethnic minority backgrounds remain at significant risk for health-related difficulties because prenatal and postnatal care is often inadequate and exposure to neurotoxins is not unusual (Covington, Nordstrom-Klee, Ager, Sokol, & Delancy-Black, 2002; National Institute of Child Health and Human Development, 2000).

School psychologists are familiar with such chronic issues as learning disabilities, attention deficit/hyperactivity disorder (ADHD), and pervasive developmental disorders. Less understood are chronic medical conditions that impact every aspect of the lives of affected children. It is no longer acceptable to view medical conditions as beyond the purview of educational institutions. The Individuals with Disabilities Act specifies that children with health impairments are eligible for services when the medical condition adversely affects her or his educational performance (Individuals with Disabilities Act, 2004). Section 504 of the Rehabilitation Act of 1973 ensures equal access to educational activities and additional supportive services when appropriate for children with a disability that limits major life activities (e.g., walking, hearing, seeing, breathing, learning). Although some chronic health-related issues may not impact a child's educational attainment or day-to-day activities, it is incumbent upon school psychologists to look beyond the rudiments of standardized achievement measures to determine what services may be beneficial (Lee & Janik, 2006). Because the pervasive effects of health-related disorders that are caused by genetics (e.g., cystic fibrosis, Turner syndrome), prenatal exposure (e.g., fetal alcohol syndrome), or environmental issues (e.g., lead poisoning, malnutrition), may be subtle, training school psychologists in the area of chronic illnesses is essential if we, as a profession, are going to effectively serve these children.

PEDIATRIC SCHOOL PSYCHOLOGY

Although knowledge about childhood chronic illnesses is crucial for school psychologists, the field has been slow to embrace pediatric health issues. Health-related publications would appear occasionally in the school psychology literature, but it has only been in the last decade that books and journals have highlighted the area referred to as *pediatric school psychology*. The first publication to do so appeared in *School Psychology Review*. Titled "Pediatric School Psychology: The Emergence of a Subspecialty," Power, DuPaul, Shapiro, and Parrish (1995) proposed doctoral and post-doctoral training models for the preparation of school psychologists with expertise in providing services to children with medical conditions. This was followed by the publication of *Health-Related Disorders in Children and Adolescents: A Guidebook for Understanding and Educating*. Edited by Phelps (1998), the book provided practitioners with a concise review of the etiology, probable outcomes, and psychoeducational implications of 96 chronic childhood illnesses. Additional books facilitated interest in the area. For example, Phelps, Brown, and Power (2002) reviewed treatment options in *Pediatric Psychopharmacology: Combining Medical and Psychosocial Interventions,* Brown (2004) edited an informative text titled *Handbook of Pediatric Psychology in School Settings,* and Phelps (2006) provided collaborative medical and psychoeducational intervention models in the edited text *Chronic Health-related Disorders in Children: Collaborative Medical and Psychoeducational Interventions.*

In the last few years, school psychology journals have followed suit by publishing numerous special issues related to pediatric school psychology. In 2007 alone, Farmer and Xie were guest editors of a special issue on aggression in the *Journal of School Psychology,* Wilczynski guest edited the special issue "Autism Spectrum Disorders in Psychology in the Schools," DuPaul guest edited "School-Based Interventions for Students with ADHD" in *School Psychology Review,* and Dumbrowski and Martin were guest editors of "Prenatal Exposure in Later Psychological and Behavioral Disabilities" in *School Psychology Quarterly.*

TRAINING ISSUES IN HEALTH-RELATED DISORDERS

There is general consensus that school psychology students preparing for practice at the 60-semester-hour level have neither adequate space in the curriculum nor time in the practica/internship sequence to participate in the intensive curriculum plan suggested for practitioners who seek expertise in pediatric school psychology (Power et al., 1995; Shaw, 2003). Nonetheless, at the specialist level, knowledge relevant to childhood health-related disorders is well within the purview of the training model. Professional preparation at the specialist level could include didactic information regarding biological bases of behavior (e.g., review of genetic transmission, the interplay of environment with genetic susceptibility, and brain–behavior relationships), integration of educational and health services via comprehensive school-based service delivery models, collaborative models and practices with medical personnel, and the provision of culturally sensitive support services to children with medical needs. It is readily acknowledged that school psychology training programs have little to no room for additional course work, but the content suggested above could be distributed throughout several courses (e.g., human development, consultation, professional practice). Using such an infusion model permits school psychology students at the specialist level the opportunity to better understand the needs of, and hence advocate more effectively for, children who have health concerns.

Within the context of the general curriculum of school psychology doctoral training programs, students seeking to become pediatric health specialists

314 Trainers of school psychologists handbook, Volume I

are expected to obtain additional instruction and supervised experience in key areas related to this population. Such topical themes include pediatric psychopharmacology (which incorporates the assessment of medication efficacy and side effects), hospital-school transition models and implementation, management of medical issues within the school setting, and the provision of prevention and intervention health-related programming (e.g., eating disorder prevention groups for at-risk adolescent females, AIDS awareness workshops, Asperger summer treatment programs). It is essential that doctoral students specializing in pediatric school psychology complete extensive practicum experiences in both school and medical settings. Appropriate internship experiences should incorporate school practice with health service provision. For example, a full-year internship placement in a school-based health center would provide the depth and breadth of experiences suitable for a student who is seeking a pediatric school psychology specialization (Brown & Bolen, 2008; Shaw, 2003). Another illustration is a hospital or clinic-based internship that requires the student to provide extensive consultation services and collaborative prevention/intervention programming with a school district. Of course, supervision by a psychologist with expertise in both educational and medical systems is essential. As the subspecialty of pediatric school psychology grows, professionals with such proficiency will become more common.

PROFESSIONAL PRACTICE FOR CHILDREN WITH HEALTH CONCERNS

Incorporated within both the specialist level and doctoral level training models outlined previously are two broad orientations toward professional practice: data-based decision making or evidence-based practice, and prevention/wellness promotion. These two service delivery models are reflected in specific NASP domains that must be addressed in order for a program to receive NASP approval (Ysseldyke et al., 1997). These issues are also integral to accreditation by the American Psychological Association within the context of *Domain B: Program Philosophy, Objectives, and Curriculum Plan* (APA, 2007).

Data-based decision making or evidence-based practice

There is a strong movement in several professions (e.g., medicine, psychology, social work) toward identifying practices that result in positive outcomes. NASP refers to such practice as *data-based decision making* (Ysseldyke et al., 1997), whereas APA has adopted the language *evidence-based practice* (APA Presidential Task Force on Evidence-Based Practice, 2006). Interest in such approaches has been piqued by poor or ambiguous intervention outcomes, the lack of application from research findings to actual practices, and external demands for accountability (Traughber & D'Amato, 2005).

NASP has embraced informed decision making, indicating in the *Blueprint for Training and Practice II:*

> Data-based decision-making and accountability should be the organizing theme for school psychology training and practice. This should permeate every aspect of the practice: school psychologists need to be good problem-solvers, able to collect information to understand problems, to make decisions about appropriate interventions, to assess educational outcomes, and to help others become accountable for the decisions they make. (Ysseldyke et al.,1997, p. 7)

The APA has also advocated strongly for a best practices model and has transitioned through a series of terms, starting with *empirically validated treatments*, to *empirically supported treatments*, to *evidence-based interventions*, and finally to the current accepted language, *evidence-based practice*. The shift in language represents the acknowledgment that variables such as the quality of the therapeutic relationship, clinical expertise, cultural context, and client/family values have an impact on outcome data (Norcross, 2002; Wampold & Bhati, 2004). After considerable debate, the APA Presidential Task Force on Evidence-Based Practice (2006) provided the following definition: "Evidence-based practice in psychology (EBPP) is the *integration* of the best available research with clinical expertise in the context of patient characteristics, culture, and preferences" (p. 273).

It is important to note the similarity between the NASP and APA practice guidelines. Both organizations stress the importance of utilizing robust scientific evidence to inform decisions regarding the selection and implementation of services. Also of significance is the acknowledgment that data-based decision making or evidence-based practice extends beyond therapeutic interventions and includes all practice decisions (e.g., assessment, diagnosis or classification, placement, direct/indirect interventions, prevention programming). Nowhere could this be more important than in the provision of services to children with health concerns.

Too often there is little communication, yet alone collaboration, between health-related service providers and school personnel. Likewise, be it pharmacological treatment, home health care, outpatient procedures, or nutritional guidelines, medical practices are assessed infrequently for efficacy using data collected systematically during the school hours. The participants in the 2002 School Psychology Futures Conference envisioned the need for increased collaboration and accountability by selecting as one of the guiding principles: "Evidence-based practices will be necessary to achieve positive outcomes for children, families, and schools" (Harrison et al., 2003, p. 381). To both address the need for better collaboration between schools and medical professionals and disseminate a timely review of evidence-based practices for children presenting with health-related disorders, *School Psychology Quarterly* will be publishing a special issue titled "Psychoeducational Implications of Neurodevelopmental Genetic

Disorders" that provides school psychologists with such information on autism, Down syndrome, Fragile X syndrome, Prader-Willi, sex chromosome anomalies, and Tourette's syndrome (Davis & Phelps, 2008).

Health-related prevention and wellness

There is an emerging service model within psychology that focuses on prevention and wellness within the context of comprehensive programming (i.e., educational, health, and social–emotional interventions; Phelps & Power, 2008). The emphasis on prevention and health promotion is highly appropriate and much needed. School psychology as a profession has been driven for much of its history by a deficit model that focused on the clear presence of a disorder (e.g., discrepancy model for the diagnosis of a learning disability). Likewise, pediatric school psychology has focused primarily on understanding medical conditions and strategies for managing diseases and disorders. Recently, the field of school psychology in general, and pediatric school psychology in particular, is starting to embrace a preventive service model. One of the guiding principles of the 2002 School Psychology Futures Conference stated: "Prevention and early intervention will be necessary to achieve positive outcomes for children, families, and schools" (Harrison et al., 2003, p. 381).

Editors of journals that focus on school psychology have facilitated the health-related prevention, early intervention, and wellness movement by supporting the publication of special issues on the topic. For example, several prevention approaches were described in the *School Psychology Review* four-part series "Emerging Models of Promoting Children's Mental Health: Linking Systems for Prevention and Intervention" that was guest edited by Power (2003). The topic of promoting wellness was highlighted in the *Psychology in the Schools* special issue "Positive Psychology and Wellness in Children," edited by Chafouleas and Bray (2004). "School-Based Health Promotion," edited by Walcott and Chafouleas (2008), further explicated measures that can be taken to integrate mental and physical health services into the schools.

Effective psychosocial prevention programming is dependent upon the identification of specific risk and protective factors. Risk catalysts are associated with higher probability of onset, greater severity, and longer duration of the disorder, whereas protective variables are affiliated with improved resistance and resilience. After successful identification of such factors, highly specific strategies can then be developed, with the prevailing intent to reduce risk factors while enhancing protective factors. Prevention efforts with children are particularly important when environmental factors place them at risk. An excellent example is the prevention of lead exposure. As with most chemical substances, lead contamination is entirely preventable. Providing parents with information about hand-to-mouth transmission, the necessity of thorough housecleaning, the advisability of new paint, and services provided through the county health agency reduces lead poisoning in preschool children (Phelps, 2005). Beyond offering parents guidance, health professionals need also to monitor infants and toddlers residing in substandard housing to prevent lead poisoning (i.e., before there is evidence of fatigue, irritability, or persistent vomiting).

Exemplar of evidence-based practice and prevention training

An excellent example of both evidence-based interventions and prevention practices is the Task Force on Family–School Partnerships (FSP Task Force). The FSP Task Force was formed on the recommendation of the 2002 School Psychology Futures Conference. Based on the theme of enhanced family–school partnerships and parental involvement in schools, the conference report stated: "Building partnerships with parents and families is one way to increase the likelihood of improvement in achievement, attendance, graduation, and other critical outcomes (Harrison et al., 2003, p. 384). The FSP Task Force has sought to identify evidence-based models of effective family–school partnerships and to ensure that school psychology practitioners and university trainers of practitioners engage in activities that view families as integral partners (Sheridan et al., 2007).

The FSP Task Force has identified five areas with preliminary evidence-based support: (a) family–school interventions with preschool children; (b) parent consultation; (c) parent education, parent training, and family intervention; (d) family–school collaboration; and (e) parent involvement (Carlson & Christenson, 2005. The listing of references that provide evidence-based practices is updated regularly.

Using the information collected by the FSP Task Force, six training modules with evidence-based support were developed: (a) overview of family–school partnerships, (b) family–school interventions with preschool children, (c) parent consultation, (d) parent education and family intervention, (e) family–school collaboration, and (f) parent involvement (Sheridan et al., 2007). Each module includes evidence-based intervention models, PowerPoint presentations, handouts, training activities, implementation guidelines, and many other helpful resources. The material is user-friendly, available at no cost, and can be adapted to a variety of settings with relative ease (Task Force on Family-School Partnerships, n.d.).

CONCLUSIONS

Chronic medical conditions may impact every aspect of the lives of affected children. Although some health-related issues may not affect a child's educational attainment, it is incumbent upon school psychologists to learn about chronic illnesses and advocate such that these children receive appropriate services. School psychologists are in an ideal position to play a primary role in consulting and collaborating with other professionals for the health and wellness of these children. Not only can school psychologists interact with medical personnel to better link home and school health care services, they can also provide school-based personnel with much-needed information and guide evidence-based intervention planning. At the specialist level of training, knowledge relevant to childhood health-related disorders is well within the purview of the NASP training model. At the doctoral level, school psychologists could become pediatric health specialists by completing additional course work and gaining supervised experience. Broad themes that are pervasive throughout both levels of training are evidence-based practice, also referred to as data-based decision making, and prevention/wellness promotion. In summary, training school psychologists in the area of chronic health-related disorders is essential if we, as a profession, are going to effectively serve these children.

RESOURCES

Carlson, C., & Christenson, S. L. (Guest Eds.). (2005). Evidence-based parent and family interventions in school psychology [Special issue]. *School Psychology Quarterly, 20*, 345–351.
This special issue provides valuable information regarding evidence-based practices in school psychology.

Phelps, L. (Ed.). (2006). *Chronic health-related disorders in children: Collaborative medical and psychoeducational interventions.* Washington, DC: American Psychological Association.
This book reviews the etiology, psychoeducational outcomes, and evidence-based practices recommended for children with health-related disorders. Collaborative models of care with health care professionals and families are delineated.

Walcott, C. M., & Chafouleas, S. M. (Guest Eds.). (2008). The practitioner's edition on school-based health promotion [Special issue]. *Psychology in the Schools, 45*, 1–90.
This is a helpful special issue that reviews wellness and prevention programming models.

REFERENCES

American Psychological Association. (n.d.). *Division 16 School Psychology.* Retrieved May 15, 2009, from http://www.indiana.edu/~div16/goals.html
American Psychological Association. (2007). *Domain B: Program philosophy, objectives, and curriculum plan: Guidelines and principles for accreditation of programs in professional psychology.* Washington, DC: Author.

American Psychological Association Presidential Task Force on Evidence-Based Practice. (2006). Evidence-based practice in psychology. *American Psychologist, 61*, 271–285.

Brown, R. T. (Ed.). (2004). *Handbook of pediatric psychology in school settings.* Mahwah, NJ: Lawrence Erlbaum Associates.

Brown, M. B., & Bolen, L. M. (Guest Eds.). (2008). The school-based center as a resource for prevention and health promotion [Special issue]. *Psychology in the Schools, 45*(1).

Carlson, C., & Christenson, S. L. (Guest Eds.). (2005). Evidence-based parent and family interventions in school psychology [Special issue]. *School Psychology Quarterly, 20*(4).

Chafouleas, S. M., & Bray, M. A. (Guest Eds.). (2004). Positive psychology and wellness in Children [Special issue]. *Psychology in the Schools, 41*(1).

Covington, D. Y., Nordstrom-Klee, B., Ager, J., Sokol, R., & Delancey-Black, V. (2002). Birth to age 7 growth in children prenatally exposed to drugs: A prospective cohort study. *Neurotoxicology and Teratology, 24*, 489–496.

Davis, A., & Phelps, L. (Guest Eds.). 2008. Psychoeducational implications of neurodevelopmental genetic disorders [Special issue]. *School Psychology Quarterly, 23*(2).

Dombrowski, S. D., & Martin, R. P. (Guest Eds.). (2007). Perintal exposure in later psychological and behavioral difficulties [Special issues]. *School Psychology Quarterly, 22*(1).

DuPaul, G. D. (Guest Ed.). (2007). School-based interventions for students with attention-deficit disorder: Current status and future directions [Special issue]. *School Psychology Review, 36*(2).

Farmer, T. W., & Xie, H. (2007). Aggression and school social dynamics: The good, the bad, and the ordinary. *Journal of School Psychology, 45*(4).

Harrison, P. L., Cummings, J. A., Dawson, M., Short, R. S., Gorin, S., & Palomares, R. (2003). Responding to the needs of children, families, and schools. The 2002 multisite conference on the future of school psychology. *School Psychology Quarterly, 18*, 358–388.

Individuals with Disabilities Act, 34 U.S.C. 300.7 (c)(9) (2004).

Individuals with Disabilities Education Improvement Act of 2004, 20 U.S.C. 1401 (2004).

Lee, S. W., & Janik, M. (2006). Provision of psychoeducational services in the schools: IDEA, Section 501, and NCLB. In Phelps, L. (Ed.), *Chronic health-related disorders in children: Collaborative medical and psychoeducational interventions.* Washington, DC: American Psychological Association.

National Association of School Psychologists. (n.d.) Retrieved from http://www.nasponline.org/resources/blueprint.html

National Institute of Child Health and Human Development. (2000). *Health disparities: Bridging the gap.* Rockville, MD: Author.

Norcross, J. C. (Ed.). (2002). *Psychotherapy relationships that work: Therapist contributions and responsiveness to patients.* New York: Oxford University Press.

Phelps, L. (Ed.). (1998). *Health-related disorders in children and adolescents: A guidebook for understanding and educating.* Washington, DC: American Psychological Association.

Phelps, L. (2005). Health-related issues among ethnic minority and low-income children: Psychoeducational outcomes and prevention models. In C. L. Frisby & C. R. Reynolds (Eds.), *Comprehensive handbook of multicultural school psychology.* Hoboken, NJ: John Wiley & Sons.

Phelps, L. (Ed.). (2006). *Chronic health-related disorders in children: Collaborative medical and psychoeducational interventions.* Washington, DC: American Psychological Association.

Phelps, L., Brown, R. T., & Power, T. J. (2002). *Pediatric psychopharmacology: Combining medical and psychosocial interventions.* Washington, DC: American Psychological Association.

Phelps, L. & Power, T. J. (2008). Integration of educational and health services through comprehensive school-based service delivery. *Psychology in the Schools, 45,* 88–90.

Power, T. J. (Ed). (2003). Emerging models of promoting children's mental health: Linking systems for prevention and intervention [Special series]. *School Psychology Review, 32*(1–4).

Power, T. J., DuPaul, G. J., Shapiro, E. S., & Parrish, J. M. (1995). Pediatric school psychology: The emergence of a subspecialty. *School Psychology Review, 24,* 244–257.

Rehabilitation Act of 1973, 20 C.F.R. Part 104 (1973).

Shaw, S. R. (2003). Professional preparation of pediatric school psychologists for school-based health centers. *Psychology in the Schools, 40,* 321–330.

Sheridan, S, Beebe-Frankenberger, M., Greff, K., Lasser, J., Lines, C., Miller, G., Woods, K., Mullaney, L., & Magee, K. L. (2007). Back to the future: The Futures Task Force on family-school partnerships. *Communiqué, 36*(3), 17–18.

Task Force on Family-School Partnerships. (n.d.). Retrieved July 21, 2009 from http://fsp.unl.edu/future_index.html

Traughber, M. C., & D'Amato, R. C. (2005). Integrating evidence-based neuropsychological services into school settings: Issues and challenges for the future. In R. C. D'Amato, E. Fletcher-Janzen, & C. R. Reynolds (Eds.), *Handbook of school neuropsychology* (pp. 827–757). Hoboken, NJ: Wiley.

U.S. Department of Health and Human Services. (2005a). *Call to action on disability: A report from the Surgeon General.* Washington, DC: Author.

U.S. Department of Health and Human Services. (2005b). *Surgeon general's call to action to improve the health and wellness of persons with disabilities.* Available from http://www.surgeongeneral.gov/library

Walcott, C. M., & Chafouleas, S. M. (Guest Eds.). (2008). The practitioner's edition on school-based health promotion [Special issue]. *Psychology in the Schools, 45,* 1–90.

Wampold, B. E., & Bhati, K. S. (2004). Attending to the omissions: A historical examination of evidence-based practice movements. *Professional Psychology: Research and Practice, 35,* 563–570.

Wilczynski, S. M. (Guest Ed.). (2007). Autism spectrum disorders [Special issue]. *Psychology in the Schools, 44*(7).

Ysseldyke, J., Dawson, P., Lehr, C., Reschly, D., Reynolds, M. & Telzrow, C. (1997). School psychology: A blueprint for training and practice II. Bethesda, MD: National Association of School Psychologists.

Part V

School psychology training: rooted in the past, practicing in the present, and contemplating the future

Summary and conclusions

18 Into the future

New directions for education and training

Enedina García-Vázquez, Tony D. Crespi, Cynthia A. Riccio, Tammy L. Hughes, and Judith Kaufman

INTRODUCTION

> When it comes to the future, there are three kinds of people: those who let it happen, those who make it happen, and those who wonder what happened.
>
> John Richardson, Jr.

School psychology as an educational and psychological enterprise has served a critical role in shaping the academic and social environments of schools for our nation's children. The future of school psychology practice begins with the education and professional training that occurs at the university, where the foundation for life-long learning and professional development and a solid foundation in standards for professional practices are established. The university trainers, together with field-based trainers (see Volume II), are partnered in developing and nurturing the next generation of school psychology practitioners and academics. At the university, training programs are faced with many challenges: what to teach, how to teach, the length of time required for students to show mastery, and what role to teach for (e.g., current vs. future; local vs. national vs. international practices). Although it is seemingly obvious, it is important to highlight that school psychology training programs exist in a context much wider than the university itself and must make decisions in keeping with university requirements, as well as state regulations (including education and psychology) and the requirements of professional practice accreditation bodies (Kaufman, Chapter 3, this volume). In addition, the populations served by school psychologists must remain a primary focus, as trainers continually examine the issues facing children, families, teachers, administrators, and local communities. Taken together, the effective training of school psychologists is an onerous challenge, but one we are prepared to meet. The chapters in this volume focus on critical training issues, such as models of training, as well as how to balance the teaching of the theoretical underpinnings that guide our decision making in concert with practical applied skills needed for the school psychologist's day-to-day work.

In addition, authors have addressed contemporary teaching of both the relevant content (e.g., consultation, assessment, and intervention from the system and individual perspectives) and also the methods (e.g., designed experiences) required for transmitting the requisite knowledge to the next generation of school psychologists.

The foundation of school psychology training has not, actually, changed significantly since school psychology was first recognized as a specialty in 1944. Ethics and professional practice standards guide decision making and professional conduct around the roles of assessment and (direct or indirect) intervention services. As Williams, Sinko, and Epifanio (Chapter 7, this volume) pointed out, legal and ethical standards continue to be the hallmark and benchmark for training programs. As the role and function of the school psychologist has evolved over the years, standards and, subsequently, the training programs, have made many adjustments to the types of training requirements needed to ensure that graduates will have the requisite clinical and research competencies.

Fagan (Chapter 2, this volume) pointed to changing demographics and needs of the school-age child over the years. For example, Arroyos-Jurado, Torres Fernández, and Navarro (Chapter 8, this volume) emphasized how multiculturalism and diversity have changed training requirements. At present, we recognize that there are a growing number of linguistically isolated households where no one over the age of 14 is English proficient. At the time of this writing, it is estimated that there are at least 5.5 million of these households (Sharpe, 2008). These children, along with their families, present a challenge to the majority of school systems. As such, Arroyos-Jurado and colleagues urged training programs to focus on working with second language learning families and to increase recruiting efforts for bilingual individuals to be prepared for school psychology positions. A second example of how changes in the demographics influence practice was presented by Phelps (Chapter 17, this volume), discussing the needs of children with chronic illness. Phelps noted that as medical health care continues to improve, it is essential for school psychologists to be aware of and have the skills to provide services for children who previously did not survive to school age or were sufficiently disabled to require home schooling. Today it has become critically important for training programs, as well as field-based school psychologists, to partner with the pediatric community so that children with chronic illness and neurological impairments can access and benefit from the educational environment. Truly, multicultural competency and the specialized needs of children with health and neurological problems in the school setting represent two areas of practice that largely did not seem paramount as the field initially developed.

Today, comprehensive care for all children is a clear focus in the field. Rosenfield, Levinsohn-Klyap, and Cramer (Chapter 14, this volume) highlighted how to meet the service delivery demands by working with teachers and parents through consultation. Similarly, Mennuti and Christner

(Chapter 13, this volume) detailed the increasing need for school-based mental health service, where programs range from universal prevention to meeting the needs of specific individuals, such as those requiring alternative education settings (Chapter 16, this volume) or those who are in need of neuropsychological assessment (Chapter 12, this volume). At the same time this does not exclude the essential training for effective assessment (Chapters 10, 11, and 12, this volume) needed for selecting evidenced-based interventions that are responsive to multicultural and diverse population needs. In short, emerging school psychologists face both the challenges that existed in the 1940s and the newer and more encompassing challenges that characterize contemporary life.

TRAINING FOR PROFESSIONAL ROLES AND FUNCTION

What has changed? The dimensions of the school psychologist's role have evolved and broadened dramatically over the past 60 years. Indeed, the discussion at meetings such as those held by the Trainers of School Psychologists at the 2008 National Association of School Psychologists convention show that school psychologists function as mental health providers, as well as consultants to teachers, parents, and administrators, in almost every community. But within these skill areas, the range of expertise has grown from assessment practices for intervention to a focus on the promotion of adequate development, mental health, and learning in all children (Braden, DiMarino-Linnen, & Good, 2001). Although changes in the roles and practices of school psychologists have been noted, and changes in standards have kept pace with this, Braden et al. contended that there are few changes in how we are training school psychologists.

In part, there is some evidence, though, that training in school psychology may be governed by the type of degree offered, where the PsyD program provides more practitioner training and the PhD program has a greater traditionally scientific research foundation (Chapter 3, this volume). There is some agreement that the first 2 years of training are intended to provide the knowledge base and skill set necessary for general school psychology certification (Chapter 4, this volume), whereas the doctorate provides the in-depth training for a specific area of expertise. The field also recognizes the role of combined–integrated training as an alternative to traditional training models (Chapter 5, this volume). Notably, there is continued discussion and controversy on the entry level for school psychology practice.

PEDAGOGICAL/SUPERVISORY ISSUES

Notably, standards require not only course work, but also practical experience and supervision. Supervision clearly is an important component in the training of school psychologists. Both the National Association of School Psychologists (NASP) and the American Psychological Association offer comprehensive guidelines regarding the total hours and type of experience required for a supervisory experience. Furthermore, most training programs recognize that there are multiple supervised activities throughout training, with the capstone experience, the internship, serving as the solidifying experience in which all requisite skills are integrated as well as solidified at an entry level for practice. Although supervision is widely touted, few school psychologists are formally trained in the process of supervision. Ross and Goh (1993) pointed out in their national survey that only one fourth of their sample of 331 school psychologists had graduate course work or training in supervision; only 11.2% had received this training in a school psychology program. Furthermore, when comparing university- and field-based supervisors, Ward (2001) found that university trainers tended to develop a more global skill set as compared with field-based supervisors' goals, where activities were more specific tasks. These topics are detailed in Volume II of this handbook; there is a critical need to bridge the gap between training and practice aimed at serving the future of school psychology practice, as well as children, families, and schools.

INTO THE FUTURE

In regards to the future, technological advances have had a major impact on the way we teach and train, on the accessibility of information, and, most importantly, on the children we serve. Not only has the world become flatter (Friedman, 2005), with information available from all over the world, but the ability to obtain such information is almost immediate. In many ways, the Internet provides increased opportunities for learning and reinforcement of skills for the training of school psychologists; however, there is an increased burden on faculty to help students evaluate the veracity of information presented on the Web. Although the use of technology has been infused into graduate programs, with online courses, blended courses, and chat rooms, not to mention the relative ease of statistical analysis, there is minimum research evaluating the impact of technology on the effectiveness of training. Few, if any, training programs offer training on the use of technology as an intervention.

Children are growing up in a "sound byte" world, where technology (instant messaging, blogging, FaceBook, MySpace, video games, etc.) presents multiple online opportunities for friendships, as well as online opportunities for problems (e.g., cyber bullying, compulsive gambling, and undesirable sexual behaviors). Today's children engage in abbreviated communication where words are truncated to letters, messages are not accompanied by facial expressions or social cues from the environment, and behavioral inhibition can be impaired through feelings of anonymity provided by the online experience (Delmonico & Griffin, 2008). In a recent study, Educational Testing Service (2008) identified cyber bullying as the most prevalent form of peer harassment. Furthermore, the impact of repeated exposure to violence prevalent in contemporary video games continues to be hotly debated (Ferguson et al., 2008), as there is some evidence that vulnerable children may be more negatively influenced by the powerful figures portrayed in the games (Anderson & Dill, 2000).

In order to address these and other ongoing practice challenges, there is the need for additional training and research, as well as the need to foster leadership and advocacy skills in our preservice school psychologists (Chapter 9, this volume). Change in service delivery models and more effective functioning can occur only when school psychologists assume a proactive rather than reactive stance. To function as effective and collaborative leaders, school psychology students need to be exposed to that body of information that can provide the framework for them to become initiators of change.

SUMMARY AND CONCLUSIONS

In reviewing the contents of this volume, it becomes clear that training of school psychologists must incorporate traditional skills along with new knowledge and approaches to address the changing needs of the student population and their families. University-based and field-based trainers, along with practicing school psychologists, need to be in a reciprocal discussion surrounding the changing demographics, populations, and issues that children bring to school and especially how these challenges translate into academic and psychological success. Specifically, for training programs to be successful, we need to address the complicated nature of the discipline with questions such as:

- What factors are influencing children?
- How are the changes in society influencing children?
- What changes in training programs are needed to address these factors and their consequences?
- What skills and knowledge do future school psychologists need in order to be effective?

Similarly, training programs need to evaluate several factors:

- How often does a program change its curriculum in response to accreditation and certification standards?
- How do we continue to become increasingly culturally competent to meet the needs of our changing populations?
- How should school psychology programs train students to address the needs of second language learners?

- How should school psychology programs train students to address the diverse needs of students with low-incidence disabilities, chronic illness, and neurological impairment, as well as those with high-incidence disabilities?
- How do we train students to deal with the negative impact that aspects of technology have on our children?
- How do we train students to become effective collaborators with the medical community in order to understand the needs of children and families with chronic illness?
- What is the most effective level of training so that future school psychologists have the fundamental skills to provide the most effective service?

Overall, school psychologists and the trainers of school psychologists cannot be satisfied with knowledge and experience that worked in the past, but must be prepared to address the concerns that children present with for the years to come. This requires flexibility and adaptability to change, as well as awareness and constant questioning and modifying of curricula. This also requires reaching out beyond the university or college setting into the various contexts in which school psychology students function— whether this is a community service agency, a medical clinic, the school, or home. It is critical to establish viable methods for building bridges between university training and field-based practice; today's technology provides for potential avenues that were not previously possible. University/field partnerships are essential in developing future generation of practitioners, researchers, and educational leaders. Volume II extends the issues generated in this volume to the integration of training, issues of supervision, and professional practice in the field setting.

RESOURCES

American Psychological Association. (n.d.). *Home page.* Retrieved May 16, 2009, from http://www.apa.org
The American Psychological Association is a scientific and professional organization that represents psychologists in the United States.

National Association of School Psychologists. (n.d.). *Home page.* Retrieved May 16, 2009, from http://www.nasponline.org
The National Association of School Psychologists represents and supports school psychology through leadership to enhance the mental health and educational competence of all children. It is the largest, most influential organization of school psychologists in the world, representing more than 21,000 members.

National Association of School Psychologists. (n.d.). *NASP-approved programs.* Retrieved May 16, 2009, from http://www.nasponline.org/certification/ NASPapproved.aspx

A comprehensive list of NASP-approved/nationally recognized graduate programs in school psychology can be found at this page. Also provided is information regarding various levels of training and the accreditation process.

National Association of School Psychologists. (2000). *Standards for Training and Field Placement Programs in School Psychology, Standards for the Credentialing of School Psychologists.* Retrieved May 16, 2009, from http://www.nasponline. org/standards/FinalStandards.pdf

The National Association of School Psychologists publishes the *Standards for Training and Field Placement Programs in School Psychology: Standards for the Credentialing of School Psychologists.* At the time of this printing, however, NASP was in the process of revising the training standards.

Trainers of School Psychologists. (n.d.). *Home page.* Retrieved May 16, 2009, from http://trainersofschoolpsychologists.org

The goal of the TSP organization is to provide support in the training of school psychologists at all levels. Additional goals of TSP are to examine current trends in graduate education programs, to provide professional growth opportunities to school psychology faculty, to facilitate communication with field-based supervisors, and to support legislative efforts that promote excellence in training.

Trainers of School Psychologists. (n.d.). *TSP Listserv.* Retrieved May 16, 2009, from http://www.trainersofschoolpsychologists.org/listserv.html

This page provides information regarding joining the TSP organization mailing list.

REFERENCES

Anderson, C. A. & Dill, K. E. (2000). Video games and aggressive thoughts, feelings, and behavior in the laboratory and in life. *Journal of Personality and Social Psychology, 78,* 772–790.

Braden, J. S., DiMarino-Linnen, E., & Good, T. L. (2001). Schools, society, and school psychologists: History and future directions. *Journal of School Psychology, 39*(2), 203–219.

Delmonico, D. L. & Griffin, E. J. (2008). Cybersex and the e-teen: What marriage and family therapists should know. *Journal of Marital and Family Therapy, 34*(4), 431–444.

Educational Testing Service. (2008, December). Cyber-bullying. Unpublished internal report.

Ferguson, C. J., Rueda, S. M., Cruz, A. M., Ferguson, D. E., Fritz, S., & Smith, S. M. (2008). Violent video games and aggression: Causal relationship or byproduct of family violence and intrinsic violence motivation? *Criminal Justice and Behavior, 35,* 311–332.

Ross, R. P., & Goh, D. S. (1993). Participating in supervision in school psychology: A national survey of practices and training. *School Psychology Review, 22,* 63–80.

Sharpe, R. (2008, November 16). English loses ground: Nearly 20% of Americans speak a different language at home. *USA Weekend.com.* Retrieved December 1, 2008, from http://www.usaweekend.com

Friedman, T. L. (2005). *The world is flat: A brief history of the twenty-first century.* New York: Farrar, Straus, and Giroux.

Ward, S. (2001). Intern supervision in school psychology: Practice and process of field-based and university supervisors. *School Psychology International, 22*(3), 269–284.

Index

A

ABPP, see American Board of Professional Psychology (ABPP)

Accountability, 33

Accreditation, of doctoral programs, 41–43

ACPWAR, see American Psychological Association (APA)

ADHD, see Attention deficit/ hyperactivity disorder (ADHD)

Administrative pressure to practice, strategies for resisting, 110–111

Administrators, school practices for, 158–159

Adolescent incarceration and children's psychiatric hospitalization, 279

clinical supervision considerations, 286–287

corrections training for school psychologists, 287–290

outcomes, 289–290

personal reflections, 290

professional roles and functions assessment and diagnosis, 282–284

consultation and collaboration, 285

counseling and psychotherapy, 284

American Board of Professional Psychology (ABPP), 36

American Education and Research Association, 298

American Psychological Association (APA), 7, 35, 39, 300, 303, 311, 314, 326

Center for Psychology Workforce Analysis and Research (ACPWAR), 68

C–I training and, 64

Commission for the Recognition of Practice Areas and Proficiencies in Professional Psychology, 71

Competencies document, 65

Education Directorate, 67

Model Licensing Act, 36

multicultural practice and training, standards for, 131

Presidential Task Force on Evidence-Based Practice, 315

Public Policy Office, 50

recommendations for school psychology training, 16–18

school-based mental health services and, 249

Shakow Committee, 66

standards for training and practice, 86, 87

American Psychological Association of Graduate Students, 67

For Product Safety Concerns and Information please contact our EU representative GPSR@taylorandfrancis.com Taylor & Francis Verlag GmbH, Kaufingerstraße 24, 80331 München, Germany

Printed and bound by CPI Group (UK) Ltd, Croydon, CR0 4YY
08/06/2025
01896998-0014